Access

for

Countryside Walking

Politics, Provision and Need

GEORGE KAY

Staffordshire University Press
2002

For Jane, Gillian and Linda,
who have walked far with me.

Acknowledgements

While the author is responsible for the arguments presented in this study, he is grateful to numerous individuals, encountered in diverse circumstances over many years, who have contributed to the development of his knowledge and appreciation of the subject matter addressed in this book. Amongst these, Stephen Williams' input has been particularly valuable.

Additionally, special thanks are due to Rosemary Duncan who not only created many of the maps and diagrams but also undertook the final composition and layout of the volume.

Published in 2002
Staffordshire University Press
College Road, Stoke-on-Trent
Staffordshire, ST4 2DE (UK)

Copyright : The Author

All rights reserved. Except for the quotation of short passages for the purposes of criticism and review, no part of this publication may be reproduced, stored in a retrieval system, or transmitted, in any form or by any means, electronic, mechanical, photocopying, recording or otherwise, without prior permission of the publishers or a licence from the Copyright Licencing Agency Limited.

ISBN 1 904133 04 5
Printed in Great Britain by Staffordshire University Press

CONTENTS

1. The NATURE and ORIGINS of COUNTRYSIDE WALKING — 1
    1. Leisure and Recreation : Motivation and Purpose — 1
    2. Walking as a Recreational Activity — 4
    3. Walking and Recreational Experiences — 8
    4. Pleasurable Walking and Designed Leisure Landscapes — 10
    5. Discerning Minds and the Countryside — 13
    6. Scientific Minds and Natural Phenomena — 16
    7. The Quest for Fitness and Adventure — 21

2. INTERPRETATIONS OF NATURE, the COUNTRYSIDE and CONSERVATION — 29
    1. World Views and Interpretations of Nature — 29
    2. The Aristocracy and the Countryside — 30
    3. Romanticists and 'Natural Beauty' — 36
    4. Scientists, Intellectuals, and Rational Pragmatism — 39
    5. People and Place : Concern and Conservation — 41

3. SOCIAL CONCERN and PROVISION for the POOR upto 1950 — 49
    1. Development, Growth and Change — 49
    2. The 'Two Nations' and Provision for Walking — 50
    3. Philanthropy and the Urban Poor — 54
    4. Countryside Access for the Urban Poor — 56
    5. Walking, Cycling and Motoring up to 1950 — 63

4. COUNTRYSIDE ISSUES and LEGISLATION : ACCESS and PARTICIPATION — 71
    1. The Political Context — 71
    2. Countryside Issues of Yesterday and Today — 74
    3. The National Parks and Access to the Countryside Act — 78
    4. Access for Whom ? The Privileged and the Disadvantaged — 81
    5. Participation and the Efficacy of Access — 84

5. COUNTRYSIDE WALKING - CURRENT PATTERNS and PROBLEMS — 92
    1. Outdoor Recreation and Countryside Walkers — 92
    2. Favourite Places and Crowded Spaces — 97
    3. Recreation in the National Parks — 101
    4. The Peak District and other National Parks — 104
    5. Open All Hours... and Free for All ? — 110

6. HIGHWAYS, BYWAYS and RIGHTS of WAY — 115
1. Concepts and Definitions — 115
2. Rights of Way : an Historical Context — 117
3. Public Rights of Way : Problems and Policies — 121
4. Public Rights of Way : The Price of Maps — 124
5. Public Rights of Way : Patterns of Progress — 129
6. Which Way Forward ? — 137

7. PUBLIC FOOTPATHS - FIT FOR WHOM ? — 140
1. 'Natural' and 'Artificial' Paths — 140
2. The Condition of Paths on PRoW in 1988 and 1994 — 142
3. Survey Findings as Weapons and Tools — 144
4. Responsibilities for Managing Paths on PRoW — 149
5. Manpower for Path Maintenance — 154
6. 'Natural Paths' and 'Managerial Disasters' — 161
7. Paths for the Public ? — 167

8. NATIONAL TRAILS, REGIONAL ROUTES and LONG DISTANCE WALKERS — 169
1. National Trails and Regional Routes — 169
2. Long Distance Walkers and Long Distance Walks — 174
3. The LDWA and its Directory of Long Distance Walks — 179
4. The LDWA and the Promotion of Walking — 185
5. The Utility and Use of Long Distance Routes — 191
6. Site Surveys and 'LDUs/SDUs' on National Trails — 202

9. PUTTING PEOPLE FIRST ? 'RECREATION 2000' and CIRCULAR WALKS — 206
1. 'Recreation 2000' - Putting People First ? — 206
2. Parish Paths and Local Walks : Policies and Priorities — 209
3. The Marketing and Promotion of Short Circular Walks — 210
4. The Countrywide Pattern of Promoted Walks — 215
5. Promoted Walks in Staffordshire — 219
6. The Utility and Use of Promoted Walks — 226

10. PROMOTING ENJOYMENT in a COUNTRYSIDE for ALL — 229
1. Ancient Rights versus Current Needs in the 21st Century — 229
2. Pseudo-Democracy Distorts Policy and Planning — 232
3. Towards a National Strategy for Countryside Walking — 235
4. Promoting Access for Countryside Walking : A Neglected Need — 242

Maps and Diagrams

Fig.1.1	Maslow's Hierachy of Human Needs with Work, Obligations and Leisure	3
Fig.1.2	Twenty Types of Walking Ranked on Five Sets of Criteria	5
Fig.1.3	Recreational Walking as an Outdoor Activity and Experience	8
Fig.1.4	Adventure Experience and Personal Development	26
Fig.2.1	World Views of Preliterate and Advanced Societies (after Redfield, 1953)	29
Fig.2.2	Interpretations of Nature (after Williams, 1991)	31
Fig.2.3	The 'Landscape of Improvement' at the Mains of Newton Garrioch	35
Fig.3.1	Edinburgh - Auld Reekie and The New Town c.1830	53
Fig.4.1	Stages in a Pressure Group Campaign for Public Awareness and Support	72
Fig.4.2	John Dower's 1943 Proposals for National Parks and other Valued Places	76
Fig.4.3	Recreational Walking by Income and Socio-Economic Groups, 1977	85
Fig.4.4	Countryside Visits and Walks by Residential Location of Participants	89
Fig.5.1	The Length of Countryside Walks	94
Fig.5.2	Major Visitor Locations in the Peak District, 1977	105
Fig.5.3	Main Visitor and Hiking Areas in the Peak District, 1987	106
Fig.5.4	Rhythms of Recreational Demand for Countryside Resources	111
Fig.6.1A	'Field-Path Map' by the Berkhamsted Citizens Association, 1945	114
Fig.6.2	Spatial Densities of PRoW, 1987	130
Fig.6.3	Expenditure on PRoW, 1987	132
Fig.6.4	Resident Population and PRoW, 1987	133
Fig.6.5	Promoted PRoW, 1987	134
Fig.8.1	National Trails in England and Wales, 1988	171
Fig.8.2	The Spatial Occurrence of 402 Long Distance Walks, 1994	183
Fig.8.3	LDWA Membership and Local Groups, 1998	185
Fig.8.4	Local Walks Organised by LDWA Groups, 1998	186
Fig.8.5	The Seasonal Profile of LDWA Walks, 1998	188
Fig.8.6	The LDWA National Events of 1998	189
Fig.8.7	Path Usage on the *Three Peaks Walk* and Adjacent Paths, 1985	201
Fig.9.1	The *Ditchling Beacon Walk*, 1999	213
Fig.9.2	*Village Walks* pinpoint 149 Prized Places in England	216
Fig.9.3	The National Trust serves Walkers well in parts of 'Beautiful Britain'	217
Fig.9.4	Short Circular Walks favour 'Valued Landscapes' in England and Wales	218
Fig.9.5	Landscape Quality and Principal Settlements in Staffordshire	221
Fig.9.6	Walks in Staffordshire Promoted by the Voluntary Sector, 1995	223
Fig.9.7	Walks in Staffordshire Promoted by the Commercial Sector, 1995	223
Fig.9.8	Walks in Staffordshire Promoted by the Public Sector, 1995	224
Fig.9.9	All Walks Promoted in Staffordshire, 1995	224
Fig.10.1	Densities of PRoW in Selected Counties of England and Wales	239
Fig.10.2	Matching Paths on PRoW to Properties of Place	241
Fig.10.3	The Gateway to Participation : A Decision-making Process	247

Photographs and Drawings

Plate 0.1	Confrontation Aggravates Conflict and Serves No Good Purpose	viii
Plate 1.1	The Diverse Satisfactions of Countryside Walking	xii
Plate 1.2	Designed Leisure Landscapes	11
Plate 1.3	The Farming Year' of 1948 : Spring and Autumn Landscapes	20
Plate 1.4	'Celebrated Tour Boots' for Gentlemen Walkers of the late 19th century	28
Plate 3.1	Octavia Hill - Heroically Portrayed in her Campaign for 'Open Spaces'	48
Plate 3.2	Sociable Strolling in Leicester Square, 1874	51
Plate 3.3	Opportunities for Recreational Travel to Countryside Resorts in 1891	59
Plate 3.4	Cook's 'Grand Tours of Europe' for the Aspiring Middle Class, c1860	61
Plate 3.5	Perry's 1896 Handbook for Manchester Cyclists	65
Plate 4.1	Pressure Groups are a Power to be Reckoned With !	70
Plate 4.2	Britain's Popular National Parks go Under Wraps	82
Plate 6.1	Central Africa in 1960 - or England in 1060 ?	117
Plate 6.2	Foundations of the Roman Road, Wheeldale Moor, North Yorkshire	119
Plate 6.3	The Medieval Bow Bridge and Causeway, Castleton, North Yorkshire	121
Plate 6.4	Enjoying the Countryside	139
Plate 7.1	Natural Paths - Overdue for Attention !	142
Plate 7.2	Compliance with the Law can be Costly to Arable Farmers	150
Plate 7.3	An Obstacle in the Guise of a Stile !	151
Plate 7.4	Woodside Bridge, Exmoor	153
Plate 7.5	A Natural Path and a Managerial Disaster !	162
Plate 7.6	Aesthetic Concerns Misdirect Path Management	166
Plate 8.1	Long Distance Walkers on the 'Anglezarke Amble'	168
Plate 8.2	LDUs or SDUs ? Hikers or Strollers ?	204
Plate 9.1	Making Countryside Visitors Welcome ?	205
Plate 9.2	The *Fair Britain* Series of Guides	214
Plate 10.1	Images of the Countryside for 'Discerning Minds'	243
Plate 10.2	The Countryside Code Inhibits the Promotion of Walking	246

Tables

Table 2.1	The Development of the Conservation Movement in Britain upto 1950	46
Table 4.1	Franchised Population and Fortunes of the Political Parties, 1900-1951	73
Table 5.1	The Principal Recreational Activities of Visitors to the National Parks	96
Table 5.2	The Mode of Transport and Distances Travelled on Day Visits, 1993	99
Table 5.3	The Duration of Day Visits and Time Spent at the Chosen Venue, 1993	99
Table 5.4	The National Parks : Visitor Use, 1990 and 1994	103
Table 5.5	Home-based and Holiday-based Visits to the National Parks, 1994	103
Table 5.6	Spatial Patterns of Visitor Use in the Peak District, 1987	107
Table 5.7	Seasonal Patterns of Day Visits in 1993	112
Table 6.1	PRoW, Population and Resources by Counties, 1987	131
Table 6.2	Spending on PRoW by 'Rich' and 'Poor' Counties, 1987	136
Table 7.1	Counties with Path Conditions Above and Below Average Standards	148
Table 7.2	Manual Labour for Path Maintenance on PRoW, 1987	155
Table 7.3	Major Employers of MSC Manual Workers on PRoW Work, 1987	157
Table 7.4	Leading Users of Volunteers on PRoW Work in 1987 and 1991	158
Table 7.5	Counties and MBs in the Parish Paths Partnership Scheme by 1994	160
Table 8.1	The National Trails, 1999	172
Table 8.2	Regional Routes, 1999	173
Table 8.3	Lyke Wake Walks reported to the Lyke Wake Club, 1955-79 & 1980-82	178
Table 8.4	Trends in the LDWA Membership, 1987 to 2000	180
Table 8.5	Long Distance Walks, Regional Routes and National Trails by Length	181
Table 8.6	LDWA Members, Groups, Local Walks and National Events by Counties	184
Table 8.7	The LDWA '100-mile Challenge Walks', 1973-2000	191
Table 8.8	The Popularity and Use of 24 Long Distance Walks	194
Table 8.9	LDWA Walkers on Long Distance Paths : The Duration of Walks	195
Table 8.10	LDWA Walkers on Long Distance Paths : The Size of Groups	196
Table 8.11	LDWA Walkers' Evaluation of 24 Long Distance Walks	199
Table 9.1	Moxham's 1995 Catalogue of Promoted Walks in Staffordshire	220
Table 9.2	Promoted Walks, Landscape, Land-use and Proximity to People	225
Table 9.3	Sources of Information Used in Planning Countryside Walks/Visits	227
Table 10.1	Rating the Countryside for Recreational Walking	236
Table 10.2	Graded Paths and their Deployment on Highways	240

Plate 0.1 Confrontation Aggravates Conflict and Serves No Good Purpose

PREFACE

Concerning the Origins and Objectives

In 1977 Madeley College, with its School of Excellence in Physical Education, merged with Staffordshire University. This provided an exceptional opportunity to create a pioneering degree in *Sport and Recreation Studies,* which admitted its first students in 1980. The author enjoyed a key role in this development; and an interest in rural geography was translated into teaching and research in Outdoor Recreation with special reference to walking, and in Countryside Management with a strong focus on access issues.

A life-long experience of the countryside, ranging from regular family walks, camping and way-faring with the Boys Brigade and much adventurous trespassing during childhood through to sociable outings with my children and grandchildren and long-distance challenge walks in more recent years, provided a useful background - but no sound basis for teaching. I entered the field like an innocent in wonderland and was repeatedly amazed by what I encountered. Relevant literature was limited. There were few general texts other than Dower's dated *Fourth Wave* (1965), Patmore's excellent *Land and Leisure* (1970) and *Recreation and Resources* (1983), and Shoard's interesting polemic on *The Theft of the Countryside* (1980). Primary sources, such as the Countryside Commission's publications and scarce academic papers, were mostly on specific topics or special issues; and much valuable survey data had been neglected or, worse, abused. In short, countryside walking was and continues to be a neglected field.

Learning and teaching went hand in hand; and field studies, notably in mid-Staffordshire, the Peak District, North-east Yorkshire and North Wales, were highly educational for both staff and students. Additional commitments - as an advisor to the Cleveland Way Management Committee, a consultant on *Outdoor Sport and Recreation* for Broxtowe Borough Council, and membership of Staffordshire County Council's *Countryside Services Committee* and its predecessors - variously provided vital insights into the contentious field of access and rights of way, for these rather than people and recreation, are the centrepiece of politics and passions. This emphasis shaped and informed part of my teaching, prompted some interim writing on contemporary issues (Kay, 1989, 1994, 1996, 1998 and 2000); and eventually, as time permitted, allowed the conversion of pedagogic materials into the present text.

The principal objectives are to examine the nature and origins of countryside walking in its historical, social and political context; and, secondly to explore the subordination of the nation's enjoyment of the countryside to the recovery, preservation and development of rights-of-way, primarily for the benefit of privileged minorities. Underlying each complex theme there is a case for social equity in terms of access to the countryside. Conventional wisdom has always denied this need, variously arguing that Nature's joys are free for all and that an over-crowded countryside, threatened by hordes of inconsiderate visitors, stands in need of protection rather than promotion. Such specious claims protect the privileged position of regular and frequent visitors while a large, disadvantaged majority rarely if ever enjoy close contact with the countryside - though they readily declare their affection for it. In reality, most of the countryside is always substantially underused by visitors, and all of it is underused for most of the time. Incontrovertible evidence to sustain these truths has for long been available, but it is neither widely known nor well publicised. Furthermore, present priorities have precluded optimal use of limited resources for the support and promotion of countryside walking; and the management of provision for walkers also is capable of substantial improvement.

The origins of this parlous state of affairs lie deep in history and politics and with the vested interests of numerous influential if not powerful minority groups. Consequently, for 200 years the countryside has been a battlefield, contested by diverse self-centred parties though often presented as a simple confrontation between ramblers and an alliance of land-owners and farmers (Plate 0.1). There is no single contest nor any master conspiracy but rather a shifting conjunction of effects achieved by numerous parties. These loosely coalesce into three broad, overlapping movements comprising countryside owners and residents; conservationists; and established recreational users. Individuals may hold a place in all three; and in protecting their own varied interests, these three have at least one thing in common - a preference to restrain access to and recreational use of the countryside while defending their own occupation and use of it.

These parties and their heartfelt beliefs and fears have a long history but their influence and their interaction has made itself felt mainly during the 20th century. Many of their idiosyncratic visions have now been endorsed by governments and translated into laws, policies and strategies which, in effect, curtail both access to the countryside and promotion of its enjoyment. Thus, not only conventional wisdom but also current policies and priorities in respect of access and provision for countryside walking are constructed on inappropriate foundations; and neither properly serves the public interest nor the people as a whole. Explanation and critical appraisal of these circumstances comprise the greater part of the second objective; but an equally important purpose is to outline, by both implication and specific proposals, a better way forward for both the countryside and the nation. In short, this study might facilitate movement in respect of a laudable cause to which the Countryside Commission was ostensibly committed for many years, namely 'to make an attractive countryside truly accessible and its benefits available to the whole public' (CCP.225, 1987). Recently, the Countryside Agency apparently pledged itself to the same cause and intends 'to help everyone, wherever they live, to enjoy this national asset [ie the countryside]' (CA.22, 1999). A major objective of this study is to facilitate firm adoption of these goals and significant progress towards them.

Concerning the Contents and Presentation

The objectives broadly define the contents, which are outlined in the following pages. A cursory glance at these might suggest there is little on offer that is not already common knowledge; but those who are readily inclined to such a view might well have most to gain from close reading of the text. Countryside walking, in its several forms, is not so much an activity as an avenue to very varied, complex experiences; and an exploration of its nature and utility, its diversity and development is necessarily and properly located within the dynamic context of cultural, political and social conditions through the relevant ages. This is attempted in the first three chapters, where an intrinsically fascinating history is illustrated by an eclectic selection of models and materials, ideas and information.

This historical material reveals how the dominant Victorian philosophy of laissez faire admitted few major initiatives by parliament in respect of either recreation or conservation; and such matters were more readily pursued by various minority interests within the fragmented voluntary sector. Consequently there was a strong maverick element in the selection of issues and concerns, and the pursuit of each cause reflects the interests of its authors. The emerging conservation movement, which embraced the protection of ancient footways, thus reflected a variety of interests but had no consistent philosophy or purpose - other than that of the advocates to do good and be good in the sight of their peers and beneficiaries. Being *ad hoc* and *ad hominem,* any problem or proposal brought to parliament was likely to be judged in terms of the weightiness of the advocates no less than the merits of the case; and while battle-lines had been firmly established, little had been achieved in respect of critical matters for countryside walking by the turn of the century.

Thereafter the political context and political processes changed quite markedly; and, eventually, the seminal National Parks and Access to the Countryside Act was passed in 1949. Chapters 4 and 5 address this turn of events; and then analyse recent and current patterns of countryside recreation, with special reference to walking, in order to examine the efficacy of prevailing policies and provision for access to and enjoyment of the countryside. They also provide the necessary context for the evaluation of later strategies and of alternative but neglected approaches. At this point it is appropriate to note that available survey data can be a valuable aid to policy-making and planning but all too often they have been ignored or even abused; and, secondly, that they afford little or no justification for current policies and practices in respect of either countryside walking or the promotion of countryside enjoyment.

In fact, the package of ill-conceived and daunting tasks generated by the Act of 1949 and eventually inherited by the Countryside Commission and Countryside Agency has continued to dominate policy and provision for access into the 21st century; and the 'right to roam' returned to parliament more than 50 years after it should have been laid to rest. In short, voices which prevailed in the post-war parliament have retained a dominant position; and too few have been raised in criticism of the present state of affairs to effect any substantial change and dispossess the dominant heresy.

The particular concern of this study is not exploration and explanation of why this should be so but rather to provide an in-depth critical appraisal of the principal elements of prevailing policies and patterns of provision in respect of countryside walking in order to demonstrate their defects and deficiencies no less than their merits; and, secondly, to point the way towards more appropriate measures. Chapters 6 to 10 are dedicated to these ends; and they are fortified by substantial research findings, often presented in maps or diagrams and supported by photographic evidence. They deal with public rights of way; public footpaths; National Trails and other long-distance routes; with 'Recreation 2000' and short circular walks; and finally with the key issues of provision for and the promotion of access for countryside walking. Each of these apparently prosaic matters is highly contentious. Furthermore, collectively they are very expensive; and, despite all claims to the contrary, present priorities and provision have generated much surplus capacity which, paradoxically, does not and cannot constitute either a satisfactory or a sufficient basis to serve the nation's needs in respect of countryside walking.

Appropriate provision is in short supply, and the sins of commission are thus compounded by equally serious sins of ommission. There is, therefore, an urgent need for a fundamental revision of policy, strategy and priorities across the entire field of provision for and promotion of access to the countryside for the enjoyment of recreational walking; and the case for this is explored in these five chapters. However, a better way forward will be practicable only when the current domination of policy by vested interests is effectively broken and a genuine concern for the people as a whole wins public and parliamentary recognition. It is an indictment of our democratic procedures that minority groups should persistently dominate policy and provision for access to the countryside so that it serves their own ends and that of like-minded persons but neglects the needs of most people. Hopefully, this book may achieve some movement to redress the situation; and the recent creation of the Countryside Agency might provide an opportunity for a new start and better prospects for countryside walking by the nation as a whole by 2020, if not sooner.

Plate 1.1 The Diverse Satisfactions of Countryside Walking are not Always Self-evident.... and should Paths Provide such a Forbidding Challenge ?
(Photo by John Woodhouse, Sports Council)

1
THE NATURE AND ORIGINS OF COUNTRYSIDE WALKING

Walking for pleasure is as old as human society. When did a lover and his lass not go roaming by banks and braes or in fairy-circled lea ? Or children not escape from their parental hearth to explore wider regions for themselves ? Such commonplace activities comprise home-based leisure; and insofar as residential areas and their hinterlands are segregated, each community will exercise its own outdoor leisure lifestyle. The countryside and the city provide the resource base and networks of multi-purpose routes serve recreational needs. Variations in geographical conditions and local culture generate vernacular variations and participation naturally follows the conventions of the day. Consequently, *everyday recreational walking* is scarcely recognised and rarely labelled as such. In contrast, several distinctive types of walking reflect particular interests of significant sub-sets of the population. These comprise an *upper circuit of countryside walking* which generates characteristic forms of behaviour that relate to preferred places, specific resources, special provision and personal attributes.

Despite the wide range of options, 'going for a walk' always implies the translation of walking from the oldest and most common form of personal transport into a leisure activity which reflects the principal purposes of the walker. This calls for some definition of leisure and recreation and the location of both within a scheme of motivation that will facilitate understanding of countryside walking as a diverse source of complex experiences.

1. Leisure and Recreation : Motivation and Purpose

> The essential elements of leisure ..... are (a) an antithesis to work as an economic function; (b) a minimum of involuntary social-role obligations; (c) a psychological perception of freedom; (d) a pleasant expectation and recollection; (e) a close relation to values of the culture; (f) the inclusion of an entire range from inconsequence and insignificance to weightiness and importance; and (g) often, but not necessarily, an activity characterized by the element of play. (Kaplan, 1960).

This considered view of leisure indicates a threefold division of time and behaviour into (a) *work*; (b) *obligations*; and (c) time free from these which is purposefully committed to recreation and pleasure and thus comprises *leisure time*. This implies a fourth category of uncommitted or *empty time;* and all too often, many individuals thus find themselves burdened with boredom. Readily accessible recreations therefore are of particular importance to the well being of individuals and society as a whole; and, if effectively marketed and promoted, recreational walking should serve this need.

This fourfold categorisation of time does not properly acknowledge that 'multiple-use' of time is commonplace, and that work, obligations and the pursuit of self-selected satisfactions may be combined in varying proportions. Thus, while walking in company to work or school or shops there is no prohibition on taking exercise for its own sake, on constructive inter-personal discourse or frivolous banter, nor on observing and enjoying the landscape. The identification of walking as either a utilitarian or recreational activity therefore is not always a simple matter; and no reasonable opportunity to improve recreational experiences during walks undertaken primarily for utilitarian purposes should be overlooked.

Nevertheless, it is often useful to categorise time with reference to the prime purpose and principal objectives to which it is dedicated. This places work, obligations and leisure firmly in the context of motivation; and a general model of motivation can assist understanding of diverse satisfactions which may be derived from leisure and, indeed, from work and obligatory duties too. Maslow's 'hierarchy of human needs' (1943 and 1970) affords an appropriate scheme (Fig.1.1). Initially it comprised five stages but was subsequently extended by elaboration and sub-division of the highest set, which figures prominently in affluent societies. The stages are in order of prepotency; and while any lower order of needs or goals is largely unmet, it will normally figure most prominently in one's consciousness and dominate use of one's time. Even so, all seven are equally co-existent and, typically, most behaviour is in response to more than one of them. Human motivation and behaviour are complex matters.

The more basic physiological needs and the over-riding desire for immediate and long-term safety and security drive us to work and commit us to vital personal, social and political obligations. Even so, multiple-use of time can mix physiological needs with leisure and thus, for example, eating and drinking are popular leisure activities. Similarly, the exercise element of recreational walking may serve physiological needs, improving health and fitness if not mental well being as desired objectives in their own right. However, recreation generally serves higher aspirations; and the most immediate of these are complex inter-personal relationships comprising 'belonginess' and 'esteem'. Therefore, the social benefits of recreational walking should never be under-estimated; and provision for walking should foster inter-personal relationships.

The highest, tripartite set of goals comprise 'self-actualisation' or the realisation of one's identity and achievement of one's potential in terms of intellectual, aesthetic and spiritual objectives. In utilitarian terms, self-actualisation comprises the least important set of goals yet their achievement is often prized above all others. Furthermore, success is dependent upon the possession and development of requisite capabilities which, unlike an appetite for food and drink, are very unevenly distributed. Nevertheless, it is possible to afford opportunities for the full development of each and every individual; and this should be a prime objective in any democratic society with a sense of social justice. This is not simply a matter of paternalism since "free time, constructively used, enriches individual lives, advances society, and produces massive cultural development" (Shivers, 1981).

There is, however, a danger, which is evident in attitudes of the respectable middle and upper classes, of directing the use of leisure to 'matters of weightiness and importance' and of disparaging its deployment on those of 'inconsequence and insignificance'. In contrast, Roberts (1978) notes that "the very concept of leisure conjures impressions of joy, amusement and euphoria. In common sense leisure is fun". He argues convincingly that apparently trivial goals deserve and demand a place not only within serious research but also within provision for and the promotion of leisure activities; and countryside walking

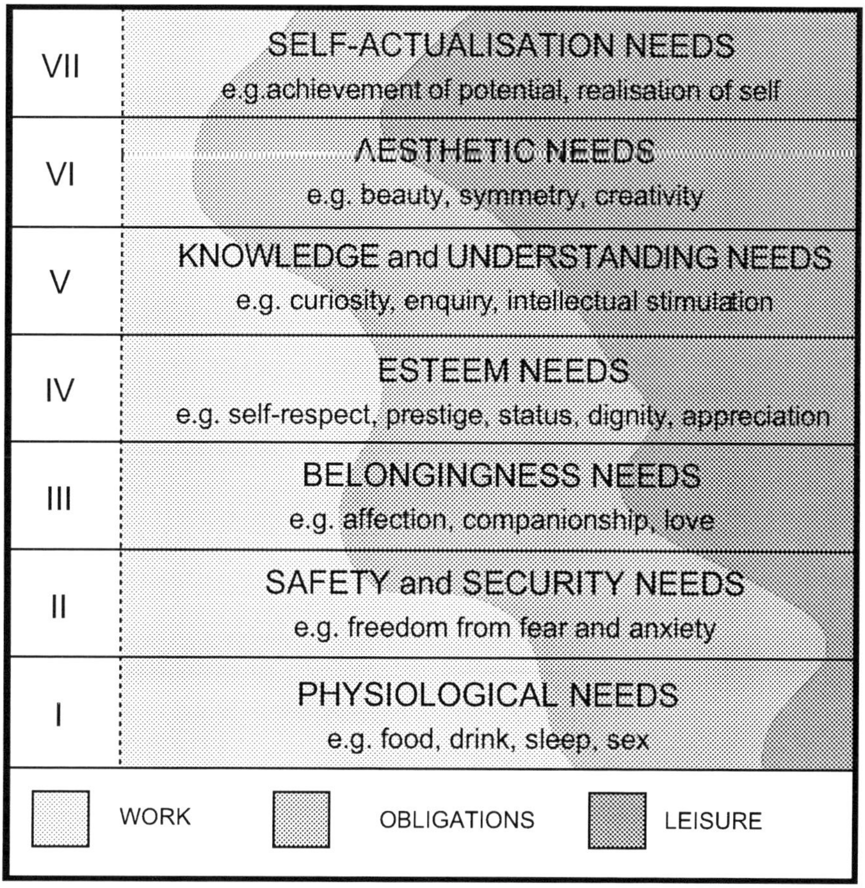

VII	**SELF-ACTUALISATION NEEDS** e.g. achievement of potential, realisation of self
VI	**AESTHETIC NEEDS** e.g. beauty, symmetry, creativity
V	**KNOWLEDGE and UNDERSTANDING NEEDS** e.g. curiosity, enquiry, intellectual stimulation
IV	**ESTEEM NEEDS** e.g. self-respect, prestige, status, dignity, appreciation
III	**BELONGINGNESS NEEDS** e.g. affection, companionship, love
II	**SAFETY and SECURITY NEEDS** e.g. freedom from fear and anxiety
I	**PHYSIOLOGICAL NEEDS** e.g. food, drink, sleep, sex

☐ WORK   ☐ OBLIGATIONS   ▓ LEISURE

Fig.1.1 Maslow's (1970) Hierachy of Human Needs and a Postulated Association with Work, Obligations and Leisure.

should be capable of providing fun no less than self-actualisation.

Recreation, renewal and self-development comprise the optimal use of leisure time, followed in turn by entertainment, amusements and pastimes. Pastimes are a form of escapism; they hold boredom at bay and dispel the gloom of empty time. Thus, beyond leisure lies the threat of empty time; and as the need for and availability of work have diminished and as individuals have been increasingly relieved or deprived of obligations because institutions have assumed a wider range of responsibilities, ennui - once a problem only for the rich and leisured class - has become more and more widespread. The unemployed and under-employed often have more free time than they can manage; and young people may be particularly vulnerable. "Studies of young people offer ample evidence that 'leisure' is far from all fun and excitement. Every recent investigation has confirmed how drab, monotonous, dull and boring spare time can be" (Roberts, 1978). If those in the formative stages of their lives do not then learn how to profit from free time, how may they begin to enjoy themselves, still less pursue 'self-actualisation', while they are in other respects best equipped to do so? The problem of 'empty time' is also frequently encountered amongst the elderly, especially since 'early retirement' became fashionable and as life has been increasingly extended beyond pensionable age. And for everyone with nothing but empty time on their hands and minds, being alive is scarcely living. In this context, relevant provision for and positive promotion of readily accessible recreations, including countryside walking, must be seen as a matter of prime importance for the benefit and well being of individuals and the nation.

2. Walking as a Recreational Activity

Walking is a biomechanical and physiological activity - one of the simpler forms of exercise; and 'Health Walks' are now being promoted in ambitious terms as "a highly effective way to recover, sustain and increase physical fitness" (Fairbanks, 1997). Gentle, short walks are recommended for this purpose; and there is a presumption that they should be located outdoors, preferably in pleasant countryside, and be taken in company rather than solitude. As always, walking is thus used as a means to an end; and a range of objectives is reflected in each type and also in the diversity of walking, which extends from a daily stroll with a dog and an occasional short walk during a family outing at one extreme, to solo back-packing over a National Trail, an organised 100-mile challenge walk and 'munro' or peak bagging at the other. This variety is one of the great virtues of recreational walking, it offers much to many; and, if properly managed and promoted, something for everyone.

To establish some order within the diversity, a student-based exercise at Staffordshire University classified 20 types of walking on the basis of five sets of dimensions which refer to the nature and accessibility of each type:

Is this type of walk ... [eg strolling, hiking, etc]
- (a) easy and casual (1)   —or—   strenuous and rigorous (7) ?
- (b) suitable for mixed-ability groups (1)   —or—   for aficionados only (7) ?
- (c) capable of spontaneous participation (1) —or— needs planning & preparation (7)
- (d) relaxing and sociable (1)   —or—   challenging and rewarding (7) ?
- (e) a conventional, mainstream activity (1)   —or—   an esoteric, minority activity (7)?

The mean score (from a range of 1 to 7) for each of the 20 types of walking together with its rank position (from 1 to 20) based on this score provided 200 bits of information. These were summarised further by adding the five mean scores and also the five rank scores for each type of walk and then plotting the single array of 20 points (Fig.1.2). Four clusters emerge. The largest has the lower scores and comprises eight types, including 'walking' per se. Thus, when perceived in general terms walking is recognised as one of the more passive, pleasurable and consequently popular forms of recreation. Together with strolling, roaming and five similar types, 'walking' is easy, casual, relaxing and sociable; and capable of spontaneous participation, individually or by groups of mixed-ability. In short, walking per se is a conventional, mainstream informal recreational activity.

On the other hand, there are five types of walking which are consistently placed at the very opposite end of the scale. These require planning and preparation; they are strenuous, rigorous and suitable only for aficionados. They provide the excitement of adventure and competition; and extend walking into the realm of outdoor pursuits with its opportunities for self-development, tangible achievement and the "challenge that has always appealed to adventurous minds which, by daring to step over the line, leave the crowd behind and enlarge their own world" (Crane, 1989). The space between these contrasting categories is held by two smaller clusters. One comprises rambling, striding and tramping; and the other, more strenuous set comprises marching, trekking, trail-walking and hiking. Overall, the important messages are that the broad field of walking provides a wide range of recreational activities and associated experiences which is capable of satisfying diverse needs of almost all sections of society; *and, secondly, that priority in respect of provision for and promotion of walking should be granted to the more accessible and more popular forms.*

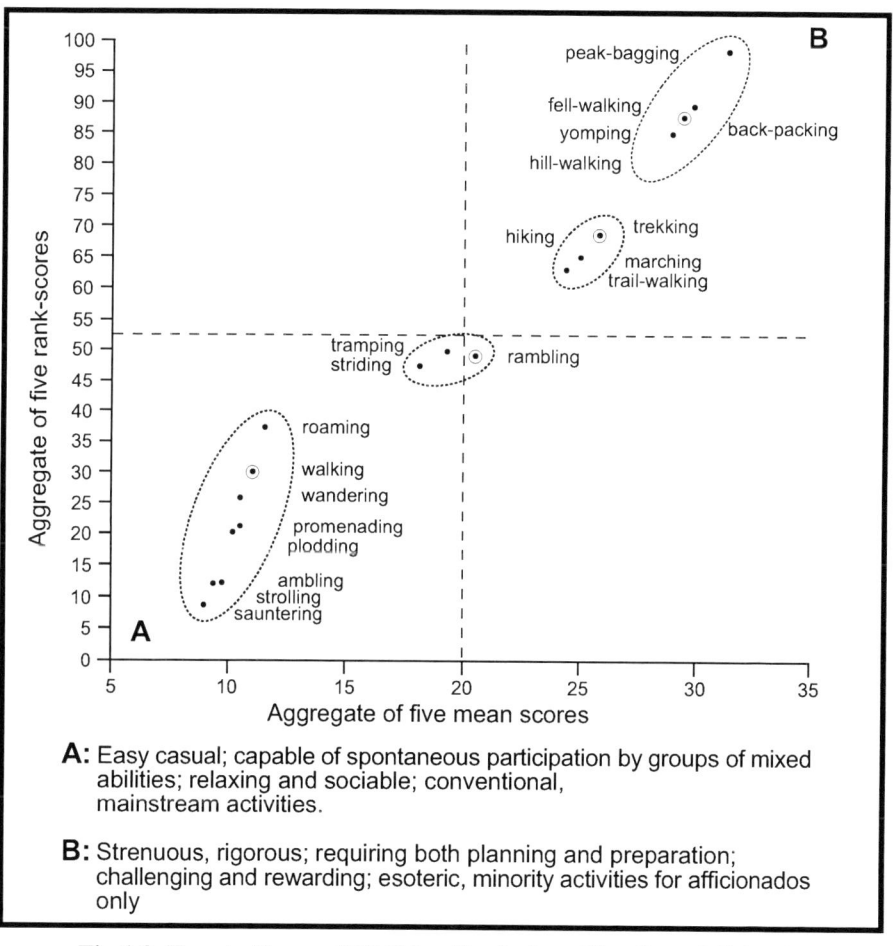

Fig.1.2 Twenty Types of Walking Ranked on Five Sets of Criteria

Unfortunately, all too often some forms of walking are seen to comprise a less appropriate use of the countryside than others; and while there is no consistency of opinion on these matters, nor any research into them, they warrant recognition. Mike Harding, comedian, enthusiastic walker and former President of the Ramblers Association, provides an introduction to some tensions in this area while addressing the question *What is Rambling?*. This discourse merits attention partly because it is entertaining but more particularly because it is incisive and informative.

> It is very difficult to define Rambling..... It is far easier to tell you what it is not !
>
> It is not, for example, *hiking*. Hiking implies a fixed purpose, an object in view, a goal or aim toward which the hiker moves. Rambling rarely has such a certitude or end-point. The destination of a ramble is often moveable.
>
> Rambling is not *yomping*. Yomping was invented during the Falklands War... It's a sort of homicidal hiking...
>
> Rambling is also not *walking*. Walking is something you do when you take the dog out or when you go to the shops. Rambling is not walking, nor ever will be!
>
> So, if Rambling is none of these things, then what is it ? A Ramble is a gentle meandering sort of walk in the countryside of anything between five and thirty miles. It might go over mountains of 3000 feet or so, or then again, it might stick to the valley bottoms. It might require the assistance of a team of mini-Sherpas and a succession of support camps but, on the other hand, it might be merely a gentle stroll along a river bank and through gently quivering hayfields, requiring nothing other than the ability to outrun the bull while reading a map.....

Mike favours some ramblers more than others, and he is not well disposed towards that influential character, 'the New Romantic Rambler' who...

> ... grows his hair long so that he looks like Shelley and always carries a notebook to record any deep thoughts he might have as he strolls through the land, head held high, eyes on a distant horizon. To him all skies are blue, all meadows green, all crags stupendous beetling marble walls, all moons are full and all blossoms fragrant... [He] is so engrossed in his mental processes as he strolls along with his head in the air, thinking his poetic thoughts, that he never looks where he's walking... Now, I go walking in the hills for the sheer joy of it. I've no misconceptions about Nature - it's red in tooth and claw and it smells and sticks to your boots - but I do believe that a leisurely ramble through wide open spaces is basically good for the soul of man...

Mike is the champion of 'the Bog-Standard Rambler' who is...

> ... a sort of ordinary, no-nonsense, John or Jane type of person, who enjoys putting a pair of boots on and going for a good walk in beautiful scenery. If you asked them

why they did it, they would probably shyly mutter something about fresh air and exercise but this is just a cover-up for the real reason they are out walking. They are playing truant. That simply is the top and bottom of it.

Truancy, getting away from places which, for the time being, have relatively little to offer, to preferred places which, at least for a while, afford greater satisfactions is, indeed, the top and bottom and the heart of the matter. However, like John and Jane, Harding continues to find it difficult to explain the real reasons for and the nature of rambling. So he addresses unwelcome 'deviants' or forms of 'crypto-rambling' and thus reveals stronger objections to particular types of walkers.

A form of crypto-Rambling that is well and truly sailing under false colours is *the picnicer*. The picnic never has been and never will be Rambling. There are even people who picnic from the boot of their car, for heaven's sake ! True, there are those who pack up a thermos and a pile of sandwiches and walk a few yards off the road to sit by the side of a stream or pond with hundreds of other folk munching away... but these are not Ramblers - any more than the folk who drive out to the countryside and sit in their cars reading the Sunday newspapers are Ramblers...

Yet another thing that I don't understand about Man, the Motorist, is why people drive to beautiful places... to spend all their time sitting in their cars facing out to sea or towards the lake or moor and after the first glance at the beauty before them they spend the rest of their day in the car, reading the newspaper or sleeping the sleep of the just-about-alive... **Can it be that they just don't know what the countryside is for ? That they don't realise they can actually get out and walk around in it ?** I believe it's much more subtle than that; these people are actually frightened of leaving the car... They actually believe, subconsciously, that if they were to stray from it, it might de-materialise in the strange moorland air and leave them stranded in a weird world full of sheep, drystone walls, and wild-haired women screaming 'Heathcliff'.

The last crypto-Rambler I want to deal with is the 'I like to get out and stretch my legs round the village' Rambler. These people clog up the roads of the country every Sunday, driving out to villages miles from their homes where they park the car and wobble around, festooned with cameras, wallets-akimbo, looking for gift shops. It must be something akin to drug addiction, this obsession with spending on things in craft shops. What do they do when they get home with them ?

Much of this is fair comment in terms of description and, to some extent, in terms of criticism of the circumstances described - which are problematic and disappointing; but the implied blame may well be misplaced. The behaviour may stem from constraints of various kinds and from response to inadequate or inappropriate provision. Many of the pseudo-walkers may not know 'what the countryside is for'; and they are frightened of straying far from their cars. *The real questions are why should this be so and what should be done about it.* The practical and deep-seated needs of walkers, hesitant walkers and potential walkers require more careful attention if their horizons are to be widened, their aspirations raised, and their enjoyment of the countryside enhanced; and the needs of children and the elderly require particular attention. Policy and provision should be directed to these ends.

3. Walking and Recreational Experiences

Recreational walking entails much more than physical exercise and its complex purposes comprise packages of interactions between people and with places, of aspirations and expectations, of satisfactions and achievements or other out-turns (Fig.1.3). Indeed, the diverse satisfactions and benefits of walking are not always self-evident, even to participants. The variety, complexity and personal nature of such goals make this a difficult field to research and understand; but it should have a central role in the formulation of policy and the determination of provision for walking. If it is misunderstood or misrepresented both policy and provision will be misdirected.

In the 1930's government health policy sought to identify something of the breadth of purposes which walking might serve:

> The Government is at present engaged on a health campaign... It is essential for any national health scheme to preserve for the nation, walking grounds and regions where young and old can enjoy the sight of unspoiled nature. And it is not a question of physical exercise only; it is also a question of enjoyment and of spiritual exercise. It is a question of spiritual values. Without vision, the people perish; and without sight of the beauty of nature the spiritual power of the British people will be atrophied. (Cited by Cherry, 1975).

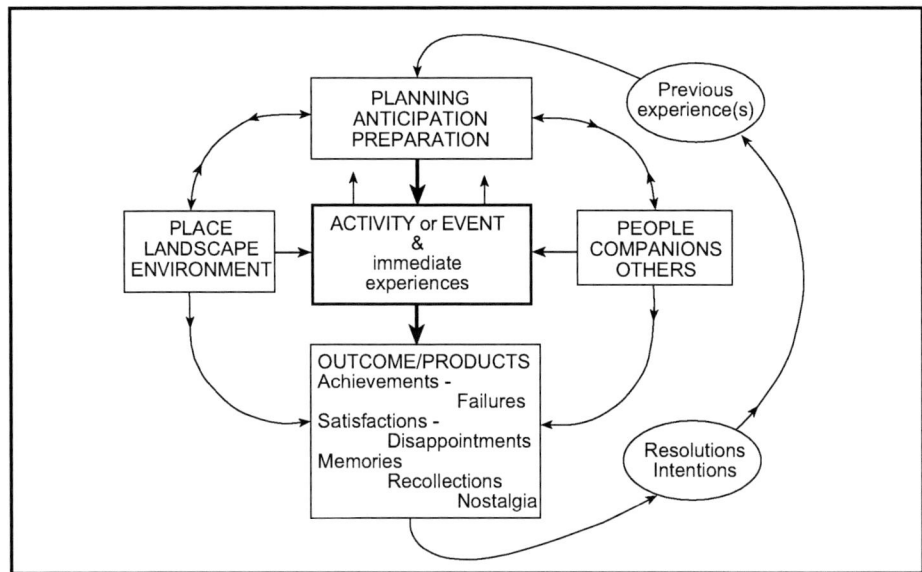

Fig.1.3 Recreational Walking as an Outdoor Activity and Experience

The merit of access for all to 'the beauty of nature' was reiterated in 1987 when it was reported that "within legislation concerning the countryside, we find no mention of the word 'landscape'... The Commission's concern is with something much bigger - with natural beauty - an awesome and complicated commodity" (*Countryside Commission News, 29, 1987*). Confirmation that 'natural beauty' is a commodity or resource underpinned the conclusion that the Commission's work "is all about sensual pleasure". The greater part of most people's response to 'natural beauty' or 'landscape' or 'the countryside' probably is sensual insofar as it is primarily dependent upon the senses and is recorded largely in emotions and feelings. On the other hand, knowledge and understanding enhance appreciation of the countryside and its constituent phenomena; and for some people, intellectual involvement with and concern for particular aspects of a place, whether historical, cultural or scientific, outweigh any sensual pleasure or spiritual satisfaction derived from the landscape as a whole.

However, personal involvement with place often extends beyond all such satisfactions to exercise creative powers of those so minded or moved to encapsulate part of their experience in some artefact. Great works of art, in music and painting, literature and poetry have been inspired by rural landscapes; and are well respected as such. In contrast, creative activities of lesser mortals are too readily dismissed as 'hobbies' rather than recognised as key elements within a package of recreational experiences. How many amateur collections of flowers or fossils, butterflies or geological specimens, carefully garnered during purposeful walks, give a wealth of lasting pleasures ? How many ordinary folk carry a camera on walks and take delight, then and subsequently, in capturing scenes which appeal to them ? How many walkers of no real artistic or literary talent are nevertheless moved to put paint or pen to paper and enjoy recording scenes, thoughts and feelings, often only for their own eyes and satisfaction or to be shared with friends ?

In summary, walking is simultaneously a means whereby individuals are involved to varying degrees in close encounters with preferred places, usually in chosen company. These experiences are rarely simple and comprise, in varying proportions, physiological and psychological benefits, sensual pleasures, intellectual satisfactions and creative achievements, together with enhancement of prior, concurrent and subsequent inter-personal relationships based on shared experiences. 'Access' to the countryside therefore should not be interpreted narrowly in terms of legal rights and footpaths but relate fully to sets of experiences which walkers knowingly or subconsciously expect, need and deserve. Such comprehensive access may be summarised in six broad categories or objectives:

- **1 Legal**   Do I have the right to be where I am, doing what I am doing ?
- **2 Physical & Social**   Can I make it safely and comfortably over the entire route in the company I wish to keep ?
- **3 Visual**   Can I see that which I might reasonably expect to observe ?
- **4 Aesthetic**   Can I appreciate that which I see, sense and feel ?
- **5 Intellectual**   Do I know what I am looking at; can I understand the 'world' through which I walk ?
- **6 Psychological**   Can I achieve the total experience, satisfactions and enjoyment which I anticipated ?

Success in respect of the first three objectives depends largely on rights and physical provision. In contrast, success in the remainder depends upon the walker's current capacity as a receptor for inputs from the total milieu encountered during the walk. This capacity is substantially a cultural construct, capable of development and direction. Therefore the promotion of recreational walking and enjoyment of the countryside should be nation-wide and should be sympathetically related to the full range of capabilities and limitations in each of these spheres. It should seek to encourage and educate current and potential participants no less than to facilitate their participation. Such a comprehensive approach to access for countryside walking is not available at present; nor is it generally accepted as an essential or desirable component of policy for the countryside. On the contrary, exclusive sectoral interests prevail and out-reach to the population as a whole is neglected.

The roots of this situation lie deep in the history of walking, and while everyday recreational walking is as old as human society influential movements have periodically produced distinctive forms which contribute significantly to the variety outlined above (Fig.1.2). These cannot be attributed to individuals but rather to schools of thought which attracted followers with similar inclinations and capabilities. Thus, in the first instance, particular forms and orientations of walking were the product of a few and the province of minorities; and while some have now become readily accessible to many, others continue as minority interests. Modern history has produced five distinctive types of continuing importance; and, broadly sequential in terms of their origins, these comprise:

- **1** Genteel, sociable strolling/promenading within designed leisure landscapes.

- **2** Educational/intellectual tours, whether at home or overseas.

- **3** Romantic pursuit of aesthetic satisfactions through 'natural beauty' and appreciation of the 'picturesque'.

- **4** Science-led nature studies and field excursions.

- **5** Ascetic quests for fitness and adventure.

While each has distinctive origins and characteristics, they are not mutually exclusive and hybrid forms have emerged. However, it is useful to identify the origins and salient characteristics of each in turn.

4. Pleasurable Walking and Designed Leisure Landscapes
The stately home, built by the aristocracy and the affluent for pleasure as much as utility, originates in the 16th century when:

> All over England there were springing up those handsome dwellings, beautifully situated, which a later generation was to know as 'gentlemen's seats', and which

were typical of a new era of luxurious living.... Around these houses were elaborately planned flower gardens, walks, orchards, parks and plantations. (Taylor, 1951).

The aristocracy were an inviolable class, protected by their privileged position, power and wealth; but for their designed leisure landscapes they were dependent on professional classes and they could readily become subject to their 'obedient servants'. The latter generally subscribed to prevailing schools of thought and were thus inclined to express the high culture of the day. But culture is responsive to change in the relevant arts and sciences and to shifts in fashion and taste; and there is a long history of leisure landscapes which is beyond the scope and needs of this study, where the aim is to illustrate some general matters relevant to provision for countryside walking.

Many 17th-century country houses were very substantial works of art and science, of architecture and horticulture. They signified man's control over nature and his ability to establish order and create beauty; and they proclaimed his intellectual achievements and appreciation of aesthetics. Beyond these they were recreation grounds: places for select gatherings where sociable strolling or solitude would be enjoyed with the benefits of a varied and pleasing environment which could, to those so inclined, be intellectually stimulating. Progress through formal gardens and carefully planted grounds was facilitated by smooth, even and firm surfaces, whether of grass or gravel; and by avenues for carriages. Enjoyment was fostered by a variety of arranged views and scenes, some comprising extensive open vistas beyond foregrounds of detailed interest, others more enclosed and intimate; some allowing appreciation of a grand design, others focusing on intricate patterns of form and colour. In short, there was comfortable access to thoughtful provision of diverse subjects at a variety of scales, most being capable of appreciation at several levels. Such things were not left to chance, nor to nature; they were designed and presented for recreational activities and experiences.

Plate 1.2 Designed Leisure Landscapes are Products of Art and Science in Concert with Nature.

In the 18th century there was a shift to classical styles of architecture and to 'simulated nature' in the design of the grounds. A new concept of 'landscape gardening'

11

was introduced by William Kent (1685-1748) though a wider impact was exerted by his successors, notably Lancelot 'Capability' Brown (1715-1783) and Repton, who completed 400 commisions between 1784 and 1816. 'Capability' was so labelled because of his careful identification of 'capabilities' in the lie of the land and its complexion that could be developed within Kent's new art and science of 'gardening', which was to improve rather than replace nature. Hoskin's (1955) introduction to their style and works cannot be bettered:

> Kent's view of landscape gardening was a reaction against the excessively formal gardens that had surrounded the seventeenth-century houses... Kent's gardens were irregular and romantic, 'with sudden changes of scene to ravish and surprise the beholders of temples, cascades, groves and statues in unexpected corners'....
> Capability Brown worked on a grand scale... In 1764 he created at Blenheim the most magnificent private lake in the country by damming the little river Glyme... He manipulated square miles of landscape in the park, planting trees on a scale consonant with the massive Vanbrugh house. Brown also made the lake at Burghley about 1775, wiped out the formal gardens of the earlier age, and 'landscaped' the park beyond them. A guide to Burghley House, published in 1797, says: 'It was the genius of the late Launcelot Brown, which, brooding over the shapeless mass, educed out of a seeming wilderness, all the order and delicious harmony which now prevail... Though the beauties with which we are here struck are more peculiarly the rural beauties of Mr. Brown than those of Dame Nature, she seems to wear them with so simple and unaffected a grace, that it is not even the man of taste who can, at a superficial glance, discover the difference'.

Although significantly different, these 18th-century parks retained key features of their predecessors. Thus, within the larger schemes, 'flower gardens, walks, orchards, ponds' and similar decorative, often formal, features generally retained a place, usually close to the house. Also, high quality provision to facilitate enjoyment of the whole was retained and extended. Short strolls were complemented by routes suitable for longer periods of exploration and exercise, whether on foot or from the vantage point of horseback or carriage. Paved paths were commonplace but comfort was always assured, even when walking on grass:

> A Prussian traveller described such provision in the following terms: "The grass in England is of incomparable beauty... Hence comes the taste for those beautiful grass walks which are smoothed and made resplendent by means of a large stone rolled over the ground: these walks are often so level, that they can play at bowls upon them as on a billiard-table. (East, 1951).

Excursions through the parks were intended to be 'eventful' through offerings of a variety of scenery and features calculated to supply immediate and memorable experiences while being equally able to titillate the minds of some and engage others in intellectual or spiritual exercise (Plate 1.2). These parks were more than picturesque. They were, for example, a sort of arboretum or botanic garden giving pride of place to various blends of indigenous and exotic plants and trees collected from far-flung corners of the world. They were show grounds for livestock, notably deer and pedigree horses, cattle and sheep, often bred for their appearance or other aspects of special interest. Again, exotic species, including the splendidly-horned Highland cattle from Scotland and highly decorative peacocks from overseas, often were deployed for display. They were galleries and museums in which the house and its contents were the centre-piece but the parks were variously equipped with artefacts representing matters of real or imagined interest. These were usually purposefully placed with scientific cunning to contribute to visual experiences, to create a 'surprise view' or draw the eye to distant features; and, alternatively, to provide a convenient and comfortable place in which to rest awhile and enjoy an exhibition of scenery and sociable company.

All such parks, their predecessors and successors, have included excellent provision for walking, providing the comfortable access which complements and facilitates enjoyment of the natural and designed landscapes. They were highly successful in their day as private places for privileged minorities comprising both residential and visiting parties. Nowadays many are open to the public and their success continues as they provide enjoyment and satisfaction to larger numbers from a wider cross-section of society who appreciate the comfortable access to the diversity of natural and man-made phenomena.

5. Discerning Minds and the Countryside

The wealthy and educated also pioneered the second and third distinctive forms of recreational walking; and Grand Tours in foreign parts, whether in Britain or Europe, were undertaken with the prime intention of increasing one's knowledge and improving one's understanding of the wider world. Bacon (1561-1626) identified the narrow and broader roles of such *Travel*.

> Travel, in the younger sort, is a part of education; in the elder, a part of experience. He that travelleth into a country before he hath some entrance into the language, goeth to school, and not to travel.

The relationship is cyclical; and travel into any 'new country' will provide intellectual and aesthetic satisfactions in proportion to ability to interact with the people and places one encounters or positively selects. The better educated will 'read' the countryside differently from those with a more limited vocabulary; but those with no lexicon are excluded from any meaningful experience, and this presents a challenge to those committed to promoting enjoyment of the countryside.

However, the mind is more than the brain. It also embraces the heart and soul and other seats of feeling; and any person can be touched and moved by visual images. These innate sensibilities may comprise the greater form of communication; and they complement or supercede intellectual perception. Both may be developed through training, direction and experience; and, since the focus of individuals may differ, it is no surprise that the pursuit of intellectual improvement and of aesthetic satisfactions should develop more or less contemporaneously. Thus the latter eventually gave birth to the 'romantic movement' with its particular emphasis on appreciation of 'natural beauty' and 'picturesque' landscapes - and to the third type of recreational walking.

In each case, travel abroad called for interpreters and guides for both novices and those extending their education and experience. Initially, guides were appropriately educated personal companions; but as travel in foreign parts increased, commercial enterprises recognised the value of literary, cartographic and pictorial 'guides'. Media intervention thus began to serve and shape patterns of recreational travel and walking for both intellectuals and romanticists. Printed guides addressed the perceived needs of an identified clientele and projected the views of their authors. Writers and publishers could benefit by adapting their products to serve more customers, but until recent times the market limits were quite narrowly defined by prerequisite capabilities, notably adequate literary skills and purchasing power. Consequently guides written for the well educated were and continue to be barriers rather than gateways to those with little or no schooling.

Where one should travel or walk for best advantage in terms of intellectual advancement or aesthetic satisfactions is also conditioned by cultural orientation, education and social convention And given that the local scene may be frequently enjoyed, travel to more distant, complementary or even exotic places within the realm of one's comprehension must appeal to enquiring minds. Furthermore, personal satisfactions from travelling may be enhanced by social satisfactions gained from the company of peers with similar experiences; and from esteem granted by those equipped to appreciate or to envy the merits of favoured places. This balance of motives, and a preference for social segregation, may generate a resolute defence by established users of their highly valued places; and early preferences of discerning minds for particular intellectual and aesthetic satisfactions have proved to be of lasting importance.

As conditions for long-distance travel improved, the geographical origins of Western civilization and the more dramatic scenery of southern Europe became fashionable. By 1776 Samuel Johnson could declare, with more than a touch of cynicism, that:

> A man who has not been in Italy, is always conscious of an infirmity, from not having seen what it is expected a man should see. The grand object of travelling is to see the shores of the Mediterranean.

Johnson was ahead of his time in highlighting shores rather than cities; and the classical heritage of Mediterranean Europe together with the mountains and lakes of Italy and Switzerland were particularly attractive to early English travellers. Both had a considerable impact in Britain. The former was a powerful influence on architecture and landscape design; and the latter was an important factor in the transformation of British mountains from detested and despised regions to highly prized places, preferred above most others for their amenity value.

The Romanticists, and Wordsworth in particular, promoted the idea that mountains and lakes were of special aesthetic significance; but to some extent he was building on an established case.

> By the time Wordsworth had embarked on writing his *Guide to the Lakes* (1810), the dons, the divines and the draughtsmen had been making the tour of the (English) Lakes for fifty years - the Lake District was already established as a fashionable resort... More than thirty accounts of tours had been published as well as several handsome volumes of views. It was a Mecca for landscape artists... And the high

priest of the Picturesque was the Cumbrian born Rev. William Gilpin. He invented the term 'Picturesque Beauty', which he defined as 'that which would look well in a picture'... (By 1798) the picturesque tour had become a subject for satire. The Rev. James Plumptree of Clare College, Cambridge, a typical 'Laker' himself, wrote a comic opera entitled *The Lakers*... (Bicknell, 1984).

In their *Guides* to the Lake District, both West (1778) and Wordsworth (1810-1846) express acute awareness of the popularity amongst Britons of the Alps and its larger lakes; and both argue strongly in favour of the intimacy of the English Lakes as the better option. In other comparative observations, Wordsworth refers to 'the scenes of Scotland' as being superior to those of Switzerland; and he also makes passing but favourable reference to Snowdon and Helvellyn, and he would be aware of Thomas Pennants' *Journey to Snowdon*, published in 1781. To what extent these other mountainous regions of Britain were preferred by early travellers and walkers is uncertain; but Pimlott (1947) reports with some authority that at the close of the 19th century "Scotland, the Lake District and North Wales were the only important inland touring areas". The railways, so much feared and detested by Wordsworth, had opened up both Scotland, where royal example had set a lead, and North Wales, which lay astride the most important route from London to Ireland. Railways had also penetrated most other parts of the country; but Pimlott specifically notes that "Cornwall was still (in 1900) comparatively unknown except to a small minority with a love for the picturesque and romantic".

While not disputing Pimlott's identification of the principal areas of 'inland tourism', local studies show that many areas with 'romantic' appeal had attracted significant numbers of walkers well before 1900. Wordsworth had twice visited the Wye valley before 1800; and where the guru leads cult members would follow to search out picturesque highlights of this remarkable valley. The Yorkshire Dales were crossed by the Keighley to Kendal turnpike road and this encouraged visitors to take in "the natural curiosities of Ingleton and Settle", if only while en route to the Lakes (Raistrick, 1967). Buxton spa, following Bath's example, was graced by its Crescent in 1786; and it drew visitors into the Peak District. Edward Rhodes' illustrated guide on *Peak Scenery for the Derbyshire Tourist* (4 vols: 1818-23) was widely read "and established for the Peak a lasting reputation as an area of beautiful scenery with many attractions for the tourist" (Edwards, 1962). White's 1851 *Directory of Staffordshire* records the recreational merits of the county's share of the Peak District:

> This bleak and alpine district exhibits many of the wildest and most stupendous features of nature, as well as some of her more chaste and fertile beauties; the latter of which are confined chiefly to the narrow and picturesque valleys of the rivers Dove, Manyfold, Hamps, Tean, Blythe, Dane and Churnet which have their sources in the high peaty moorlands and rocky mountains which rise in picturesque disorder and shut in the fertile pastures of the glens... At Ilam, further up the Dove, is a very pleasant seat [Ilam Hall] which, from its romantic situation, suggests the idea of a glen in the Alps. [Here] two considerable rivers rush from under the limestone hills... the precipices that surround the valleys are well clothed with oak and other woods... the sides are furnished by nature with a profusion of flowers of no ordinary

appearance... and the bold romantic Hills of Thorp Cloud and Bunster may be seen on either side of the Dove. The pleasure walks from the Hall are diversified and beautiful...and the warmest imagination can scarcely conceive a spot more wild and romantic than some parts of the Vale of Manyfold...

Such examples may be multiplied and it is certain that by 1900 Romanticists had discovered all promising picturesque areas in Britain and, with or without the aid of Claude glasses*, had 'picked out the eyes' in each. Spatial patterns thus established at several scales have proved to be enduring, with ongoing consequences of real substance for recreational walking and rural tourism.

> * Claude glasses, named after the 17th-century painter, were concave, slightly darkened and usually oval mirrors which allowed the selection of condensed views by an observer or painter who had, metaphorically perhaps as much as physically, partly turned away from the landscape in question. Their modern counterpart may be the view-finders of cameras with wide-angle and telephoto lenses which allow selection of scenes for the purpose of picture-making.

6. Scientific Minds and Natural Phenomena

Meanwhile, modern science and the extension of formal education had generated a more analytical view of nature which gave birth to the fourth distinctive form of countryside walking, comprising field studies and excursions that were more sharply focused than those of earlier intellectuals and romanticists. Professionals led the way; and *James Forbes' Alpine Tour of 1832* illustrates the scientific focus of such investigative walkers but also shows that it need not exclude appreciation of picturesque places. Forbes (1809-68) was a distinguished graduate of Edinburgh University and subsequently its Professor of Natural Philosophy with special interests in geology and glaciology. His tour from Geneva occupied 65 days:

> On most of these he covered 20 to 30 miles, and occasionally more... Forbes was in no doubt that only furtherance of knowledge justified his exertions, although aesthetic enthusiasm was an allowable bonus... The Lauterbrunnen Valley was already famous, not only for its scenery but also as the prototype of a 'valley of disruption'... the result of a great wrench in the earth's crust... Forbes then visited the lower Grindelwald glacier, another a tourist attraction... but his intention was to carry out a series of actinometrical observations on the valley floor... Three days later he enjoyed a splendid view of the snout of the Rhine glacier where, ten years on, he evolved his original theory of glacier structure; in 1832 it was just scenery... His Tour was concluded with an ascent of Rigi for its magnificent panorama, which was already so famous that tens of thousands of travellers ascended annually (Cunningham, 1979).

Professional scientists such as Forbes were the archetype of science-led walkers and leading figures in the formation of institutions to promote and eventually popularise the expanding field of science. National organisations were complemented at regional and local levels; and the Manchester societies may be representative of developments throughout the country:

      1781   Manchester Literary and Philosophical Society
      1821   Manchester Society for the Promotion of Natural History
      1827   Manchester Botanical and Horticultural Society
      1838   Manchester Geological Society
      1860   Manchester Field Naturalists (and Archaeologists) Society
      1884   Manchester Geographical Society.

The Literary and Philosophical Society reflected the classical holistic approach to education and embraced a very wide range of cultural and scientific interests. As the senior institution it sought to retain its comprehensive hold on all disciplines and was reluctant to admit amateur scientists. Tensions were inevitable between such conservative bodies and the more relaxed societies which emerged as a growing range of sciences were extended into schools and 'evening institutes' and thence into middle-class and even working class homes. Amateur archaeologists, botanists, entomologists, geologists, historians, zoologists and others, soon greatly out-numbered the professionals; and many of them combined home-based hobbies with field excursions and a social life based on both. Many joined such 'learned societies' to enhance their knowledge and skills and the enjoyment derived from them; some established societies sought to accommodate this new and numerous clientele, and new ones were formed in response to it.

Founded in 1860, the Manchester Field Naturalists Society illustrates such developments. It was open to:

> ladies and gentlemen who are specially interested in natural history (which includes geology, botany and zoology); and it is open also to those who, without paying minute scientific attention to the objects of nature, delight to ramble in the country and find pleasure in the contemplation of its loveliness... and to people fond of topography, archaeology and all the pursuits, literary, artistic and scientific, that give life and reward to rural excursions. (Shercliffe, 1987).

This generously catholic approach espoused recreation, notably countryside walking, no less than erudite enquiry; and it may well have admitted romanticists. The Society flourished; and many others in the local region followed its lead. For example, the Stockport Society of Naturalists, founded in 1884, restyled itself the Stockport Field Club in 1896 in recognition of the diversity of its members' interests - which evidently embraced a growing concern for conservation:

> Natural History remained the first listed objective on the membership card, along with Photography, Topography, Antiquities and History... Those seeking both pleasure and instruction (were) invited. And aid (was) sought to protect those plants made rare or extinct by reclamation of moss and moorland and agricultural

improvements, such as sundews, primroses, cowslips and daffodils. The club intended to form a collection of specimens for the town museum.

At this time, the membership of such societies was largely middle-class but it also embraced a growing number of artisans and working-class enthusiasts too. In contrast, the Manchester Literary and Philosophical Society resisted all such popularisation and became the refuge of senior intellectuals, academics and professional scientists. In 1862 it refused admission to the best known amateur botanist of his day, Leo Grindon (co-founder of the Mancheter Field Naturalists Society), who fostered both 'nature study' and countryside walking:

> Grindon's first book, *Manchester Walks and Wild Flowers*, (1858) aimed to help ordinary people to explore their beautiful surroundings... He was full of praise for the outdoor investigation of natural beauty: *Rambling in the fields, the town cobwebs get dusted out of one's lungs and the whole frame becomes buoyant and elastic.* He noted social blessings brought by the railways... and the Saturday half holiday... and the prospect of a comfortable farm-house tea.. (He also noted that) natural history provides perennial employment for leisure hours at home *forming little museums of natural objects such as plants, insects, fossils and shells...* In 1866 Grindon produced his second book on *Summer Rambles in Cheshire, Derbyshire, Lancashire and Yorkshire...* in which the chapters are arranged around the railway system. (Shercliffe, 1987).

Grindon epitomised the convergence of popular scientific interests with countryside walking and, increasingly, with conservation; but he and others were so successful in promoting nature rambles and home collections of botanical species in North East Cheshire that certain rare plants disappeared from some popular districts. New codes of behaviour were evidently necessary; and established enthusiasts were soon concerned to protect both their favoured phenomena and their privileged position.

All local history is unique, but Manchester's experience may be indicative of general trends; and attention may be drawn to some particular points. First, whereas the Romanticist's mystical view of nature called for 'an eye to perceive' which was not to be found among the 'imperfectly educated classes', the more practical orientation of science-based approaches and their inclusion in the school curriculum made them more accessible and more appealing to wider sections of society. Secondly, whereas the Romantic movement sought out distinctive areas of outstanding beauty, scientific enquiry and related interests are more capable of being pursued universally and, therefore, most conveniently within local regions. Thirdly, practical involvement with particular sets of natural or cultural phenomena rapidly generated protective feelings for them; and many regular 'nature walkers' became committed to the cause of conservation. Finally, preoccupation with selected natural or cultural phenomena diverted attention from the composite nature of the countryside as a whole. Major architects of the contemporary landscape, namely farming and forestry, were not readily recognised as such but rather were perceived as threats to the well being of valued but minor components of it; and special interests diminished respect for the countryside as a whole in which the continuing work of man has a key role.

Promotion of the countryside thus broadly followed and strengthened the several foci of attention associated with the four distinctive types of recreational walking outlined above, particular attention being given to specific themes, notably 'historic heritage' (including the early designed leisure landscapes); 'natural beauty'; and 'wildlife'. This fostered alliances of established recreational users of the countryside with conservationists, and set them both in tacit if not open opposition to the principal agents of change - notably owners and users of rural land, property developers, and excessive numbers visitors to their preferred places. These circumstances were largely a product of convergent interests and sympathies rather than conspiracy; and they were often reflected in innocent but influential literature rather than polemic tracts.

For example, *Lovely Britain* (Mais and Stephenson, c.1935) exudes nostalgia while pursuing the theme that 'The face of Britain is most lovely where it is most ancient'. A similarly excellent book of its type and age on *The Countryside and How to Enjoy It* (Mais, 1948) adopts a thematic approach which allows a more analytical exploration of its emphases. 10% of its 310 pages comprise an introductory chapter on *The Varied Scene* which reports that:

> The native of these islands has never lost his desire for what he has learned to call natural beauty and rightly regards it as his most precious heritage. So whenever he finds an opportunity for leisure, he may be seen, rucksack on back, cycling along the lanes and walking over the downs in pursuit of the varied countryside scene ...in the South Downs, the North Downs, the Chilterns, Wiltshire and Dorset; the uplands of the Quantocks, Exmoor, Dartmoor, the Bodmin Moors, the Moorlands of Wales, and the Yorkshire Moors; together with the Mountains of Scotland, Wales and the Lakeland.

The implicit claim that *all natives* regard natural beauty as their most precious heritage and the presumption that no truly lowland region deserves inclusion in a review of 'the varied countryside' reflect emphases destined to become more deeply entrenched; a minority presumes to speak for all, and arguments based on selected parts are applied to the countryside as a whole. Furthermore, this 'comprehensive guide for all country lovers' reduced the countryside to selected elements of it :

ANIMAL and PLANT LIFE (36%)		**CULTURAL HERITAGE** (37%)	
Butterflies and Moths	18 pages	Villages	18 pages
Wild Birds	22	Historic Towns	16
Wild Animals	08	Churches and Cathedrals	22
Wild Flowers	30	Castles and Abbeys	14
Fungi	06	Old Buildings	20
Ferns	06	Ancient Landmarks	11
Wild Fruits	08	Curious Customs	
Trees	13	& Ceremonies	14

Only four short chapters are devoted to general matters. Three of these relate to practical concerns of walkers - *The Weather*; *How to Plan a Journey*; and *Footpaths*. The exception sketches *The Farming Year*; and its illustrations highlight the massive contribution of farming to valued landscapes (Plate.1.3). It thus challenges the book's claim to be 'comprehensive' since it evidently lacks a substantial section on *FARMING: Farm Houses and Farm Yards; Field Boundaries and Buildings; Crops and Livestock; Equipment and Implements; Field Operations.* Such vital material relates to the dynamic use of rural Britain but it evidently has a limited place in the new agenda for the 20th century which

Plate 1.3. 'The Farming Year' of 1948 : Spring and Autumn Landscapes.

A.J. Street's review of *The Farming Year* (in Mais, 1948) does nothing to extol the contribution of farming to valued landscapes but alerts newcomers to the countryside to the need to respect the farmer's use of it. '*Untutored townsfolk** should be quite clear... that the countryside which they would treat as a free playground is the countryman's business premises... And that, generally speaking, the farming community does not welcome the visitor, in fact, in the main resents his coming. Therefore, if an ever-increasing invasion of the countryside by untutored townsfolk is not to lead to an ever-widening breach between town and country, the invader must... realise that most of the countryside is private property... have manners enough to ask permission to trespass... and have at least some elementary knowledge of what is being done on farms at different seasons of the year... why it is being done... and what sort of behaviour by the visitor will hinder or not hinder its efficiency'.
  * A term probably borrowed from C.E.M. Joad's (1946) book -
  The Untutored Townsman's Invasion of the Countryside.

favours a countryside in which Heritage, Natural Beauty, and Wildlife are all while farming and forestry are, at best, a necessary context or, at worst, an enemy of both the countryside and its regular recreational visitors.

This agenda is well suited to current adherents of four of the five distinctive types of walking outlined above, and the enthusiastic participants are all protective of their preferred environments and their particular response to them. Indeed, their defence of particular places has been substantially extended to the countryside as a whole at the expense of promoting its enjoyment by the nation as a whole. Ironically, the fifth distinctive type of walking embraces a relatively recent adventurous response to 'wilderness' and thus relates to parts of the countryside which, until recently, held little or no attraction to anyone. It was, however, destined to have marked effects on both attitudes towards access to the countryside and provision for countryside walking.

7. The Quest for Fitness and Adventure

The ascetic quest for fitness and adventure was taken up in numbers during the latter part of the 19th century, largely but not exclusively by professional and middle-class men as an antidote to sedentary working-lives in confined spaces. Without eliminating other interests in the landscape nor enjoyment of select company, the principal emphases were on rigorous exercise and 'the adventure alternative'. A specific example has been brought to light by Butler's 1986 publication of *A Gentleman's Walking Tour of Dartmoor, 1864*. This is a delightful account of an expedition by two young gentlemen who travelled by train from Exeter to South Brent and then walked back to the city by a circuitous route over more than 60 miles of difficult terrain.

Several general points are noteworthy. First, planning and preparation were necessary (Fig.1.2). The walkers required special equipment including 'thick boots', knapsacks, an Ordnance map and a compass. Without the map and compass and some skill in their use, route planning and navigation would have been very difficult and hazardous. Pipes and tobacco also were indispensable; and the pair 'never walked so much or smoked so much' as in four days' vigorous relaxation on Dartmoor. Secondly, on the Moor the pair rarely found definite paths. Much of their walking was 'knee-deep in heather; over Turkey Sponge'; across boulder-strewn, rocky ground; and even 'on boulders in the river, covered with spray-sprinkled moss which made them uncommonly slippery'. What right they may have had to follow their chosen route, or their unplanned and unbeknown deviations from it, are not discussed; but they were never questioned as trespassers. Next, even though they visited several well publicised 'attractions', on the intervening stretches of moor they met no other walker, despite it being mid-summer. Long-distance hiking and remote moorland were not yet popular; and, apart from their own company, their meanderings were solitary.

This may have been as they would have it; and their successful, planned detour to search for Cranmere Pool illustrates the asceticism associated with adventure. 'All who have attempted to reach the pool will concur as to its seclusion and utter dreariness... Its inaccessibility is its charm; and the fun of the whole thing is to get there, and when there, to find it'. Wordsworth and his fellow romanticists would have wasted no time on such barren places, totally devoid of everything picturesque. They sought a 'concentration of interest which grants a decided superiority' to places, and they did nothing to recommend uplands as distinct from mountainous and hilly regions.

> In Scotland and Wales are found individual scenes, which, in their several kinds, cannot be excelled. But, in Scotland, particularly, what long tracts of desolate country intervene ! So that the traveller, when he reaches a spot deservedly of great celebrity, would find it difficult to determine how much of his pleasure is owing to excellence inherent in the landscape itself; and how much to an instantaneous recovery from an oppression left upon his spirits by the barrenness and desolation through which he has passed. (Wordsworth, 1835: Bicknell, 1984).

Although later ecologists paired 'mountains and moorlands' (Pearsall, 1950), they are distinctly different; and, assisted by sheep-farming and grouse-shooting which civilised the uplands, it was adventure seekers who popularised the latter. Thus, for example, they translated the miserable, miniscule Cranmere Pool into a 'great celebrity'; and William Crossing outlines its early history as such in his 1909 *Guide to Dartmoor*.

> According to tradition the pool is haunted by the spirit of a former Mayor of Okehampton... In 1854 a little cairn was built in the pool by the late Mr. James Perrott of Chagford, so long known as the Dartmoor guide. In it he placed a bottle for the reception of visitors' cards. Fifty-one years later, that is, in April 1905, Mr H.P. Hearder and Mr H. Scott Tucker of Plymouth, both enthusiastic moorland ramblers, placed a visitors' book there. The number of signatures to the end of 1908 is as follows:-
> *1905   1906   1907   1908   1905-1908*
> 609   962   1262   1741   4574.
> [Two-thirds of the signatures were provided in the four summer months, and August accounted for 25 %. There were just 9 visitors in February. - gk]

If Perrott was the founder, Hearder and Tucker were the pioneers of 'letter-boxing', a peculiar form of Devonshire asceticism whereby nowadays at any one time upto 3000 'boxes' are hidden at obscure locations within the 365 square miles of Dartmoor's wilderness, to be sought by aficionados with the aid of enigmatic clues.

Our unknown gentlemen adventurers of 1864 were summer walkers, and the 'attractions' which they visited within the Moor deserve attention. At 'Prince Town' the Duchy Hotel was 'decently comfortable' and the 'inhabitants were civil', but the place as a whole was 'dreary' and the church, 'a dismal object'. Even the 'celebrated Dartmoor Prison' aroused curiosity but nothing more; so the pair evaded an option to inspect the interior and escaped to the moors. At Lydford, *The Castle* proved to be 'a very poor Inn' but the ancient castle justified 'a contemplative moonlit stroll among its ruins, with those great aids to reflection - our pipes'. As a whole, however, Lydford was no more than a 'group of squalid houses' which belied its previous existence as 'the principal town in the Stannary'. Lydford gorge and its 'celebrated waterfall was the only thing worth seeing' but access to this 'smart little water-privilege' was available only 'by a judicious application of that dirty dross, money, to the Miller's palm'. [The dues now go to the National Trust]. Clearly tourism had done little by the 1860s for Princetown or Lydford; but Chagford was somewhat busier and, arriving too late to obtain beds at anything but a lodging-house, the pair were met by 'hosts of people strolling out in the evening to see and climb over the old ruins at Gidleigh'.

To solitary adventurers, a host might comprise a dozen; but the following day they encountered substantially more visitors at Fingle Bridge, where 'Nature is most lavish of her gifts'.

> This is a great place for Pic-Nics, indeed a Pic-nic is a pretty sure 'find' on any day from the middle of May to the middle of August. We found two Pic-Nics going on at once to the tune of a hideous German band... Very shortly the rain came down in torrents, and we were fain to seek shelter with the dripping Pic-Nicers and draggle-tailed musicians in the picturesque old mill that lies below the bridge. The Pic-Nicers, though damp, were affable and most kindly insisted on our drinking several glasses of their sherry, nor did their kindness come at all amiss, for we had more than twelve miles to walk before we could get to Exeter that night.

Evidently, Dartmoor was already attracting a diversity of walkers; adventurers might have the moors to themselves, but genteel promenaders, sociable strollers and elegant picnicers held sway in more accessible, picturesque places. Each such minority group thus established customary rights to particular locations which their contemporaries and successors would resolutely defend from invasion by uninitiated common folk.

Seventy years later, 'moorland tramping' was firmly established as a branch of countryside walking, especially in northern England where the proximity of extensive uplands to industrial towns facilitated its promotion amongst working-class men. Its charismatic qualities generated an influence out of all proportion to its size; and A.J.Brown's *Striding Through Yorkshire* highlights both the nature and appeal of adventure walking and the case which its proponents presented to the wider world and politicians of the day.

> In an age that craves and discovers more and more fantastic sports, **it is astonishing that so few people know the thrill of crossing a moor from end to end** in a direct line without any sort of guide. Yet, given the right kind of day, it is to be doubted whether there is any sport in the world to vie with it. Mountaineering... lacks the sustained lyric thrill; the joy of free movement; the bluff assault and repulse of the wind; the feeling of fighting one's way forward in the teeth of the elements, of contesting every yard of the way, of being beaten back and still struggling on. To cross a stretch of moor like this in a gale is something like sailing a yatch single-handed over an angry sea. There is the same absolute dependence on one's own vigilance and strength, with the added satisfaction of making one's own pace. One lays a course and attempts to steer by it, tempest-tossed and buffeted perhaps for hours on end... Sometimes one has to tack a little, to avoid a treacherous swamp; sometimes one has to scramble down the bank of a steep gill and crawl, panting, up the other side... And always one must keep one's eye fixed sharply on some directing point on the horizon,

and reach it, or risk being benighted in the high secret places. (Brown, 1938). [Brown's *Striding Through Yorkshire* appeared in 1938 but it comprises revised versions of two books published in 1931 and 1932; and it was reprinted in 1943, 1945 and, perhaps significantly, in 1949].

In summary, it was argued that 'moorland tramping is to walking what poetry is to prose'. Most might not agree but many were persuaded; and Tom Stephenson, another adherent and an effective persuader, was bold enough to declare in 1935 that the Lake District, the precious hearth of the romanticist, 'is not planned on a grand scale and an energetic walker might traverse it in a day'. In the same year he suggested a continuous footpath of some 250 miles over the tops of the moorland spine of northern England; and this was to have unfortunate consequences for national policy and provision for countryside walking.

Moorland tramping, fell and hill walking, peak and munro 'bagging' are all demanding, minority forms of recreational walking which relate to particular landforms and terrain that occur largely if not entirely in 'Highland Britain' (Figs.1.2 &.8.1). However, the quest for fitness and adventure was never restricted to these exceptional and often bleak, dour and forbidding places. Within softer, pleasant, verdant landscapes, key elements of the challenge, notably the length of the route and the pace of the walkers, are determined by man rather than the land, though this does not preclude simultaneous enjoyment of the countryside. These key properties are measurable and thus permit contests and competition between individuals; and from the mid-18th century these led to extraordinary feats over incredible distances by both professional 'pedestrians' and amateur gentlemen. Prize money for the few performers of real excellence and easier, more substantial earnings for promoters and gamblers were prominent features of this sport until, in the latter part of the 19th century, an emphasis on amateurism in public schools, universities and the upper echelons of society in general became a dominant force in the broad field of athletics. This underpinned the emergence of the Olympic Games in 1896; and, of more immediate importance, it fostered the rapid growth of numerous amateur sports, including race-walking. Participants employed their local countryside as a training and testing gound but, insofar as its character and their inclinations allowed, they also pursued other satisfactions associated with countryside walking (Figs.1.1 & 1.3).

The ascetic pursuit of fitness and adventure and of more leisurely satisfactions in the green and pleasant countryside of south-east England is covered in the story of *One Hundred Years of Walking with Surrey Walking Club, 1899-1999* (Brown, 1999). This club, the first in the world devoted solely to competitive walking, was formed on 8th October 1899 "by a group of ardent men who had for some time gathered together for the exercise of walking, at speed or merely strolling, in the County of Surrey, chiefly from Croydon from their base at the Swan and Sugar Loaf Hotel". On the 22nd of October the club's first Sunday 'stroll' covered the 18.5 miles from Croydon to Godstone and back; and this favourite route became the venue for one of the Club's three regular races, the others - introduced in 1902 and 1903 - being the 52 miles between London and Brighton and the 104-mile return trip on the same route.

Preparation for such rigorous events comprised regular Sunday 'strolls at 11 am for both the fast and slow packs... the latter proceeding at a speed of not more than 4 mph'. They included a stop for a light pub lunch and, after covering some 20 miles, concluded with dinner at the Club's HQ. The weekly 'stroll' was complemented by shorter but faster 'spins' of upto 10 miles on Wednesday and Thursday evenings and Saturday afternoons. At first, such training was on roads but to minimise impact-damage through the use of light shoes on hard and often cobbled or broken surfaces a strong preference for 'field paths' and bridleways soon emerged; and 'the club made an early decision to purchase the OS map of Surrey'.

Longer strolls soon became frequent and memorable events. The first to be minuted was the *Midnight Stroll to Brighton* which left the Croydon HQ at 11.00 pm on Saturday 23rd May 1903. It was very well attended; and was repeated annually for 70 years, but only one man completed it in 1973. Holiday periods allowed members to undertake longer excursions, perhaps for pleasure as much as training.

> In August 1906 members enjoyed a delightful field-path ramble, covering some 70 miles of woodland and riverside scenery from Orpington station... along a route devised by careful study of *Walker Miles Guidebooks*. Walker Miles was the pseudonym of Edmund Seyfang Taylor, author of a series of guides to the footpaths of Surrey and Kent which were published at the end of the 19th and the start of the 20th century. He did more than anyone else to popularise walking through the countryside south of London. (Brown, 1999).

It is evident from the outset that while pursuing serious training members also enjoyed social interaction and the intrinsic qualities of a varied and visually attractive countryside; and a wider range of club activities developed in response to these ancillary objectives.

> In 1907 a series of short social strolls for ladies who were friends of Club members [was introduced]... and on 7th September several members and friends met at Bromley station and strolled to Chislehurst where they were met by a guide who conducted them around the famous caves. The strollers afterwards proceeded to the Bickley Hotel, where an excellent tea was served. Then a ladies 100 yards running race was held...(and) after singing songs round the hotel's piano, the participants walked back to Bromley station....
>
> A turnout of 70 members and friends was recorded for a ladies stroll and garden party on Saturday 5th of June 1909. About 30 met at Sutton station and walked through Cheam village to Nonsuch Park. A Lady Stroller noted that "towards the end of the park a field path was followed, the natural attractions of which were added to by various kissing gates". Shortly afterwards, the walkers reached the Glyn Arms in Ewell where they joined the rest of the party. Strawberries and cream were served, and a concert and dancing followed... (Brown, 1999).

Against this broader context of diverse enjoyment of the countryside, it is easy to overlook the fact that the Surrey Walking Club was highly succesful, locally, regionally and nationally, in competitive events. And to win 'gold awards' in its own trio of races, members had to walk the 18.75 miles from Croydon to Godstone inside 3 hours; the 52 miles between London and Brighton in less than 8h.45m; and the 104 mile round trip inside 22 hours. To reach such standards and achieve one's full capabilities in races required sustained dedication to rigorous training; attractive though it may be, the Surrey countryside was a testing ground for athletes no less than a pleasure ground for them and their companions.

The 1914-18 war interrupted all such activities; but in 1920 the club celebrated its 'coming of age' with a race and a dinner party. The club was back in its stride; and its continued emphasis on training for long distance events, together with that of other walking clubs, may well have been instumental in eventually equipping the south-east with National Trails and other long-distance routes (Ch.8). However, it would be a mistake to imply that only walking clubs have a long and continuing history of using the wider countryside as a training ground. Running, rather than walking, along 'field paths', bridleways, tow-paths, 'green lanes' and other highways has for long comprised a major element in the quest for physical fitness by adherents of a wide range of sports, notably cross-country and road running, track and field athletics but also, if only periodically, by other seasonal team sports. Thus, for example, in 1867 members of the Thames Rowing Club agreed to run and race over fields to keep fit for the rowing season; but some substituted running for rowing and thus gave birth to the Thames Hare and Hounds Club (Brown, 1999). In short, an ascetic quest for fitness if not adventure has a long and diverse history and a substantial, continuing input to the use of 'field paths' and the countryside as a training ground; and nowadays participants are drawn from a wider spectrun of society than was the case when the Surrey Walking Club was founded.

Furthermore, although walking in search of adventure and a challenge has always been a minority activity (Fig.1.2), it has a long hisory as a matter of 'weightiness and importance'. At the beginning of the 20th century the achievements of great explorers and

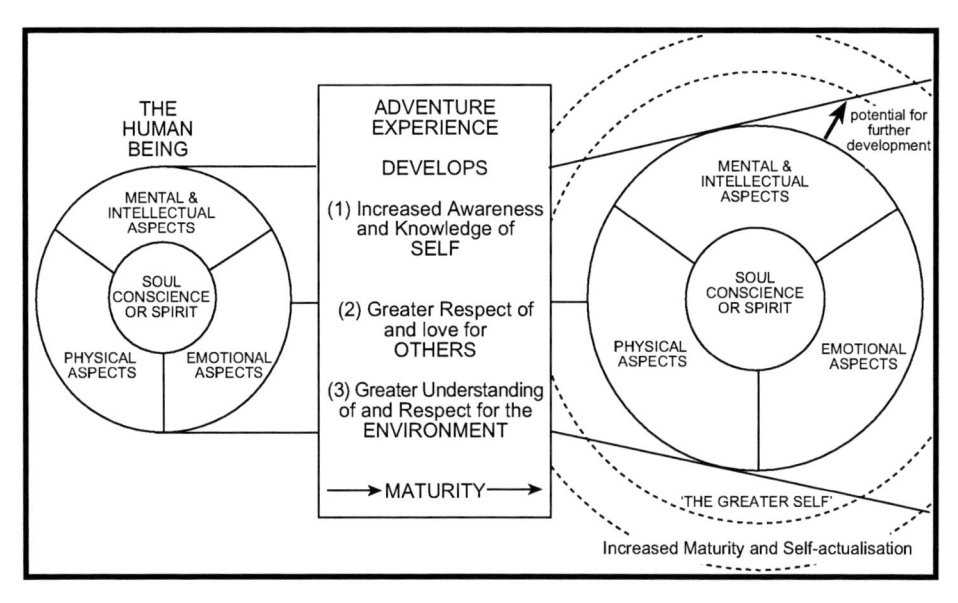

Fig.1.4 Adventure Experience and Personal Development.
(after Mortlock, 1978)

the need to improve the physical fitness of the nation combined to give it a prominent place in many respectable youth organisation; and, alongside other 'outdoor pursuits', it found a place in the curriculum of many schools (Hawkins, 1987; and Smith, 1987). Eventually, the case for 'adventure education' was documented by Mortlock (1973 and 1984). He identified a comprehensive set of benefits comprising increased self-actualisation and maturity in three broad fields: awareness of self, respect for others, and understanding of the environment (Fig.1.4). Progress in each may be achieved until the limit of one's potential precludes further development - or until misadventure and accident restrict or terminate participation. The general case is convincing provided the latter are rare and, secondly, that the competition which adventure entails is perceived as a personal, self-contained experience (Fig.1.3). Outdoor adventure thus should be seen primarily as a challenge posed by the activity and the environment for the individual participants, rather than a rule-bound sport which is characterised by inter-personal and group rivalry.

In recent years a rapid growth in leisure activities and an excessive concern for safety have had adverse effects on outdoor pursuits, but a new *Study of Opportunities for Adventure and Challenge for Young People* confirms their intrinsic value and their utility as educational devices:

> We do not claim that physical activities in a natural environment provide, by themselves, a panacea for our social problems... But... It is vitally important to encourage all young people to be enterprising and adventurous, and to help them - through education, training and leisure pursuits - to widen their interests. We are in no doubt about the pleasure and benefit which experience of outdoor challenges gives to young people... [and] that programmes based upon, or embracing this element can be of immense benefit to young people and to society in general. (Hunt, c.1990)

The case for special provision for young people is indisputable; but is anyone too old for adventure ? And is not countryside walking a particularly suitable and appropriately varied field to offer a challenge to boys and girls, men and women of any age ? Within the limits of physiological capabilities, it is never too early nor too late to enjoy adventure; and a report on the Long Distance Walkers *Invicta Hundred* lends weight to this view:

> It is a notable achievement to walk a hundred miles in one walk [within 48 hours]. To win a 'Ten Hundreds Badge' is the mark of a very special walker. Henry Bridge has done it as he approaches his 82nd birthday. He took up long distance walking when he was 68, and walked his first Hundred at the age of 69... 'Age is only a figure on a piece of paper' says Henry, modestly; but his numerous admirers think his achievement magnificent. (*Strider*, 63, August 1992).

There are few activities that can offer both senior citizens and young people a rigorous challenge and an opportunity to 'leave the crowd behind' and can equip initiates with 'a mystique that sets them apart' (Crane, 1989). However, walking can be understood by all, is open to all, and can provide a challenge for all. Having a low threshold requirement in terms of personal attributes - including skills, strength and courage - walking is capable of being presented in a variety of forms and at a wide range of graded levels or standards (Fig.1.2). It can therefore introduce most individuals to an adventure and challenge and it can also provide for their subsequent development to the limits of their potential. Nevertheless the merits of 'adventure walking' and 'challenge walks' are subject to some debate, even dispute; and Mike Harding is granted the last word on this matter.

> There are varieties of pseudo-Rambling which have ensnared many of the unwary and are to be avoided like the very plague... One [such] form of ersatz Rambling is *the challenge walk*... It seems crazy to me that hundreds of people will pull on boots and anoraks and, wearing badges and numbers like common criminals, will set off on a hundred-mile, overnight hike through the harshest of landscapes in the most abysmal of conditions. Off the hills they come hours later, sopping wet and freezing cold, bandy-legged and delirious, steam coming from their boots, eyes like bloodshot pickled onions and tongues like rhubarb sticks, crying for water, liniment and their mothers, and so dehydrated that they are a fire hazard. I see nothing sensible in that sort of carry-on. (Harding, 1986).

Plate 1.4. Waukenphast's 'Celebrated Tour Boots' for Gentlemen Walkers of the late 19th Century, at Home or Abroad. (from Butler, 1986)

2
INTERPRETATIONS OF NATURE, THE COUNTRYSIDE AND CONSERVATION

The several relationships between distinctive types of walking and preferred places within the countryside reflect different, dynamic sub-cultures. These are underpinned by different interpretations of nature which, in turn, are affected by over-riding 'world views'. These are matters of 'weightiness and importance', but a simple exposition of their role in recent times may facilitate understanding of significant shifts in the development of the countryside, the selection of valued places, and the origins of the multi-faceted conservation movement which, in turn, have marked effects of continuing importance on access to the countryside.

1. World Views and Interpretations of Nature

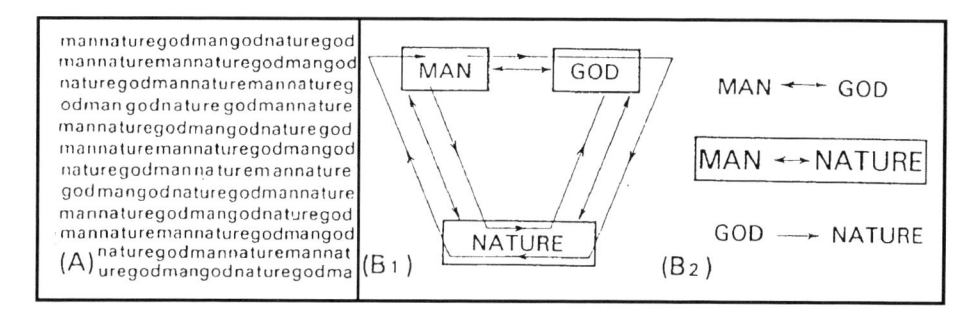

Fig.2.1 World Views associated with (A) Preliterate Societies and (B) Advanced Societies of Today (after Redfield, 1953).

All human societies have always recognised (i) Man (*homo sapiens*), (ii) Nature (all other physical manifestations and forces comprising the known universe), and (iii) God (all supernatural non-man and non-nature), as distinct components of a structured cosmology (Redfield, 1953). As human capabilities and perceptions have changed, so too has man's view of relationships between these three components. Pre-literate societies generally recognise Man, Nature and God as one might see the colours of a plaid; each is identifiable but none can have a separate existence. They are closely interwoven as the warp and weft of the fabric of life. Mutuality, inter-dependence, and a moral order bind Man, Nature and God into a single dynamic entity, and communal rather than individual rights are dominant. In contrast, monotheistic world views and technologically more advanced societies generally attribute a separate and primordial role to God and to His creations, Nature and Man; and they postulate an intricate, interactive network of relationships between the three in which the rights and responsibilities of individuals assume a major role, subject to the over-riding authority of the law (Fig.2.1).

With further developments in science and technology which provide 'convincing and cumulative evidence of man's control over his natural environment' (Balogh, 1969), modern, scientific societies have increasingly divorced Man and Nature from God. They even question His active involvement, since the Creation, with either Nature or Man; some doubt His existence and the need for theistic religion; and the law of the land assumes a more dominant and pervasive role. While these alternative world views may be seen as successive independent sets of ideas, they are better regarded as additional layers within man's collective, stratified memory. Thus, while recent beliefs may well be more in evidence, the range of world views and the possibility of hybrid variants has multiplied through time; and the option of invoking 'history' or 'precedent' as an alternative to current practice and the law has never been surrendered.

These world views underpin four important interpretations of Nature (Fig.2.2). The first and second are closely related and reflect well established Judeo-Christian traditions. In each case, Nature is a divine creation; but in the first, its purpose is to serve Man who is granted dominion over the Earth, to develop, shape and use it in his interests and to bring glory to God as the maker of both Nature and Man. The second, broadly compatible view is that Nature is a prior entity with its own worth which God sees to be good. Therefore, as God's steward, Man's use of the Earth lies within an over-riding responsibility for its well being. While the niceties of the differences are significant, both ecclesiastical and secular authorities have been able to live and work within either or both of these schemes.

The third interpretation is markedly different. It recognises Nature as an independent entity with a meaning and purpose of its own. As the only reflective product of Nature, Man is capable of independent action but his ultimate well being is dependent on recognition and accommodation of the role of Nature itself. Man at war with Nature could be disastrous for both. Secondly, God is not perceived as having a necessary role; and Man-Nature relationships are seen to be independent of or isolated within any scheme involving Man and God. Such flexibility allows deployment of this interpretation of Nature within either theistic or non-theistic beliefs. The fourth view is a harsher version of the third; it is essentially non-theistic and sees Nature as an indifferent, self-generating and potentially self-destructing machine. Man is its only intelligent product and has a peculiarly powerful role in shaping both his own future and that of substantial parts of the natural world. In these matters, Man will be his own judge; and God is granted no part in this interpretation except, perhaps, as the force which initiated the cosmos.

World views and interpretations of nature inform religion, politics and everyday life. They have under-pinned changing attitudes towards man's possession, use and protection of the land; and current views on the countryside, its use and conservation cannot be understood without appreciation of their antecedents. These matters are explored through a series of cameos which reviews contributions of the aristocracy, romanticists and scientists to the complex legacy of ideas that affects current attitudes and practices in respect of the ownership, use and conservation of the countryside and access to its component parts. Illustrative material is partly derived from hymns, which were widely influential prior to the age of universal literacy. It complements the more common use of poetry and it may have some interest in its own right.

2. The Aristocracy and the Countryside

Second only to royalty, the land-owning aristocracy were the most powerful and influen-

> [1] **NATURE is a DIVINE creation to serve MAN who is made in the image of GOD and is bound to His glorification.**
>
> [2] **NATURE is a DIVINE creation, good in itself; MAN is GOD"s steward granted the use of NATURE to sustain himself and glorify GOD.**
>
> [3] **NATURE is an independent entity with meaning and purpose which reflective MAN must ascertain, accommodate and respect. (GOD is not a necessary part of this view).**
>
> [4] **NATURE is neutral, indifferent, without meaning: an independent self-generating machine. MAN, as the only intelligent product of NATURE, may confront and exploit his environment to the benefit or peril of both. (GOD has no part in this view).**

Fig.2.2 Interpretations of Nature (after Williams, 1991).

tial, the richest and the most leisured class in Britain until the latter part of the 19th century. Together with the church, they generally espoused the first of the four interpretations of nature outlined above (Fig.2.2). Its meaning was extended so that it not only granted man dominion over the earth but also placed royalty and the aristocracy at the head of the political and social hierachies. When this view was tempered by a perception that all men may be equal and each a steward of God, one might detect shifts of emphasis; but while society was dominated by the land-owning aristocracy there was no fundamental change in philosophy. It is, however, a little surprising to find that as late as 1848 the divine origins of this 'natural order' were endorsed in a hymn, written especially for children, and destined to become an all-time favourite:

All things bright and beautiful,   Each little flower that opens,
All creatures great and small,   Each little bird that sings,
All things wise and wonderful,   He made their glowing colours,
The Lord God made them all.   He made their tiny wings.

> The rich man in his castle,
> The poor man at his gate,
> God made them, high or lowly,
> And order'd their estate.
> Cecil Frances Alexander (1818-1895).

It is not surprising, however, that the third verse went out of favour and is not to be found in modern hymnaries. Popular affection for the pleasant face of nature has long outlived acceptance of aristocratic rule as part of the 'natural order'.

These verses clearly show that nature was seen as God's creation. This had been largely unquestioned for centuries; and man's dependence on God, directly and through nature, has been proclaimed in church and chapel throughout the ages in many great hymns:

I sing the almighty power of God,
That made the mountains rise,
That spread the flowing seas abroad,
And built the lofty skies.

I sing the goodness of the Lord,
That filled the earth with food;
He formed the creatures with His word,
And then pronounced them good.

There's not a plant or flower below
But makes Thy glories known;
And clouds arise and tempests blow
By order from Thy throne

Lord, how Thy wonders are displayed
Where'er I turn mine eye,
If I survey the ground I tread,
Or gaze upon the sky !
      Isaac Watts (1674-1748).

Untamed nature and destructive 'acts of God' were and still are threatening to man; and they were often presented and received either as a punishment or, more usually in later times, as a trial and test of both faith and ingenuity:

> Though vine nor fig-tree neither
> Their wanted fruit should bear;
> Though all the field should wither,
> Nor flocks nor herds be there;
> Yet God the same abiding,
> His praise shall tune my voice;
> For, while in Him confiding,
> I cannot but rejoice.
>   William Cowper (1731-1800).

The hostile image of nature receded as man's scientific and technological advance - or the sheer weight of his numbers - increasingly granted him the upperhand. Then the benefits of a successful tripartite partnership could be celebrated with little reserve:

> We plough the fields and scatter
> The good seed on the land,
> But it is fed and watered
> By God's almighty hand.
>   Mathias Claudius, (1740-1815).

> To Thee, O Lord, our hearts we raise
> In hymns of adoration;
> To Thee bring sacrifice of praise
> With shouts of adulation.
> Bright robes of gold the fields adorn,
> The hills with joy are ringing,

> The valleys stand so thick with corn
> That even they are singing.
>   William Chatterton Dix, (1837-98).

Against this background of fundamental beliefs, the cultivated lands and closely settled tracts of rural Britain, with their remarkable regional and local diversity, were highly prized and regarded with pleasure no less than thanksgiving by the aristocratic and labouring classes alike. 'Where the grass the hills adorn, and smiling fields are clothed with corn', the purposes of God, Nature and Man were met in a natural way with the added merits of being hard-won, through the ages and year by year. These preferred places were virtuous and beautiful; and such prospects could be equally pleasing to strangers:

> I cannot but remember, with some satisfaction, having two Foreign Gentlemen in my Company... how they were surprized at the Beauty of this Prospect [of the Vale of St. Albans]... One of them said to the other, That England was not like other Countrys, but it was all as a planted Garden... In a Word, it was all Nature, and yet look'd all Art. (Daniel Defoe, 1724 ; cited by East, 1951).

Furthermore, as and when resources allowed, the aristocracy enhanced the countryside not only by providing designed leisure landscapes (Plate.1.2) but also by improving the aesthetic quality of the countryside as a whole. A range of measures to this end was advocated in 1712 by Joseph Addison in *The Spectator* :

> Why may not a whole Estate be thrown into a kind of Garden by frequent Plantations, that may turn as much to the Profit as to the Pleasure of the Owner? A Marsh overgrown with Willows, or a Mountain shaded with Oaks, are not only more beautiful, but more beneficial, than when they lie bare and unadorned. Fields of Corn make a pleasant prospect, and if the Walks were a little taken care of that lie between them, if the natural Embroidery of the Meadows were helped and improved by some small Additions of Art, and the several rows of Hedges set off by Trees and Flowers, that the Soil was capable of receiving, a Man might make a pretty Landskip of his own Possessions. (cited by Daniels and Seymour, 1990).

Trees and other woody plants had a key role in the efforts to 'put husbandry into a pleasing dress'. In clumps, coverts and coppices as much as small woodlands; within hedgerows, in lines along winding lanes and arrow-straight avenues, and in windbreaks; encircling ponds, edging lakes and hiding quarries; and in many other formations, trees became vital components of most lowland scenery and some of the uplands too. Native species dominate; and while the vast majority of the 10,000 plant introductions to Britain by 1900 still remain in gardens, parks and plantations, a number of exotics do contribute significantly to the wider countryside (Jarvis, 1979). Furthermore, many key points within the landscape were enhanced by architectural features, often in the form of monuments and follies; and these artificial jewels provide highlights in many highly prized places. In summary, while the contribution of nature is vital, the highly varied and intricate British landscapes would all be nothing but for the hand of man. And landscape itself is nothing if not an experience; but if a 'Man (should) make a pretty Landskip of his own Possessions', for whom was it intended ?

While the productive and pleasant tracts of cultivated land were held in high esteem, it follows that wilderness and unimproved lands, whether rocky mountains, bleak moorlands, open heaths, watery wastes or other products of Nature, did not commend themselves in any way to the aristocracy nor to society in general. Joseph Addison, (1672-1719), captured their preferences very well in his adaptation of Psalm XXIII:

When in the sultry glebe I faint,	Though in a bare and rugged way
Or in the thirsty mountain pant,	Through devious lonely wilds I stray,
To fertile vales and dewy meads	Thy bounty shall my pains beguile;
My weary wandering steps he leads,	The barren wilderness shall smile
Where peaceful rivers, soft and slow,	With sudden greens and herbage crowned,
Amid the verdant landscape flow.	And streams shall murmur all around.

Camden expressed similar sentiments when describing the Pennines above Richmond:

> The prospect among the hills is wild, solitary and unsightly... There is a safe harbour in this tract for [wild] goats, deer and stags... The road into Westmorland and Cumberland lay across Stanemore and is entirely desolate and solitary, except for one inn in the middle for the entertainment of travellers. (Taylor,1951).

Early in the 18th century, Gregory King reported that more than a quarter of England and Wales still comprised 'barren lands'; and these stood as a reproach to the land-owning aristocracy for failure to harness all of Nature to the service of Man and the glory of God.

However, a new spirit of enterprise and the slow dawn of modern science were at hand to foster a remarkable 'age of improvement'. At first, intensification of production on enclosed farmland received priority over spatial expansion of farming and forestry, hunting and shooting into recalcitrant and often remote land. Thus, for example, in 1775 even 'within thirty miles of the capital there was not less than 200,000 acres of waste land'. Hounslow Heath and Finchley Common were 'fitted only for Cherokees and savages', while the Forests of Epping and Hainault remained 'good cover for the more finished and hardened robber retiring from justice' (East, 1951). And in 1800 one-fifth of England and Wales and the greater part of Scotland were still uncultivated and scarcely used in any productive way.

Then, for 70 years, the rapid growth of population, industrialisation and urbanisation underpinned a more determined search for greater agricultural production. Driven by an economic imperative and opportunity, aristocratic and other land-owners subdivided, enclosed and humanised the uttermost parts of the kingdom. Farming was pushed to its furthest limits to embrace all but the highest hills, the least fertile heaths, the worst wetlands and bogs - and all but the most resolutely defended common lands - leaving grouse, deer and conifers to complete the task of taming virtually the whole of Britain. Where 'improvement' came late it often assumed its most ruthless form with dramatic effects on both landscape and society. The 'Highland Clearances' are the best known and most publicised episode of such proportions; but the capture of the Pennine flanks within a geometric network of stone walls, crossed by roads drawn with mathematical precision and dotted with near-identical farmsteads had more profound and permanent effects on scenery. Such scientific and systematic rape and re-dressing of wild open spaces produced landscapes destined to become highly valued parts of our visual heritage; and had there been an effective conservation movement some 200 years ago, British scenery might well have been the worse for it.

Prior to and during this colonisation of wilderness and wastelands, the established farmlands of Britain also were subject to agrarian and agricultural revolutions which effected major changes to the countryside and rural society. No landscape or community

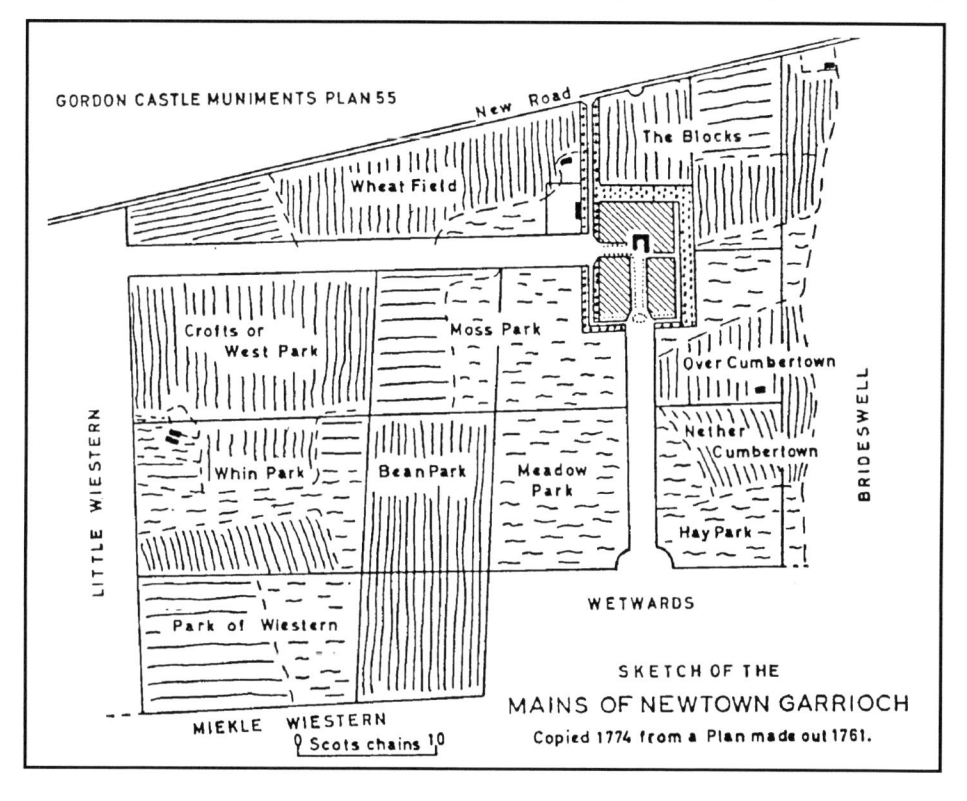

**Fig.2.3 'The Landscape of Improvement'
at the Mains of Newton Garrioch, Aberdeenshire.**

The eighteenth-century rectilinear pattern of large fields, avenues and roads was drawn and constructed without regard for the former system of land-use and settlement, which are indicated in a generalised form. The new replaced the old. This farm-plan, typically, forms a segment of a regional scheme on part of the Duke of Gordon's estate; and four of the adjacent farms are named. The new farm house, garden and drives are fancifully designed but were not always built in the prescribed fashion. Nevertheless the intention to beautify the landscape is evident and was usually achieved. (Kay, 1962).

was left untouched, and where comprehensive 'enclosure' was effected on extensive areas of open fields, pasture, rough grazing and common land the transformations often were 'so drastic and widespread that few signs of previous settlements and land-use systems [including previous highways and byways] remained intact (Fig.2.3). Patterns then established, however, have persisted... and many features of the present landscape can be dated to this revolution' (Kay,1962). Rural society emerged with a more diversified and structured system. The aristocracy naturally retained their superior position; but other land-owners, yeoman and tenant farmers on sizable holdings, and the upper echelons of the new agricultural workforce also benefitted substantially. On the other hand, those left with insufficient land to support their families; those reduced to the ranks of hired labourers and day-workers; and those totally dispossessed, all fared badly. These comprised the greater number, and such cataclysmic social change generated protest, which embraced the loss of paths. For example, John Clare, an exceptional, articulate peasant writing about the time of Waterloo had nothing good to say about enclosure:

> Inclosure, thou'rt a curse upon the land,
> And tasteless was the wretch who thy existence planned. (cited by Hoskins, 1955).

> These paths are stopt - the rude philistine's thrall
> Is laid upon them and destroyed them all.
> Each little tyrant with his little sign
> Shows where man claims earth glows no more divine
> On paths to freedom, and to childhood dear.
> A board sticks up to notice, 'No Road here'. (cited by A.D. Wallace, 1993).

The Manchester Association for the Preservation of Ancient Public Footpaths, established in 1826, proved to be a more lasting expression of protest; but other movements, including those by 'levellers' which took a more violent form, had little or no positive effect; and, over time, urbanisation or emigration extracted most of the more serious victims from the modernised countryside. The aristocracy and land-owning classes together with the clerical establishment thus retained time-honoured world views and interpretations of nature. They welcomed the new landscapes, 'smiling with cultivation... and parcelled out into beautiful enclosures' (Briggs, 1983), for Nature now served Man better than ever before and Man acknowledged God's blessings.

In more recent times, broadly comparable changes effected through mechanisation and modernisation of farming in a highly scientific age also generated outrage and protest, but on this occasion environmental and aesthetic issues have generated prominent, persistent and effective protest movements. Dominant world views and interpretations of Nature have changed (Fig.2.2); democracy empowers a wider range of voices; and the multifarious conservation movement has acquired a particularly strong voice.

3. Romanticists and 'Natural Beauty'
In fact, the aristocracy's orthodox world views and attitudes towards nature and the countryside were increasingly questioned from the mid-18th century. Scientific advances which then underpinned the transformation of Britain's economy, society and landscape, and

equally momentous socio-political changes in Europe and America, disturbed significant minorities and encouraged adoption of the more radical world views and interpretations of nature outlined above (Figs.2.1 & 2.2). Disillusioned by the turmoil and degradation of the 'natural world' but unable to dictate a new, ideal state of affairs, middle-class 'romanticists' sought refuge and reassurance in a philosophy which distanced themselves from the harsh realities of the times in which they lived. And those who could afford to do so took up residence in or frequently visited their preferred, picturesque places. They were destined to have a profound effect on today's policies for the countryside.

Romanticism, as inspired in Britain by Wordsworth (1770-1850), Coleridge (1772-1834), Byron (1788-1824), Shelley (1792-1822), and Keats (1795-1821), disassociated itself from the establishment's view of the world without positively enunciating a realistic alternative. This ambivalence led them to embrace a flexible view which grants Nature a central position as an avenue to God, or as a surrogate for Him, or as an independent subject of reverence and source of spiritual satisfactions. An evident difficulty of this flexibility is uncertainty as to 'the purpose and meaning' of Nature; the Romanticists were neither precise nor dogmatic and they mixed dreams with reality, and observed landscapes with spiritual images:

> ...... I have learn'd
> To look on Nature, not as in the hour
> Of thoughtless youth, but hearing often times
> The still, sad music of humanity,
> Nor harsh nor grating, though of ample power
> To chasten and subdue. And I have felt
> A presence that disturbs me with the joy
> Of elevated thoughts; a sense sublime
> Of something far more deeply interfused,
> Whose dwelling is the light of setting suns.
> And the round ocean and the living air,
> And the blue sky, and in the mind of man:
> A motion and a spirit, that impels
> All thinking things, all objects of all thought,
> And rolls through all things. Therefore am I still
> A lover of the meadows and the woods
> And mountains, and of all that we behold
> From this green earth; of all the mighty world
> Of eye and ear - both what they half create,
> And what perceive; well pleased to recognize
> In Nature and the language of the sense
> The anchor of my purest thoughts, the nurse,
> The guide, the guardian of my heart and soul,
> Of all my moral being...   from Wordsworth's *Tintern Abbey*.

If 'all that we behold from this green earth' is deemed to be as one, then the Romantic concept of what is 'natural' evidently embraces those products of Man which are seen to be harmonious with the works of Nature. These are the good and beautiful; and those which are seen to be discordant and damaging are neither. 'Natural beauty' thus can be appreciated and judged as art; and while cynics might question the purpose and competence of anyone who attempts to transfer this view into practical politics, it is no less tenable than views which identify Nature as a divine creation and grant its interpretation to ordained authorities. The Romanticist's view cannot be dismissed as erudite ramblings of nature mystics; nor has it been treated in this way. On the contrary, the diverse legacy of Romanticism has proved to be very influential.

Indeed, the authors of the Romantic Movement were not mystics. They were great travellers and walkers; and their writing reflected genuine recreational experiences. Even when absorbed by 'natural beauty', they could be drawn close to God; and from a walking tour in the Alps in 1790, Wordsworth told his sister that 'the impressions of three hours of our walk among the Alps will never be effaced. I had not thought of man, or a single created being; my whole world was turned to Him who produced the terrible majesty before me' (cited by Williams, 1991). However, aware, as they were, of the real world, the Romanticists were less than content with much of what they saw and anticipated:

> The world is too much with us; late and soon,
> Getting and spending, we lay waste our powers:
> Little we see in Nature that is ours;
> We have given our hearts away, a sordid boon !
> This sea that bares her bosom to the moon;
> The winds that will be howling at all hours,
> And are up-gather'd now like sleeping flowers;
> For this, for everything, we are out of tune;
> It moves us not. -Great God ! I'd rather be
> A Pagan suckled in a creed outworn;
> So might I, standing on this pleasant lea,
> Have glimpses that would make me less forlorn;
> Have sight of Proteus rising from the sea;
> Or hear old Triton blow his wreathed horn.
>   Untitled verse by Wordsworth.

The desire to 'be a Pagan' - to return to simpler, primitive times when man-nature-god were one (Fig.2.1) - was unrealistic; but it was a cry of discontent from a perceptive and apprehensive mind as the industrialisation and urbanisation of Britain was foreseen, and not desired.

The Romanticists did enjoy their comfortable circumstances and the opportunity to find refuge, solace and happiness in their love affair with the natural beauty of picturesque places; but the leading Romanticists were not mere dreamers and idealists. They were brilliant, creative writers who would have the world better than they found it. Nature and natural beauty, especially in remote countryside, evidently provided deeply pleasing prospects; but their inability or reluctance to pronounce a clear, complete and rounded view of 'Nature, Man and God' which was compatible with practical politics deprived the Romantic Movement of real power in its own day. That remained for some time with the aristocrats; but the dreams of the Romanticists were highly infectious, durable and influential.

Unfortunately, both their message and language suffered much in translation. Honest simplification is justifiable to make the essence accessible to a wider range of people but it was soon popularised, then vulgarised beyond recognition. Many of its imitators found greater satisfaction and profit from the dissemination of imaginative rustic presentations, often in pictorial forms and possibly based on but far removed from reality. Bucolic idylls and fanciful falsehoods of rural scenes may well delight and distract, but they also deceive. Nevertheless, once natural beauty and the countryside had become marketable commodities, commercial interests generated an outpouring of pleasing if somewhat less than truthful images.

Misuse or abuse of the Romantic legacy as this may be, such presentations continue the tradition of portraying nature and the countryside as beautiful and beneficent; and while they unduly heighten and distort expectations, they have fostered a widespread affection for picturesque rurality. The Romanticists of old would deplore the debasement of their currency, but they may find some solace in the fact that the concept of 'natural beauty' has been perpetuated in conservation legislation; and that a large part of the nation has taken to its heart some sort of favourable image of the countryside which they wish to protect, while many 'truants' walk within it for aesthetic if not spiritual satisfactions as a central part of their recreational experience.

4. Scientists, Intellectuals and Rational Pragmatism

While the Romantic movement was still gathering momentum, scientists and intellectuals in diverse fields unleashed a flood of findings and ideas that were so much at variance with conventional world views and interpretations of nature that conflict was inevitable. Science seemed to demand a radical view that would treat Nature as an autonomous and dynamic complex whose origins and characteristics, predictable out-turns and aberrations, can all be explained in terms of its own inherent processes; and it gave credence to the fourth interpretation of Nature outlined above (Fig.2.2). Empirical evidence and rational argument therefore could replace theology and faith in the explanation of the natural world. This scheme was at odds with Judeo-Christian beliefs, and while Romanticists' views were accommodated by the clerical and aristocratic establishments, the advance of modern science and related ideas were more contentious. Eventually, the British genius for resilience and flexibility would triumph, but within the context a more diverse and divided society.

Thus, later poets, bordering on the Romantic school, were able to 'praise indifferent Nature' as an independent entity. In *Quiet Nature*, Matthew Arnold (1822-1888) urged Man to learn from *'the sleepless ministers of Nature'* who will persist *'when man is gone'* ; and Laurence Binyon (1869-19..) provided an eloquent introduction to *Nature* as an indifferent participant in the lives of Man but a potential tutor of individuals:

> Because out of corruption burns the rose,
> And to corruption lovely cheeks descend;
> Because with her right hand she heals the woes
> Her left hand wrought, loth nor to wound nor mend;
> I praise indifferent Nature, affable
> To all philosophies, of each unknown;

> Though in my listening ear she leans to tell
> Some private word, as if for me alone.
> Still, like an artist, she her meaning hides,
> Silent, while thousand tongues proclaim it clear
> Ungrudging, her large feast for all provides;
> Tender, exultant, savage, blithe, austere,
> In each man's hand she sets the proper tool,
> For the wise Wisdom, Folly for the fool.

However, neither church or chapel could readily accept the notion of an 'independent' Nature; but nor could they maintain a futile denial of the facts of modern science. They had to accommodate new knowledge, and to that end the fundamental, comprehensive qualities of the 'God of all power, and truth, and grace' were re-presented; and the divine origins of Nature and its role as a messenger of God were re-emphasised:

> Yes, God is good: in earth and sky,
> From ocean-depths and spreading-wood,
> Ten thousand voices seem to cry,
> "God made us all, and God is good".
> J.H.Gurney (1802-1862).

A tripartite 'world view' with God at its apex was thus confirmed, if not proven; and modern science was attributed as a gift of God to Man:

> From Thee all skill and science flow,
> All pity, care, and love,
> All calm and courage, faith and hope
> O pour them from above !
> Charles Kingsley (1819-75).

> Thine is the loom, the forge, the mart,
> The wealth of land and sea;
> The worlds of science and of art,
> Revealed and ruled by Thee.
> John Ellerton (1826-1893).

Such readjustment has continued as an on-going effort of Christian faith to retain its comprehensive world view and pronounce its relevance to each and every age and generation:

> We limit not the truth of God
> To our poor reach of mind,
> By notions of our day and sect
> Crude, partial and confined;
> No, let a new and better hope
> Within our hearts be stirred;
> The Lord hath yet more light and truth
> To break forth from His word.
> George Rawson (1807-89).

> Solar systems, void of meaning
> Freeze the spirit into stone;
> Always our researches lead us
> To the ultimate Unknown.
> Faith must die, or come full circle
> To its source in God alone.
> F.Pratt Green (1903-19xx).

The greater 'reach of mind' granted through modern science thus allows a re-interpretation of the destructive and recalcitrant elements of Nature as a test of Man, the scientist, in his role as God's steward. He need not surrender to Nature but should discover more of God's truth and purpose in order to successfully manage the Earth for the benefit of Man and the glory of God. Conventional wisdom has retained a tri-partite world view.

On the other hand, within an increasingly secular society, the guidance or restrictions of such a world view have been widely rejected or set aside from time to time. And, consciously or by default, the third and fourth interpretations of Nature have been widely adopted. Consequently, Man - greatly empowered by science - is now often perceived as the greatest threat to Nature and his own worst enemy. *Laissez faire* is no longer acceptable, and a more active role is expected of the government in order to conserve and preserve the one world available to Man. To that end, numerous individuals and groups have taken up a wide variety of environmental issues in which they have a close, often personal, interest and have pressed their case upon the government, all too often with adverse consequences for other groups or, in some cases, the majority of the population; and access to the countryside is not yet generally available.

5. People and Place : Concern and Conservation

The Victorian era thus gave way to an age of uncertainty and minority interests, and those comprising the broad conservation movement have become increasingly prominent. Conservation is essentially self-centred; and the protection of aspects and elements of places which have special value and meaning to particular individuals and groups has been the driving force of a kaleidoscopic movement. Any movement that can embrace Nelson's column, the natterjack toad and natural beauty merits some exploration of its underlying values and objectives. World views and interpretations of Nature are relevant; and while the perceived purpose of Nature is to sustain Man, it will be recognised as a prime source of resources. Thus 'in asserting a need for conservation of resources we imply that present or future welfare would be less if such action were not taken... Conservation means taking special steps to prevent depletion or deterioration of a resource' (Whitby, 1974). This approach is essentially utilitarian; and it was evident, for example, in the formation in 1826 of the Manchester Association for the Protection of Ancient Public Footways, which reflects competition for a specific resource which, in turn, facilitates access to less tangible aspects of the countryside.

However, the attribution of meaning and purpose to Nature provided a moral and aesthetic basis for conservation; and the subsequent emphasis on the rights of good and beautiful aspects and endangered elements of nature sits uncomfortably alongside a crude utilitarian concern for resources. For example, 'animal rights' led to the early and protracted campaign to abolish bull-baiting, and with it a recreational activity based on a perception of animals as resources, which is still paramount in horse and dog racing, fishing and farming. Nevertheless, a wide range of living creatures have now been selected for protection, including specified birds which were protected by law in 1880. Such specific concerns may be unlimited; but they are matched by the view that valued places merit comprehensive protection. This approach underpins the conservation of 'nature reserves', 'wilderness' and 'natural beauty'. It gathered strength in the mid-19th century in Britain and America; and it is reflected, for example, in the designation of America's Yosemite Valley as a 'protected area' in 1864; and the formation of the Lake District Defence Society in 1883. Meanwhile, educated and scientific minds had disseminated interests in numerous elements of both urban and rural landscapes; and the preservation of Ancient Monuments in 1882 was an early step in the extension of conservation by law to a wide range of phenomena, collectively designated nowadays as 'heritage' or 'wildlife' or both.

It is useful to identify the utilitarian, aesthetic and scientific bases for conservation although, in reality, combinations of motives and purposes are commonplace; and conservation is often confused or fused with similar concepts such as preservation, protection, restoration and rehabilitation. In every case there are conflicting interests; and conservation always implies the prevention or diminution of change led by natural processes or market forces, which, in other quarters, may be perceived as beneficial rather than a threat. The opportunity costs of conservation therefore may be substantial; but nowadays this rarely weakens its popular appeal and, whatever else it may be, 'conservation' has become a very complex and powerful movement (Goldsmith and Warren, 1993).

It was not always so, and for most of the 19th century market forces ruled the day. Nevertheless, a fine example of conservation occurred in Georgian Bath. Barton Fields, immediately south-west of The Royal Crescent, were set aside as an open space 'never to be built upon'. The adjacent High and Low Commons also were preserved for their amenity value, though part of the latter was surrendered in 1830 to the 'delicious Royal Victoria Park'. However, Bath was a special case - a pleasure ground for gentlemen and their ladies; and this early example of conservation for 'the public good' was not widely repeated. On the contrary, agricultural and urban development rapidly absorbed open spaces and ancient commons. Whether or not intervention to conserve these and their opportunities for recreation would have achieved a better outcome is debatable. Much must depend on the circumstances of each place and time, and the vantage point of each commentator; and some of the complex issues may be illustrated by brief exploration of one peri-urban common.

Oldham's experience may exemplify the typical process and consequences of rapid urban growth.

> An Act of Parliament permitted the enclosure of the moors around Oldham in 1803. Up to that time a full circle of large open commons, [including Greenacres Moor], surrounded the parish church... When the enclosure commissioners finished their work in 1807... the land was divided between the owners of property adjoining the waste... [and it] became the centre of speculative building. Edwin Butterworth [writing in 1849] has left a vivid picture of the transformation of Greenacres Moor... *In 1807 the hundred acres of waste land had all been effectually reclaimed, and manufactories and habitations were all starting into existence as if by magic. By 1820 (there were) ten cotton mills and nearly 450 houses where before had been an almost uninhabited wilderness.* In 1841 Greenacres formed the largest suburb of Oldham, with a population of 10,000 and twenty-three mills... even today it stands out as a dense cluster of chimneys lying at the foot of the Pennines... Only its name commemorates the pleasant heath that was signed out of existence by an Act of Parliament. (Millward, 1955).

The tone of Millward's account is critical of enclosure and development. Butterworth's 'waste land' or 'wilderness' is retrospectively translated into a 'pleasant heath'; and its transfer to 'manufactories and habitations' is presented as the execution of a death warrant issued by Parliament. Where would the 23 mills and housing for 10,000 people have been located if Greenacres Moor had been preserved as such ? What use would it have been put to in 1841 and subsequently ? Would the welfare of Oldham's populace have been better served by its preservation ? These questions are neither asked nor answered by Millward who implicitly deplores the loss of an amenity and its transformation into a resource.

Throughout the country the loss of commons and open spaces to urban growth and to improved farming was a frequent occurrence, and eventually *The Commons, Open Spaces and Footpaths Preservation Society* was formed in 1865 to campaign for the protection of public access to several types of space. Octavia Hill was a leading activist; and *Punch* portrayed her as an heroic champion of the urban poor (Plate 3.1), thus linking conservation with philanthropy, though at that time 'commons, open spaces and footpaths' were essentially recreational places for the middle-classes. In any case, by 1865 tramways and railways had burst the bounds of the 'walk-about city' for those who could afford to use them; and competition for land would be continued in a more spacious arena as suburbanisation, commuting, and recreational travel to peripheral open spaces and the wider countryside became realistic options for many, other than the poor. The purpose of *The Open Spaces Society* was facilitated by these changed circumstances; and its achievements are impressive. They are concentrated in the south where it sought to protect:

> the great natural heritage of commons and woodlands in the London area... The view being that commons within reach of large towns, particularly London, were of greater value to the public as open space for health and recreation than as cultivated land or building sites. (Cherry, 1972).

The Society was instrumental in saving more than 400,000 acres for 'public use' (Shercliff, 1987); but for the greater part of a century this common heritage of open spaces was dominated by the middle-classes and they have yet to be made readily accessible to the population as a whole. In this sphere, as elsewhere, carefully targeted, positive promotion is overdue.

Deeper in the countryside, a movement for the protection of places highly regarded for their natural beauty had preceded the efforts of the Open Spaces Society by 30 years but had no real success until 1949, largely because it related to extensive areas of the rural Britain rather than designated commons. The romanticists, like other middle-class minorities, lacked the will and generosity to modify their values or compromise the satisfaction of their personal aspirations, even in the cause of democracy. Consequently, the admission of crude standards and vulgar tastes, no less than the pressures of heavy use, were seen as threats to valued, picturesque places; and in 1835, at a time when he was 'deeply affected by changes and their bad effects' that had occurred since the publication of West's *Guide to the Lake District,* Wordsworth put his case in the following terms:

> [Since 1778] the lakes have become celebrated; visitors flocked hither from all parts of England; the fancies of some were smitten so deeply that they became settlers... no one can now travel through the more frequented tracts without being offended, at almost every turn, by an introduction of discordant objects...

> It is then, much to be wished that a better taste should prevail among these new proprietors... **In this wish the author will be joined by persons of pure taste throughout the whole island, who, by their visits, often repeated, to the Lakes in the North of England, testify that they deem the district a sort of national property, in which every man has a right and interest who has an eye to perceive and a heart to enjoy.** (*Wordsworth's (1835) Guide to the Lakes* edited by Bicknell, 1984.)

Wordsworth's, in fact, spoke for no one but the small minority of 'persons of pure taste' who, like himself, had an educated mind, a sophisticated eye and a jealous love for 'the Lakes' and similar picturesque places. A decade later, towards the end of 1844, Wordsworth protested vigorously against the Kendal to Windermere railway; and he was more explicit on the origins of 'pure taste', 'an eye to perceive' and 'a heart to enjoy' which he considered the necessary passport for appreciation of and therefore admission, whether as a resident or a visitor, to the Lakes.

> A vivid perception of romantic scenery is neither inherent in mankind, nor a necessary consequence of even a comprehensive education... Rocks and mountains, torrents and wide-spread waters, and all those features of nature which go to the composition of such scenes as this part of England is distinguished for, cannot, in their finer relations to the human mind, be comprehended, or even very imperfectly conceived, without processes of culture or opportunities of observation in some degree habitual... The imperfectly educated classes are not likely to draw much good from rare visits to the Lakes... (and) the humbler ranks of society are not, and cannot be, in a state to gain material benefit from this beautiful region. (Wordsworth, 1844, cited by Bicknell, 1984).

Wordsworth was not alone in his fears and others of a like mind included James Payne who later complained that 'excursion trains bring thousands of curious, vulgar people to the Lakes and *our* hills are darkened by swarms of tourists; *our* lawns are picnicked upon twenty at a time'. Eventually, in 1883 *The Lake District Defence Society* was formed by Canon Rawnsley; and no doubt a large number of residents and regular visitors hoped that this might protect their interests no less than those of the romanticist. Nor was the Lake District the only valued place to produce a protest movement but successive governments were reluctant to review fundamental policies based on *laissez-faire*; and perhaps partly as a consequence of such reticence, the turn of the century witnessed a substantial growth of middle-class organisations campaigning for the preservation of rights and privileges and the conservation of valued places (Table 2.1). Perhaps the Council(s) for the Preservation of Rural England, Scotland and Wales had the most comprehensive outlook which incorporated the range of concerns anticipated and outlined by Wordsworth. But the Americans took the lead in setting aside tracts of land for their amenity value, and their experience has been widely influential.

A Scotsman, John Muir - 'wilderness sage and founding father of the American conservation movement' - was largely responsible for the setting up in 1864 of California's Yosemite Valley Park for public use, resort and recreation; for the creation in 1890 of the USA National Park System; and for the foundation in 1892 of the Sierra Club to promulgate the cause of conservation throughout the USA. The opening paragraph of his book on *Our National Parks*, published in 1901, is full of interest:

> The tendency nowadays to wander in wilderness is delightful to see. Thousands of tired, nerve-shaken, over-civilised people are beginning to find out that going to the mountains is going home; that wilderness is a necessity; and that mountain parks and reservations are useful not only as fountains of timber and irrigating rivers, but as fountains of life. Awakening from the stupefying effects of industry and the deadly apathy of luxury, they are trying as best they can to mix and enrich their own little goings on with those of Nature, and to get rid of rust and disease. Briskly venturing and roaming, some are washing off sins and cobweb cares of the devil's spinning in all-day storms on mountains; sauntering in rosiny pinewoods or in gentian meadows, brushing through chaparral, bending down and parting sweet flowery sprays; tracing rivers to their sources, getting in touch with the nerves of Mother Earth; jumping from rock to rock, feeling the life of them, learning the songs of them, panting in whole-souled exercise, and rejoicing in deep long-drawn breaths of pure wildness. This is fine and natural and full of promise. So also is the growing interest in the care and preservation of forests and wild places in general, and in the half-wild parks and gardens of towns. Even the scenery habit in its most artificial forms, mixed with spectacles, silliness, and kodaks; its devotees arrayed more gorgeously than scarlet tanagers, frightening the wild game with red umbrellas - even this is encouraging, and may well be regarded as a hopeful sign of the times. (Muir, 1901: republished 1992).

There is much here to delight and alarm the British middle-class conservation-oriented lovers of the countryside. They would not welcome 'whole-souled exercise, silliness and red umbrellas'; and in the early 1930's the Ramblers Federation reported that:

> a majority of (its) members believe that there are too many rambling clubs who merely went out to enjoy each others' company in the countryside, often in rather an aggressive way with fantastic hats and scarves, making no effort to understand the way of life they were invading or to appreciate the delicate balance of nature all round them. (R.F. Handbook 1930/34, cited by Shercliff, 1987).

This unfortunate reluctance to accept fun as part of legitimate packages of countryside enjoyment is still influential today; and there are other continuing differences between America and Britain. In particular, large tracts of unoccupied 'wilderness', unaffected by prior rights of property-owners, were readily available in the USA for allocation solely for 'public use, resort and recreation'. When delineated as a commercial venture in 1872, the Yellowstone National Park covered 3,344 square miles; subsequently, it was nearly doubled in size.

1826	Manchester Association for the Preservation of Ancient Public Footways
1833	Select Committee on Public Walks
1864	Yosemite Valley Park (State of California)
1865	Commons, Open Spaces and Footpaths Preservation Society
1866	The Metropolitan Commons Act
1872	Yellowstone National Park, USA (A commercial venture)
1876	Hayfield and Kinder Scout Ancient Footpaths Association
1878	The Epping Forest Act
1880	Wild Birds Protection Act
1882	Ancient Monuments Act
1883	Lake District Defence Society
1884	Access to the Mountains (Scotland) Act
1889	Royal Society for the Protection of Birds
1890	USA National Parks: scheme approved by Congress
1892	Yosemite National Park, USA
1892	Sierra Club, USA (founded by John Muir)
1894	Peak District and Northern Counties Footpaths Society
1895	National Trust for Places of Historic Interest and Natural Beauty
1904	British Vegetation Committee
1907	National Trust Act (Trust granted unique statutory rights)
1907	Country Landowners Association
1908	British Association for Shooting and Conservation
1912	Society for the Promotion of Nature Reserves
1913	British Ecological Society
1926/7/8	Council(s) for the Preservation of Rural England/Scotland/Wales
1929	Addison Committee (on desirability and feasibility of National Parks)
1932	Town and Country Planning Act (largely ineffective)
1935	Ramblers Association (replaced Ramblers Federation, 1930-35)
1936	Standing Committee on National Parks
1942	Scott Committee and Report on Land Utilisation in Rural Areas
1942	Dower Report on National Parks commissioned (published 1945)
1945	Hobhouse Committee on Dower's proposals for National Parks
1947	Hobhouse Report on National Parks
1947	Huxley Report on Wildlife Conservation
1947	Town and Country Planning Act (Development subject to Local Authority planning approval; farming and forestry specifically excluded)
1949	National Parks and Access to the Countryside Act
1949	Nature Conservancy created by Royal Charter

Table 2.1 Selected Events in the Development of the Conservation Movement in Britain up to 1950

> The withdrawal of this large tract from the public domain did no harm to anyone; for its height, 6,000 to over 13,000 feet above the sea, and its thick mantle of volcanic rocks, prevent its ever being available for agriculture or mining, while on the other hand its geographical position, reviving climate, and wonderful scenery combine to make it a grand health, pleasure and study resort - a gathering place for travellers from all over the world. (Muir, 1901: republished 1992).

'Yellowstone' was evidently more useful as an amenity than a resource. In contrast, Britain's task was to introduce conservation and provide for new and growing forms of recreation, notably countryside walking, within a heavily utilised, privately owned domain. It was easier for all, governments and protagonists, to start with specific, limited concerns - commons and footways; birds and ancient monuments. It was also easier, and more practicable, to delegate and disperse authority and responsibilities to local government, to charitable bodies and, eventually, to quangos. This diaspora led to a proliferation of policies, strategies and practices - some more successful than others; and it effectively prevented the development of any policy for countryside walking that would serve the people as a whole.

The general outcome led Pennington (1996) to argue that 'the history of countryside policy represents a catalogue of bureaucratic mismanagement and special-interest manipulation... [and that] ... Conservation depends on an end to political interference and a return to full private property rights'. A return to times and conditions when market forces and the rights of land-owners were beyond question is neither practicable nor desirable. However, Pennington usefully draws attention to the success of organisations such as the Wildlife Trust, the RSPB, and the National Trust which are able to reinforce their conservation role through their position as land-owners.

Founded in the Lake District by Canon Rawnsley, Sir Robert Hunter and Miss Octavia Hill in 1895, *The National Trust for Places of Historic Interest or Natural Beauty* does provide a limited success story in terms of access and provision for walking. It takes property deemed worthy of permanent protection out of the private domain and public ownership to hold and conserve it on behalf of the nation and for the enjoyment of the public. It depends on the voluntary support of its members and on income from its commercial enterprises, including entry charges to many of its properties. It generally maintains high quality footpaths to facilitate access within its varied properties. These embrace 248,000 ha and comprise:

> 1,000 scheduled monuments, 200 historic houses, 160 gardens and 49 industrial monuments... over 590,000 acres of beautiful countryside and almost 590 miles of outstanding coast... These properties include mountains and moorland, coastland and woods, commons and pasture, lakes, waterfalls, bridges and canals. Many of its open spaces are designated as nature reserves or country parks. Its buildings include prehistoric and Roman antiquities, medieval chapels and castles, villages, cottages, mills, inns, barns and dovecotes. Its parks and gardens illustrate many different types and periods. Its country houses - large and small - contain important collections of pictures, furniture, tapestry,

books, sculpture, silver, china and musical instruments. (The National Trust, 1985 and 2000).

This variety reflects a catholic and eclectic philosophy; and a pragmatic approach to both conservation and recreation; and it regularly attracts 11 million visits annually to those properties which levy a charge. The Trust has 2.6 million members and is extremely popular with its established, largely middle-class, clientele of regular visitors. However, in common with the countryside as a whole, the Trust does not serve the population as a whole; nor does it actively promote its opportunities for countryside walking to all sections of the public. And as a private, quasi-commercial land-owner it may exercise its discretion in such matters.

Furthermore, the National Trust could not address a widely held deep felt-need, clearly expressed by Wordsworth, for both access to and conservation of 'valued' parts of the countryside if not of the countryside as a whole. Consequently, influenced by American experience, during the early decades of the 20th century diverse voices campaigned for 'National Parks' and other protected areas out of self-interest rather than concern for the public good. Eventually, in 1949, some achieved a degree of success in the National Parks and Access to the Countryside Act and the creation of the Nature Conservancy. However, before locating access for countryside walking within the context of this seminal legislation, it is appropriate to review the plight of those 'untutored townsmen' who, for far too long, have been seen by many, such as Wordsworth, to be unfit for admission to valued places.

Plate 3.1 Octavia Hill - Heroically Portrayed by Punch during her campaign for 'Open Spaces'. (from Blunden and Curry, 1990).

Set amongst the urban poor, Octavia Hill is associated with both philanthropic and conservation movements, with concern for needy people and for valued places. However, the over-riding image is of 'two nations'; and in terms of access to the countryside and open spaces a comparable division is still evident (Ch.4.4).

3
SOCIAL CONCERN AND RECREATION FOR THE POOR UP TO 1950

1. Development, Growth and Change

From the middle of the eighteenth century, Britain was subject to profound change which affected all aspects of life, including access to recreational activities. The population of England and Wales grew very rapidly from 8.9m in 1801 to 17.9m in 1851; and then to 32.5m in 1901 and 43.8m in 1951. The growth of towns and cities was more dramatic. The urban population soared from 1.5m (16.9 %) in 1801 to 9.0m (50.2 %) in 1851; and thereafter the nation could be fairly described as 'urbanised'. In 1901, when agricultural workers and domestic servants were still the largest occupations, some 25 million people were 'urbanites'; and by 1951 four-fifths of the population lived in towns and cities. Thus, while the rural areas remained relatively sparsely settled and were characterised not only by out-migration but, after 1861, by depopulation too, most poor people were born and bred in large, over-crowded and often squalid urban areas, with limited mobility and consequently restricted access to the countryside.

On the other hand, the scientific advances and technological change which drove agricultural improvement, industrialisation and urbanisation also brought unprecedented wealth and mobility to the nation, or rather initially to some sections of it. The aristocracy continued as a class apart but the *nouveau riche* became serious rivals not simply in terms of their purchasing power but also through their greater numbers and political strength. They in turn were greatly outnumbered by the aspiring middle-classes who, insofar as their relatively limited resources and education would allow, generally took the aristocracy and plutocracy as their role models. Below this increasingly stratified but generally affluent superstructure, a large majority of the population remained poor; and, while many were truly poverty-stricken, generally they were differentiated more by their various occupations and geographical locations than by their earnings. This dynamic diversity was reduced by Disraeli to 'two nations'; and this innocent deception has the advantage of simplicity which may compensate for a loss of detail. In any case, the contrast between the upper and lower classes, the rich and the poor, the educated and the near-illiterate is valid; and it has a key role in any discussion of contrasting capabilities and needs, of privilege and deprivation in terms of access to resources and opportunities, including those of the countryside as indicated above (Ch.1.4-7).

Throughout the 19th century *laissez-faire* and private enterprise prevailed and the government's attention was focused on national rather than local issues. Any hint of comprehensive or central planning was anathema, unless it was promulgated by the ordained ruling class in support of the national interest. Parliament, the Lords, the Crown and the Church were not unmindful of environmental and social issues, but they had to be persuaded to act on such matters. Action and, indeed, inaction reflect concern and motivation no less than capability; but those most in need of intervention and planning on their behalf were the least well equipped on all three counts. Thus, both rural and urban poor lacked an effective and coordinated voice. The weight and force of their numbers were sporadically rallied; but mob-rule was readily suppressed and, in any case, it is no substitute for good government. They were, therefore, heavily dependent upon or subject to philanthropy and advocates lobbying on their behalf. In contrast, as noted above (Table 2.1), environmental issues did generate substantial concern amongst the well informed middle-classes, though they too had to press their case onto politicians and parliament, often with little success.

Consequently, the 19th century not only produced a multitude of pressing needs and worthy causes but also a number of affluent and influential individuals who, personally and through pressure groups, were able and willing to crusade on their behalf. Maslow's model of motivations (Fig.1.1) helps to explain this. With basic and social needs fully satisfied and esteem derived from opulence already won, sensitive minds were more likely to be directed to the achievement of greater public recognition and 'self-actualisation' through intellectual, aesthetic and moral pursuits. Affluence fosters philanthropy. For example, while millions at home were being reduced to drudgery in appalling conditions alien to their origins, in the wider world enlightened Britons were successfully campaigning for the abolition of the slave trade and slavery. And in 1800 the first Bill for the abolition of bull-baiting was presented to parliament; and its aim was eventually realised in 1835. On the other hand, neither John Clare's protest against 'stopt paths' nor Wordsworth's defence of the Lake District won an effective response until 1949 (Ch.2.2&5).

Several important consequences with immediate and lasting significance thus emerge from any dependence on philanthropy and voluntary action. First, the selection and pursuit of each cause reflects a particular perspective and interpretation of the situation; and these are usually from an external and superior viewpoint. Secondly, there is a strong personal preference in the selection of problems and issues to be addressed, and a maverick element in the likelihood of them being pursued to a positive outcome. Thirdly, positive responses from governments and other authorities are often variously compromised by the need to address the nature and weightiness of the advocates and of their opponents as much as the specific merits and needs of the problem laid before them. Fourthly, because the issues often are brought to and pressed upon them rather than generated from within, governments are likely to deflect, devolve and disperse responsibility for their resolution rather than take up the burden of duty themselves. Finally, in terms of modern planning, the whole process is inherently flawed because it is essentially *ad hoc* and *ad hominum* - reactive and piecemeal. It reflects no consistent philosophy, other than that of the advocates to do and be good; and its products often lie outside established schemes for implementation and regulation of policy, planning and development.

2. The 'Two Nations' and Provision for Walking
The poor of the countryside presented the greater need for care and pity; but they largely escaped the attention of those with ample means to exercise philanthropy. They were more dispersed and disguised by greenery; and a cosy notion of comfortable communities enjoying traditional bucolic pleasures in idyllic settings cast a veil over all unpleasantness. Thus, for example,

> Most Victorian artists were painters of pretty pictures... They do not present a truthful, realistic or comprehensive picture of the countryside or of life as it was really lived by country people... The overwhelming impression they create is

Plate 3.2 Sociable Strolling in Leicester Square, 1874.

> one of a rural paradise... that is how most Victorian artists saw country life, and how their patrons wanted to see it... They preferred their own image of the countryside - a beautiful, healthy, pure, innocent arcadia where peasants went happily about their labour, children played on the village green, mothers sat by the fireside in neat picturesque cottages, all watched over by a benevolent gentry and clergy. (Wood, 1988).

Migration from rural Britain denied such romantic notions; and in 1768 Arthur Young reported that:

> Young men and women in the country fix their eye on London as the last stage of their hope... The number of young women that fly there is incredible... What induced them to quit their healthy clean fields for a region of dirt, stink and noise ? (cited by Williams, 1973).

This neatly summarises the misconception of conditions in the countryside and the somewhat more realistic appraisal of those in urban areas, where the poor were accepted as a necessary part of the industrial system but were perceived as a threat to harmony and peace; to personal and social well being; and to health, morals and human dignity. In urban areas the contrast between 'two nations' was too stark and too immediate to be disguised; and provision for walking, which was now focused on urban areas, reflected this dichotomy.

Not all towns are of a kind; and some market towns and service centres were integral and attractive parts of the countryside, and many remain so today. Others were built primarily as health and pleasure resorts for the wealthy, leisure-rich classes. 'Spa towns' are a prime example; and amongst these Bath, rebuilt between 1760 and 1810, set the fashion. Georgian Bath comprises sweeping classical facades, the first-ever crescent, a circus and squares equipped with formal, fenced and gated gardens, generous pavements, and commons dedicated to recreation . Spas had become complex resorts in which the landscape played a major role (Denbigh, 1981). Like the designed leisure landscapes of country seats, they provided for walking, talking and courting; for parading and promenading; for seeing and being seen; all in a pleasing and stimulating setting equipped with comfortable walkways. The basic resources of the spas comprised natural waters and a contrived environment; and the latter proved the more efficacious and enduring.

From the late 18th century, the spa towns were rivalled by coastal resorts and 'visitors came to the seaside for the same reasons as to the spas, and amongst them health and pleasure are not easily disentangled' (Pimlott, 1947). What is quite certain, recreational walking within designed leisure landscapes and provision for comfortable walking again played a major role. Sea-front promenades, esplanades and piers, parks and gardens, became hallmarks of the Victorian seaside resort, where sociable perambulation and even some energetic walking were central to a range of satisfying experiences.

When the urban plutocracy and middle classes could afford the splendour of Bath for a summer season, it was unlikely that they would settle for much less on city properties where most of their life and leisure were spent. Naturally, the 'greening' of London set the prime example (Plate 3.2); but the creation of Edinburgh's 'New Town' was more dramatic. By 1750 Scotland's capital was a disgrace to civilised society. Built high and packed tight along the royal mile from castle rock down to the former abbey and palace of Holyrood, its squalor and disorder were medieval. 'Auld Reekie' had become an affront to the aspirations and pecuniary capabilities of the middle classes, and they determined to distance themselves from it by engineering a leap across the northern loch, into 'The New Town' and fashionable modernity with full recognition of the recreational value of green spaces.

> The New Town - symmetrical, clean and classical - was not born until the Town Council adopted James Craig's plan in 1767; and the middle classes had not completed their movement into it until some time after 1800... It was built on different principles, for a new and quite different mode of middle-class living. Laid out in classical squares and long, straight streets with splendid houses and spacious gardens, and with circuses and crescents added later, it was the cold, clear and beautiful expression of the rational confidence of the middle-class... [It reflected] a vision for a metropolis that would break with the chaotic past [of Auld Reekie] and testify in stones and mortar to an ordered and harmonious world. The mob, the caddy, and the chamber-pot emptied out of the top-floor windows had no place in Anne Street or Charlotte Square, Heaven forbid ! (Smout, 1969).

By 1830 Edinburgh had become 'two towns', each evident in environmental terms on any map (Fig.3.1), and equally evident in social terms to anyone with an eye to perceive:

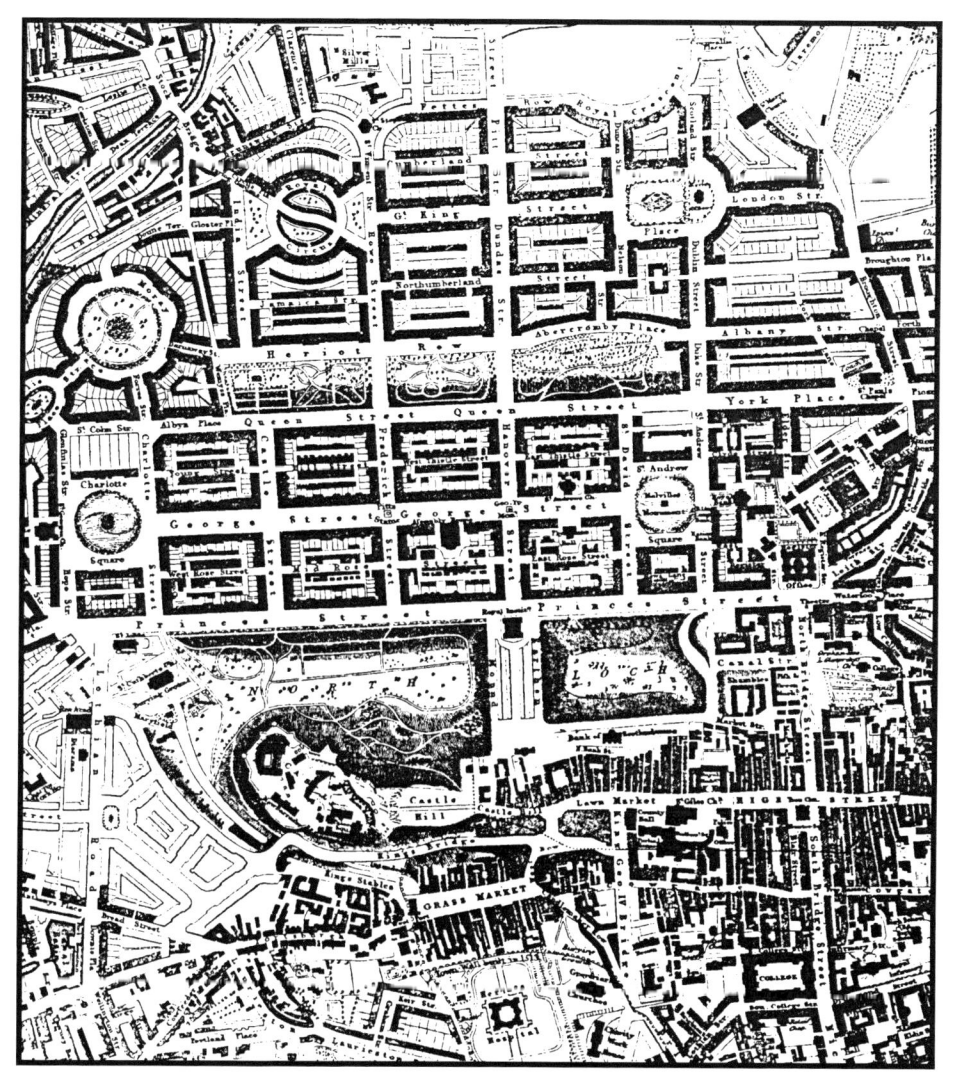

Fig.3.1 Edinburgh - Auld Reekie and The New Town c.1830.
(from Laing & Forbes Map by Baldwin & Craddock, Edinburgh, 1834)

Edinburgh is, in fact, two towns in more ways than one. It contains an upper and an under town - the one a sort of thoroughfare for the children of business and fashion, the other a den of retreat for the poor, the diseased and the ignorant. (Chambers, 1833 cited by Smout, 1969).

Spatially separate and secure within their avenues and green squares, the fine gentlemen and ladies in Edinburgh, London and other cities were not entirely lacking ideas about the urban poor, but they were too readily perceived as an anonymous mass - and typified as such in Dicken's 'Coketown'. Divorced from the land and 'natural social order' of the countryside, they had apparently lost their character and sense of proper behaviour to become a necessary but faceless adjunct of urban mechanisms. A serious lack of affinity and common ground, other than the workplace, thus fostered antipathy between the two nations; and if bridges rather than barriers were to be built between them, positive steps were necessary by those most able to pursue constructive projects.

However, in the field of leisure provision for the poor, the publicans were unrivalled. The tavern, ale-house, inn or pub is a flexible institution and it had rapidly become the leisure and sports centre of working-class quarters. Its diverse roles have been variously described and criticised by contemporary commentators and historians:

> In 1844 Frederick Engels complained that 'next to intemperance in the enjoyment of intoxicating liquors, one of the principal faults of English working men is sexual licence'... Men and women turned to drink and prostitution for a wide variety of reasons - for enjoyment, comfort, relief or escape... and these 'sinful pleasures' were enormous industries catering for leisure needs of millions; they were among the first of the mass commercialised leisure occupations of the new urban age, providing pleasure on an unprecedented scale... Apart from the pleasures of drink there was a range of recreations originating in and organised through the pub. Many early Victorian sports were arranged by the drinking [and gambling] fraternity, particularly those which were either illegal or attracted a strong criminal element. Boxing was perhaps the best example... (Walvin, 1978b).

Such questionable leisure life-styles may be partly explained in terms of parlous environmental and social conditions, which they actually aggravated. But all too often, the poor were victims of their poverty and prisoners of their environment, ignorance and base emotions; their aspirations were negligible and their hopes invested in gambling. The conditions of both people and place were urgently in need of improvement; and philanthropic paternalism eventually intervened to these ends.

3. Philanthropy and the Urban Poor

Escape to the countryside was not practicable for most of the urban poor; and, prompted by the *Health in Towns* movement, a Select Committee on Public Walks submitted its Report to parliament in 1833. This provides insights into a problem as seen from above and a response preferred from on high. The Committee was appointed:

> To consider the best means of securing Open Spaces in the Vicinity of Popular Towns as Public Walks and Places of Exercise calculated to promote the Health and Comfort of the Inhabitants... [It reported that] "it cannnot be necessary to point out how requisite some Public Walks or Open Spaces in the neighbourhood of large towns must be, to those who consider the occupations of the Working Classes who dwell there; confined as they are during the weekdays as Mechanics and Manufacturers, and often shut up in heated factories. It must be evident that it is of the first importance to their health on their day of rest to enjoy the fresh air, and to be able (exempt from the dust and dirt of the public

thoroughfares) to walk out in decent comfort with their families"... (Patmore, 1970).

Its findings reflected the situation of the day - namely that certain towns *had* come open spaces - but that inadequacies were the general rule. The Committee favoured the provision of Public Walks and Open Spaces, suggesting legislation... but not until the Recreation Grounds Act of 1859 was there a general Act. (Cherry, 1972).

Neither health issues nor leisure needs were being addressed directly; and 'it was perhaps typically Victorian to treat the symptoms rather than the cause' Patmore (1970). It was equally typical to seek improvements within the framework of approved middle-class conventions; but the promotion of walking as a health measure rather than as a source of enjoyment and fun was unlikely to attract the masses from the taverns.

Nevertheless, the 19th century will be remembered for 'Victorian parks'. However, no matter how benevolent their intentions, philanthropists, public corporations and landscape designers, all found it difficult to provide these pleasure grounds except as projections of their own expectations and those of respectable society; and they were greatly influenced by prevailing concerns for romantic places and science-based interests rather than the preferences of the poor (Ch.2. 3&4).

The idea of the park attracted the financial support of many a Victorian benefactor, and the open space movement to which it was linked took firm root throughout the middle classes with the result that towards the end of the century there was widespread support for measures for improving health, reducing overcrowding, and preserving open air amenities. This was a complex amalgam, but the Victorian public park was part of a total concern, including the improvement and enhancement of the urban landscape, the question of health and morality of the masses, attitudes to public recreation, and belief in the natural benefits of air and sunlight in over-crowded cities. (Cherry, 1972).

Such provision ultimately might facilitate convergence of the diverse classes, but it called upon the humble poor to bridge the gulf; and most parks were better able to serve the aspiring middle classes than the labouring masses.

Victorian parks were not always placed in the best location to serve the majority of the local populace... The extent of the existing built-up area suggested peripheral sites... Many were also private benefactions, and while such gifts were often genuine philanthropic gestures, others were concerned to create a buffer between working-class and middle-class areas of towns... Individual or corporate desire for a fitting memorial frequently made grandiose schemes beyond real need. A Middlesex magistrate of the 1850s 'regretted that these large parks should be formed at the public expense, in preference to squares of four or five acre pieces, in particular districts... The parks are too far off from the poor districts for [the poor] to avail themselves of them to the extent which they might otherwise do'. (Cherry, 1972).

The content of Victorian parks no less than their location was 'too far off from the poor'. For example, the first park to emerge in the light of the 1833 report on Public Walks may be Derby's *Arboretum* - eleven acres laid out in 1839 by J C Loudon and a gift to the public by Joseph Strutt (Patmore, 1970). Others followed but few if any were designed for 'the poor, the diseased and the ignorant'. Liverpool's Sefton Park may serve as an example. Provided at a cost of £400,000 and opened by royalty in 1872, it included a Grand Conservatory, a Horseman's Gallop, Moorish kiosks, deerhouses, restuarants, cricket and croquet pavilions, a Great Aviary, lakes, cascades, a rhododendron glen, grottoes, a bandstand, a giant flagstaff with a banderole... and Swiss chalet-style cottages as lodges. (Channon, c.1975). These amenities were located within 269 acres of idyllic, sylvan parkland calculated to satisfy the refined sensibilities of the cultured classes and to offend no sabbatarian. They would have little appeal for boisterous workers on the one day they were released from their noisy labour; and clearly the park was not intended for them. As in so many other cases, the commendable and apparently simple recommendation of 1833 - that Public Walks and Open Spaces be provided for the working classes - had been subverted or ignored.

Perhaps the first real attempt to provide for working-class interests was made in Blackpool in 1922 when Stanley Park was laid out as both a park and a play-ground. From the outset it comprised not only an ornamental lake, an Italian garden and a Rose garden but also a golf course and putting green, an athletics track, football pitches, a cricket square and bowling greens - all served by a social centre (Patmore, 1970). Eventually, Sefton Park and many others were able to accommodate such new features without destroying their traditional character; and even the smaller Victorian parks have exhibited a similar degree of flexibility. It is as well that they should do so, for their localities have been increasingly abandoned during the present century by the more affluent classes; and so 'Victorian parks' at last have become recreation grounds for those whom Victorians would describe as the 'humbler classes of the towns'.

4. Countryside Access for the Urban Poor.

Like their countryside cousins, the urban poor generally were confined to commonplace forms of walking within their various local environments; but most found themselves in unpromising places such as the Potteries, which Hoskins (1951) argued 'should not be avoided by anyone who wishes to know Britain'.

> Their ugliness is so demonic that it is fascinating... Coming down into it from the eastern or western hills, one savours its more intimate horrors... The canal, that aorta of the Potteries, flows - no, it does not flow, it simply lies inert - hidden between potbanks, and one has to look hard for it and, having found it... the water is the colour and consistency of cocoa... but the young men dive cheerfully into its opaque depths and swim under the dark bridges.

And they may have fished in it - if fish were to be had; and they certainly walked by it; what other options did they have ? In fact, the small scale of the Six Towns and the widespread sprawl of the Potteries offered some escape to local countryside where the 'townies' might share the basic pleasures of the rural poor, if only on the Sabbath. Broadly comparable geographical circumstances provided similar opportunities for workers and their families in the textile towns which straggled up Pennine valleys and the dispersed mining communities on many coalfields. On the outskirts of such places 'opportunities afforded by woods and fields gave children their greatest chance for fun... (and)... children everywhere seemed to find endless enjoyment climbing, fishing, hunting, collecting food, fruit and eggs - sometimes illicitly (Walvin, 1983). Men and women may have been more prone to rest at home or relax at a local ale-house but some few undoubtedly shared their children's enjoyment of the countryside.

However, the greater part of the urban poor were soon trapped deep in the dismal inner areas of the more massive conurbations; and comparable benefits for them required significant improvement of their capabilities and development of their aspirations. This depended heavily upon external forces which would increase their income and mobility, improve their minds, and widen their horizons. Education and sympathetic promotion of countryside recreation were key factors; and significant inputs were necessary to uplift and brighten the lives of such deprived sections of society. Unfortunately, for far too long, too little was forthcoming from the government and institutionalised philanthropy; and considerably more was achieved by commercial enterprises, symbolised by the publican, which provided the 'sinful pleasures' that were a major force in urban lifestyles.

The churches and chapels initially stood aloof; and the urban poor largely lost contact with religious institutions, if not with God:

> As a clergyman remarked in 1896, 'It is not that the Church of God has lost the great towns: it has never had them'. People moving into towns lost the habit of worship and working-class people born in towns never acquired it. (Inglis, 1963)... The religious census of 1851, showed that 'the labouring myriads of our working population... are never or seldom seen in our religious congregations'... Fewer than one person in ten attended church or chapel on census day in Birmingham, Liverpool, Manchester, Sheffield and Newcastle... and the metropolis was equally indifferent to the call for regular worship. (Briggs, 1963).

Furthermore, Victorian churches and chapels generally embraced a spirit of paternalism if not puritanism which discouraged pursuit of earthly pleasures and stressed the virtue of strict sabbatarianism. This could only distance them from those who found refuge in the ale house; but sabbatarianism for long affected all respectable households:

> Sunday was the grimmest day in the week... No inclemancy of the weather ever freed us from morning service... Games of any kind were forbidden... (though) a walk was tolerated as part of my father's open-air religion... Our own story books being strictly banned, we had to read a good book... History, fortunately, was counted suitable for Sunday reading. (Lockhart, 1937).

The respectable establishment would not openly criticise the 'dreadful Victorian sabbath'; and there is some justice in the fact that the severity of its exclusiveness was instrumental in the 1860s in liberating Saturday afternoons from work. Sunday had to be protected from football!

Such moral rectitude inhibited and coloured the secular mission of all religious organisations; and they generally agreed:

> with most men and women of property (who) felt the necessity for putting the house of the poor in order. The remedies proposed might differ... (but) the message to be given to the poor was simple... *'Patience, labour, sobriety, frugality and religion should be recommended to them; all the rest is downright fraud'*. (Thompson, 1963)

Religion was inclined to teach 'that man must expect his chief happiness, not in the present, but in a future state'; *There is a Happy Land, far, far away !* Whether this was fraud or not, such beliefs and values were comforting to the converted but they did not endear their advocates to common sinners. Church and chapel members, Sunday school teachers and scholars thus were set apart to a significant degree within the working class and even within their own families. Nevertheless, they were widely tolerated and respected; and they were disproportionately influential in their own communities.

The Sunday schools and associated Day schools soon occupied a central role in the social life and improvement of a substantial minority of the urban poor.

> Beginning in the 1790s, the Sunday school movement rapidly established itself in lower class communities, providing education - in reading, writing, religion and occasionally other subjects - for periods of four to six hours each Sunday. By the early nineteenth century, the Sunday schools had taken on a distinctly plebeian tone and style, with working-class teachers ministering to working-class children through an educational structure which was unusually democratic. Moreover it was a voluntary yet time-consuming business for teachers and pupils, and the fact that millions passed through the system speaks for both its appeal and importance... There were some 1,400,000 children attending Sunday schools in 1833; 2,100,000 in 1851. (Walvin, 1978b).

Literacy was one of the most significant achievements of the Sunday schools, enabling members of the labouring masses to see beyond the gulf which isolated them from mainstream life and culture. Furthermore, the Sunday schools promoted 'respectable recreations'. For both teachers and scholars, going to Sunday school itself - thoroughly washed and cleanly dressed in the best available - generated a sense of occasion; and, increasingly, the schools also catered for the free-time of their members and, indirectly, of the communities from which they were drawn.

> Sunday school anniversaries and prize-givings, choral concerts, public parades on festive days, and even excursions and trips, punctuated the weekly routines... bringing a degree of mass organised leisure where in general none existed... Many of the early pioneering excursion trains were filled in the 1840s by Sunday schools heading for the coast... Three thousand children travelled from Birmingham to Cheltenham in 1846; a similar number that year journeyed from Macclesfield to Stockport; and no fewer than 6125 parents, children and teachers were taken by train from Norwich to Yarmouth. (Walvin, 1978b).

> Every MONDAY, WEDNESDAY, and SATURDAY (except on Saturdays, August 4th and 11th to L. & N. W. Stations), until further notice,
> Cheap Excursion Tickets to
> # TRENTHAM, STONE, †BOSLEY,
> ## †RUSHTON (for Swythamly and Dane Valley), †RUDYARD LAKE,
> †Rudyard, Oakamoor, Alton, Ashbourne,
> # THORPE CLOUD, TISSINGTON, HARTINGTON,
> (for Dovedale) AND
> # †MANIFOLD VALLEY
> will be issued
> ## From BOLLINGTON & MACCLESFIELD
> (HIBEL ROAD or CENTRAL).
>
> | TO | FARES FOR THE DOUBLE JOURNEY.—THIRD CLASS. | |
> |---|---|---|
> | | From Bollington. | From Macclesfield |
> | Trentham | 2 3 | 2 - |
> | Stone | 2 9 | 2 6 |
> | †Bosley | 1 - | - 9 |
> | †Rushton | 1 3 | 1 - |
> | †Rudyard Lake or Rudyard | 1 6 | 1 3 |
> | Consall, Oakamoor, Alton | 2 6 | 2 3 |
> | Ashbourne | 2 9 | 2 6 |
> | Thorpe Cloud (for Dovedale) | 3 3 | 3 - |
> | Tissington | 3 3 | 3 - |
> | Hartington | 4 - | 3 9 |
> | †Waterhouses | 2 9 | 2 6 |
> | †Manifold Valley | 3 3 | 3 - |
>
> **Hartington, Tissington, Thorpe Cloud, Ashbourne, and Alton Tickets** will be issued by any Train, and all others by any Train after 10.0 a.m. which reaches the destination in time for the Passengers to return by the last Train by which there is a through connection on the day of issue.
> **For Train Service** see special Bills and Time Tables.
> †—Tickets are issued on Sundays also from Bollington and Macclesfield (Central Station) to these places.
> **Rudyard and Rudyard Lake Tickets** are available to alight at or return from either Station.
> **Holders of Tickets** to Rudyard can obtain Day Tickets for Fishing in the Lake (which has recently been re-stocked) from the Station-master there at 1s each, and Boats can be obtained by arrangement.

Plate 3.3 Opportunities for Recreational Travel to Countryside Resorts offered by the North Staffordshire Railway in 1891. (from Shercliff, 1987)

Such Sunday school outings became highlights of the year. They reflect a combination of organisation by the voluntary sector and commercial provision of low-cost, bulk passenger transport - at first by canal, then and much more significantly by railway (Plate 3.3) and later by motor-coaches. Within the range of destinations offered by the transport systems, the particular choice of venue reflected the preference of the organisers; but from 1850 it was difficult to ignore the popularity of the seaside. However, the gaiety and frivolity of the resorts did not readily appeal to the churches, which argued on moral and health grounds for sober visits to the countryside. In towns far removed from the coast, this case was reinforced by the cost and inconvenience of long journeys for large numbers of children. Consequently, for more than a hundred years, the Sunday schools introduced many thousands to the countryside and walking therein, creating awareness and images that might well lay foundations for independent participation in later life.

> In June 1843, after the opening of the line in 1842 from Manchester to Crewe, the ladies of Alderley reported the pleasure of 2-3000 Sunday school children brought out by their teachers at Whit to the Edge, as far from the evils of the Manchester racecourse as possible, to enjoy 'the scenery and breathing such pure air, despite wet and windy conditions'. They walked round the Edge in pairs; then farmers' fields were hired to play in, drinks and buns were provided. But later on Henrietta Maria Stanley noted a quantity of dirty paper had been left, and the ferns trampled... *The Manchester Guardian* commented (some years later) that such excursions were a lot more healthy and more conducive to social and domestic life than the disorderly scenes at the racecourses. (Shercliffe, 1987).

Inevitably, all such outings took hundreds if not thousands of visitors at a time to particular locations; and this underpinned Wordsworth's opposition to the railways and his desire to protect 'the Lakes' from untutored townsmen (Ch.2.5). However, excursion trains served the middle-classes no less than the working class; and White's (1851) *Directory of Staffordshire* records some effects of early commercial initiatives in countryside tourism in the Peak District:

> In the highly picturesque township of Rudyard, an extensive reservoir had been formed for purposes of feeding the Caldon Canal. Since the opening of the Churnet Valley Railway, this extensive sheet of water has been dignified by the name of Lake Rudyard, and is visited in summer by numerous pleasure parties from the Potteries, Manchester, Macclesfield and other towns, especially at Easter and Whitsuntide when there is usually a grand fete and regatta attended by many thousands of people brought by cheap trains.

Sociable strolls, promenading and picnicing by the Lake would no doubt be popular, as would longer walks within the 'highly picturesque' parish. And it is, perhaps, a little known fact that the parents of Rudyard Kipling first met at this resort.

Four general consequences of lasting importance may be noted. First, particularly attractive and accessible places thus became popular and they responded to market opportunities; 'honeypots' were created long before the term was invented. Secondly, 'an outing' comprised a package of activities and experiences, almost invariably including walking and picnics or purchased meals. Thirdly, day-trippers conveyed by public transport were necessarily gregarious; and even in the countryside they accepted and probably preferred close company. Wordsworth and his fellow romanticists were now the minority but the 'democratisation' of travel had done little to reduce class consciousness. Indeed, the revolution in leisure travel provided new opportunities for the aspiring middle classes to emulate the gentlemen of the previous century and enjoy affordable 'Grand Tours of Europe' organised by Thomas Cook, thus continuing to distance themselves from the urban poor (Plate 3.4). Finally, as Henrietta Stanley noted, proletarian outings would inevitably have some adverse consequences for the host environment, and this allowed discerning minds environmental grounds for objections to supplement or camouflage their reluctance to share their preferred places. Enjoyment of the countryside was thus further embroiled with class consciousness if not conflict.

Plate 3.4. Thos. Cook's 'Grand Tours of Europe'
for the Aspiring Middle Classes of the 1860's.

Towards the end of the century access for working-class people to respectable recreations was addressed by a wider range of philanthropic institutions, voluntary organisations, commercial concerns and employers. For example, in 1892 the Fresh Air Fund was launched by C.A. Pearson, and it had the merit of bringing the deprivation of the poor to the notice of wealthy, who were invited to supply the necessary funds:

> By 1909 it had financed day trips for more than two million children; and while the seaside was the most popular destination, children were also frequently taken into the countryside..... To bring home its point to the wealthier (upon

whom these ventures ultimately relied for finance), the Fresh Air Fund published a telling poem:

> Pity the children of the poor
> Who've never plucked daisies;
> Who've never watched the skylark soar,
> Or heard it singing praises;
> Who've never trod the fresh green sward,
> Or rambled by the river;
> They need a holiday, ye rich -
> May God reward the giver.   (Walvin, 1978b).

Such occasional outings provided at least a flash of colour, which might be inspirational, for millions of people whose lives continued to be dominated by work within the towns and cities; and, sponsored by various agencies, they became a relatively common feature:

> Hordes of children were packed into trains for visits to coast and country, onto steamers for trips down river or round the bay. Schoolmasters, clergymen, social workers and others with access to poor quarters, rallied willing armies of children for these trips. In 1887 a Glaswegian businessman treated some 15,000 of the city's poor to an outing to Rothesay... Wealthy industrialists opened the grounds of their stately homes to the curious gaze of their employees, who were ferried into the country by fleets of trains and coaches... In 1897 Lever Brothers treated 2,300 employees to an excursion to London for the Queen's Diamond Jubilee... In 1909 the staff of W.H. Smith's warehouse in Fetter Lane travelled to the countryside at Pinner, where they enjoyed dinner, tea and a cricket match... Many such trips were epics of organisation on an almost military scale. (Walvin, 1978b).

For many their effects were likely to be transient, but for others they may have been seminal; and the Cooperative Holidays Association provides an example of innovatory provision for those with some commitment to countryside recreation and the means to pay for a holiday:

> The CHA began in 1891 with informal excursions by members of the Social Guild of the Rev.T.A. Leonard, a Congregational Minister at Colne, and became a non-profit making company in 1897. Its purpose was to provide recreative and educational holidays by purchasing or renting and furnishing houses and rooms in selected centres, by catering in such houses for parties of members and guests, and by securing helpers who will promote the intellectual and social interests of the party they are associated with. It was an honest attempt towards the better use of the people's holidays. "The CHA offers guests the healthful ways of an out-of-door life among the hills, instead of the rowdy pleasures of popular holiday resorts... and helps people to find joy in music, literature, nature-study, and that best of all exercises, walking, with all that it brings to mind and body". (Pimlot, 1947).

The intention was to emulate and disseminate experiences enjoyed by those with discerning minds; and such opportunities were likely to appeal to aspiring members of the newly educated classes. In this respect the CHA was a pioneer, to be followed by the Holiday Fellowship, the Workers' Travel Association and the Youth Hostel Association. Such endeavours are admirable, but they often became victims of their own success, eventually serving converts and established customers rather than addressing new cohorts of inexperienced persons. It was essential that they should always retain and renew their sense of mission if enjoyment of the countryside was to become accessible to all.

However, by the close of the century all such outings and holidays were overshadowed by the massive growth of urban-based leisure for all sections of the population. Countryside recreation as a whole was dwarfed by 'the emergence of organised, spectator and participatory sports (which effected) a major revolution in social life' (Walvin, 1978b). Football, cricket, rugby, swimming, athletics, boxing, rowing, tennis, hockey, golf and many other sports were all supported by commercial enterprise, local government provision, and both professional and amateur or voluntary organisations. They were practised and promoted in schools throughout the country; and taken up by thousands of clubs for children and young persons.

Some of these were based at chapels and churches, but many were secular. Some, such as the Boys' Brigade and Boy Scouts, specifically promoted outdoor activities, including countryside walking, as a part of their 'training for life'; but they were a small minority and most youth organisations granted pride of place to organised sports and social activities. A similar emphasis was to be found in schools. Comparable growth and diversification occurred simultaneously within the broader field of entertainment and home-based leisure. Consequently, at a time when most untutored minds were being significantly enlightened, they were also being captured by accessible urban-based sports and recreation. Furthermore, resource limitations still restricted their participation in out-of-town activities at a time when those with discerning minds and ample pockets were being better equipped with improved transport to enjoy the best of both worlds - the countryside and the city.

5. Walking, Cycling and Motoring upto 1950

At the turn of the century, while walking within close proximity of home was probably a commonplace recreation, its more specialised forms, with the possible exception of sociable strolling in pleasant civilised places, were still the preserve of small minorities.

> Rambling - or pedestrianism, to use the ugly contemporary term - was less popular than might perhaps have been expected. In some parts, especially in the north, it was a favourite pastime of young working men, but on the whole it was confined to the sedentary and the intellectual. One reason was no doubt that in his short leisure periods the manual worker sought rest rather than exercise; another was that he rarely possessed the education or the sophistication to appreciate the delights of the countryside...and, as is shown by the guide books, it was assumed as a matter of course that the pedestrian's equipment would include interest in the botany, geology, archaeology and history of the districts he visited. Public opinion regarded with disfavour the association of unmarried

> members of both sexes in the intimacy of a walking tour; and rambling is not a pastime well suited to a family... (Pimlott, 1947).

Wordsworth's fears for the Lake District had not materialised. The untutored townsmen had been deflected to Blackpool and distracted by football; and countryside walking was still dominated by the upper-strata of the social hierachy.

Furthermore, participation was affected by new forms of transport and changes in personal mobility; and walking was being seriously challenged by cycling. Developed in Paris in the early 1860s, the 'velocipede' was little more than an expensive toy; but there are documented reports of some early club activities. For example, in 1869 two members of the Liverpool Velocipede Club cycled to London, which seems very much like an ascetic quest for adventure. In the same year the Manchester-based Levenshulme Club organised an afternoon excursion to Wilmslow, which appears to have much in common with a ramble.

> At Davenport [the cyclists] were travelling at great speed upon the footpath when a policeman rushed before one of the riders and upset him. The velocipedist fell heavily... Two members were later fined 4s.6d. each for being on the footpath... It was not clear whether such machines should be on the footpath where pedestrians did not like them; or on the road where drivers of horses did all they could to upset them... All the gentlemen being experienced riders, the speed attained was from seven to eight miles an hour; and downhill, ten miles... They had tea at the White Swan, Alderley, and a few of the gentlemen went on to enjoy Alderley Edge. (Shercliffe, 1987).

The velocipede or 'bone-shaker' craze was confined to a few, if only because the machines were very expensive and the roads, very bad. New machines, better in every respect, were soon developed; but as custom-built products they remained prohibitively expensive. Cheaper, mass-produced bikes could be made if they could be sold in large numbers; and the key to this 'chicken-egg' problem lay in promotion, something which walking had rarely if ever enjoyed. The formation, in 1878, of the Cyclists' Touring Club and the National Cyclists' Union were backed by manufacturers; and these national bodies promptly campaigned for better roads and conditions for cyclists and for the formation of clubs; and they provided channels of communication for all matters relating to cycling, including the products of commercial companies. The cycling boom was launched. Membership of the CTC rose from 142 in 1878 to 6,705 in 1882 and to a peak of 60,449 in 1899. Its pioneering work was done by then, and the power of an authoritative voice at national level, which walkers had yet to achieve, had been demonstrated.

> The members of the CTC formed only a small proportion of the vast army of cyclists who filled the roads at week-ends and during the holiday season. As yet not seriously challenged by the motor-car, the bicycle was popular with all classes, but it meant most to young men and women of the factories, the shops and the offices. For them it was a liberating agency... The appeal of the bicycle lay partly in its novelty, partly in the freedom and the scope for individual en-

Plate 3.5. Perry's 1896 Handbook for Manchester Cyclists. (from Shercliff, 1987)

terprise which it gave as compared with the railways. It was cheaper than any other method of travel (not excluding rambling, which ordinarily necessitated expenditure on travel at the beginning and the end of a tour); and it was important not least because of its contribution to the rediscovery of the countryside... The contribution of the bicycle was summed up by Lord Balfour: *There has not been a more civilizing invention in the memory of the present generation... open to all classes, enjoyed by both sexes and by all ages.* (Pimlott, 1947).

This is fulsome praise; but a more detailed analysis by Walvin (1978b) qualifies Lord Balfour's sweeping truth. Open to all classes and ages it may be, but cycling was not taken up equally by all. Also, the prominence given to female participation may be explained by its association with the fashionable movement for the emancipation of women.

The most notable female sporting prescence (except perhaps horse-riding) was in cycling... For many women the bicycle involved more than mere sport when, from 1870 onwards, a fierce political debate arose about the propriety of women cyclists. Cycling was thought to be unladylike (originally, of course, only *ladies* tended to ride); it was claimed to be unhealthy... and indecorous... American women had already shown the attractions and possibilities of cycling, developing the scandalous 'bloomers' specially for the purpose. Bolder spirits in England insisted on following the American - and French - example, wearing the new clothes and embarking on cycle races. By the early 1890s women had generally won the argument by simple force of habit... Women's cycling clubs proliferated... By 1895 cyclists often usurped the place of horse-riders in fashionable London parks. Aristocratic ladies, middle class ladies and fashionable society in general vied with each other to be seen astride a bike. Poorer women could only hope for a ride at the seaside, where bikes could be hired for a short spin... As with other sports, cycling was carried along by entrepreneurial guile and propagated by a spate of cycling publications.

It would be false to suggest that for ladies the cycle was primarily a symbol of political protest. In 1896 Perry's *Handbook for Manchester Cylists* gave prominence to lady riders (Plate 3.5); the *Manchester Ladies' Oxford Cycling Club* was founded in 1897; and *The Country Diary of an Edwardian Lady*, (written in 1906 by Edith Holden and eventually published in 1977), shows how walking and cycling were combined by ladies in the exploration of the countryside. Nevertheless, Shercliffe's study of cycling in and around Manchester shows that participants were predominantly male. It also shows that recreational cycling and walking served similar ends, and the former offered several advantages:

> The joys of cycling with the YMCA Cyclist's Club included... the pleasures of social and friendly intercourse... the ability to reach country impossible to see any other way except by great expense... and its value for health... The body is being exercised all the time whilst pedalling in addition to which the rider is inhaling the pure fresh air of the country, and whilst riding merrily along there is an endless panorama resplendent with the works of nature... The cyclist goes where he pleases, stops where he feels inclined, and finds great pleasure in planning tours for several days... the prettiest and quietest routes are chosen for runs rather than the shortest or the main roads. This manages to keep us pretty clear of the motor cars and such like which raise the dust and pollute the air... Most of the runs are 20 to 40 miles... (Shercliffe, 1987).

Countryside recreation was thus diversified forever by another user, comparable in many respect with walkers. Whether cycling did attract more fashionable ladies and young men and women of the factories than walking is uncertain; but it certainly was a popular option, and the overall growth of walking, especially amongst the urban poor, probably was slowed if not diminished. Like walking, cycling has utilitarian and recreational functions, and it would be imprudent to cite the number of cycles in general use as an indicator of recreational cycling - but in 1931 there were ten million bikes in Britain and only one million cars in private ownership.

Nevertheless the car was destined to transform the spatial organisation of Britain although, unlike the bicycle, its use was for long restricted to the wealthy.

> The first motor-car owners were plutocratic. Early motor cars were superb hand-made vehicles which retained a luxury image down to 1914... For a well-off traveller it had been a major weakness of the rail road that 'you were shunted here and there along fixed tracks'. By contrast, if you had the money, a motor car was your own... you had 'the freedom of the road'. (Briggs, 1983).

This freedom was sometimes abused; and there were major problems in accommodating the car on roads scarcely fit for a horse and cart. In 1914, when there were only 132,015 licensed private cars, there were no less than 1,328 fatal motor accidents. But, supported by the Royal Automobile Club from 1897 and the Automobile Association from 1905, the rich and powerful were not to be denied. Harry Graham (1874-1936) captured something of the times:

Lord Gorbals

Once, as old Lord Gorbals motored
Round his moors near John 'o Groats,
He collided with a goatherd
And a herd of forty goats.
By the time his car got through
They were all defunct but two.

Roughly he addressed the goatherd:
"Dash my whiskers and my corns !
Can't you teach your goats, you dotard,
That they ought to sound their horns ?
Look, my AA badge is bent !
I've a mind to raise your rent !"

Tragedy

That morning, when my wife eloped, With James, our chauffer, how I moped !
What tragedies in life there are ! How can I live without the car ? (Graham, 1986).

Highways and highway authorities were soon dedicated to motor vehicles at the expense of horse-riders, cyclists and walkers - with little more than a wimper of protest. The reconstruction of roads and creation of by-passes was soon reminiscent of the era of railway-building. Yet seasonal and peak-period traffic congestion remained recurrent problems 'as the car, coach, char-a-banc and lorry began to transform the face of English society'.

> While the aspiring middle class saved for their cars (emulating the style of their betters before 1914), working people took to the roads in motor coaches and char-a-bancs, heading for favourite haunts and new delights... For millions it was a major emancipation, even when enjoyed only on the occasional day... It also meant that trippers could now visit previously inaccessible parts of the country. As a result large parts of the nation's natural beauty spots were laid bare to motor-borne tourists - the beginning of a phenomena which ever since has plagued the country's rural assets... (Walvin, 1978b).

Walvin's evident censure of the 'millions of trippers' is reminiscent of Wordsworth's fear of the railways. Both reflect the contemporary and continuing view of self-centred if not selfish middle-class minds as and when they perceive a threat to their privileged position and their valued places. No *evidence* of damage to 'rural assets' (as distinct from middle-class enjoyment of them) is offered, but the implicit argument places the 'problem' into the sensitive field of conservation. However, Pimlott (1947) provides more detailed information on the early motorised 'invasion' of the countryside, noting diverse benefits rather than the disadvantages of 'rural tourism':

> By 1939, there was hardly a village which did not provide some facilities - teas, bed and breakfast, camping sites or a garage - while in the hilly districts and in most of the hinterland of the coast holiday-catering had become an important source of income. Derelict hotels and inns were rejuvenated, cottage parlours blossomed forth as tearooms, the village blacksmith became a motor mechanic and a petrol station sprang up where once the village smithy stood. The cyclists and youth organisations had pointed the way. The motorists followed, and of over 2,000,000 private motor vehicles in 1939 there were few which were never used for touring...... The new tourists were to be found wherever there was beautiful country... (and) Cook's *Holiday Guide* for 1946 - admittedly an abnormal year - listed 53 inland resorts in England and 7 in Wales as compared with 71 seaside resorts. Their variety is illustrated by the dozen first on the list: Ambleside, Bovey Tracey, Bradford-on-Avon, Brotherswater (Westmoreland), Burford, Buxton, Caterham (with 'rural delights that can be swiftly exchanged for the pleasures of the capital'), Chagford, Cheltenham, Chester, Chiddingford (Surrey - 'a splendid centre for a walking holiday, proud of its 14th-century inn and its 20th-century unsophistication'), and Coalbrookdale (Shropshire).

This list presents a clear message; scenic touring now complemented cycling and walking in the countryside, and selected rural resorts and regions were becoming more heavily used and their economies benefitted. The car had became an adjunct to rambling since it 'could cut out the long plod before you actually started your walk'; and while recreational cycling probably was an alternative to walking for the poor, the car facilitated countryside walking by the middle-classes.

In summary, the first half of the 20th-century continued in much the same vein as the preceding fifty years but significant innovations gave a new edge and urgency to established concerns. Increased recreational use of the countryside, generated mostly by the middle-classes, fuelled fears for the privileged position of regular users; and a greater host of conservationists feared for the well being of their valued places and for a wide range of phenomena dear to their hearts and minds. Secondly, while many land-owners and holders had been tolerant of limited and considerate walking over their property, increased usage proved more damaging and less acceptable. While meekly surrendering the roads to motorists, walkers' organisations responded by campaigning more vigorously for ancient and inalienable rights of access to the wider countryside. Finally, the increased participation in outdoor recreation, including hunting, shooting and fishing, by the upper and middle classes strengthened the voice and influence of privileged minority groups for the protection of their preferred places and of their particular recreational interests; and the alleged threat to the countryside of unidentified hordes of untutored townsmen was implicitly and openly deployed. No one argued for a place in the countryside for the public as a whole; but numerous parties generated public support for their particular causes and privileged positions (Fig.4.1).

More than ever before the countryside had become an amphitheatre (Pl.1). Acute, discerning minds should have seen, and surely did see, that trends evident in the 'thirties would escalate in any prolonged period of prosperity; a new world did lie just beyond the horizon. Dower's 'fourth wave' was delayed by depression and war but it was entirely predictable. It called not only for a sound appreciation of the legacy and lessons of history in terms of ongoing conflicts, but also and more importantly, of the likely problems and needs of the future. Priority should have been given to positive and comprehensive policies, planning and preparation for the countryside as a major recreational asset for the nation as a whole. This may have been considered in some quarters but it was never publicly proposed, largely because too many influential parties with vested interests relentlessly pursued their own self-centred agenda. Additionally, Victorian sentimentality and romanticised half-truths have continued to turn heads and hearts and cloud real issues - and are still purposefully propagated to those ends.

> England's countryside is not only one of the great treasures of the earth, it is also a vital part of our national identity. All of us - even those who rarely step outside our towns - cherish somewhere in our souls the same vision of our real homeland: a rural vision.. of England's patchwork quilt of fields, downs and woods, separated by thick hedgerows, mossy banks, sunken lanes and sparkling streams. (Shoard, 1980).

Plate 4.1 Pressure Groups are a Power to be Reckoned With !
(Sean Smith, The Guardian, 7 January 1999)

Some 50 Ramblers, including their President, Mr Andrew Bennett MP, undertook a protest walk over a blocked path on Mr van Hoogstraten's 100 acre estate in East Sussex prior to successful pursuit of their case in court. The millionaire's determination to defend his privacy by reducing rather than eliminating paths across his land and the Ramblers' apparent determination to score a victory could well lead to a lengthy, bitter and expensive dispute.

4
COUNTRYSIDE ISSUES AND LEGISLATION: ACCESS AND PARTICIPATION

1. The Political Context

From the early Middle Ages British society has always been highly stratified; that was the 'natural order' of things, and the more contentious divisions were regional and religious. However, Victorian *laissez faire* and capitalism wrought such marked changes that the image of 'two nations' gained credibility and political views were increasingly polarised and focused on social issues. Political philosophies such as republicanism, socialism and communism became more prominent; and, being dissatisfied with a slow and piecemeal improvement in socio-economic conditions, their proponents sought fundamental and comprehensive change rather than progressive modification of a continuing 'steady state'. Williams (1973) has expressed the frustration which can beset such movements:

> Capitalism, as a mode of production, is the basic process of most of what we know as the history of country and city. Its abstracted economic drives, its fundamental priorities in social relations, its criteria of growth and of profit and loss, have over several centuries altered our country and created our kinds of city. Seeing the history in this way, I am convinced that resistance to capitalism is the decisive form of the necessary human defence. Many particular defences stop short of seeing the decisive process...and others get through *as defences*, as forms of opposition to what is called the modern world... but with no available confidence in any different way of life, or with such confidence replaced by utopia or apocalyptic visions...

However, a better way of life is not dependent on a revolutionary philosophy; but during periods of rapid change the value of looking forward to 'a different way of life' and of constructing new, positive policies for the future is beyond question. Unfortunately, all too often there is a marked tendency to grant history a reverence it may not deserve and to build for the future on obsolete and inappropriate foundations. The Victorians were ambivalent in such matters, and especially so in respect of the countryside. On the one hand, driven by an economic imperative, improved use of rural resources was vigorously and effectively pursued, often with adverse effects on the lives of many, and on physical access to the countryside (Ch.2.2). On the other hand, numerous amenity values of the countryside were subject to 'particular defences' to improve, preserve, protect and conserve valued places and phenomena (Table 2.1). The several privileged minorities promoting this broad conservation movement simultaneously defended their hold on their particular preferred places and amenities, and on their perception of the best means of access to the countryside (Ch.2.3-5). This defence of particular rights and privileges developed in a piecemeal fashion over a long period, and with limited success while Victorian *laissez faire* held sway; but a degree of affinity between numerous bodies gradually developed, giving added strength to each without sacrificing the identity of any. Furthermore, while

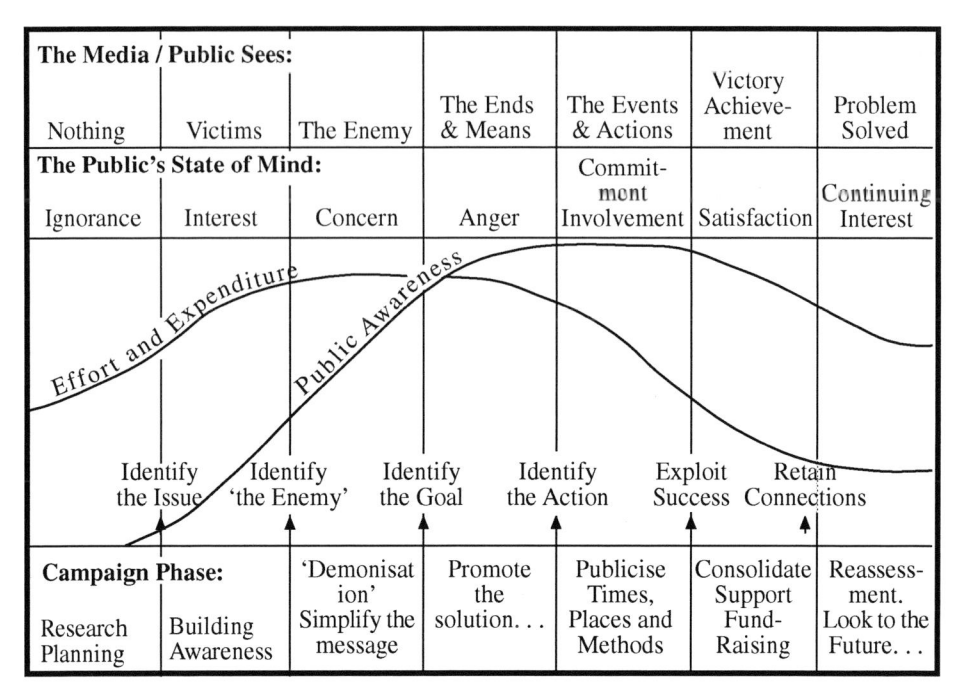

The Media / Public Sees:						
Nothing	Victims	The Enemy	The Ends & Means	The Events & Actions	Victory Achievement	Problem Solved
The Public's State of Mind:						
Ignorance	Interest	Concern	Anger	Commitment Involvement	Satisfaction	Continuing Interest
	Identify the Issue	Identify 'the Enemy'	Identify the Goal	Identify the Action	Exploit Success	Retain Connections
Campaign Phase:						
Research Planning	Building Awareness	'Demonisation' Simplify the message	Promote the solution...	Publicise Times, Places and Methods	Consolidate Support Fund-Raising	Reassessment. Look to the Future...

Fig.4.1 Stages in a Pressure Group Campaign for Public Awareness, Support and Involvement. (after C.Rose, 1993)

> The modern militant pressure group was born of universal literacy, the growth of the mass media, and political change during the first-half of the 20th century. Lobbying has continued as an important function in decision-making, but it has been increasingly matched by winning the hearts of 'the people' via sensational and, arguably, newsworthy stories. Consequently, emotive appeals count more than rational argument; complex issues are reduced to simple morality stories; these are highlighted by dramatic events; and confrontation is preferred to conciliation. Truth and democracy are thus dispossessed; sectional rather than national issues are pursued with vigour and, all too often, are pressed upon parliament which, from time to time, is persuaded to make bad law.

Wordsworth acknowledged that his defence of 'the Lakes' was for 'persons of pure taste' (Kay, 2000), it subsequently became common practice for numerous parties to claim that their particular case is in the public interest, though in reality it evidently does not serve the needs of the people as a whole and, in many cases, is detrimental to large sections of the population.

In many cases progress depended on legislation, but the 19th century was characterised by a high degree of stability and continuity in parliament, which was responsible for the nation but answerable to a narrow electorate. This favoured two major parties with a strong element of 'me-too-ism'; and neither was inclined to persistently antagonise the aristocracy or the upper and middle classes. Then, as the franchise was repeatedly wid-

Year	Conservative (%)	Labour (%)	Liberal (%)	Others (%)	Votes Cast (Millions)
1900	51	2	45	2	3.5
1906	44	6	49	1	5.6
1910-Jan	47	8	43	2	6.7
1910-Dec	46	7	44	3	5.2
1918	36	24	26	14	10.8
1922	38	29	29	4	14.4
1923	38	30	30	2	14.5
1924	48	33	18	1	16.6
1929	38	37	23	2	22.7
1931	55	32	11	2	21.7
1935	54	38	6	6	22.0
1945	40	48	9	3	25.1
1950	43	46	9	2	28.8
1951	48	49	3	-	28.6

Table 4.1 The Growth of the Franchised Population and Changing Fortunes of the Major Political Parties, 1900-1951. (Ryder and Silver, 1970)

ened, there was increased opportunity for and probability of two or more parties with distinctively different philosophies, since each could appeal to opposite ends of the socio-economic spectrum - to the proponents and beneficiaries of capitalism or to its victims. The rise of the Labour Party reflects the opportunity and the process; and both may be summarised in votes cast in general elections from 1900 to 1951 (Table 4.1).

Secondly, the political importance of mass media greatly increased with the spread of literacy which supported the expansion and growth of national, regional and local newspapers and encouraged greater use of pamphlets, tracts and posters. Then the emergence of new forms of media transmission, notably the radio, films and eventually television, gave the mass media greater immediacy and authority. Governments have always been subject to petitions and lobbying, but now they became very susceptible to 'public opinion' and more sensitive as to how it might affect the distribution of votes. Newsworthy items could be rapidly converted into 'national issues' and be broadcast with ready-made opinions throughout the land. This led political activists to recognise the value of a 'national voice'; and thus to the emergence of national organisations, such as the Country Landowners Association (1907) and the Ramblers Association (1935) to represent amalgamations of local concerns with shared interests (Table 2.1). This was particularly important as the government increasingly became involved in a widening spectrum of affairs and functions, notably planning and monitoring change. Many organisations and movements thus discovered that the government had an interest, or could be made to take an interest, in their particular concerns; and the modern, militant 'pressure group' was born.

Such groups know that approaches to parliament and administrative authorities must be backed with popular support; and they know how to acquire popular appeal through the mass media (Fig.4.1). Typically, this requires an emotive issue, a sharp focus on a specific objective, and simplification of the message They also know it is no part of their purpose to show any sympathy for 'the other man's point of view'; except, perhaps, when sitting together in diplomatic circles. It is necessary 'to know thine enemy' in order to unseat him - to destroy or discredit his cause by all practicable means, including the breach of minor 'unjust laws' provided such action will win media attention and public support. In the political arena, all too often the end justifies the means; but in the context of countryside access all too often the end is a narrow objective defined with reference to the past rather than the future. Furthermore, most crusaders enjoy the battles more than their campaign; they win medals in the field rather than round the table; and insofar as their real goal may be self-expression and self-development, the conduct of the contest is an end in itself. Each victory is sweet; but compromise is failure. Such pressure groups may not be 'a good thing'; but they are a power to be reckoned with !

Despite their importance, they receive little attention in literature on the countryside. For example, in a book on *Countryside Recreation*, Glyptis (1991) promises a chapter on *Planners, policy makers, providers and pressure groups*, but the last are not mentioned in the text nor the index. Readers are left to wonder to what extent The National Trust - 'which sprang from upper-class horror at the impact of industrial and urban expansion' - and the Countryside Commission or Agency are 'pressure groups'. Each embraces strands which could earn them that title; and it may be difficult for such institutions and their members not to have sympathy with particular causes. Neutrality is a rare quality in countryside affairs.

2. Countryside Issues of Yesterday and Today

Rapid change generates contentious problems relating to prior and future conditions; and while the past is widely revered, the future is often feared, except by those who readily perceive and amply receive benefits from the new world. Conflicting interests and opinions are inevitable; and many problems are seen to have moral dimensions no less than practical concerns. Consequently many countryside issues have generated much continuing passion which serves no good purpose. It often polarises positions; reduces complex issues to simplistic arguments; and facilitates recruitment of public opinion by pressure groups in support of minority interests. It thus defeats democracy and provides no sound basis for legislation (Plate 1). Various 19th-century concerns are outlined in the preceding chapters; and those which are continuing issues may be summarised broadly in order of their origins:

- *Prohibition of animal-abuse and prevention of cruelty to animals.*
- *Protection of landowners' and farmers' privacy and property rights.*
- *Preservation of 'ancient footways' and rights of way.*
- *Protection of areas of picturesque scenery, natural beauty and wilderness.*
- *Exclusion of vulgar/untutored folk from valued places in particular and the countryside in general.*
- *Preservation of 'open spaces' and 'public access' to them.*
- *Conservation of specified elements of 'wildlife' and 'heritage'.*
- *Protection of rural landscapes and rural life.*

Several of these complex issues have something in common; they may be variously inter-woven, and also merged with philosophical questions concerning the proper relationships between man, nature and God (Figs.2.1 & 2.2). However, attention now must be focused on physical access to the countryside for its enjoyment via recreational walking in recent times and in the future.

For 200 years or more, change in farming and related activities has had adverse effects on time-honoured practices in respect of public access over private land. Discontent led to protest; and in 1826 the 'Manchester Association' became the first of many local organisations dedicated to 'the Preservation of Ancient Public Footways'. Walkers, walker's clubs, and other regular users of 'field paths' generally supported similar aims (Ch.1.5-7); and eventually this paved the way for the centralisation of such protests through the Ramblers' Association. Since 1935 it has been the most powerful and most militant pressure group in respect of access to the countryside; and most of its allies echo its voice. However, the Ramblers' Association has always been a privileged and influential body of regular and frequent walkers and it has always represented minority, middle-class interests. An internal survey of its membership indicates the basis of this orientation (The Ramblers' Association, 1994). Based on current and former occupations, 39% of the RA are in Socio-economic Groups A/B; 43% are in C1; 15% in C2; and only 3% in Groups D/E. 46% are graduates; 28% have A-levels and/or equivalent or higher qualifications; and 26% have 'upto O-levels'. 44% are members of the National Trust; 24% belong to a walking club; 21% to the RSPB; 17% to the YHA; 12% to the Holiday Fellowship; and 12% to Greenpeace. This is not a profile of the nation; but ready acceptance of the RA's voice within parliament and government agencies has dispossessed the population as a whole of effective representation in respect of access to the countryside and has seriously misled policy and priorities for countryside walking.

In fact, the Ramblers' Association generally has looked to the past rather than the future and has campaigned on a range of narrow issues rather than for strategic plans; and in 1935 'it immediately began lobbying for access to the hills, as well as for long distance footpaths, national parks, and better protection for rights of way' (Ramblers' Association, 1984). The RA thus allied itself with several minority recreational interests and a broad front of preservation and conservation movements which were opposed to any 'invasion of the countryside'; and consequently positive promotion of the more popular forms of recreational walking (Fig.1.2) has not yet been granted any priority in the wider countryside.

The principal array of parties with interests in countryside access has thus frequently merged into two rather than three camps. The land-owners, farmers and long-standing residents of the rural areas comprise a loose federation which has an uneasy alliance with client development agencies. Their roots lie deep in the past, but their livelihood and prosperity lie with the future; and this common ground brings them together despite their evident differences. The land owners, farmers and farm labourer, game-keepers and the poachers all depend on the same land; and rural services support and depend upon both rich and poor. This does not deny conflicting interests within this 'natural unity' but, under pressure, truly rural society generally supports a single voice.

The second camp has no common territorial base but rather a concern, now widespread amongst both urban and rural populations, for the conservation of valued places and phenomena which are widely distributed in the countryside but also occur in towns and cities. This is essentially a middle-class movement driven by intellectual no less than emotional interests. Furthermore, its hostility is directed against all harmful change, whether of rural

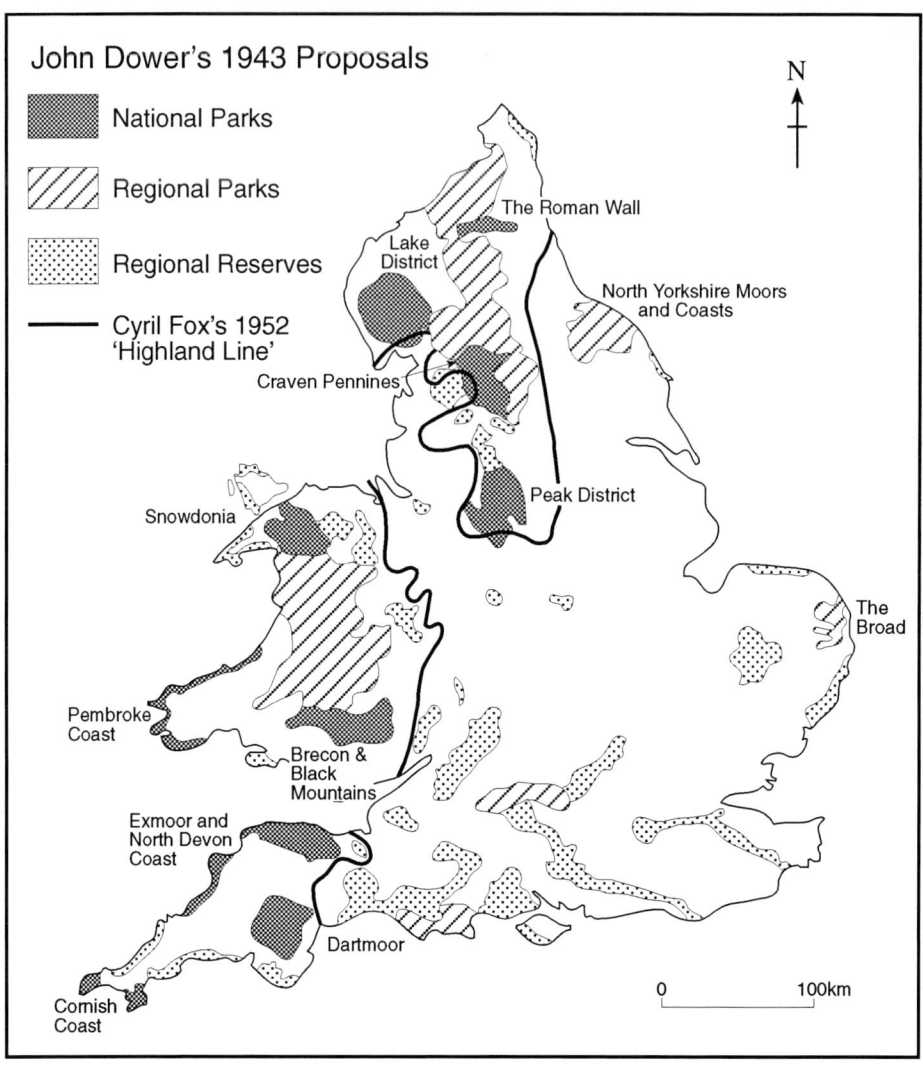

Fig.4.2 John Dower's 1943 Proposals for National Parks and other Valued Places.

> Cyril Fox's (1952) 'Highland Line' identifies the contrasting roles of the ancient palaeozoic rocks of the north and west and the softer sedimentary rocks of Lowland England in determining the diverse *Personality of Britain*. John Dower appears to have been of a similar mind; as, indeed, were the Romanticists and those walkers in search of ascetic adventure on upland moors (Ch.1.5 & 7).

or urban, local or distant origins; and it thus holds ambiguous and variable relationships with the 'countryside lobby'; and with recreational and sporting users of the countryside that comprise the potential for a third camp. However, they are so diverse that each is inclined to act independently and consequently they have no united voice and are rarely active at national levels. This grants the Ramblers' Association a peculiar strength and, as the self-appointed representative of all countryside walkers, physical access to the countryside has become its principal concern. However, its origins, composition and inclinations are all middle-class, and this frequently leads it to support and seek support from the conservation movement, particularly those branches concerned with the protection of 'amenity value' since this at least implies support for appropriate and modest recreational use of valued places.

Historically, parliament has favoured the established rural voice rather than the relatively modern conservation movement. or the nascent recreational lobby. Consequently, while there has for long been a Ministry of Agriculture, Fisheries and Food, the aesthetic, scientific and recreational qualities of the countryside received scant attention until quite recently (Table 2.1) After decades of indecisive campaigning by diverse organisations, John Dower (1945) argued for a *Ministry of Amenities* with a composite agenda intended to embrace the other major interests in the countryside:

Wherever real quality or need occurred the Ministry should ensure that:
    (a) the characteristic landscape beauty is strictly preserved;
    (b) access and facilities for public open-air enjoyment are amply provided;
    (c) wildlife, and buildings and places of architectural and historic interest, are
        suitably protected.

This useful agenda was not without its critics. 'It begged the question of how these concepts might be reconciled with all the other activities and aspirations of private and public life... and how they would relate to individual tracts of countryside and sectors of rural and urban life ? (Sheail, 1981). Indeed, how would any policy based on such concepts be implemented at local levels, where various interpretations and modifications of the several strands were certain to occur ? Local government is conducted within spatial units which reflect political and human history rather than the nature of the land and which represent local populations rather than the general public. No radical revision of the structure and processes of local government was proposed, though in 1931 Pepler had wistfully conceived a scheme so that:

> 'for every part of our country there shall be a plan, each plan being designed with the purpose of ensuring that every inch of our beloved land shall be put to its most productive use, with full regard to health, amenity, convenience and economy'. (Sheail, 1981).

In practice, despite all campaigning and careful thought dedicated to countryside issues, little was achieved until the post-war Labour government sought to make up for time lost to the depression and World War II.

The Town and Country Planning Act of 1947 was a monumental achievement which placed land-use planning and control of 'development' in the hands of local government, subject to parliamentary supervision and review. However, agriculture and forestry were specifically excluded from this powerful and durable legislation; and some other major users of rural land, notably the armed forces, water authorities and major transport systems, also retained independence from local management and had an ear if not an arm of the national government. Conservation and recreation had neither; and proponents of each had to depend on raising public opinion and lobbying influential individuals to achieve progress. The outcome was substantial but far from satisfactory. Neither could be granted high priority within the government's crowded timetable and each received hurried attention during 1949. The scientific arm of the conservation movement had the most organised voice; and its concise, cohesive and convincing case was sharply focused on the merits of safeguarding specified species and defined habitats. It did well to distance itself from the less tangible case for protection of aesthetic qualities of the landscape; and at the eleventh hour:

> The national Nature Conservancy, created by Royal Charter in 1949, was granted considerable autonomy, power and resources. In contrast to the limited powers given to the National Parks Commission, the Nature Conservancy, was an autonomous research, advisory and land-holding council. Thus, a far more powerful State organization was created for the promotion of national nature reserves from which the public are largely excluded than had been provided for the promotion of national parks. (Pacione, 1984).

The Nature Conservancy (now English Nature) was thus well equipped; and its success is largely due to the positive pursuit of specific objectives. Broadly created to care for the welfare of wildlife, it can embrace the aspirations of many groups with scientific and/or recreational interests in diverse categories of natural phenomena. It developed demonstrable priorities and won substantial resources to secure them. It focused on specific sites of special importance for particular purposes wherever they occurred within the whole country; but has also protected particular items throughout the entire country. Finally, it developed an authoritative voice, won much respect and attracted little criticism or controversy. Perhaps its most serious weakness is the limited provision for recreation on many of its holdings but, as yet, this has not been seen as a major issue. In short, in 1949 nature conservation was well equipped for the future; but the more enigmatic and contentious countryside issues were bundled into the more famous or infamous Act of that year.

3. The National Parks and Access to the Countryside Act
This was a dog's breakfast if ever there was one ! Yet, dressed as a dainty dish for a nation still on ration books, it was presented as a feast fit for heroes. *The Times* (17.3.49) anticipated it with generous acclaim:

> The Bill will promote the creation in England and Wales of national parks in parts of the country famous for their natural beauty; and for the designation and special protection of other similar areas. The general purpose of the Bill is to provide urban populations fuller access to and enjoyment of the countryside. In addition to the provision of national parks, it will make possible rights of access to the wilder parts of the country anywhere. The Bill also provides for a national survey of existing footpaths and bridleways, for the creation of new

public rights of way, and for the establishment of nature reserves. (Blunden and Curry, 1990).

The Bill was presented to the Commons in rather different terms as :

> A People's Charter - a people's charter for the open air, for the hikers and ramblers, for everyone who loves to get out into the open air and enjoy the countryside. Without it they are fettered, deprived of their power of access and facilities needed to make holidays enjoyable. With it the countryside is theirs to preserve, to cherish, to enjoy and make their own. (Rt.Hon Lewis Silkin, M.P. *Hansard*, 31.3.1949; cited by Blunden and Curry, 1990).

The intention to serve 'the hikers and ramblers... and...everyone who loves to get out... and enjoy the countryside' refers to a quite different clientele than the 'urban populations' identified by *The Times*. This apparently passed unnoticed; and so too did both the spatial correlation of 'natural beauty' and 'the wilder parts of the country' with the preferred places of particular groups (Ch.1. 5&7), and the fact that 'hikers and ramblers' comprise a very small proportion of those who enjoy walking (Fig.1.2). Indeed, the Act is shot-through with an exclusive view of the countryside as a recreational resource for particular minority groups; but the presentation and the rhetoric ignore or deny this. The pressure groups had won the day; and for more than half-a-century the population has been denied a rational policy for access to the countryside for recreational walking.

The National Parks were never intended for the nation; and their asymmetrical distribution and specific locations reflect their association with special concerns rather than urban populations (Fig.4.2).

> John Dower [had] recommended that national parks should be extensive areas of beautiful and wild country, consisting largely of mountains and moors (with the associated farmlands of their valleys and fringes), heaths, rocky and infertile coastlines and the rougher parts of numerous downs, hills and forests. (MacEwen & MacEwen, 1987).

The spectacular and picturesque scenery of cliff coasts and intricately varied mountainous or hilly regions were for romanticists; the extensive, bleak uplands and moors were for adventure-seekers. The Act confused matters further by embracing all valued landscapes within a single ambigous concept - 'natural beauty'; and then establishing the purposes of the National Parks Commission as 'preserving and enhancing their natural beauty and promoting their enjoyment by the public'. Dower had specified no precedence for preservation or enjoyment; but the Act apparently gave priority to the former. In fact, natural beauty, picturesque or romantic scenery, wilderness and wide open spaces, or amenity by any other name are all imputed qualities. They are essentially resources, providing pleasures and satisfactions which cannot be separated from recreation. Unused, they are nothing; under-used, they are wasted; and while abuse and neglect will damage and diminish them, mis-use is a matter of judgment.

Such resources or amenities have a long history of devotees; and when equipped with articulate leaders several have produced pressure groups, each jealous of its own perspective and disdainful of the views of others (Table 1). Wordsworth set a prime example; and in 1844 he acknowledged that his wish to protect the Lake District from 'the humbler ranks of society' may be interpreted as selfishness. He defended his position because he held it for 'all persons of pure taste throughout the whole island'; his was a national cause!

> The time of life at which I have arrived may, I trust, guard me from the imputation of having written from any selfish interests... If gratitude for what repose and quiet in a district hitherto, for the most part, not disfigured but beautified by human hands, have done for me, and hope that others might hereafter be benefited in the same manner and in the same country, *be selfishness*, then, but not otherwise, I plead guilty to the charge. (Wordsworth, 1844; Bicknell, 1984).

For more than 150 years, the basic elements of Wordsworth's argument have been taken up by pressure groups to protect their privileged access to their preferred places; and the promotion of greater public enjoyment of these has been sacrificed - in the interests of conservation and the preservation of privilege.

The 1949 Act also provided for the designation of *Areas of Outstanding Natural Beauty* which soon became more numerous, more widespread and collectively more extensive than the National Parks. The country was thus implicitly divided into four categories by ambiguous use of a nebulous concept. The National Parks and the AONBs are presented as the best and second best landscapes that England and Wales have to offer; then there is the rest of the countryside; and then the urbanised areas. This map has been further complicated over time by 'peri-urban zones' and, in some cases, their translation into Green Belts; by Nature Reserves and Sites of Special Scientific Interest; by numerous small Conservation Areas established by local authorities; and by rural areas designated by County Councils as being of 'Great Landscape, Historic or Scientific Value'. The strength of the conservation movement is thus reflected in the fact that, by the mid-sixties, 40% of England and Wales comprised protected land of one sort or another (Patmore, 1983); *but no rational policy for enjoyment of the countryside or for countryside walking had emerged.*

Within the 1949 Act, overt provision for recreation was limited to three items. First, to the bitter disappointment of the Ramblers' Association, the much-vaunted 'freedom to roam' over all extensive open or uncultivated tracts of land was granted only where Access Agreements could be negotiated with landowners by local authorities. The most important item refers to 'rights of way'; and Highway Authorities 'were intended first to identify and protect the public's rights of way (PRoW) that had been built up over centuries; and then, where necessary, to adapt the system of footpaths and bridleways to the needs of modern recreation' (MacEwen & MacEwen, 1987). The Act thus calls for reclamation of a largely derelict product of bygone times prior to assessment of its utility with reference to the 'needs of modern recreation'. There was very limited provision for making good any deficiency in that product; and no reference to pedestrians' rights on other highways, even though these were being severely eroded by motorised traffic, And, paradoxically, the Act left responsibility for PRoW with the Highway Authorities which were and are preoccupied with obtaining improved provision for motor vehicles. Finally, almost as a footnote, the Act authorised the creation of Long Distance Footpaths (LDFPs), now known as National Trails, and several routes were specifically named. This may seem to be an item of little consequence but it neatly illustrates the extraordinary influence that a small, special interest group could and did achieve; and this clause was destined to have profound and long-lasting effects of questionable merit.

With all its faults and limitations, the National Parks and Access to the Countryside Act marks a watershed in terms of policy and provision for countryside recreation in general and walking in particular. Few genuinely new initiatives have been achieved in respect of access to the countryside since 1949, and much legislation has been built upon foundations, flawed though they be, which were laid at that time. Thus an Act which relates to issues of the 19th century is still the cornerstone for policies seen to be relevant for the 21st; but to what extent this continuity is justified is an open question.

4. Access for Whom ? The Privileged and the Disadvantaged.

Implementation of the Act has focused on specific items - the creation of National Parks, AONBs and LDFPs and the more prosaic plotting of PRoW. The prime task of promoting enjoyment of the countryside was neglected; and rumours of 'an invasion by untutored townsmen', (Joad, 1946 and Mais, 1948), led to a greater emphasis on protection than promotion. In fact, at that time there was no likelihood of a marked increase in country-side recreation; but trends evident prior to the War were destined to emerge sometime later as an unprecedented growth of free time, affluence and personal mobility generated Michael Dower's 'fourth wave':

> Three great waves have broken across the face of Britain since 1800. First, the sudden growth of dark industrial towns. Second, the thrusting movement along far-flung railways. Third, the sprawl of car-based suburbs. Now we see, under the guise of a modest word, the surge of a fourth wave which could be more powerful than all the others. The modest word is leisure. (Dower, 1965).

During the '60s the weight and force of this 'fourth wave' were being felt throughout the land, raising issues and concerns which could not and should not be ignored.

> The layman can scarcely fail to be aware of the pressures this has generated... Outdoors, congested roads and crowded beaches seem the inevitable concomitant of the summer weekend, and the lover of rural solitude seeks often in vain for the peace and isolation he values so highly. For the planner, these pressures present an urgent and varied challenge, *a challenge bedevilled by the inherent paradox of the need not only to conserve the scarce resources of land and amenity, but also to provide for their fuller use and enjoyment.* (Patmore, 1970).

The paradox was not properly addressed and the government responded to the growth in leisure needs in a piecemeal fashion. The Arts Council had been established by Royal Charter in 1948. Now attention was focused on the Wolfenden Committee's 1960 report on *Sport and the Community,* which led to the establishment of the Sports Council in 1965.

Its main aims are:

- *(a) to promote understanding of the social importance and value of sport & physical recreation.*
- *(b) to increase provison of new sports facilities and stimulate fuller use of existing facilities.*
- *(c) to encourage wider participation in sport & physical recreation.*
- *(d) to raise standards of performance.*

This is a 'People's Charter'; and the Council became widely known through its emphasis on *Sport for All*. However, its role in respect of sport and physical recreation in rural areas has always been ambivalent, partly because the Countryside Act of 1968 created the Countryside Commission with a wide range of duties and responsibilities throughout England and Wales, the 1967 *Countryside (Scotland) Act* having done likewise in 'North Britain'. However, the Countryside Commission ignored the opportunity to promote enjoyment of countryside recreation in conjunction with the *Sport for All* campaign. Then in 1969 the English Tourist Board was set up (Blackie *et al*, 1979). Consequently, while one might agree with Travis (1979) that 'it is extraordinary to find that we have no [single] central government agency overviewing provisions for our major recreations', a more cynical observer might be thankful that we should, at last, acquire so many with countrywide responsibilities.

The Countryside Commission inherited the conflicting responsibilities of conserving the amenity value of the countryside and promoting enjoyment of it; and given that 'the fourth wave' was seen to be flooding the countryside with visitors, regulation rather than promotion of its use was seen to be appropriate. The Commission reacted to perceived priorities of the day. The National Parks appeared to be threatened by over-crowding so the popular ones set out to deter visitors (Plate 4.2) while Country Parks and Picnic Sites were created to intercept and divert demand. Wordsworth's (1844) advice from the Lake District was thus adopted: 'if a scene is to be chosen suitable for persons thronging from a distance, it may be found elsewhere at less cost of every kind'. Within 15 years nearly 200 Country Parks and more than 200 Picnic Sites had been established by local authorities with the help of grants from the Commission. And Marian Shoard, if no one else, saw this

Peak N.P. c.1975

We are not trying to deny people the right to visit the Park. Everyone has the right to visit the Park but in some areas numbers have reached a level where visitors are beginning to destroy the very thing they have come to enjoy.

The Board must try to balance the different needs of a variety of different groups and people. These are often in conflict. It is not possible to please all people all the time.

Plate 4.2 Britain's Popular National Parks go Under Wraps.

provision as an elaborate conspiracy:

> The setting up of Country Parks... as miniature Red Indian reservations for the urban underclasses marked a moment when the hegemony of the landowner was as complete as it ever had been... the idea of townsfolk being decoyed into Country Parks before they got as far as the real countryside suited landowners very well... (and) planners have sought to cage visitors in carefully confined locations. (Shoard, 1987)

In reality, the varied nature and widespread locations of the parks reflect a range of interests; and, like the Victorian urban parks, the Country Parks programme was often subverted if not hi-jacked by the middle-classes. It was not until 1982 that a policy revision was made to concentrate 'new country parks and picnic grounds in the urban fringe, making the best possible use of neglected or reclaimed land close to centres of demand' (CCP.151, 1982). This revision reflects a late shift to more appropriate priorities, especially since the later Parks were designed and promoted as 'gateways' to the countryside; but it was too late to be particularly effective because the Country Parks movement had already lost its momentum.

A more general consequence of numerous national bodies with responsibilities for leisure and recreation was over-due recognition of the value of survey information. Such diverse, dynamic and nebulous fields do not yield much incontrovertible data, especially since survey design and the presentation of findings are often significantly affected by perspectives and motives of interested parties. Genuine problems of data capture and the positivist rather than behavioural approach of the early surveys also add to the difficulties of interpretation; and misinterpretation may well feed myths. Nevertheless, if addressed with care and caution, much of the output on participation in countryside recreation can facilitate understanding of fundamental questions as to who does what, when, where, how and why. Nevertheless, progress was slow and a 1978 review of all *Countryside Trip Making* concluded that:

> After ten years of research a complex web of factors has been revealed as having *some effect* on countryside trip-making, albeit in a wide variety of largely unspecified geographical and social contexts and at different levels of analysis... However, conceptual and data deficiencies appear to leave many observed variations in behaviour unexplained. (Elson, 1979).

This faint praise reflects the need for a behavioural approach which would put individual action and motivation at the heart of analysis and interpretation, if not as the basis for data collection.

In fact, Elson's 1970 survey of *Weekend Recreation Motoring Trips* was informed by Chapin's 'human activity system' comprising 'behaviour patterns of individuals, families and institutions'; but guided or distracted by factor analysis of 19 variables it showed that 'possession of a driving licence was the most important single influence on the probability of making a day trip for recreation'! Elson asked 2054 heads of households in Lewes, Sussex, if they owned a car. 41% had no car; *and these 'non-participants'- who deserved special attention - were excluded from his study.* Survey findings led to the classification of the car-owners as *Highly Active*, *Less Active* and *Least Active*; but 'explanation' of these groups in terms of 'factors' such as age, income, social class, terminal education and size of household proved less than convincing. However, the behavioural approach was valuable in its own right but Elson did not look closely for 'messages' from it. Reworking one of his tables has revealed the following pattern:

Category of Tripper	Share of all Households	Motorised Trips	Share of Trips
Frequent	12 %	20 %	45 %
Regular	19 %	31 %	34 %
Occasional	19 %	32 %	18 %
Rare	10 %	17 %	03 %
'No Car'	40 %	00 %	00 %

Half of all the households in Lewes generated, and enjoyed, only 3% of the trips; and if the promotion of walking and enjoyment of the countryside were taken seriously, they would be the focus of concerned attention. On the other hand, while crowding of the countryside was the centre of concern, the small minority (12%) of frequent users who created nearly half of the total 'pressure' should be the principal subject of close management. No such reading of Elson's work is evident; and consequently it could dispel no myth nor have any impact on policy. Furthermore, the ability to ignore such lessons has persisted.

5. Participation and the Efficacy of Access

The efficacy of 'access' is reflected in patterns of participation which, in turn, reflect both the distribution of enjoyment of the countryside and the sources of pressures upon it. The measurement of participation is a function of *the participation rate x the frequency rate x the duration of participation*. The participation rate is the percentage of a 'population' undertaking the activity within a defined period, usually four weeks or a year; the frequency rate is the number of times the activity is undertaken by a participant during the same period; and the duration is the average length of the several occasions. There is a general dearth of data on the third element, but in many leisure activities it is reasonably accepted as a constant factor. However, a visit to the countryside and the length of a walk are highly variable, but fortunately some information on their duration often is available. Even so, the frequency and duration of visits and walks are often ignored while crude participation rates are too readily used and often abused. They do not provide a sound basis for understanding countryside issues, and they should be treated with caution.

Detecting patterns of countryside recreation therefore calls for critical examination and careful use of survey data (Kay, 1996); and the General Household Survey (GHS) of 1977 is the earliest reliable source providing both participation and frequency rates. Annual participation rates in *Walking 2 miles or more (including rambling and hiking)* showed a positive relationship with income and with socio-economic groups; but the frequency of participation showed marked contradictory patterns of behaviour, particularly in relation to income (Fig.4.3). Proportionally, the very poor produced half as many walkers as the very rich; but as individuals the poor walked twice as often. Similarly, 100 professional workers produced three times as many walkers as 100 unskilled manual workers; but on average, the latter walked more often (ie 8 times rather than 6 times per month). This clearly shows that the financial costs of walking are not a significant barrier. On the contrary, the higher incomes of the wealthy may admit them to more expensive leisure activities and thus reduce both their time and inclination to walk more frequently. Demands of their professional and social lives may further erode their opportunity to walk as often as that smaller proportion of low-income workers who, having become committed participants, evidently can and do find the resources and time to walk more frequently.

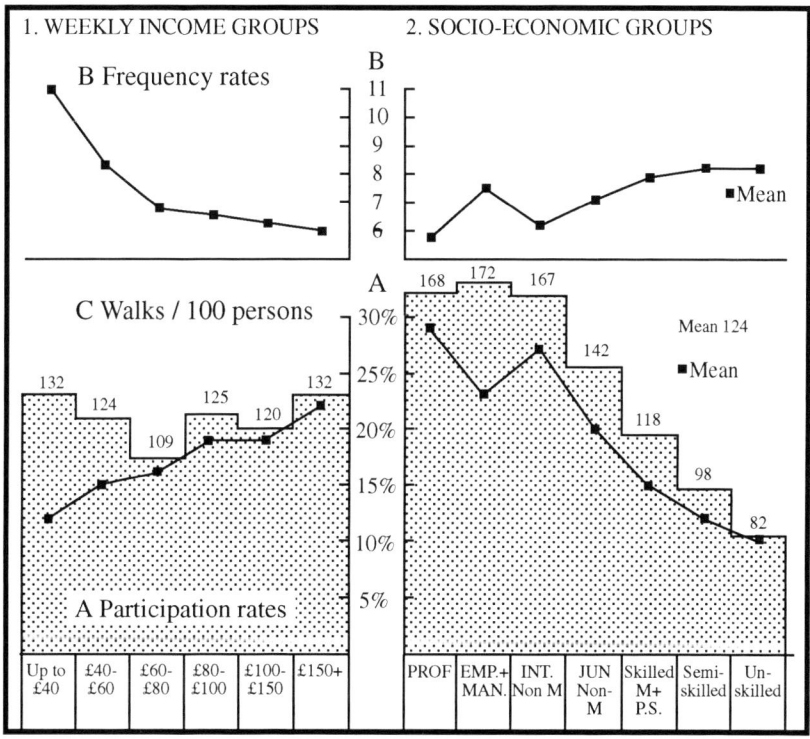

**Fig.4.3 Recreational Walking
by Income and Socio-Economic Groups, 1977.**

In each case the lower line-graph (A) plots the percentage of each cohort that participates in recreational walking (over 2 miles or more). The upper line (B) shows the frequency of participation (ie the average number of walks in the 4 weeks prior to interview). A x B provides C - ie the number of walks generated in four weeks by 100 participants in each cohort; and this is shown in the bar-graphs and numerical statements. The mean value of the participation rate, the frequency rate, and number of walks generated by 100 participants in 4 weeks are shown in the right 'margin' of the diagram. (Data source: GHS, 1977).

This evidence raises serious questions as to the nature of effective channels for admission and barriers for exclusion in respect of recreational walking. If the poor and the unskilled can and do produce the most active walkers, why do relatively small proportions of these groups participate? Elson's (1970) detailed factor analysis had provided no answer; but the 1977 GHS may provide a significant pointer by recording participation rates against the highest educational qualification attained:

Highest Qualification	% Participating in Recreational Walking	% of respondents
Degree or equivalent	37 %	04.5%
Other Higher Education	27 %	06.9 %
GCE A-Level or equivalent	24 %	05.3 %
GCE O-Level, CSE Grade 1 or equivalent	22 %	14.5 %
Other CSE Grades, Appprenticeship, etc.	21 %	12.2 %
No such qualification	14 %	56.7 %

The correlation is striking; while the small cohort of graduates had a participation rate more than double the national average (17%), the majority of the population (57%) with no qualification other than basic schooling had a participation rate significantly below that of all other categories. *Can it be that the majority of them just don't know what the countryside is for ?* (Harding, 1986). On the other hand, this large cohort, comprising more than half of the population, did produce many frequent walkers, out-numbering those with higher education by 20%. And there is evidently no inherent reason why the participation rate of the poor should be so low. In the '70s linear distance from the countryside may have been an inhibiting factor for those without car, but as this factor has declined there has been no corresponding increase in participation. This calls for well prepared and carefully targeted 'promotion' of walking to extend enjoyment of the countryside to those sectors of the population which lack the necessary knowledge and understanding, skills and confidence to participate; and who apparently have no *satisfying experience* to encourage them (Fig.1.3).

Subsequent GHS data sets do not provide frequency rates nor analyses by income and education; but attention has been repeatedly focused on relationships with the enigmatic concept of 'socio-economic groups'; which, as in 1990, consistently show a correlation with participation in recreational walking:

Socio-Economic Group	12-month Rate	Four-week Rate
Professional	81 %	51 %
Employers & Managers	72 %	45 %
Int & Jun Non-Manual	69 %	43 %
Skilled Manual.Own Ac.Wks	61 %	40 %
Semi-Skld. Personal Services	55 %	35 %
Unskilled Manual	49 %	31 %
ALL GROUPS	65 %	41 %

The loss of detail has continued to misdirect attention to socio-economic conditions rather than educational and cultural differences as the principal source of disadvantage in terms of walking. And this in turn located responsibility for improvement to the state of the economy, the wealth of the nation, and the incomes of the poor. This apparently has excused the inexcusable - a persistent dearth of carefully designed and targeted promotion of countryside walking.

It might be expected that the Countryside Commission's own *National Surveys of Countryside Recreation* (NSCR) would produce information that would directly inform policies and strategies for the countryside walking; and they do indeed provide some valuable insights. However, they too call for careful interpretation. The 1977 NSCR identified the wide appeal of countryside recreation and its domination by a small minority of visitors.

> *In 1977 over half the population visited the countryside at least once in a summer month and three-quarters of the population visited the countryside at least once a year... **Against this must be placed the high concentration of trips made by a small number of people - 10 per cent of the population accounted for over half of all recorded trips.***
> These highly active countryside recreationists were not confined to any identifiable group within the population, but the chances are that the majority of them were in the 25-45 age-group, in the upper income and social groups, and - most important of all - had access to a motor car. (CCP.152, 1982).

Elson's (1974) undiscovered findings (12% generated 45% of all trips) were confirmed; but only the widespread use of the countryside found its way into the general *Conclusions* of the report and the more important information on the mal-distribution of countryside recreation was suppressed.

The inequitable reality in access to the countryside continued and is documented in the NSCR of 1984 (CCP.201) and that of 1990 (Walker, 1995):

Category of Visitors	Trips in any 4 weeks.	% share of Population. 1984 1990	% share of all Visits. 1984 1990
Regular & frequent users	9+	17% 11%	68% 61%
	5-8	12% 9%	17% 19%
Committed but casual	2-4	20% 18%	13% 17%
Occasional users	1	11% 12%	2% 4%
Infrequent users	Nil	40% 50%	Nil Nil

Both show that more than half of the population [62% in 1990] rarely visit the countryside and enjoy only 2-4 % of all visits. On the other hand, "a small keen section of the population is responsible for the majority of visits"; and comparison of the 1984 and 1990 data shows that a reduced number of regular, frequent visitors increasingly dominate the recreational use of the countryside. 29% of the population generated 85% of all visits in 1984 while 20% accounted for 80% in 1990. It follows that the alleged continuing growth in the number of visitors may well be a misinterpretation of an increased number of visits by such privileged minorities. Indeed, the proportion of the population making no visit had increased from 40% to 50% of the population.

All such evidence suggests that positive outreach to promote 'rural tourism' and walking is required if the decline in the number who do, in practice, enjoy the countryside is to be reversed and if the disadvantaged who rarely if ever enjoy a visit are to be encouraged and persuaded to do so. However, the Countryside Commision's 1991 consultation paper on *Visitors to the Countryside* chose to give prominence to the view that 'countryside recreation remains immensely popular, with three-quarters of the population visiting the countryside in 1990, making a total of 1,640 million trips' (CCP.341, 1991). Myth-making prevails; and the whole truth in respect of participation in countryside recreation is still neither widely available nor generally understood.

Identification of the critical factors that differentiate the privileged, frequent visitors and the disadvantaged continues to be elusive. The 1977 GHS data still provides the best commentary; but the report on the NSCR of 1984 (CCP.201) also came close to the heart of the matter when it observed that those in the lowest socio-economic classes *'who have made the commitment to go to the countryside, tend to do so more or less as frequently as others irrespective of their different [socio-economic] circumstances'*. This observation should have prompted a search for the key cultural attributes, personal qualities and experiences which motivate the frequent visitors from different classes - and those which deter all non-participants, regardless of their socio-economic status. The findings should inform a carefully constructed programme to promote countryside visiting and walking - if and when any such promotion receives serious consideration. Meanwhile, complacency has prevailed; and the messages of available data have been over-looked or ignored.

Thus, for example, the 1990 NSCR survey provides new data on participation rates in relation to 'distance from the countryside' which offers some new light on patterns of privilege and disadvantage in respect of access to the countryside.

> *People who live in the country or close by (within 1-3 miles) are more likely to make recreational visits and to be frequent visitors than people living farther afield, particularly over six miles away. However, having a car has more influence on visiting the countryside than how close people live to it. (Walker, 1995).*

The unnecessary re-statement of the benefits of having a car deflects attention from the characteristics of the four zones *as places where people live*. 'Living 7+ miles away from the countryside' in effect means living 7+ miles deep in the heart of large, built-up urban areas, with all the changes in imagery and reality that this invokes. Thus, the zones may be purposefully re-defined as rural, suburban, urban and inner-city respectively. Pursuit of the necessary basic data through labyrinthine appendices has allowed an alternative analysis; and participation in visiting and walking in the countryside in relation to these inferred spatial patterns of human conditions is summarised in Fig.4.4.

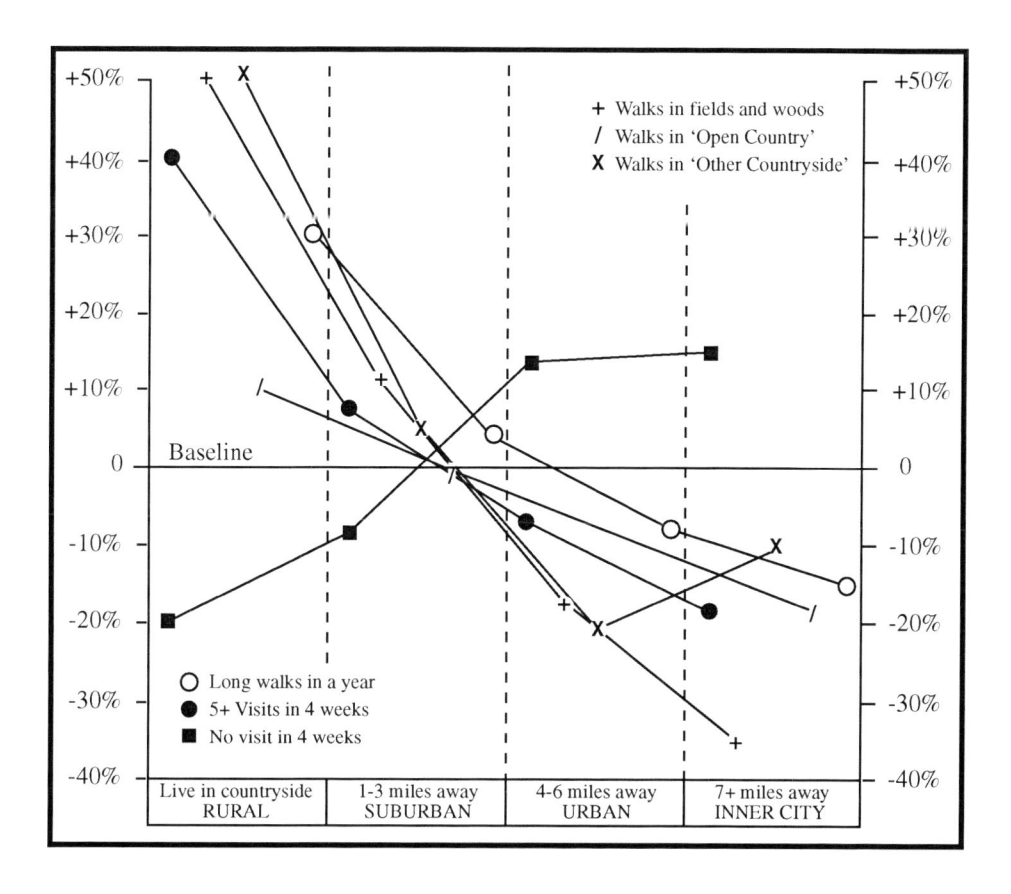

**Fig.4.4 Countryside Visits and Walks
by Residential Location of Participants, 1990.**

The 'Baseline' represents the average level of participation for the population as a whole in respect of each of the six activities shown. The level of participation achieved by the population of each residential zone in each activity is plotted as a percentage of this baseline. Thus, for example, those living in rural areas score 50% 'above par' in respect of *Walks in Fields and Woods* while inner-city populations score 35% below the benchmark. Particpation rates in the six activities show marked and consistent differences across the sequence of residential zones; and those living in the countryside, proportional to their numbers, are by far the heaviest recreational users of it.

Source: Tables 1 and 5 of Appendix 4 of the Report on the NSCR of 1990 (Walker, S. 1995). What appears to be a technical/printing error in these tables is identified in the diagram as a 'rogue figure'; it has been ignored in the construction of the diagram. This rare data appears to be much under-used, perhaps because access to it is difficult.

To what extent distance or human conditions underlie the patterns of behaviour thus revealed may be a matter of judgment; but the patterns are clear, consistent and pronounced. Country dwellers generate and benefit from the heaviest use of the countryside; city dwellers are the most deprived. Increased distance from the countryside - or living deeper in urban areas - shows strong and consistent correlations with decreased activity rates for both general visits to the countryside and for walking in each of three types of countryside. There is only one point of exception. This relates to 'walking in other countryside', which comprises developed sites such as 'country parks, historic parks and gardens, villages and country lanes'. Inner-city residents are shown to have a greater predilection to visit such locations than those living in other urban areas. Perhaps more than any, 'they just don't know what the (wider) countryside is for' and therefore developed sites have a stronger appeal to them; but distance is not a factor since these sites are mostly located within the wider countryside.

The prevalence of different personal attributes and cultural characteristics in these several residential zones are probably the key factors affecting the contrasting patterns of participation; and these, rather than linear distance, need to be addressed. The 1990 NSCR also provides rare and useful data on respondents' declared knowledge of their local countryside; and this too can be analysed in relation to their residential location. Again the relationship is pronounced; and the summary scores of 'awareness' highlight differences between the spatial zones or, more realistically, between the different levels of countryside experience in each of them.

% of People Who Know Their Local Countryside:

Residential Location	Very Well (+5)	Fairly Well (+3)	Not Very Well (+1)	Not At All (-5)	Overall Awareness Score
Rural (Live in the Countryside)	38%	28%	21%	13%	230
Suburban (Live 1-3 miles away)	28%	30%	24%	18%	164
Urban (Live 4-6 miles away)	21%	27%	31%	21%	112
Inner-city (Live 7+ miles away)	22%	21%	30%	27%	68

[The allocation of relatively arbitrary scores (from +5 to -5) to the four levels of knowledge allows a summary comparison of the 'overall awareness' of their local countryside by the people in each of the four zones. Thus, 'inner-city people' have an overall score of $(22 \times 5)+(21 \times 3)+(30 \times 1)-(27 \times 5) = 68$].

These patterns of mental awareness invite exploration of the experiences and limitations of people in the several zones with reference to the origins and the functional importance of their different degrees of 'knowing' and 'not knowing' one's local countryside and of what it can afford. For example, if 22% of inner-city dwellers know their local country side very well, why is it that 57% are virtually ignorant of it? Answers might well inform and direct promotion of countryside walking; and this would not be at the expense of privileged minorities if sufficient appropriate provision for walking is available and if mutual tolerance and respect is engendered between all members of a multi-cultural nation.

Several important conclusions may be drawn from this data-based review of the current efficacy of access as reflected in patterns of participation in countryside recreation. First, recreational use of the countryside continues to be dominated by privileged minorities of frequent and regular visitors who are drawn, albeit unequally, from each major socio-economic sector of society. Secondly, although low-income and unskilled workers now comprise a small but significant proportion of the privileged users, the myth of a destructive 'invasion of the countryside by untutored townsmen' has not materialised, though it has yet to be dismissed. Thirdly, it is the pressure of numbers, not their origins, which may comprises a threat to the countryside; and the regular, frequent users generate a large majority of all visits. Finally, in any society with a commitment to social justice and that values the countryside as a public good rather than private property, the disadvantaged majority who rarely if ever are able to enjoy it should be the focus of concern. There is, therefore, a long-overdue need for carefully designed and purposefully targeted promotion of the countryside as a recreational resource; and any such promotion must be underpinned by the existence of a marketable commodity in terms of facilities no less than resources. This requires a sympathetic and comprehensive recognition of the needs and aspirations, capabilities and limitations of those whose level of participation indicates that they do not know what the countryside is for; and it would be an act of positive injustice if promotion of the countryside amongst those who at present rarely enjoy its delights continues to be neglected in order to protect the position of the privileged minority of regular users, whether they be middle or working class. As Professor Coppock put it in 1973:

> There are real dangers in adopting, whether consciously or unconsciously, moral attitudes towards recreation... We must avoid the judgement of rosy-cheeked young men in shorts striding over the hills as a good thing, and try rather to ensure that everyone has the opportunity to experience and participate in a wide range of recreational activities. We are still very bad at being able to determine what the public wants, as opposed to what we, or planners or other professionals, think they ought to want. (in Rodgers, et al, 1973).

5
COUNTRYSIDE WALKING - CURRENT PATTERNS AND PROBLEMS

"While the Peak District offers scope for special forms of outdoor activity such as angling, grouse-shooting and rock-climbing, the great majority of people find their enjoyment in traversing the hilly ground, observing the magnificent views and breathing the upland air. The good roads of today enable sightseers by car and by coach to see much of the National Park in a single outing... and vehicles can reach most of the well-known viewpoints... There is also little doubt, although there are no statistics to prove it, that away from the main roads, the largest category of persons seeking open-air recreation is that of the hikers and ramblers".

1. Outdoor Recreation and Countryside Walkers

Edwards (1962) thus captured the essence of outdoor recreation in the Peak District. Each specific activity has its own niche but traversing expanses of attractive countryside and visiting well known places appealed to 'the great majority of people'. The popularity of scenic touring is noted, alongside that of 'rambling and hiking' although recorded participation in these particular forms of walking was then only 3% (General Household Survey, 1965). It was, however, symptomatic of the concern with minority interests that these particular forms figured prominently in early surveys; and it was not until 1984 that any data became available on participation in respect of walks of different lengths (Fig.5.1). Eventually, in 1990 the GHS achieved effective communication with respondents in respect of the plurality of recreational walking (Fig.1.2); and it was then revealed that walking is indeed the most popular 'activity' with an annual participation rate of 65%.

Consequently, there are no reliable data to plot the growth or decline of countryside walking; and it may have been as popular in 1965 as it was in 1990. Furthermore, detecting patterns of outdoor recreation is still no easy matter (Kay, 1996); and the best data to illustrate the merit of walking as a life-time activity, popular with both men and women of all ages, is to be found in the GHS of 1977:

	Participation Rate (%)				*Frequency Rate Days in 4 wks.*			*Activity Rate Walks by 100 People in 4 wks*
Age	Men	Women	All 16+		Men	Women	All 16+	
16-19	14%	17%	16%		6.0	5.9	5.9	94.4
20-24	17%	22%	19%		5.3)	5.8)	5.5)	104.5
25-29	20%	20%	20%		5.3)	5.8)	5.5)	110.0
30-44	20%	20%	20%		6.2	6.2	6.2	124.0
45-49	17%	16%	17%		7.4	7.5	7.5	128.0
60-69	20%	16%	18%		11.0)	10.3)	10.7)	193.0
70 +	13%	7%	9%		11.0)	10.3)	10.7)	96.3

Except at the extremes of the age range, there is little departure from the mean participation rate (then seriously under-recorded at 17%); but the activity rate clearly increases with age due to the retention of high levels of participation and a greater frequency of walking, three or four times a week in the case of active elderly people. Later data sets, though less detailed, confirm that walking is a very effective life-time recreation; but preferences for particular types of walking differ according to age, life cycle stage and, probably, gender. These are important matters in planning for provision, but unfortunately, most data sets treat all walking as one. However, the systematic classification of 20 types (Fig.1.2) does indicate forms that are more suitable than others for different age groups and for parties with young children; and commonsense if nothing else ought to ensure that the needs of different demographic groups are duly noted in policy, planning and provision. Unfortunately, in the greater part of the countryside there is little evidence that this is so; and provision for walking is too often dictated by ancient rights rather than current needs.

The fact that 'going out for the day' and 'going for a walk' are commonplace but nebulous labels for very varied forms of behaviour has undoubtedly aggravated the difficulties of data capture in respect of countryside recreation; and the NSCR relates to 'day visits' to 'the countryside' rather than to everyday use of local space. Consequently it deals with special, valued places and embraces a wide range of chosen locations. In 1984 (and 1990) it showed that those whose *prime purpose* was 'to walk two miles or more' comprised only 18% of all countryside visitors. 34% of these walked over fields or farmland; 32% through woodlands; 14% over heaths and moors; 13% by rivers or canals; 12% on beaches or sea-cliffs, and 10% by lakes or reservoirs. And nearly all of them enjoyed several other activities in addition to their walk. This allowed the several pertinent summary observations (CCP.201,1985):

- **People tend to be 'general countryside goers'** rather than specialists concerning themselves with just one or two different activities.
- **The majority of recreational activity takes place quite informally** without outside organisation or special equipment or high profile management.
- **The 'wider countryside' accounted for three times as many trips as managed sites.**... and the use of the wider countryside for walking requires that greater consideration be given to it as a recreational resource.
- **The farmed countryside is the major destination for walking trips**; the classic recreation areas of heathland and moors accounted for only a small proportion, and the image of walkers rambling over heather and mountains is not typical; but water is a significant attraction.

This summary properly emphasises that most visitors, including those responsible for most walks are, in fact, 'general countryside goers' in search of a complex package of experiences (Fig.1.3). Also, it is properly critical of the romanticised image of ramblers walking over heather and mountains in search of solitude; but it fails to emphasise the importance of social interaction during most walks, and the statement that 'the farmed countryside' is the major venue for walking is quite misleading. It was marginally host to

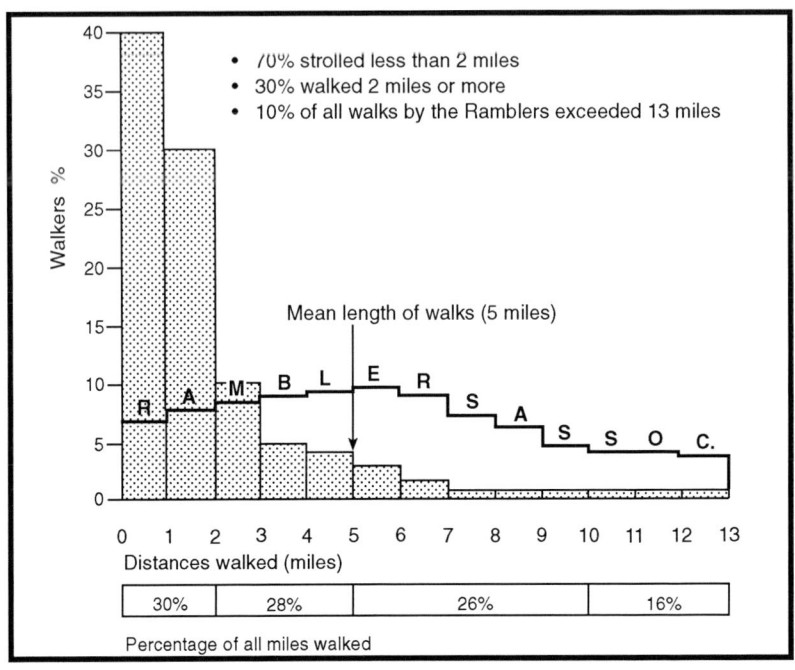

Fig.5.1 The Length of Countryside Walks by 'General Countryside Goers' and Members of the Ramblers' Association
Sources: NSCR of 1984 and the RA, 1994.

- 70% strolled less than 2 miles
- 30% walked 2 miles or more
- 10% of all walks by the Ramblers exceeded 13 miles

Mean length of walks (5 miles)

Percentage of all miles walked: 30% | 28% | 26% | 16%

The length of a walk is a key dimension affecting the time and stamina required for its completion; and the demand for walks over various distances is a vital element in planning for provision.

In 1984 the 70% of walkers who strolled less than two miles generated only 30% of the total miles walked, and thus only 30% of the wear and tear on footpaths. However, their enjoyment of the countryside, and their impact upon it, is highly localised within favourite places. These hesitant walkers and their valued places merit the investment necessary for quality provision which promotes enjoyment and protects paths.

The 12% whose walks habitually exceed 5 miles are the dominant users of the wider countryside. They generate more than 40% of the miles walked, and of the wear and tear on paths, often in vulnerable places. They obtain the greater and more varied benefits of the countryside; and both policy and provision should aim to achieve more equitable access to these rewarding experiences.

The Ramblers are exceptionally keen, committed walkers, and their experience is far removed from that of the typical countryside walker. Only 15% of their walks are short strolls; most of them exceed 5 miles; and 10% are not shown because they exceed 13 ! However, both profiles question the preoccupation in surveys with 'walks of two miles or more' - and in policy, with National Trails and Regional Routes.

more walkers than any other type of land but given its extent it would be surprising if it were otherwise findings. Indeed, most walks (66%) took place elsewhere, and the importance of woodlands as a close rival to farmland and the attraction of water are both overlooked in the summary statement.

Policy-makers and planners deserve better guidelines; and information on people *per se* is no less important than that on their use of place. The 1984 NSCR found that only 10% of all visiting parties consisted of one person; and most of these were 'by people living very near the countryside', and probably using their local space. On the other hand, the relatively novel UK Day Visits Survey (UKDVS) of 1993 dispensed with all restrictions on the duration and location of 'visits' and showed that one-third of all countryside visits, including those in peri-urban areas, were made up of lone persons, with or without a dog. This supplements rather than contradicts the findings of the NSCR by incorporating everyone's local countryside and embracing everyday recreation; and all surveys conducted deeper in the countryside do emphasise the importance of small groups. A survey conducted in North York Moors National Park provides information on these matters and reveals differences between visitors encountered within villages and small resorts and those interviewed some little distance along the Cleveland Way and into 'the wider countryside' (Kay, 1990).

Group Size	*In Villages/Resorts*		*On Footpaths*	
	Parties	*Persons*	*Parties*	*Persons*
1	12 %	4 %	23 %	12 %
2	50 %	38 %	59 %	59 %
3	14 %	17 %	11 %	16 %
4	16 %	24 %	5 %	8 %
5	5 %	10 %	2 %	3 %
6	3 %	7 %	1 %	2 %

Lone walkers comprised 12% of all persons encountered on the paths, and couples accounted for a further 59%; only 13% were in groups of four or more - and very few children of any age were out walking. In the villages and small resorts, only 4% of the parties were singletons; and groups of four or more, including many children, accounted for 24% of the parties and 41% of the visitors. This must raise questions as to why family groups are relatively rare on countryside footpaths; and what can be done to promote countryside walking amongst the young.

The survey also encountered 30 groups of '7 or more persons' which, together, accounted for 828 people - an average of 28 per group. These large groups, like the bands of participants in organised walks, rarely figure in visitor surveys; but they do comprise distinctive and significant elements of countryside recreation. They merit more attention than they seem to receive; and if provision for visitors and walkers fails to provide for the sociable satisfactions sought by all groups, it will neglect a vital aspect of enjoyment of the countryside.

History shows that distinctive types of walking developed in special environments (Ch.1.4-7); and data on visitor use of special places may add an additional dimension. The first *National Parks Visitor Survey*, (CCP.503, 1996), generally supports the findings of the NSCR noted above, but the Parks attract a particularly active clientele; and holiday-makers, who have longer days at their disposal, are more active than day-visitors (Table 5.1). As Edwards noted in 1962, 'sight-seeing' is the most popular recreation and this highlights the importance of 'landscape' as a resource. However, sight-seeing from the dubious vantage point of a mobile car is somewhat more popular than sight-seeing strolls, and especially so with holiday-makers who drive in from resorts outside the Parks. This situation must present recreational planners with a range of challenges, and more effective marketing and promotion of 'sight-seeing on foot' might prove beneficial to visitors and could reduce traffic within the Parks.

Including the sight-seeing strolls by 63% of the visitors, walking is the dominant activity in the Parks, and a majority of visitors walked at least twice a day. In addition to these strolls, 45% undertook walks of less than 60 minutes duration; but 61% walked for longer, including 18% who enjoyed arduous walking for more than four hours. Edwards' observation in 1962 that 'hikers and ramblers' were prominent users of the Parks is confirmed; and the character of the National Parks evidently generates heavy usage of selected footpaths by dedicated walkers. On the other hand, it may be noted that guided walks are not popular while two of Mike Harding's dislikes, picnicking and shopping, were pursued by more than a third of the visitors.

Activity	*All Visitors*	*Day Visits from Home*	*NP Holiday Visitors*	*Holiday Visitors from Outside*
Walking				
Up to 1 hour	45%	37%	48%	54%
1 to 4 hours	43%	31%	57%	41%
4 hour + (Hill/Fell)	18%	14%	27%	13%
Guided Walk	2%	1%	2%	1%
All Walking	**108%**	**83%**	**134%**	**109%**
Sight-seeing				
-driving	70%	56%	74%	88%
-strolling	**63%**	**52%**	**73%**	**68%**
Having a meal or drink	55%	42%	68%	57%
Picnicing	36%	30%	38%	42%
Shopping - gifts, souvenirs, etc.	38%	25%	47%	48%
No. of activities per person	**5.57**	**4.12**	**6.72**	**6.08**

Table 5.1. The Principal Recreational Activities of Visitors to the National Parks, 1994.

[Walkers in the North York Moors NP also are significantly more active than countryside walkers as a whole (Fig. 5.1). While most (51.0%) strolled or walked less than 2 miles, 33.0% walked 2-6 miles; 9.5% - 6-10; 5.0% - 10-20; and 1.5% over 20 miles. Kay, 1990.]

2. Favourite Places and Crowded Spaces

Loveliest of trees, the cherry now
Is hung with bloom along the bough,
And stands about the woodland ride
Wearing white for Eastertide.

Now, of my threescore years and ten,
Twenty will not come again,
And take from seventy springs a score,
It only leaves me fifty more.

And since to look at things in bloom
Fifty springs are little room,
About the woodlands I will go
To see the cherry hung with snow. (Housman, 1859-1936).

Any systematic exploration of spatial patterns of countryside recreation requires a general framework; and it is important to note that most humans, like most animals and birds, are creatures of habit. This may be due to force of circumstances. When free time and the means to travel are in short supply, necessity may restrict outings to the vicinity of one's own home, and commonplace activities will prevail. Even so, within the limits of terrain thus accessible, individuals will develop networks of favourite places and related behaviour. If demand for particular types of place is substantial these will become popular and, perhaps, under considerable pressure. Sharing favourite places will become habitual and everyday recreation, gregarious; and within local communities it may well be enjoyed as such.

While each home-based domain gains substantial value from its proximity, their merit in terms of intrinsic qualities will differ markedly. The picturesque Lake District provided Wordsworth with his 'dear native regions' while the Potteries were notoriously somewhat less salubrious; but in each case the resident populations would select the best accessible places within their local space. Accidents of birth-place and address thus are major determinants of the nature of one's home territory, unless residential mobility allows some freedom of choice. Aristocratic and other wealthy households have for long been able to locate their homes within attractive countryside, and to enhance them with designed leisure landscapes. More recently, 'the fourth wave' has granted much larger numbers considerable freedom of choice as to where they will live or, indeed, have their 'second home'. Although travel time always remains a factor, this has led to colonisation by the middle classes of highly prized places in much attractive countryside beyond the urban fringe. And within the smaller, more dispersed settlements of commuter countryside, sociable sharing of home-based domains is unlikely to lead to unbearable pressures on favourite places. On the other hand, any substantial invasion of highly prized areas by outsiders may well be resented and even resisted. Established residents and new immigrants are likely to be protective of their domain; both may espouse the cause of 'conservation' as their champion; and both may be loth to promote their territory in wider circles. Wordsworth set the classic example more than 150 years ago.

Turning to recreational visits beyond everyday life within home territory, each significant increase in expenditure of time or finance will anticipate a substantial additional return in beneficial experiences (Ch.1.3). More expensive outings will not be to places known or believed to be inferior to those available locally but rather to places with a greater reputation for quality and charisma in relation to the objectives of the outing. Although novelty may occasionally be an attraction, there is a common propensity to acquire lasting affection for favourite places which are then subject to repeated return visits. In short, a hierachical network of favoured venues in successively more distant zones is constructed. Favourite places close to home and within the sphere of everyday life are visited most frequently; those within the more distant circuits are used regularly but less frequently; and the extreme frontiers of one's space may be subject to occasional, special or perhaps exploratory visits.

There will be exceptions. In particular, many households (probably 40% or more) make little or no use of their local countryside, especially if it is some distance away and/ or is not readily and comfortably accessible. Nevertheless, from time to time, perhaps on special occasions, they may visit a well known distant place; and these infrequent visitors many be resented by its regular users. On the other hand, some very active minority groups may not focus on particular favourite places but delight in visiting many different but similar places. Thus, 'munro-baggers' seek to climb each and every one of the 284 Scottish summits higher than 3000 feet; and some long-distance walkers are committed to publicised 'challenge walks' or even to traversing several National Trails in turn. However, most 'general countryside goers' are creatures of habit and probably act in accordance with the model outlined above.

Survey data provides ample supporting evidence, and the model is partly derived from such data. The 1984 NSCR relates to lengthy trips with a mean duration of 5.5 hours; but it shows that nearly half of all visits were within ten miles of home and reveals a pronounced decline in the number of visits with distance travelled:

Round-trip Distance	*% of Visits*
Upto 20 miles	49 %
21-40	17 %
41-60	11 %
61-80	7 %
81-100	4 %
Over 100	12 %

The UK Day Visits Survey (UKDVS) of 1993 provides more detailed information on the location and duration of home-based leisure outings to the countryside and other special environments (Table 5.2). 53% of all outings to countryside locations took place within 2.5 miles of the visitor's home; and 49% are completed within a couple of hours. The recreational use of woods and forests is even more concentrated within these short distances (65%) and periods (69%); but canals and rivers (23% and 24%) do not provide comparable opportunities for such immediate use of home-based territory. Very heavy use and dependence on truly 'local' countryside is thus revealed whereas previous national surveys of countryside recreation have employed restrictive clauses and labelling which prevented proper identification of this important truth.

UKDVS data on the duration of leisure outings (Table 5.3) illustrates of another aspect of the model outlined above. Allowing travelling time as part of the total experience, short recreational visits (upto 2 hours) comprise 49% of all trips but account for only 18.8% of the total time given to enjoyment of the countryside. In contrast, the 15% of trips lasting 5 hours or more may well have provided 40.4% of the hours of enjoyment.

Round-trip	Countryside	Woods/Forests	Canals/Rivers
Up to 1 mile	12%	5%	2%
1 - 5 miles	41%	60%	21%
5 - 10 miles	16%	10%	20%
10 - 20 miles	10%	10%	13%
20 - 40 miles	9%	6%	15%
Over 40 miles	9%	4%	24%
Not known	3%	5%	5%
Mean Distance	*16.4 miles*	*11.1 miles*	*32.8 miles*
Mode - CAR	53%	30%	44%
Mode - FOOT	38%	61%	26%
Mode - BIKE	4%	5%	7%
Personal Transport	95%	96%	77%
All Visits	*637 million*	*210 million*	*41 million*

Table 5.2 Distances Travelled and the Mode of Transport on Home-based Visits to Countryside, Woods and Forests, Canals and Rivers, 1993.

Duration of Visit	Countryside		Woods/Forests		Canals/Rivers	
	Visits	Time	Visits	Time	Visits	Time
Up to 1 hour	27%	6.5%	44%	14.9%	12%	1.8%
1 - 2 hours	22%	12.3%	25%	19.7%	12%	4.3%
2 - 3 hours	18%	15.8%	10%	12.4%	13%	7.3%
3 - 4 hours	12%	14.4%	8%	13.5%	12%	9.2%
4 - 5 hours	7%	10.6%	5%	10.7%	12%	11.6%
5 - 6 hours	4%	7.4%	3%	7.8%	14%	16.4%
Over 6 hours	11%	33.0%	6%	21.0%	25%	49.4%

Table 5.3 The Duration of Visits and Share of All Time at Each Venue on Home-based Visits to Countryside, Woods and Forests, Canals and Rivers, 1993.

Notes: (1) Tables 5.2 & 5.3 : 88% of the visits to woods and forests were within the countryside; 11% were in urban areas; and 1% was on the coast. 55% of the visits to canals and navigable rivers were within the countryside; 42% were in urban areas; and 3% were on the coast. **(2) Table 5.3** : The average duration of visits to the countryside, woods and forests, canals and navigable rivers is 3.1, 2.2 and 4.9 hours respectively. Therefore 100 representative visitors would generate a combined trip-time of 310, 220 and 490 hours respectively. *Assuming* that the average length of visits of less than an hour is 0.75 of an hour, and that for visits between 1 and 2 hours it is 1.75 hours etc, the percentage share that each of the six closed classes contributes to the total trip time can be calculated. The unallocated residue must be attributed to those visits which exceeded 6 hours; and this suggests the average duration of these longest visits to the countryside was 9.4 hours; to woods and forests 7.8 hours; and to canals and rivers 9.7 hours. All visits include the time of travel to and from home. (Source UKDVS, 1993).

Committed 'countryside goers' thus generate demand for a wide range of provision to support lengthy visits to their selected destinations; and they sustain pressures within and on the approaches to these places for lengthy periods. These conditions together with the relatively rare intrinsic qualities of these favourite places adds to the prominence which they receive in surveys, publicity and policy. In contrast, the 'local countryside' comprising the domestic domain of the public as a whole remains relatively anonymous; but it accommodates more than half of all countryside visits and should be a high priority, if not the highest for investment.

The two special environments selected by the UKDVS invite brief comment. Visits to woods and forests generate profiles comparable with but more pronounced than those for the countryside as a whole. 65% occur within 2.5 miles of the home and 69% last for less than two hours. They are the least likely to be car-based (31%) and most likely to be entirely on foot (60%). The average size of groups is only 1.9 and 45% of all visits to woods and forests are by lone persons. These snippets of information suggest and support the hypothesis:

> that many, perhaps most visits to local woods are accompanied or led by at least one dog. And all members are in search of regular exercise and relaxation close to home but beyond the limitations of more organised open spaces and irksome regulations in respect of sanitation. Supplementary explanations may comprise preferences for local woodland paths and trails of some informal activities, such as jogging, running and mountain-biking. More focused, in-depth local surveys may validate, qualify or refute these ideas. (Kay, 1996).

A study of path-users in an urban-fringe wood within Bracknell Forest Borough provides supportive evidence. The 'average walker' used the paths 44 times a year; tended to be middle-aged; lived about 5 miles away; and spent just under £50 a month on leisure. Some 40% had left full-time education at 21 or over; more than 40% had an annual household income in excess of £40,000; and half of them belonged to one or more 'countryside organisations' such as the National Trust (Tranter, 1994). This profile is consistent with that of privileged, regular users of the wider countryside; and it indicates that such people are also likely to be frequent users of their local environs for commonplace recreation.

Visits to canals and navigable rivers are quite different in terms of distances travelled and duration. They exhibit an even distribution of visits between the five shorter periods and a concentration (39%) in those lasting more than 5 hours, which account for two-thirds of all time spent visiting waterways. This pattern partly reflects heavy use of more distant waterways (29% of the round trips exceeded 40 miles) but the greater part of the explanation probably lies in the main purpose of the visits. Walking accounted for only 30% of them; other, more time-consuming, water-based activities, including fishing, would appear to be more prominent.

Both the NSCR and UKDVS thus highlight the importance of proximity to home as a key factor in determining spatial patterns of everyday recreation, but they do little to identify the location of favourite places within either the domestic domain or the wider countryside. The nation's vaunted 'love affair' with the countryside implies a uniformity of affection but this is certainly not reflected in recreational behaviour. On the contrary, a principal argument in the model outlined above is that each significant step in investment and importance attached to a visit will be reflected in the selection of more valued locations. And a principal purpose of foregoing historical themes (Ch.1-3) is to show that today's selections are heavily conditioned by successive legacies of influential minority groups; today's 'honeypots' were created, and defended, long before the term was invented. There is, however, no national register of favourite places or crowded spaces; and illustration of the markedly uneven use of the countryside must depend on case material.

3. Recreation in the National Parks

The National Parks were designated largely on grounds of inherent qualities valued by dominant minority interest groups; but their merit is perceived by the public at large to be beyond question. There is, therefore, a prima facie case that they should comprise popular favourite places, if only with significant minorities. In 1990 data from the most recent visitor survey of each Park were collated to inform a review of their future (Edwards, 1991). This exercise indicated a total of 103 million visitor-days per annum (Table 5.4.Col.1) and, at first sight, this is an impressive figure. However, it comprises only 5% of all countryside visits indicated by the NSCR of 1984 or 7% of the number suggested by the 1993 UKDVS; and, given that the Parks cover 9% of England and Wales, in each case this is less than would be expected from their areal extent without any consideration of their inherent qualities. Furthermore, in 1994 the first independent survey of all the Parks, The Broads and The New Forest was carried out by consultants for the Countryside Commission (CCP.503, 1996), and it indicates that the Parks received only 69.3 million visitors, 33% less than was cited in 1991. The methodology of the National Parks Visitor Survey (NPVS) differs from those of the several Parks' authorities; it excluded leisure travellers who passed through but made no stop within a Park - and this change may be largely responsible for the reduction in visitor numbers. Unsurprisingly, it has been received with some scepticism but it provides the only uniform set of data for all the Parks and it thus offers the best material for a comparative study of them (Table 5.4).

Leaving aside the Pembrokeshire Coast and The Broads where peculiarities of geography and data collection clearly did affect findings, the Lake District and the Peak District, with 20% and 18% of all visitor-days, are confirmed as the most popular National Parks; and the latter (with 22,900 visitor-days per square mile) is by far the most heavily used. The Yorkshire Dales (12%) and the North York Moors (11%) follow in order of both popularity and pressure; and, although more lightly used, Snowdonia is the fifth most popular Park. However, The New Forest, with 6,620,000 visitor-days, is almost as popular as Snowdonia and substantially more popular than six other National Parks. Three of these, Dartmoor, Exmoor and the Brecon Beacons have seen their apparent popularity halved by the NPVS, though Dartmoor is still identified as one of the more heavily used. The Northumberland National Park benefited from the NPVS but, with only 1.4 million visitor days, this remote Park shares the distinction with Exmoor of being the least popular. Alton Towers, a theme park on the edge of the Peak District, has regularly received more than 2.5 million visitors annually and they have paid handsomely for the privilege of admission. While it offers a different package of experiences, its popularity may help to put that of some of the National Parks in a broader perspective than that automatically granted them as a special genre.

The NPVS shows that a clear majority (61%) of visitor-days spent in the National Parks are generated by persons on holiday away from home, 40% by holiday-makers staying in the Parks and 21% by those travelling from resorts beyond their boundaries (Table 5.5). Holidays represent substantial investments of leisure time and resources, and this marks the National Parks as highly valued places by their patrons. This is reinforced by the fact that 73% of the holiday-makers are on return visits:

> Many were regular repeat visitors. 61% of holiday visitor-days were accounted for by those who had been on a previous holiday in the same Park in the past five years. Of these 29% were by those who had visited six or more times during this period' (CCP.503, 1996).

The propensity to visit the Parks regularly while on holiday, and their use by home-based visitors may be partly a function of the location of the Parks in respect of the distribution of population. Those with small populations within 20 miles of their borders (Table 5.4) and those remotely situated in respect of the national distribution of population may thus be relatively protected from low-cost, local visits and reserved largely for holiday-makers able and inclined to undertake more expensive outings.

Collectively, the National Parks do attract holiday-makers from all parts of the country; but from some more than others. For example, Greater London has 11.8% of the national population but generates only 5.4% of the holiday-visits to National Parks, that is only 46% of the number its population size would suggest. In contrast, the South East with 18.6% of the population accounts for 23.7% of the visits, 121% of its proportional share. Since both regions are similar in terms of distance from the Parks, this serves as a reminder that urban populations in general and inner-city dwellers in particular are the least likely to be 'countryside goers' (Fig.4.4); and while the National Parks have a countrywide clientele of frequent visitors, they do not serve the nation as a whole.

1 Peak District	6.7 m. 29.9 %	2 North York Moors	2.8 m. 12.5 %
3 Lake District	2.7 m. 12.1 %	4 Yorkshire Dales	2.2 m. 9.8 %
5 Brecon Beacons	1.7 m. 7.6 %	6 Snowdonia	1.6 m. 7.1 %
7 The Broads	1.6 m. 7.1 %	8 Dartmoor	1.5 m. 6.7 %
9 Pembrokeshire Coast	0.8 m. 3.6 %	10 Northumberland	0.5 m. 2.2 %
11 Exmoor	0.3 m. 1.3 %	(New Forest)	2.6 m ——

Home-based Visits by Car to the National Parks in 1999

Proximity to the Parks is particularly important in respect of the 22,400,000 home-based visits made by car. The Peak District is unrivalled as an attraction for day-visitors and this reflects a high rate of activity amongst the 1.6 million people living within 20 miles of its boundary. The Peak Park Survey of 1986/87 recorded '500,000 visits by local walkers making direct entry on foot'; and that '65% of [all] day visits are made by people who live within 20 miles of the Park ... Visitors from further afield tend to be infrequent visitors' (PPJPB, 1988b). This implies that some 2.3 million visits were made from 'further afield'; and in this context proximity in terms of linear distance is less important than travel-time.

National Park	Visitor Days(m) 1990	1994*	% Change	Area sq ml	Visitor Days	Pop. (m) within	Pop. '91
Lake District	20.0	13.93	-30%	880	15,800	0.58	42,239
Peak District	20.0	12.40	-38%	542	22,900	1.60	38,100
Yorks Dales	9.0	8.30	-8%	680	12,200	2.76	17,980
N. York Moors	11.0	7.79	-27%	533	14,600	0.55	25,348
Snowdonia	8.0	6.75	-18%	838	7,800	0.45	40,000
Dartmoor	8.0	3.83	-52%	365	10,500	1.05	32,292
Brecon Beacons	7.0	3.62	-48%	519	7,000	1.97	32,500
Northumberland	1.0	1.41	+41%	398	3,500	No data	3,500
Exmoor	3.0	1.40	-53%	265	5,300	0.25	10,650
The Broads*	3.0	5.36	+77%	111	48,300	0.35	5,500
Pembroke Coast*	13.0	4.66	-64%	225	20,700	0.30	24,000
All Parks	**103.0**	**69.27**	**-33%**	**5356**	**12,900**	**9.86**	**272,109**

Table 5.4. The National Parks : Visitor Use, 1990 and 1994

The basic data are derived from Edwards (1991) and CCP.503 (1996); and the Parks are listed in rank order of their popularity as recorded in 1994. The '1990' data refer to the most recent pre-1990 surveys of the several Parks. The percentage change, calculated by the author, should, perhaps, be read with caution given the changes in methodology.

*The Visitor Days for The Broads and the Pembrokeshire Coast are generally considered to be over-estimates because of the inclination of respondents to refer to wider areas than the designated Parks; this weakness applies to both the pre-1990 and 1994 data, and comparisons with the other Parks should be made with caution. (The New Forest had 6,620,000 visitor-days in 1994.)

National Park	Home-based Visits	Holiday-based visits from:	
		(a) in the Park	(b) elsewhere
Pembrokeshire Coast	20 %	68 %	12 %
Exmoor	23 %	31 %	45 %
Lake District	26 %	62 %	13%
The Broads	30 %	64 %	6 %
Snowdonia	32 %	43 %	25 %
Yorkshire Dales	34 %	20 %	46 %
North York Moors	40 %	31 %	29 %
Northumberland	40 %	07 %	53 %
Dartmoor	44 %	11 %	45 %
The New Forest	45 %	27 %	28 %
Brecon Beacons	53 %	17 %	30 %
Peak District	65 %	22 %	13 %
All National Parks	**39 %**	**40 %**	**21 %**

Table 5.5. Home-based and Holiday-based Visits to the National Parks and The New Forest, 1994.

The position of both home and destination in relation to motorways and other 'expressways' then assumes considerable importance; and so do traffic conditions. Outward and return journeys of 90 minutes or more on open roads may well be an enjoyable or acceptable part of an outing; but 20 minutes in near-stationery traffic will mar if not ruin the day. In this context, the Peak District has a particularly favourable location in respect of several densely populated regions. The Lake District, Yorkshire Dales and the North York Moors are similarly accessible from one or more populous regions; but the others lack either comparable accessibility or appeal for day-visitors. There is evidence that growing problems of access, notably those associated with traffic flows, and alternative opportunities offered by increased affluence have led to some substitution of day trips with 'short-break' holidays; and this trend would seem to confirm that the National Parks are highly prized by their established clientele who can afford to make such adjustments.

As noted above, most visitors are regular users of the Parks; and most of the population rarely if ever visit them. The 1994 NPVS noted this point: *'The high proportion of repeat visits, and high satisfaction levels show how popular the Parks are with current visitors. This may beg the question whether enough is being done to present opportunities to potential new visitors to the Parks'* (CCP.503, 1996). This is a part of the wider question concerning the privileged and the disadvantaged who are currently excluded not only from the National Parks, but also from the wider countryside as a whole (Ch.4.4-5). However, history shows that favourite places will be resolutely defended; and the defence of the National Parks is often focused on the misplaced argument that they are over-crowded and threatened by over-use (Plate.4.2). These issues will be explored with particular reference to more specific information on the recreational use of the Peak District and other National Parks.

4. The Peak District and other National Parks

In 1977 the Peak Park Planning Board identified 42 'major visitor areas' comprising the more popular places, each of which generated heavy recreational use (Fig.5.2). These dominate the visitors' 'mental map' of the Park though in reality they occupy only a small proportion of it. Most of them were favoured locations during Victorian days, many having been popularised by railway excursions. However, success fosters growth; and post-war growth of countryside recreation focused attention on established visitor attractions as both honeypots and problem spots. Crowding and congestion and diverse pressures on the limited resources and facilities of such favourite places thus have a long history. These persistent features are recognised and to a large degree accepted by most regular visitors, who will not lightly abandon that which they highly prize; though they may wish that others would !

Ten years later, a second survey (PPJPB, 1988a) undertook a more systematic analysis of visitor use which compensates for a loss of pictorial impact with striking statistical information (Table 5.6 & Fig.5.3). Twenty-two 'Landscape' or 'Natural' areas identified for planning purposes provide the framework for plotting the distribution of (i) all stops within the Park; (ii) sight-seeing visits; and (iii) hiking visits. Five areas comprising only 27% of the Park accommodate 70% of the 15,940,000 stops and 80% of all 'landscape visits'. The three most popular areas - the Lower Derwent, Wye and Hope Valleys - sustain 50% of all stops and 66% of all landscape visits on 11% of the Park's surface. The

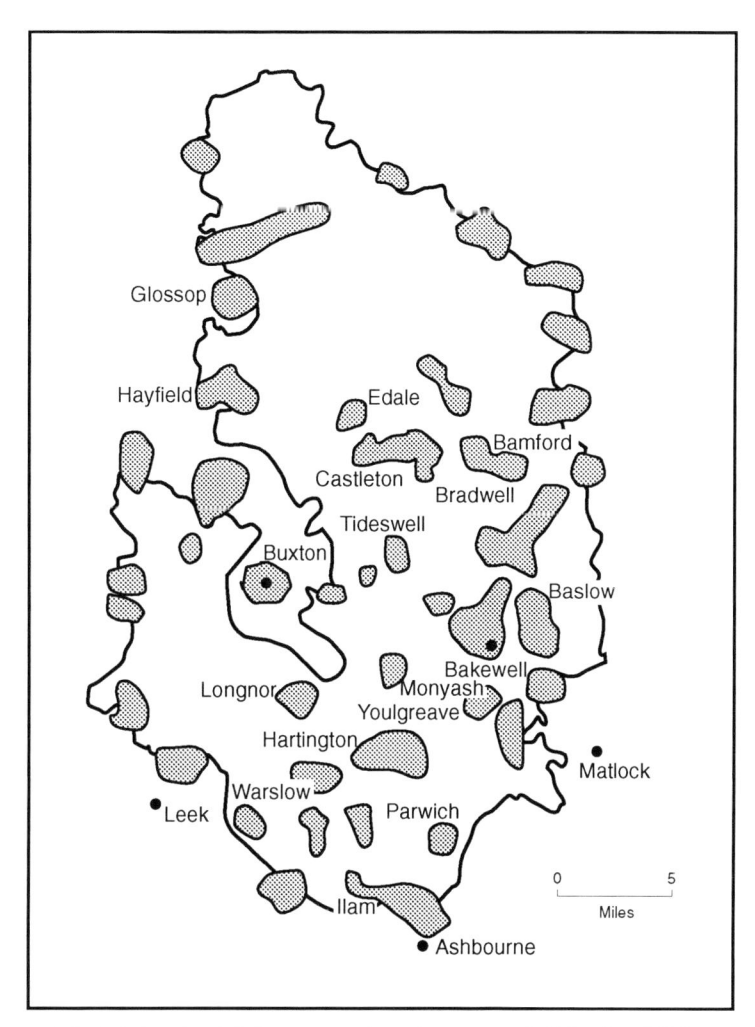

Fig.5.2 Major Visitor Locations in the Peak District, 1977.

Wye, Hope, Dove and Manifold valleys together with Edale are also the main locations for holiday accommodation, notably camp and caravan sites; and they provide for 75% of all visitor-nights spent within the Park.

Beyond these five, three relatively small areas adjacent to the Park's boundaries also attract attention through the scale and/or density of their use. These are (5) the Meltham and Holmfirth Fringe; (9) the High Peak (Hayfield) Fringe; and (17) Lyme Hall and Park.

Hikers' (walking 2 miles or more) comprise a small set of visitors but they are active users with significant contact with the open countryside. They are rather less concentrated, but five areas comprising 26% of the Park accommodate 60% of them; and four of these are coincident with the five noted above for their prominence as visitor attractions. Nine areas covering half of the Park account for 82% of all hiking visits.

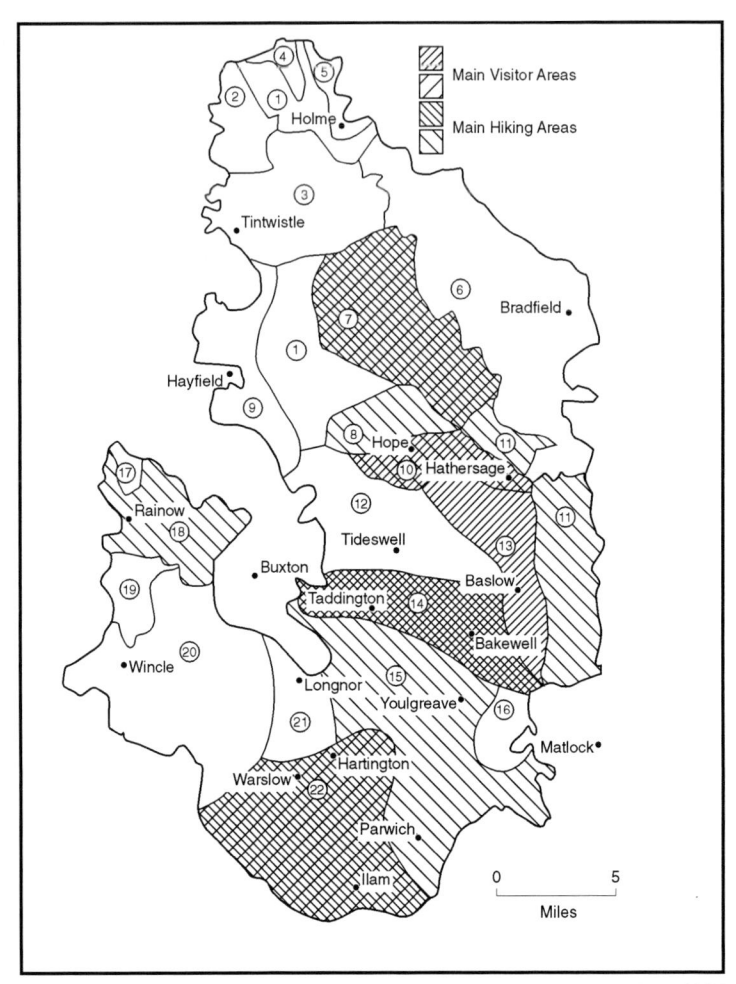

Fig.5.3 Main Visitor and Hiking Areas in the Peak District, 1987

Landscape or Natural Area	All Stops		Landscape Visits		Area	
	%	Acc.%	%	Acc.%	%	Acc.%
13 Lower Derwent Valley	19.6%	19.6%	33.0%	33.0%	3.61%	3.61%
14 The Wye Valley	16.1%	35.7%	18.0%	51.0%	5.22%	8.83%
10 The Hope Valley	13.9%	49.6%	15.0%	66.0%	2.14%	10.97%
22 Lower Dove and Manifold Valleys	12.2%	61.8%	8.0%	74.0%	9.52%	20.49%
07 Upper Derwent and Woodlands Valleys	7.8%	69.6%	6.0%	80.0%	6.90%	27.39%

Landscape/Natural Area	A Area %	B Stops %	C Sight- seers %	D Hikers %	B/A x100	C/A x100	D/A x100
1. The Northern Moors	6.42	1.2	01	03	019	016	047
2. Dove Stone	1.76	0.5	—	—	028	—	—
3. Longendale	5.43	2.3	01	02	042	018	037
4. Wessenden-Marsden	0.48	0.2	—	—	042	—	—
5. Meltham-Holmfirth	0.75	1.3	3.0	1.0	*173*	*400*	*133*
7. Upper Derwent & Woodlands Valleys	**6.90**	**7.8**	**6.0**	**13.0**	*113*	087	*188*
8. Edale Valley	1.92	1.6	1.0	8.0	083	052	*417*
9. High Peak Fringe	3.10	2.4	4.0	3.0	077	*129*	097
10. The Hope Valley	**2.14**	**13.9**	**15.0**	**8.0**	*650*	*701*	*374*
11. The Eastern Moors	5.05	5.1	1.0	6.0	*101*	020	*119*
12. Northern Limestone Plateau	5.48	2.1	2.0	2.0	038	036	036
13. Lower Derwent Valley	**3.61**	**19.6**	**33.0**	**4.0**	*543*	*914*	*111*
14. The Wye Valley	**5.22**	**16.1**	**18.0**	**11.0**	*308*	*345*	*211*
15. Southern Limestone Plateau	0.8	3.8	3.0	7.0	035	028	065
16. Stanton-Birchover	2.23	0.4	—	1.0	033	—	081
17. Lyme Hall & Park	0.48	2.2	1.0	—	*458*	*208*	—
18. Goyt, Todd Brook & Lamaload	4.50	2.4	1.0	5.0	053	022	*111*
19. Macclesfield Forest & Wildboarclough	1.11	0.2	—	—	018	—	—
20. South West Moors	9.27	2.2	1.0	3.0	024	011	032
21. Upper Dove & Manifold Valleys	2.42	0.7	1.0	1.0	029	041	041
22. Lower Dove & Manifold Valleys	**9.52**	**12.2**	**8.0**	**20.0**	*128*	084	*210*
PEAK DISTRICT NP	100	100	100	100	100	100	100

Table 5.6. Spatial Patterns of Visitor-use in the Peak District, 1987

Col.A: The relative extent of each Area was calculated by the author from PPJPB maps by counting the occurrence in each of the 22 areas of 4159 grid squares comprising the National Park as a whole.

Cols.B, C and D show the distribution of 'Stops' made by all visitors, and of Sight-seers and Hikers; and the last three columns show the relative 'density' of the three users in each Area. '100' represents the mean density which would occur if the use was evenly distributed in proportion to the size of the Area. Above-average densities are shown in italics; and the five most popular Areas are emboldened. They comprise 27% of the Park and accommodate 70% of the 15,940,000 stops and 80% of the sight-seeing.

The principal features of this Table are illustrated in Fig.5.3. (Source, PPJPB, 1988a)

Landscape or Natural Region	Hiking Visits		Area of Park	
	%	Acc.%	%	Acc.%
22 Lower Dove/Manifold Valleys	20.0%	20.0%	9.52%	09.52%
07 Upper Derwent/Woodlands Valleys	13.0%	33.0%	6.90%	16.42%
14 The Wye Valley	11.0%	44.0%	5.22%	21.64%
10 The Hope Valley	8.0%	52.0%	2.14%	23.78%
08 Edale Valley	8.0%	60.0%	1.92%	25.70%
15 Southern Limestone Plateau	7.0%	67.0%	10.80%	36.50%
11 Eastern Moors	6.0%	73.0%	5.05%	41.55%
18 Goyt/Todd Brook/Lamaload	5.0%	78.0%	4.50%	46.05%
13 Lower Derwent Valley	4.0%	82.0%	3.61%	49.66%

Additionally, the Meltham and Holmfirth Fringe (05) is notable, again, for a high density of hikers. It is, however, evident that the 'Valleys' dominate the pattern of all visiting, including that by walkers. The moorland regions comprise 41% of the Park but accommodate only 6% of all sightseeing, 13% of all stops and 15% of all hiking visits. Only the Eastern Moors (11) suffer any above-average use. These 'environmentally sensitive' upland areas are vulnerable, and it is well that they should escape heavy use. Despite their history of 'mass trespasses', uncontrolled 'open access' to them should be out of the question.

It is evident from the above analyses that, while extensive areas may well contribute visual inputs to the overall experience of many who do not invade their space, direct visitor-use of most of the Peak District is sparse. This is a corollary of the spatial concentration of most visitors; which is repeated throughout the countryside. For example, in the North York Moors on an August Sunday in 1980, 58.5% of all parked cars were located 'in 24 villages or small areas which together cover only a minute part of the National Park'; and 35% were in the eight more popular locations (NYMNP, 1981). In 1991 this level of concentration was repeated on Sundays, and exceeded on Wednesdays when 38% of all parked cars were found in eight favourite places (Kay, 1996).

Nevertheless, the realistic view that the greater part of the Park - like the greater part of countryside - is only lightly used is not readily recognised by visitors nor by the public at large. This may well be because most visitors, including the occasional and infrequent visitors, actually spend most of their time within such popular areas at popular times. Furthermore, on roads leading to and from these favourite places and at particular sites and points within them, crowding, congestion and pressures of all kinds will be frequently encountered. Such conditions often comprise the sharp interface between people and place and immediately affect the experience of many, perhaps most, visitors. They are rare in space and time but they characterise most visits and are likely to shape opinions and perspectives, not only on conditions at the particular places but also on more general related issues.

At first sight, the 1966 White Paper on *Leisure in the Countryside of England and Wales* (Cmnd.2928) might seem to have grasped the principal issue. *'The problem is to enable [the people] to enjoy this leisure* without harm to those who live and work in the country and without spoiling what they go to the countryside to seek'. Enabling people to enjoy their favourite places calls for positive management and adequate provision for people; but too often prevention is perceived to be better - and cheaper - than problem-solving; and exclusion is prefered to provision for and promotion of enjoyment. Inflation of the threat to the countryside therefore is accepted if not fostered; and the fact that the greater part of the countryside, even in the National Parks, is but lightly used for recreation is too readily overlooked.

Comparable evidence to that set out above has long been available. In 1973 'the limited areal extent of visitor pressure' in Snowdonia was emphasised:

> In the National Park, outdoor recreation areas are used intensively during brief periods of time, moderately at others; some are wholly unused for much greater periods of time; while other areas are completely unused... **Extreme time-peaking and the resulting areal impact is one of the major management challenges in the field of outdoor recreation...** The impact of recreation in areal terms (comprises) a series of corridors and nodal points, **reinforcing the view often made by well informed observers, that it is nonsense to speak of an overcrowded countryside.** (Gittins; in Rogers et al, 1973).

By 1983 Patmore could authoritatively state in *Recreation and Resources* that:

> Countryside recreation is concentrated not only in time but also in space... The degree of concentration is evident in a variety of studies, most notably in surveys of recreational patterns in many of the national parks. The patterns differ markedly in detail... but all belie the idea of a widespread 'wave' of recreational users, ubiquitous in their impact.

By that date, Patmore's denial of any widespread threat was urgently needed but it has had little impact on either public or apparently informed opinion:

> We know from surveys that 18 million people visit the countryside on a sunny Sunday. More will come in the next 30 years... Will these English counties of yours be suffering direly in 2020 from the feet of hordes of visitors... eroding the footpaths and providing positive hurt to the countryside and its wildlife ? It is indeed very likely unless we develop, quite rapidly, some imaginative policies... We have been slow to understand and construct sensistive, acceptably discrect ways of applying practical management to our fellow citizens... Perhaps in the field of access, the (Countryside) Commission's target of reopening the 135,000 mile footpath and bridleway network of England and Wales will help spread the load of public pressure. What is clear is that the public are coming in increasing numbers and will in one way or another have to be accommodated. (Barber, 1990).

The countryside as a whole, in fact, faces no such threat from hordes of visitors; and it is less probable that 'visitors are coming in increasing numbers' than that the relatively few established, regular users are coming more frequently. Imaginative polices are required, together with appropriate resources, to tackle problems within popular places; and, more importantly, to provide for and promote access to countryside walking by many more people. But they will not be produced by any approach that treats the countryside, rights of way, and their users all as more or less uniform entities.

5. Open All Hours... and Free for All ?

The wider countryside is open all hours, all year round; and walking through the night or in wintry conditions (Plate 8.1) adds an extra dimension to the appreciation of landscape and terrain and to the exploration of one's self. However, recreation is concentrated within limited periods; and crowding therefore might be reduced, not by denying access to favourite places, but by dispersal of visitors through time, though established patterns have proved persistent and will not be readily surrendered nor easily changed.

The main features of the temporal pattern are well documented. The 1977 GHS shows that walking is an all-year-round activity with a marked seasonal pattern of participation. The steep increase in July-Sept coincides with summer holidays and reflects a concentration of activity by occasional walkers at a time when regular walkers are most active:

	1st Qtr	*2nd Qtr*	*3rd Qtr*	*4th Qtr*	*Year*
Participation Rate (% of Pop)	15.3	16.6	22.1	14.1	17.1
Mean Frequency (days/4 wks)	0.74	7.1	7.7	7.8	7.5
Walks/100 persons/4 weeks	113.2	117.9	170.2	110.0	128.3
% of the mean	88.2%	91.9%	132.7%	85.7%	100 %

The 1984 NSCR confirms this pattern but also illustrates the more striking short-term rythms of countryside recreation (Fig.5.4). Very strong daily variations are revealed, with the visits ranging from a low of 2 million on a typical winter weekday to a high of 18 million on a summer Sunday. (CCP.201, 1985). The weekly rythm is most pronounced in winter when brevity of daylight is probably a critical factor. Sunday use is then six or seven times that of weekdays; and winter Saturdays also are relatively heavily used. In summer, long evenings and holidays are key factors in raising the level of weekday use to about one-third that of Sundays; but summer weekdays still generate less than half the visits of winter Sundays.

Throughout the year, countryside recreation is highly sensitive to weather, with a general preference for long, dry and sunny days and for warm, even hot, rather than cold conditions. Wet weather is the least acceptable. Favourable weather on a summer Sunday or bank holiday weekend therefore accentuates the weekly peak; and adverse weather, especially in winter, produces exceptionally low levels of use. Leaving aside such refinements, favourite places are regularly subject to quite intense use on most Sundays in each and every season; and information on the timing and duration of trips indicates acute congestion for short periods at popular times during the days of heaviest use.

However, the same data sets (Fig.5.4) also show that the countryside's capacity for providing enjoyment is grossly under-used for the greater part of every week throughout the year. This point is often lost in concern with problems created by brief periods of peak

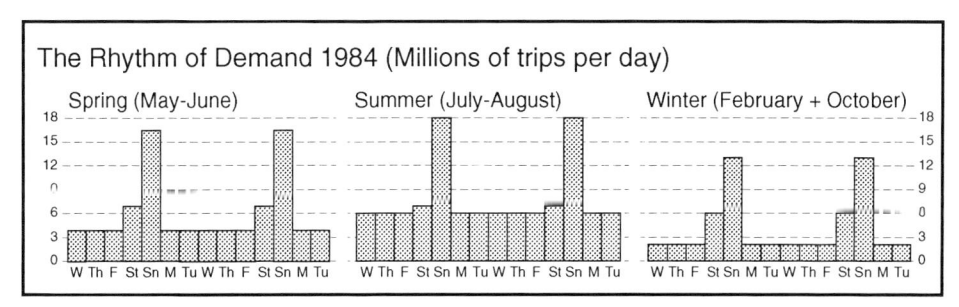

The Rhythm of Demand 1984 (Millions of trips per day)

Spring (May-June) Summer (July-August) Winter (February + October)

Fig.5.4 Daily and Seasonal Rhythms of Recreational Demand for Countryside Resources
Source: CCP.201, 1984.

use; and the benefits of a more even distribution are rarely granted the attention they deserve. The year-round concentration of countryside recreation on Sundays has its roots in culture and history no less than in contemporary leisure habits; and it is widespread throughout the population and the country. On the other hand, some seasonal differences are revealed in place-specific studies. For example, where holiday-based visitors are prominent, as in most National Parks (Table 5.5), emphasis on the summer months is above average - and mid-week use by both holiday-makers and retired persons is then more pronounced. In contrast, in the Peak District the winter decline in weekday use is much less marked and this may reflect the importance of regular, all-year, mid-week visits by those living within or close to the Park who are not restricted to weekend outings. Peak Park data also show that persons over 60 years of age comprise 27% of all weekday visitors and only 13% of Sundays visitors; and this pattern may well occur elsewhere.

The 1993 UKDVS shows that towns and cities command popularity all year round while the seaside - the classic destination for day visits - has a very marked seasonal rythm:

	Winter Use as % of Summer Use.	*Users Making No Winter Visit.*
Towns and Cities	86%	5%
Countryside	70%	17%
Canals & Rivers	60%	46%
Woods & Forests	56%	28%
Seaside/Coast	49%	44%

The rythm of countryside visiting lies closer to that of the cities; it is popular throughout the year and only 17% of its users stay away in winter. However, while small minorities of frequent visitors make more than 70% of all visits in both summer and winter, considerably larger groups of occasional users achieve only 5-6% throughout the year (Table 5.7). In short, UKDVS data confirm and emphasise the unequal distribution of countryside recreation through the year. The profile for woods and forests (where walking was the main purpose of 74% of all visits) is similar but more pronounced; smaller minorities dominate its use in summer and, even more firmly, in winter - when 29% of woodland users chose to make no visit. Canals and rivers, where walking was the prime purpose of only 29% of the visitors, have a more idiosyncratic profile. Throughout the year frequent

	COUNTRYSIDE			
	Summer		Winter	
Type of Visitor	Visitors	Visits	Visitors	Visits
Frequent	25.0%	72.5%	17.0%	72.0%
Regular	37.0%	22.5%	24.0%	22.0%
Occasional	38.0%	5.0%	42.0%	6.0%
Seasonal				
Non-Visitor	00.0%	00.0%	17.0%	00.0%

	WOODS & FORESTS				CANALS & RIVERS			
	Summer		Winter		Summer		Winter	
Type	Visitors	Visits	Visitors	Visits	Visitors	Visits	Visitors	Visits
Frequent	18.0	72.0	09.0	68.0	05.5	48.0	03.0	60.0
Regular	27.0	20.0	16.5	22.0	16.0	30.0	06.5	21.0
Occasional	54.0	8.0	46.0	10.0	77.5	22.0	44.5	19.0
Seasonal								
Non-Visitor	1.0	00.0	28.5	00.0	1.0	00.0	46.0	00.0

Table 5.7 Seasonal Patterns of Visits to the Countryside, Woods and Forests, Canals and Rivers in 1993. (Walker, 1996).

visitors are very small but very active minorities; and the occasional users are particularly numerous. However, nearly half of the canals' customers are absent in winter; and these rather exceptional features may well be a product of water-based recreations rather than walking.

The countryside is indeed open all hours, all year round; but it is subject to marked temporal concentrations of use that generate serious problems for its management, especially in respect of the provision of supporting services, facilities and amenities and the control of visitor behaviour. The countryside *per se* is also free for all, and control of access via market mechanisms is strongly opposed by visitors and the public at large; and it is not generally deployed in the wider countryside. The National Trust is an exception; it is a land-owner and it does make charges for entry to many of its properties (Ch.2.5).

> It spends all of its income on the care and maintenance of the land and buildings in its protection but cannot meet the cost of all its obligations. It is always in need of financial support and it relies on the generosity of its supporters, through membership subscriptions, gifts, legacies and the contribution of some 30,000 volunteers' (National Trust, 1996).

In 1998-99 the Trust's income from all sources was £182,400,000. The wider countryside lacks comparable commercial opportunities; nor can it readily turn goodwill into hard cash. On the contrary, the public generally expect that the countryside will not only be open all hours but also, as a gift of nature to the people, it will in every respect be free for all.

Such ill-founded but widely held beliefs and attitudes underlie much confusion and conflict which, in turn, adversely affect policies for and management of the countryside for recreation. The Countryside Commission's 1995 survey of public attitudes reflects and propagates such confusion (Ashcroft, 1996). 91% of respondents were encouraged to state that 'the countryside is an important part of our heritage' and 89% to declare that 'the English countryside should be protected at all costs'. Do these beliefs justify exclusion and restrictions on access ? Or, since 72% of the public agreed that 'people will have to pay more to enjoy the countryside', do they imply that direct charges should be levied on visitors, or that public spending should be increased at the tax-payers' expense? The latter may be the prefered option since 71% of the respondents agreed that 'nowhere near enough government effort is invested in protecting the countryside'; and proper provision for users, rather than exclusion, will greatly help in this respect.

Nevertheless inconvenience, loss and damage do and will occur; costs are incurred and money does matter. The indirect costs and losses incurred through impacts of recreational use on the countryside are considerable and varied; and while the Countryside Code and similar measures seek to address this issue, rural communities, land-owners, farmers and other land-users, still pay a heavy price. Crowds and congestion may be more harmful than low levels of use, but the latter are still fraught with dangers. It requires but a single match, cigarette end or piece of glass to cause a fire; one loose dog may terrorise sheep or cattle or disturb wildlife; one discarded plastic bag may endanger the health or life of an animal; one walker failing to close a gate or breaking through a fence may allow stock to stray; and one ill-placed parked car may block a lane to farm machinery and wide loads. In short, although excessive visitor pressures are highly localised, there is widespread potential for cost - and conflict - wherever careless or inconsiderate behaviour occurs on other peoples' land or domestic domain. Most visitors and walkers probably are innocent of any such gross act; but most do contribute collectively to disturbance, disruption and even damage. For example, if only by considered departures from the precise location of authorised footpaths, 'trespass' is widespread with consequent damage to crops or grass. The law of trespass is virtually unenforceable; and farmers once felt their best defence was in a campaign to inform walkers that *'Your Feet Are Killing Me'*. A greater general awareness of the costs of countryside recreation and a willingness by all parties to reduce or share them could improve relationships to the benefit of all.

Finally, the impacts and costs of recreational use can and do generate dissension amongst participants and between them and potential users; and they have done so for more than 150 years (Ch.1-2). Congestion and crowding, queues and competition for key spaces, hustle and bustle, noise and litter, may all characterise favourite places at popular times; and may be perceived by the more sensitive persons even in sparsely used locations. Many visitors may positively enjoy convivial company; and many may be reasonably tolerant of the need to share prime sites with large numbers of their fellows. On the other hand, significant minorities find that crowds and noise cost them too much in terms of damage to their expected experiences. Some retreat to less popular places and times; but many positively seek to protect their enjoyment of their favourite places, often by representing pressures as a threat to the countryside. Consequently, unwittingly or purposefully, influential minority groups thus align themselves with farmers and land-owners, country dwellers and conservationists of all kinds to argue for lower levels of recreational use in significant parts if not all of the countryside. The effects of their combined case, historically and currently, fall largely, if only indirectly, upon the very substantial numbers of infrequent visitors and non-users whose right to access is implicitly if not openly contested or denied; whereas, if justice is to be done, the development of their latent potential for access to and enjoyment of the countryside should be a prime objective. The management of the countryside as a recreational ground is neither easy nor cheap, but it should not be simplified by denying access to potential visitors.

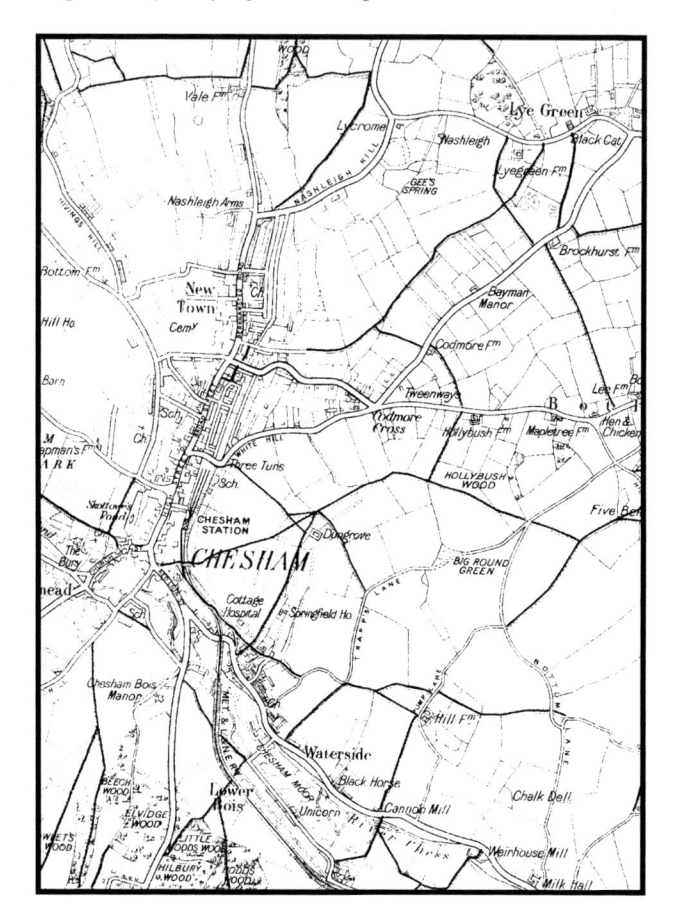

Fig.6.1 A 1945 'Field-Path' Map of Berkhamsted, Ashridge and District Compiled by the Berkhamsted Citizens Association and published by Ed.Stanford Ltd.

'Field-paths' were precursors of PRoW; and both are discontinuous remnants of previously integrated transport systems. They do not form a 'network'; and it is unrealistic and misleading to present PRoW as an entity. Policy and provision for countryside walking should be devised with reference to the utility and merits of all highways that are accessible to pedestrians; and by mapping 'field-paths' the Berkhamsted Citizens were securing an extension to the options available to them.

6
HIGHWAYS, BYWAYS AND RIGHTS OF WAY

Rights of way are a subtle inheritance from the past and a vital gift for the future. Footpaths and bridleways were made by foot, hoof and custom, as people trod their daily route to work, school or church. Formalised during the enclosures and recorded on the first ordnance survey maps, they formed the intricate veins in the mature leaf of the countryside. Then the growth of industrial cities drew people away from the countryside, and many paths fell into disuse. Over the last century, the reverse flow of people - first in recreation, then in home-seeking - has renewed the wish to walk and ride through the countryside. People again wish to penetrate the ways, to exercise the rights... What our forebears created, our grandchildren will enjoy. (Dower, 1993).

1. Concepts and Definitions

An alternative interpretation might consider the legacy of 'rights of way' as a mixed blessing comprising largely redundant remnants of discarded transport systems (Fig.6.1). And while many are persuaded that ancient rights are a priceless heirloom, a more perceptive reading could present them as the contents of a well filled junk-room which merit careful sorting and appraisal against a measured assessment, first, of needs which they might serve in conjunction with other highways and, secondly, of prospects for equipping selected routes with appropriate paths suitable for walkers and, in the case of bridleways, for horse-riders and cyclist too.

Concern and protest over 'stopt paths' began early in the 19th century (Ch.2.2 & Table 2.1); and eventually the defence of Public Rights of Way (PRoW) was achieved through the efforts of pressure groups in 1949 when highway authorities were charged with identifying and mapping them (Ch.4.3). Then, in 1968, the Countryside Commission inherited responsibility for rights of way but initially focussed its attention on protecting natural beauty from the people rather than facilitating access to the countryside as a whole for the nation as a whole (Ch.4.4-5). Twenty years passed before a comprehensive, proactive policy for PRoW was adopted as the centre-piece of *'Recreation 2000'* (CCP.234, 1987); and this was promptly subject to a comprehensive challenge:

The Commission's unyielding aim 'that the entire rights of way network be legally defined, properly maintained and well publicised by the end of the century' may well be unrealistic, unnecessary and unhelpful.
- Unrealistic, because of the absence of any reliable estimate of the costs involved and of ways and means of funding this operation.
- Unnecessary, because preoccupation with the total network can distract attention and resources from a more useful plan for recreational walking which focuses on selected routes of particular merit.
- Unhelpful, because it seems to align the Commission with the interests of a small number of crusaders for the total recovery for public use of every yard of the rights of way. (Kay, 1989).

This challenge calls for substantial revision rather than rejection of current policies. There is neither room nor need for a U-turn but there is urgent need for new approaches if the public and the countryside are to be served better and scarce resources used more effectively.

Semantics can be instructive; and definition of some basic terms may be helpful. *Public Rights of Way* are lines on definitive maps and on the ground along which pedestrians and other specified users have the right to travel. A PRoW is essentially a legal concept; and, although identified by reference to an actual or previous path, bridleway or track, its authority does not depend on continuous concurrence with any such phenomena. Unless it ceases to exist because the land on which it rests disappears (as, for example, by cliff-top or river-bank erosion), a PRoW will continue until removed by due legal process. Comparable rights of way for pedestrians exist alongside or within every public highway and byway except the motorways. The separate identity of rights of way and physical provision for traffic, including footpaths, is important; and much misunderstanding and mismanagement arises from confusion or fusion of the two.

A footpath is a visible, linear, physical feature produced by or provided for pedestrian use; each is a product of erosion or construction or a combination of both. Where they are coincident with 'highways', including PRoW, paths are available for public use; but some may be 'permissive' or 'concessionary' paths available to the public by arrangement with the land-owner; and others may be private. *Roads and lanes* are comparable physical features provided by construction for a range of traffic, including pedestrians, though provision for the latter is not always evident. The specific provision of an identifiable 'walkway' offers an additional facility, but where no such facility exists pedestrians still retain priority on the roads.

'Open access land' is available to the public by customary or statutory law or by concessions negotiated with land-owners which admit walkers and other identified users to defined paths in specified areas or, in some cases, allow people to 'wander at will' over them. Notice of such rights usually is publicised locally. On the other hand, much 'open country' of a similar nature is private property and entry thereon comprises trespass. Nevertheless, access often is taken for granted, if only because land-owners have no effective means to prevent it. The claim for a universal 'right to roam' through or over all such 'open spaces' was rejected in 1949 but it has continued as a focus for protest by the Rambler's Association and a problem for the government (Kay, 1998).

Trespass, whether committed accidentally or intentionally, is a civil offence caused by a person's physical presence where he/she has no legal right to be; departure from a PRoW onto private property thus comprises a trespass. The law of trespass may be a useful control measure; but wilfully causing damage and/or a nuisance are more serious offences and trespass alone is unlikely to sustain successful prosecution and is rarely pursued in the courts. Furthermore, most damage caused by or during trespassing cannot easily be laid at the feet of individuals and consequently prosecutions are rare.

Finally, attention must be focused on a key concept which relates to the interface between people and place, namely *a route*, which is a purposeful selection of PRoW and other highways. Routes for countryside walking serve leisure rather than utilitarian needs; and they comprise an important means whereby enjoyment of the countryside may be achieved. The location, selection, development and promotion of appropriate routes therefore should be the centrepiece of policies for physical access to the countryside.

2. Rights of Way : an Historical Context
When walking was the principal if not the only form of transport, the pattern of most pedestrian movements was reflected in a network of footpaths along routes selected by people, individually and collectively, in pursuit of their total lifestyles. Parts of rural Africa where such conditions still prevail afford useful illustrative material without the burden of polemics (Plate 6.1).

Plate 6.1 Central Africa in 1960 - or England in 1060 ?

In such hard-pressed communities time is of the essence in calculating the net balance of diverse costs and benefits, and while naturally respecting the 'lie of the land' individuals and groups select their own 'shortest' - ie quickest - routes to and from their various destinations. The net result is a multiplicity of well worn paths because:
- (i) the outlay on making them is minimal, the main process being incidental erosion;
- (ii) the perceived 'opportunity costs' are negligible since land is a common or public good rather than a personal possession or resource; and
- (iii) the productivity of the land is low.

Significant change in any of these three factors will affect several interested parties differently; and, brokered within a shifting balance of powers, the net effects will be reflected in new networks of and roles for highways, byways and rights of way.

Within and beyond this network of well worn paths, the much lighter effects of dispersed travel for legitimate purposes over open spaces may not be immediately visible. However, a 'right to roam' is important; how else could firewood and fruits be collected, or birds and animals be trapped and hunted? Even so, there are recognised limits to this apparent freedom of movement. The most important is the cohesion between land and people reflected in the spatial coincidence of socio-political groups - household and village, chiefdom and tribe - and their territory. The right to move freely exists only within one's own domain. Secondly, there are restrictions and controls on movement into and within locations allocated to particular functions. Thus, for example, plots granted to any household, together with the immediately adjacent areas, are exclusively for its use and should not be subject to any wilful entry. This does not preclude general use of any path through, rather than into, such areas; but behaviour on the path must respect those with rights of usufruct over adjacent land. Finally, if any individual has cause or desire to travel beyond his/her own domain, approval and permission should be negotiated with the socio-political leaders of the territories through which his/her route lies. And on any such journey, behaviour by both parties is governed by conventions surrounding visitor and host respectively.

In times long past, broadly comparable transport technologies, economic conditions, and socio-political rights and responsibilities prevailed in Britain; but marked change in these fields has had widespread consequences. Thus the piecemeal shift over 2000 years from communal rights of usufruct to individual rights of property ownership reflected fundamental changes in beliefs which affected the nature and structure of the law and rights in respect of land and access. Also, gradually at first but with greater rapidity during the last 250 years, many ancient paths, bridleways, drovers' roads and cart-tracks were made redundant by successive technological developments in land-use and transport. And the shift from paths and tracks created by pedestrians and horses to roads constructed for vehicles introduced new actors - a succession of 'highway authorities' of various kinds, including private companies which collected tolls. Consequently, in recent times, 'natural' surfaces produced by erosion generally have been found wanting in quality and, more particularly, in physical carrying capacity; and they have been largely abandoned. Their recovery and maintenance for any use is a difficult and costly business (Fig.6.1).

The earliest systematic construction of roads in Britain is attributed to the Romans. They built durable roads over long distances; and they built them straight, partly because this provided the shortest journey between key points but probably because it incurred the lowest costs of construction and maintenance, which were weighty matters. Such roads were the highways of their day; and they are marvels of our time (Plate 6.2). Other constructed paths of bygone days, such as 'monk's trods' and pannier or packhorse trails, also reflect significant efforts to acquire better products than those induced by erosion; and they too contribute to valued sites (Plate 6.3). However, unlike the Roman roads, many of these followed lines worn down by walkers' feet; and through the ages highway authorities often have prefered to modify and upgrade parts of pre-existing networks selected for their importance in relation to new needs, including those generated by new modes of transport (Spratt and Harrison, 1989; Breakell, 1992). Thus, there is as much truth as humour in the adage that 'the rolling, drunken Saxon marked out the English roads'. There are, of course, some clear exceptions. For example, rapid and systematic reclamation of large areas involved the making of new and often straight roads. Ruthless reorganisation and enclosure of well settled areas could similarily impose new lines on both maps and landscapes (Fig.2.3); and the modern motorway is a recent example. Nevertheless, most

**Plate 6.2. The Foundations of the Roman Road, Wheeldale Moor.
(North Yorkshire County Library)**

British highways, byways and paths have a lengthy history; and together they comprise a hierachical network which incorporates rights of way for pedestrians as a first priority within *all* of its constituent parts except private roads and paths and the motorways.

Motorways, Roads, Lanes, Tracks and Paths identified on OS Maps.

(1) Motorways (M6) and Upgraded Trunk Roads (A74M).
(2) Trunk Roads (A38T) and Main Roads (A377).
(3) Secondary Roads (B3215).
(4) Unclassified Roads (i) generally more than 4m wide.
    (ii) generally less than 4m wide.
(5) Other roads, lanes, drives or tracks.
(6) Paths.

OS Maps also identify 'public rights of way' as plotted on Definitive PRoW Maps in four categories: Footpaths, Bridleways, Roads Used as a Public Path (RUPPs) and Byeways Open to All Traffic (BOATS). On some maps, notably the 1 : 25,000 series, they take care to point out that 'Public rights of way shown on this map may not be evident on the ground'; *ie there may be no path*. In England and Wales, there are some 51,000 km of roads, 200,000 km of PRoW, and some 10-15,000 km of RUPPs/BOATs which have been described as 'the hidden network', partly because they are not comprehensively mapped and partly because their past, present and future status and legitimate use are less than clear.

Despite their history and present importance, pedestrian rights of way within or alongside roads all too often are over shadowed in countryside affairs by limelight granted to PRoW. Many rural roads and lanes afford recreational experiences which are complementary and often superior to those obtainable on paths. In addition to the advantage of their surface and the sense of confidence which they confer, they allow intimate inspection of villages and other features of the built environment which contribute significantly to many countryside outings. Also, broad and relatively untended verges and hedgerows provide easy visual access to a rich variety of flora and fauna which is relatively scarce elsewhere, and especially in fields subject to herbicides and insecticides (Kay, 1989). Consequently, observation and surveys show that roads and lanes are heavily used by people walking in the countryside.

The principal objections to their use seem to be an aversion to and dangers posed by vehicular traffic; and to their eternal shame, pressure groups campaigning for PRoW have, for 100 years or more, been willing to cede by default the right of pedestrians to walk safely along public highways in rural areas (Ch.3.5). And nowadays, while toads crossing the road not only benefit from warning signs but are granted protective tunnels under some new roads, pedestrians are insulted at crucial locations with warnings declaring 'No Walkway'. This is an obscure reminder to all road users, especially motorists, that pedestrians always have priority on the Queen's highways except when suicidal or wilfully causing an obstruction. And this state of affairs suggests that highway authorities, conservationists, motorists and, above all, proponents of countryside walking lack a proper recognition of the rights and needs of pedestrians on all highways, otherwise more appropriate labelling would be employed.

While the more important elements of the network were being selected and upgraded by highway authorities for use by wheeled vehicles, most of the lesser paths, bridleways, tracks and trails continued to hold an ambivalent place within what had become 'private property'. This located their standing and future in the vexed field of socio-political structures and relationships which readily attracts diverse campaigners. The ascendancy in the Western world of Judeo-Christian principles had long since established the freedom of the individual subject to the law of the land; but it had also established the absolute ownership of land and personal property and the individual's right to privacy. Rights of usufruct administered by socio-political leaders for and on behalf of present and future generations - so characteristic of ancient times in Britain and the present day in much of Africa - were largely superceded but not forgotten. Thus, we still gather blackberries; and the use of paths over private land by members of local communities for time-honoured purposes is rarely contested. But two critical issues emerged some 200 years ago. First, was such use achieved through exercise of a paramount and continuing right of usufruct or was it dependent upon implicit consent of the land-owner? And, secondly, did use by local people, largely for utilitarian purposes but doubtless for some recreation, establish a precedent for unspecified but largely recreational use by the public at large and, indeed, by visitors from other countries? Freedom to roam over open spaces where few if any clear paths existed was and is subject to similar questions.

The importance of these issues to land-owners, land-users and members of the public increased with the growth of modern recreational use of the countryside and with the greater investment in and productivity from much of rural Britain which, in turn, raised

Plate 6.3. The Medieval Bow Bridge and Causeway,
Castleton, North Yorkshire. (Breakell, 1982)

the direct and indirect 'costs' of granting public access to farmland and other parts of the countryside. In short, both risks and stakes increased substantially, especially in recent times. Furthermore, the conservation movement no less than landowners, farmers and rural residents has argued for curbs on public access to the countryside. Something of the history based on contrasting interpretations of these various parties circumstances has been outlined above (Ch.2-4); and the attempt in 1949 to provide a resolution left much room for continuing conflict, campaigning and legislation concerning PRoW, to the neglect and detriment of the basic needs of countryside walking.

3. Public Rights of Way : Problems and Policies

Divergent interests and interpretations of rights led to conflict in the courts no less than the countryside; and the Manchester Society for the Preservation of Ancient Footpaths was formed in 1826 to fight one of the early battles between walkers and land-owners who sought to exclude them. The Highways Act of 1835 made wilful obstruction of any public path an offence; but users had to prove to the satisfaction of the courts that the path was indeed a public right of way. A century of case law did nothing to achieve a concordance and more legislative intervention became inevitable. Eventually the *Law of Property Act (1925)* granted 'the public right to take air and exercise on any common or manorial waste within an urban area'. It was appropriate to deal with accessible commons first, but comparable rights were not granted over the more extensive rural commons and open spaces which were of more importance to land-owners and more interest to minority groups of walkers. *The Rights of Way Act (1932)* followed in an attempt to standardise the conditions and limit the period of public use necessary to prove the existence of a right of way; but all such piecemeal legislation did not satisfy the demands of pressure groups, and in 1947 the Hobhouse Committee was persuaded to recommend:

- *(i) that a complete survey of all rights of way should be put in hand forthwith;*

- *(ii) that footpath law should be drastically revised and simplified;*

- *(iii) that a way used by the public for 20 years should, in all cases, be deemed sufficient to establish a right of way' (Brown, 1949).*

The first and third points were incorporated in the National Parks and Access to the Countryside Act of 1949. The second proved too much for the law-makers; and footpath law has proliferated to such an extent that a definitive book on the subject was revised in 1992 'to take account of the many changes in law and practice since 1983. These include 25 Acts of Parliament and 29 court cases' (Riddall and Trevelyan, 1992).

This study is concerned with policies rather than intricacies of law; and policy is best reflected in purposes. Unfortunately, the 1949 Act has objectives rather than policies and it focuses on means rather than ends. It sought to terminate more than a century of indecision by the production of a countrywide definitive map of all off-road public rights of way; and the intention to secure and publicise all PRoW was a genuine effort to serve walkers rather than land-owners. The underlying notion was that improved maps would promote enjoyment of the countryside, but in terms of access achieved this has perpetuated a very uneven distribution of benefits (Ch.4.4-5). Subsequent revisions of policy have similarly favoured small minorities of established walkers and have shown scant regard for equity and social justice, Consequently, there is still an urgent need for policies based on a clear vision of the future and a purposeful prioritisation of people's needs within a realistic assessment of the means to satisfy them. Unfortunately this was lacking in 1949 when political pressures demanded a solution to the 'rights of way question'; and this tactical concern has continued as a substitute for policy in respect of access for countryside walking.

The identification and mapping of off-road rights of way was already being undertaken in some areas by voluntary groups (Fig.6.1); and it might have been achieved relatively quickly throughout the country if it had been prescribed and properly funded as a purely administrative duty of highway authorities in conjunction with the Ordnance Survey. However, adequate resources were never forthcoming; and psuedo-democratic procedures were not to be by-passed. Furthermore, neither land-owners nor ramblers were ready to yield to arbitration; and each could exercise influence, if not power, at both local and national levels. Consequently, the 1949 Act in effect set new terms of reference for controversy and conflict and relocated them within local government circles, which are much more diverse and probably less impartial than the courts. Shoard (1980) suggests that "the county councils were dominated by landowners. And to make matters worse, they turned for help in the mapping task to a set of administrative units in which the power of the landowners was even more strongly felt - the parishes". On the other hand Denman and Clarkson (1992) report that:

> A determined member of the Suffolk Area Ramblers' Association has made more than 500 claims for amendments to the definitive map, largely through examining detailed historical documentary evidence... Not only does he get

great satisfaction from such an achievement, but he also feels that it is a fascinating activity in its own right.

Such intervention by parties with vested interests was facilitated, intentionally and incidentally, by the complexity of procedures set down for the preparation of definitive maps and written statements identifying each PRoW.

> Under the 1949 Act, before a definitive map may come into existence there has had to have been produced earlier draft and provisional maps; each of these being open to public inspection. Any representations or objections from members of the public about the inclusion or ommission of ways on the draft maps have had to be taken into account, following a local inquiry, in producing the provisional map, with a right of appeal to the Secretary of State against the local authority's decision. Objections by landowners to ways shown on the provisional map have been determined by appeal to the Crown Court. The provisional map has then been followed by the definitive map... All county councils had completed their [initial] maps by mid-1982. (Garner & Jones, 1991).

Long before they were finished, the validity of these maps was challenged on grounds of inaccuracies and ommissions. Furthermore, given the requirement in law for local authorities to respond to requests for Diversion, Creation or Extinguishment Orders in respect of particular PRoW, the maps were rarely static nor ever up-to-date. This unending process of amending the definitive map by Public Path Orders (PPOs) is subject to the same complex procedures of public scrutiny as those outlined above for the creation of the map; and the following organisations secured the right to be notified of all PPOs: the British Horse Society, the Byways and Bridleways Trust, the Cyclists Touring Club, the Open Spaces Society, and the Ramblers' Association; and, for certain parts of England only - the Chiltern Society and the Peak and Northern Footpath Society; and for Wales only - the Welsh Trail Riders' Association. Controversy and conflict were thus extended to new ground; the probability of obtaining a truly definitive map receded; and the Wildlife and Countryside Act of 1981 required that PRoW maps be kept under *continuous review*.

Meanwhile, two significant developments had occurred. First, the size and complexity of the task had called into being a growing and increasingly sophisticated cadre of 'Rights of Way' personnel - and of training courses for them. This extract from a recent advertisement illustrates the point:

> The Senior Rights of Way Officer is responsible, with a staff of seven, for updating and maintaining the Definitive Map, preparing Rights of Way Orders, including giving evidence at inquiries, resolving complaints received, and promoting the use of rights of way... You must possess a degree and have at least three years broad-based Rights of Way experience at a decision-making level. Knowledge of Rights of Way legislation and a valid driving licence are also essential... Membership of RTPI, RICO or equivalent experience of staff management, of public inquiries, and the possession of computer skills are desirable...

By the 1980s a well defined field of employment focused on 'Rights of Way' had emerged; and PRoW were no longer the subject of a finite exercise but of an on-going industry with a life and momentum of its own making. Secondly, in 1981 the Wildlife and Countryside Act granted the Countryside Commission independence of the civil service and greater freedom to define its own role and policies. This allowed a more active interest in PRoW but it was some time before it was moved to action and its 1982 *Prospectus* makes only indirect reference to 'Rights of Way'.

At that time, the Commission's intentions for access and recreation were founded 'on the concept of a multi-use countryside' and depended on a three-point plan to:

- *Review* the provision of country parks, picnic sites, recreational paths and bridleways and small-scale access on farms to see what more is needed.
- *Promote* new facilities and ways of working in the urban fringe and on reclaimed and neglected land.
- *Grant aid* the Ramblers' Association to service a special forum designed to bring together national representatives of farmers, landowners, walkers, riders,and all concerned with countryside access and rights of way.

The distribution of financial support indicates its priorities. The 'three main areas of spending were tree-planting, ranger services, and country parks'; each received more than £1,250,000. In contrast, spending on Long Distance Footpaths was in the region of £150,000 and a similar sum was spent on all other 'recreational routes'. At the same time the Commission intended to distribute some £200,000 p.a. to help voluntary bodies; and organisations cited as examples comprise the National Trust, the Woodland Trust, the British Trust for Conservation Volunteers, the Council for the Protection of Rural England, and the Ramblers' Association. The emphasis on conservation is evident; and the narrow representation of recreation is both disappointing and disturbing. The affinity between the Countryside Commission and the Ramblers' Association recurs in 1984 when the latter was contracted to report on the implementation and effects of recent *Rights of Way Legislation* (CCP.202, 1985). Shortly afterwards the Commission published its ill-conceived tri-partite policy that 'the entire PRoW network be legally defined, properly maintained and well publicised by the end of the century' (CCP.234, 1987).

4. Public Rights of Way : The Price of Maps

Having declared its policy, the Countryside Commission *then* sought basic data whereby it might discern the nature and magnitude of its task and monitor progress towards its targets. Key reports include a survey of *Local Authorities' Involvement with Rights of Way in England and Wales in 1986-87* (CCD.43, 1991); a broadly comparable survey four years later on *Local Authorities' Expenditure on Rights of Way, 1990-91* (CCP.395, 1993); and a *Review of Local Authorities' Charging for Public Path Orders* (Curry, 1996). Collectively, these highlight first, the gargantuan nature and costs of the requirements of PRoW legislation; secondly, the wide range of progress achieved and, perhaps, of levels of commitment by the numerous local authorities; and, finally, the persistent pursuit of unattainable objectives for no clearly defined purpose. Information from the reports may validate these conclusions and provide insights into 'rights-of-way work'.

By 1983 reviews of provisional and definitive PRoW maps were in progress in most local authorities; the earliest had commenced in Northamptonshire in 1968 and Staffordshire in 1969, and the most recent in Durham and West Yorkshire in 1979. 32 authorities responded to a parliamentary request for progress reports and, collectively, they revealed that 20,697 objections had been lodged; inquiries had been held in respect of 5324 of these leading to decisions in 3132 of them. In the light of this information, 15 counties (where a conclusion was in sight) were directed to complete their reviews, and a further 26 were instructed to abandon theirs. The Ramblers Association expressed regret that "the abandonment of these reviews is, in effect, a decision by the Department of the Environment and Welsh Office that they will not be dealing with 15,036 objections made to draft revised maps." (CCP.202, 1985). This view reflects a total disregard for priorities. It also fails to recognise that the concept of a definitive PRoW map is an ideal and, as with any topographical map, only continuous, forward-looking revision may achieve a close approximation to reality. An endless pursuit of history is an academic exercise.

Public Path Orders seeking amendments to definitive maps were already a major component of PRoW work and one which has shown no sign of decline. From 1985 to 1990 there were, on average, 1375 PPOs p.a and in the following five years there were 1744 p.a. (Curry, 1996). The composition of this ongoing task reflects something of its nature. Development Planning generated 26.4% of the 8719 Orders made in 1990-95 ; and a large majority (73.6%) of all PPOs relate to PRoW within the countryside. These may be classified according to their intended function:

Purpose of PPO	*1983-84*	*1990-95*	*Confirmed as Unopposed 1990-95*
Diversion of PRoW	74.3 %	77.4 %	66.7 %
Extinguishment of PRoW	19.5 %	14.3 %	53.2 %
Creation of PRoW	4.0 %	6.1 %	54.7 %
Joint Orders*	2.2 %	2.2 %	58.3 %
ALL Orders	100 %	100 %	63.8 %

* Any combination of the single options.
Sources: CCP 202,1985 and Curry, 1996.

Curry (1996) indicates that 'owners, occupiers and lessees' comprised 85.5% of the principal applicants for such PPOs; and the Ramblers' Association report relates the 1983-84 PPOs to 'the interests of the following parties':

Owner	59.6 %
Owner and Public	14.5 %
Public	10.0 %
Owner and Occupier	6.0 %
Occupier	3.2 %
Owner, Lessee and Occupier	1.6 %
Lessee	0.9 %
Owner and Lessee	0.6 %

Owner, Occupier and Public	0.6 %
Occupier and Public	0.1 %
Not Known	3.0 %

Each source shows that, whereas prior to 1949 the defence of threatened rights of way fell upon user-groups, the onus of initiating amendments to the dynamic pattern of PRoW now lies largely with landowners and occupiers; and they do so primarily in the interests of efficiency in land management and privacy. In 1983-84, only 25% of all PPOs overtly served any 'public interest'. However, taking a wider view, path users no less than land owners and occupiers benefit from any reduction of aggravation and conflict that is achieved by the diversion of a path from a problematic location. This is often recognised; and nearly two-thirds of all PPOs are not formally contested. On the other hand, some protagonists are always inclined to place PPOs in a political arena and challenge them as an erosion of the people's heritage and 'natural rights', though they may well base their overt case on less emotive grounds. In short, diverse vested interests can and do affect the progress of many PPOs; and local authorities have the unenviable duties of broker, arbiter and manager of the whole process until each case is resolved or passed to higher authorities, where they must continue to represent the public.

Furthermore, local authorities have to bear the greater part of all costs; and 'on the evidence available (in 1984) it was far from clear that the resources would prove adequate for the task ahead' (CCP.202, 1985). This has proved to be the case. In 1987 legal work absorbed 26% of all time spent by professional and administrative staff on PRoW work and it cost £1.76m or 13% of all expenditure on PRoW (CCD.43, 1991). By 1991 the cost had risen to £2.44m or 10% of an enlarged budget; and little or none of this contributes to new provision for or promotion of enjoyment of the countryside. To provide some relief, in 1993 legislation extended the option of local authorities to recover part of their expenses on administrative and advertising costs up to a maximum of £400 for an order relating to one path plus £75 for each additional path. Curry (1996) examined the efficacy of such legislation; and identified 'mean and maximum costs in 1993/94 of the stages in the making a PPO'.

STAGE	*Mean (£)*	*Maximum(£)*
(1) Making a PPO, prior to representations or inquiries:	£758	£3000-5000
(2) Written representations:	£502	£1500-3000
(3) Public inquiries:	*£1388*	*£4300-5000*
(4) Determined PPO that is confirmed:	£415	£2800-3500
(5) Determined PPO that is not confirmed:	£200	£1500.

Thus, a PPO that is made, determined without objections, but remains unconfirmed (rows 1 and 5 only) had an average cost in 1993/94 of £958, with a possible maximum of between £4500 and £6500. A PPO that is made, is dealt with through written representations and is subsequently determined and confirmed (rows 1, 2 and 4) had an average cost of £1675, with a possible maximum of between £7300 and £11,500. These two examples indicate mean costs that are susceptible to being recovered under the 1993 Regulations. They are clearly in excess of the £400 maximum... The costs of PPOs that go to public inquiry are, on average, higher than these composite costs, but inquiry costs are specifically excluded from the 1993 Regulations (Curry, 1996). Costs associated with the few cases which reach the courts can escalate in an alarming fashion; but once committed on behalf of the public to the due process of law, local authorities find it difficult to withdraw. In summary, Curry's report reveals the high cost to the public purse of complex administrative and quasi-democratic procedures; and, secondly, the paltry effects the 1993 regulations would have on such spending. More recent legislation allows local authorities to recover somewhat larger sums; but any substantial transfer of costs to PPO applicants could have adverse effects on the public good if those feeling in need of path diversions should be persuaded to turn to less costly but potentially more aggravating means of achieving their objectives.

Pursuit of the law in respect of PRoW for a half-century has achieved much of value and real benefit to the countryside walker. However, established procedures empower minority groups at the expense of the public; and the need for more cost-effective procedures was aired in a Discussion Paper of 1988 which concluded that:

> Although generally accepted as being fair and judicious, the present procedures make heavy demands on everyone's scarce time and resources... A way forward has therefore to be found so that the rights of way network can be adapted better to meet today's demands and expectations *and truly become a resource for all to enjoy...* In 1947 Sir Arthur Hobhouse's committee referred to the need for "a simple and effective machinery (to adapt the path network) to meet changing local conditions and farming practice as well as the changing needs of the public"... The Commission (now) looks forward to the comments and suggestions that will be made, and to working with its partners to develop solutions which will stand the test of time for the next forty years. (CCP.254, 1988).

Unfortunately, the discussion was partly pre-empted by a statement in *A Study by the Ramblers' Association'* which concluded that:

> It may be that there is scope for speeding up the handling for applications for orders, although without consultation there would be no way, prior to the making of an order, for ascertaining the likely degree of opposition to the proposal. There may also be scope for authorities and central government to handle orders more expeditiously. *But we do not find anything which suggests that the basic procedures can easily be modified without denying to one or more of the parties rights which are currently protected by the procedures.*

Rights rule ! And another decade has passed and a new millenium has begun, and there is still urgent need for 'simple and effective machinery' to deal with PPOs.

Given the experience and expertise developed over the years, there is a strong case for radical change which builds on established strengths. Full and final executive authority could be exercised in each highway authority by a small panel comprising professional Rights-of-Way officers assisted, perhaps, by two or three elected councillors. Interested parties should continue to be notified of each PPO and allowed to submit written comments within a specified period; and any interested party inclined to dispute the findings of the panel should have access to the courts as a first and last resort. This is a relatively authoritarian approach, but it grants professional officers the respect they deserve and may well serve the public better than costly procedures which exploit and abuse democracy and impose excessive demands on the public purse.

An item from the 1987 survey of local authorities' involvement with rights of way adds weight to this proposal. The request for an estimated date of completion of the definitive PRoW map and the number of person-years required for the task generated many 'politically correct' replies. In 1987 30 county councils expected to have finished by 1995 - and none of them did so! Ten more realistic responses revealed 'major outstanding work':

County	*1987 Predicted Completion Date*	*Person-years Required in 1987*
Devon	2040	50
Cornwall	2008	60
Suffolk	2005	48
Northumberland	2005	25
Shropshire	2000	48
Bedfordshire	2000	20
North Yorkshire	1997	30
Warwickshire	1997	30
Leicestershire	1993	20
Surrey	1991	35

Eventually, in August 1998, the Isle of Wight became the first County to achieve the triple target of completing its map of PRoW, maintaining paths along all of them, and publicising them - if only by use of signposts. However, this holiday island with only 827 km of PRoW is a rather special case. More generally, the mapping of PRoW and processing of PPOs are major, ongoing tasks; and, as noted above, the relentless pursuit of an elusive definitive map merits early reconsideration.

> Was it necessary in 1987 for the Countryside Commission to grant first priority to completion of the task of giving legal definition to every known, presumed or alleged public right of way ? Where a very large majority of all possible PRoW have been so defined and proven, is urgent completion of the map a necessity, a question of law, or a point of principle and pride ? Residual tasks often are particularly difficult and expensive, and may not provide a sound or the best return on resources. Before pursuing any such case the costs and benefits together with the 'opportunity costs' of not being able to deploy elsewhere resources thus expended should be carefully assessed. At some stage, priorities must take precedence over policy... Decisions to defer for an indefinite period progress towards legal definition of disputed, probable or possible bits of the growing 'network' should be logged in outline - and the case be suspended *sine die* while retaining the option to take it up at some later date. Such positive inaction should not adversely affect walking over

paths not yet underpinned by a legally defined PRoW; and any legal action against or by 'trespassers' would probably re-activate the case. (Kay, 1994).

5. Public Rights of Way : Patterns of Progress

The merit of unquestioned acceptance of ancient rights as the basis for present and future access to the countryside is challenged not only by the cost of mapping PRoW but also by the patchwork patterns of key relations produced by recent and current policies and practices. For example, if PRoW were uniformly distributed through space, the aggregate length in each county or highway authority would be a function of its size; but PRoW, people and resources are not evenly spread and 'densities' of each are weighty matters. Thus, for example, with a population of only 338,000 and a rights-of-way budget of £527,000, Dyfed has more PRoW (9362 km) than seven other counties with a combined population of 3,577,000 and budget of £1,044,000 (Table 6.1). Can Dyfed afford to maintain so many PRoW ? Does its population require them ? Does any 'national need' require them ? and if so, who should pay for their 'development' ?

The densities of PRoW in the several counties (Fig.6.2), no less than the size of the counties and of their populations (Table 6.1), are products of geography and history; but even at this crude scale some general patterns emerge. The lower densities are broadly coincident with the well farmed counties of Eastern and Midland England and, secondly, with the sparsely settled upland regions of Northern England and the South-West peninsular. The higher densities occur in the closely settled counties of the South-East; in the 'down and scarpland' counties of Dorset, Somerset and Wiltshire, and on through Monmouth and Worcestershire, with an off-set extension into the hills and vales of the Welsh Marches; and, finally, along a smaller axis from Lancashire, through Derbyshire and possibly into Leicestershire. London and the other Metropolitan Boroughs comprise another distinctive set of places; and all such diversity calls for *a co-ordinated national scheme of place-related policies and priorities* Without an adequate spatial scheme for directives, guidelines and resource allocations, independent initiatives by local authorities within a simplistic national policy are likely to accentuate the diversity of conditions affecting access to and enjoyment of the countryside. People will benefit or suffer according to their address.

Expenditure on PRoW work supports this argument. Under present policies and directives, there is a *prima facie* case for expenditure to match the length of PRoW; and this would be reflected in a narrow range of spending per km of PRoW. In fact, this index extends from £176.80 per km in Surrey and an average of £154.04 in the 'top' five counties to £20.50 in Powys and an average of £25.74 in the 'bottom' five (Table 6.2 & Fig.6.3). How may this be explained? Differences in the length of PRoW each county is blessed or burdened with are a significant factor. Table 6.1 is structured on the rank order of length of PRoW in each of the 44 counties; and the list falls neatly into quartiles with 'mean rank scores' of 6 (ie the mean of 1-11), 17, 28 and 39. If any other factor is distributed in comparable order, it too will have this profile of mean scores for its quartiles. Conversely, an entirely random distribution of any factor would provide a mean rank score of 22.5 for each quartile, a base-line from which departures may be measured. In the case of expenditure per km of PRoW there is a marked and consistent reversal of the mean scores for each quartile:

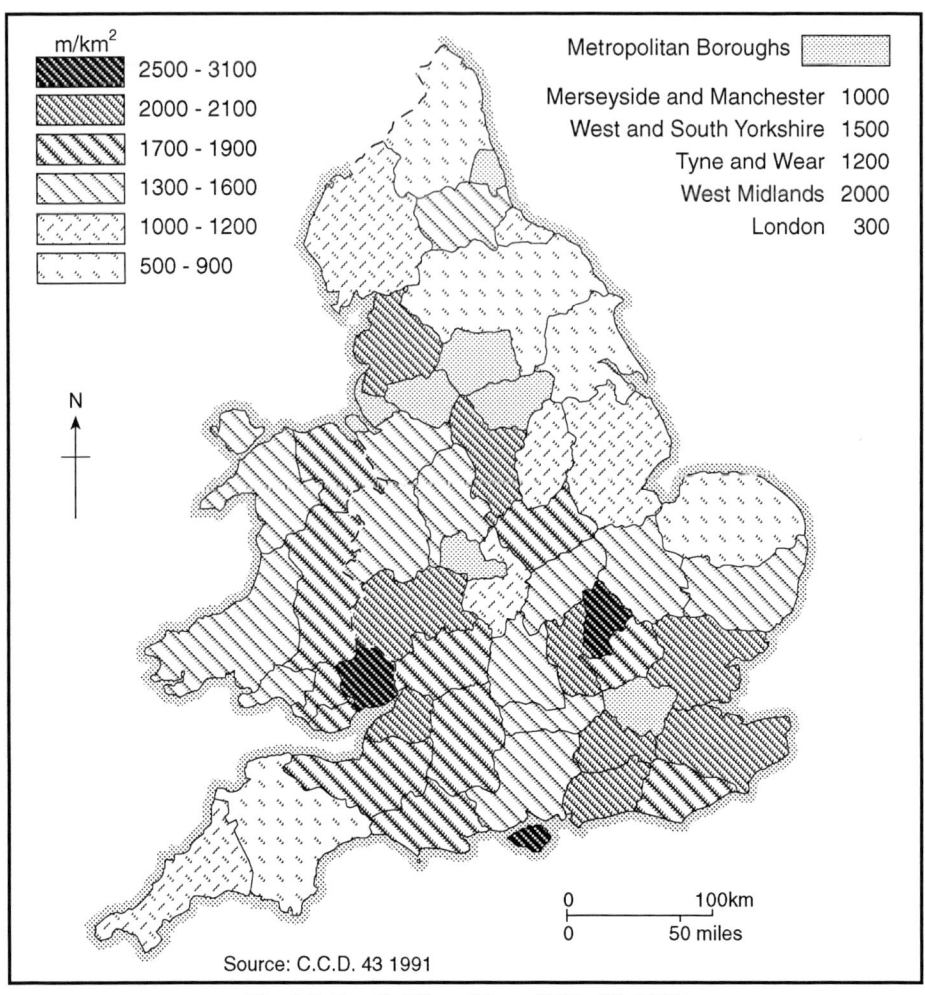

m/km²
- 2500 - 3100
- 2000 - 2100
- 1700 - 1900
- 1300 - 1600
- 1000 - 1200
- 500 - 900

Metropolitan Boroughs
- Merseyside and Manchester 1000
- West and South Yorkshire 1500
- Tyne and Wear 1200
- West Midlands 2000
- London 300

Source: C.C.D. 43 1991

Fig.6.2 Spatial Densities of PRoW, 1987

The 1987 and 1991 surveys of local authorities' involvement with rights of way - CCD.43, 1991 and CCP.395, 1993 respectively - are key sources and have provided the data for Tables 6.1 and 6.2 and for Figs.6.2-6.5. In 1987 three of the 47 county councils in England and Wales did not respond and while they participated in 1991, six others did not; so the common base lacks nine (19%) of the principal actors. The 1987 survey provides the prime bench-mark data and the more comprehensive coverage; and 1991 data therefore are cited only when they signal important changes or afford significant new insights. Both surveys encountered some difficulties in the collection and interpretation of data, but much of real value is systematically documented for the first time; and even taken as indicators rather than definitive statements, many findings show an urgent need for fundamentally new directions. These somewhat obscure reports deserve more attention than they appear to have received.

Place	PRoW (km)	PRoW/Sqkm Metres	Rank	Pop/km PRoW Number	Rank	£s/km PRoW £s	Rank	MSC Labour Person-years
Eng & Wales	200,039*	1300	—	237	—	£69.9	—	1670
England	163,637*	1300	—	275	—	£72.8	—	1410
London & MBs	10,164*	1350	—	21541**	—	£189.2	—	242
All (44) Counties	189,875*	1300	—	169	—	£60.6***	—	1428
1. Dyfed	9362	1600	22	36	43	£56.3	25	57.5
2. Powys	9000	1800	13	12	44	£20.5	44	6.7
3. Here'd & Worcs	8000	2000	8	82	37	£59.9	22	50.0
4. Kent	7725	2100	4	194	19	£55.4	26	5.4
5. Cumbria	7500	1100	37	65	41	£30.2	40	0.1
6. Essex	7300	2000	8	207	17	£56.9	24	132.2
7. Lancashire	6395	2100	4	216	14	£75.6	19	35.0
8. Lincolnshire	6000	1000	38	95	34	£45.5	34	100.0
9. Wiltshire	6000	1700	18	91	35	£33.3	39	31.5
10. Somerset	5980	1700	18	75	39	£49.4	33	12.0
11. Gwynedd	5819	1500	24	40	42	£51.3	30	84.5
12. Suffolk	5714	1500	24	109	32	£58.1	23	6.0
13. N. Yorks.	5600	700	41	125	30	£55.0	27	60.0
14. Shropshire	5077	1500	24	77	38	£22.1	43	70.0
15. Devon	5000	700	41	197	18	£103.9	06	89.8
16. Cambridge	4800	1400	27	131	27	£41.2	35	10.0
17. Leicestershire	4800	1900	12	182	21	£26.4	42	16.0
18. Gloucestershire	4777	1800	13	107	33	£52.3	28	57.5
19. Clwyd	4461	1800	13	90	36	£41.1	36	11.0
20. Northumberland	4438	900	40	68	40	£29.5	41	28.0
21. Staffordshire	4265	1600	22	340	7	£36.6	38	2.0
22. West Sussex	4025	2000	8	172	23	£81.9	18	0.0
23. Gwent	4024	2900	2	109	31	£98.2	10	30.0
24. Bucks	4000	2100	4	431	3	£50.8	31	6.0
25. Bedfordshire	3880	3100	1	134	26	£49.4	32	0.0
26. Oxfordshire	3751	1400	27	150	25	£90.6	14	1.0
27. Cornwall	3575	1000	39	126	29	£95.5	12	10.2
28. Cheshire	3327	1400	27	284	12	£103.1	07	124.3
29. Surrey	3279	2000	8	311	9	£176.8	01	0.0
30. East Sussex	3247	1800	13	209	16	£71.3	20	0.2
31. Durham	3149	1300	32	191	20	£51.4	29	20.0
32. Northampton	3040	1300	32	182	21	£38.6	37	0.0
33. Avon	2882	2100	4	327	8	£90.0	15	10.2
34. Hertfordshire	2832	1700	18	348	6	£98.9	09	2.0
35. Norfolk	2681	500	44	268	13	£62.7	21	15.0
36. Nottinghamshire	2677	1200	34	374	5	£147.0	04	0.0
37. Warwickshire	2254	1100	36	213	15	£90.8	13	50.1
38. Humberside	2082	600	43	410	4	£99.4	08	19.0
39. Mid-Glam.	1828	1800	13	297	11	£149.8	02	3.7
40. Berkshire	1712	1400	27	431	3	£96.3	11	1.0
41. West Glam.	1184	1400	27	308	10	£82.8	17	37.0
42. Isle of Wight	965	2500	3	127	28	£89.9	16	10.0
43. South Glam.	724	1700	18	541	2	£149.7	03	30.0
44. Cleveland	718	1200	34	785	1	£146.9	05	0.5
1991 data								
(a) Derbyshire	5266 - 13	2000	8	176	23	£96.8	(11)	
(b) Dorset	4800 - 17	1800	13	137	26	£57.5	(24)	
(c) Hampshire	4887 -15	1300	32	316	9	£87.9	(17)	

Table 6.1 PRoW, Population and Resources by Counties, 1987

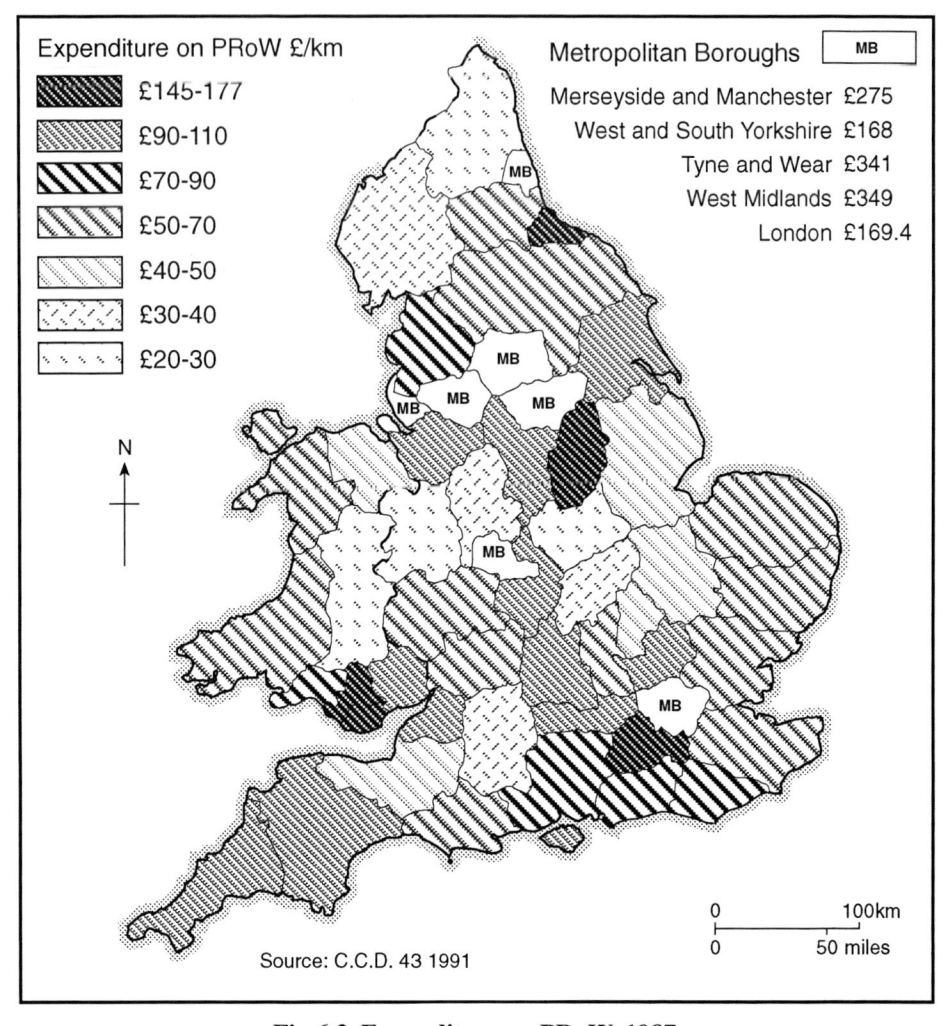

Fig.6.3 Expenditure on PRoW, 1987

Expenditure per Km PRoW (b) by 44 Counties Ranked by Length of PRoW (a).
(a) Length of PRoW.   Mean Rank Score.   (b) £/km PRoW.   Mean Rank Score.
    1st Quartile   06th   1st Quartile   30th
    2nd Quartile   17th   2nd Quartile   30th
    3rd Quartile   28th   3rd Quartile   20th
    4th Quartile   39th   4th Quartile   10th

In short, while there are some exceptions - Devon generously spent £104 on each of its 5000 km while Northamptonshire spent no more than £38.6 on each of its 3040 - *generally, the more PRoW a county has, the less it has to spend on each km.* In particular, the 11 counties with least PRoW on average were able to spend 55% above par while the 22 with most PRoW on average spent 33% below par (Fig.6.3). Clearly resource allocations do

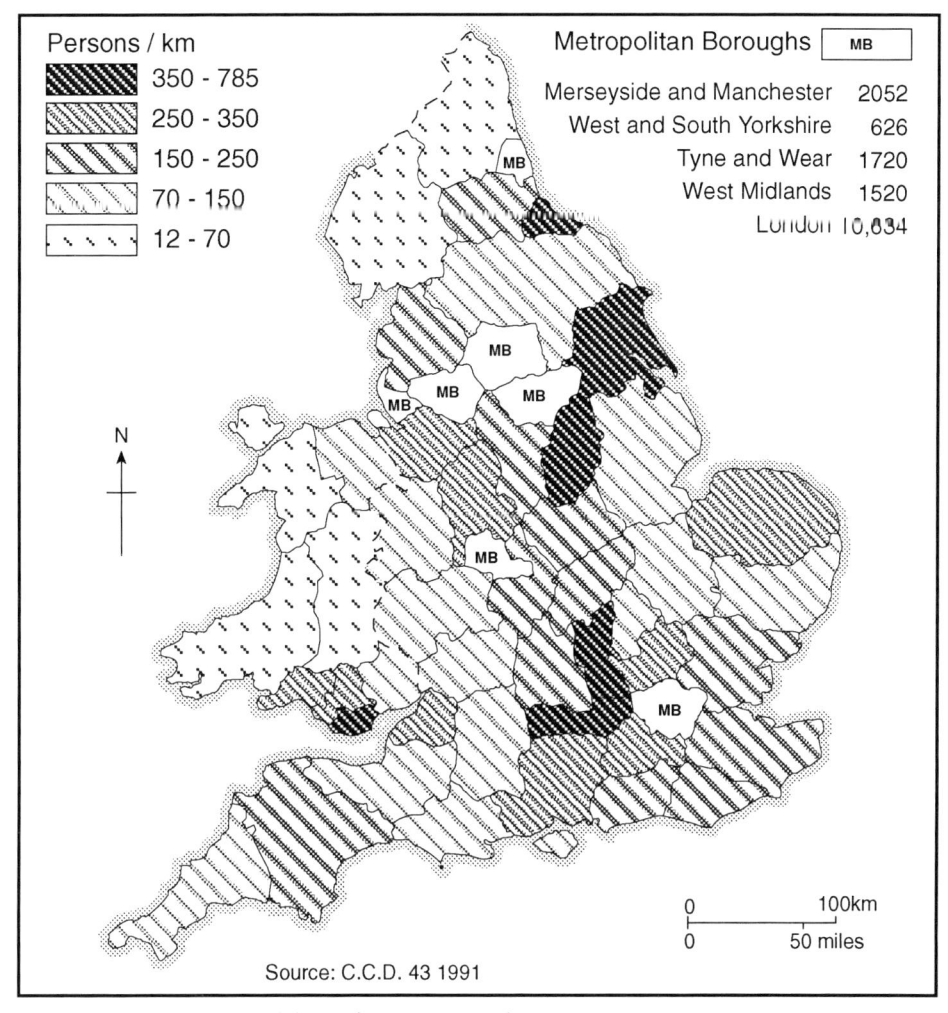

Fig.6.4 Resident Population and PRoW, 1987

not remotely match need as reflected by length of PRoW; and this must create markedly different capabilities to respond to any universal policy requirement of substance which relates to all PRoW.

Spending on PRoW, in fact, generally exhibits a close relationship with the size of the county's population, and the latter may well affect the revenue available to the local authority. Populations per km range from 785 in Cleveland and an average of 508 for the 'top' five counties to an average of only 44 per km in the 'bottom' five (Table 6.1 and Fig 6.4). Comparison of the two rank-order data sets on lines set out above shows a close and consistent relationship between population/km and resources/km:

133

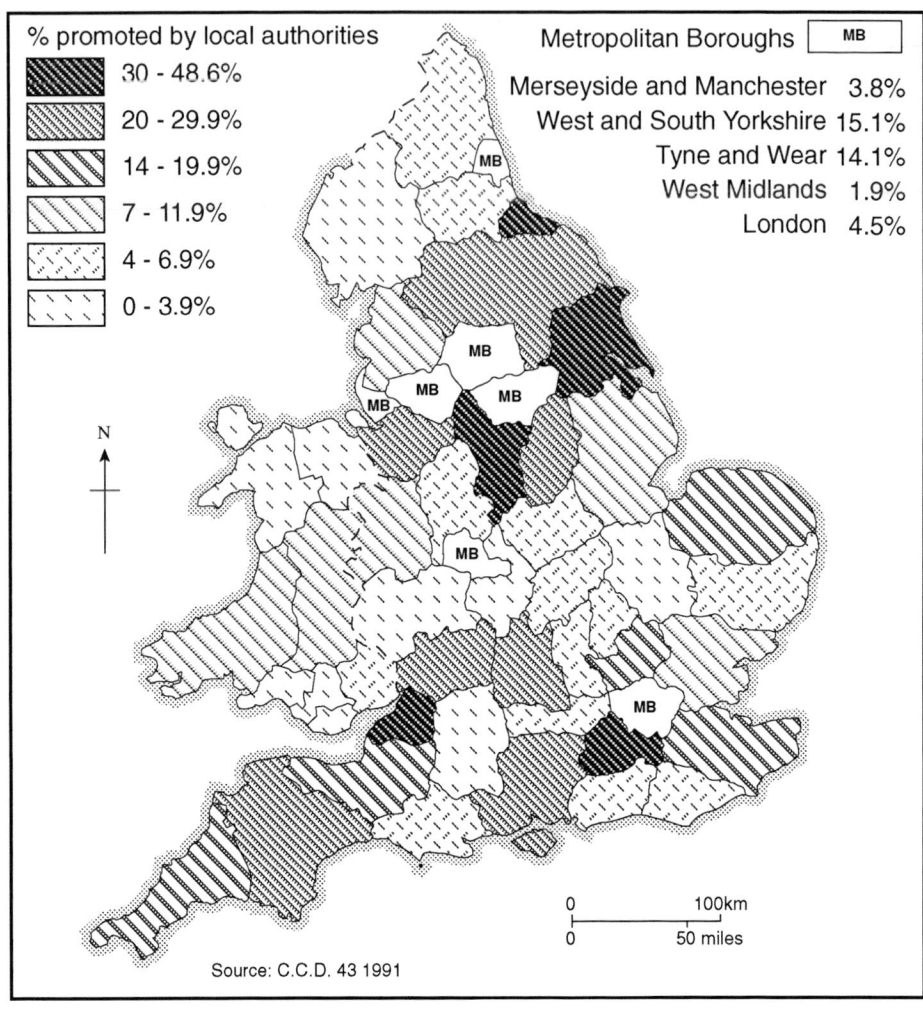

% promoted by local authorities
- 30 - 48.6%
- 20 - 29.9%
- 14 - 19.9%
- 7 - 11.9%
- 4 - 6.9%
- 0 - 3.9%

Metropolitan Boroughs MB
- Merseyside and Manchester 3.8%
- West and South Yorkshire 15.1%
- Tyne and Wear 14.1%
- West Midlands 1.9%
- London 4.5%

Source: C.C.D. 43 1991

Fig.6.5 Promoted PRoW, 1987

(a) Expenditure/Km PRoW by 44 Counties Ranked by (b) Population/Km PRoW.

(a) £./Km.	Mean Rank Score.	(b) Pop./Km	Mean Rank Score
1st Quartile	06th	1st Quartile	09th
2nd Quartile	17th	2nd Quartile	20th
3rd Quartile	28th	3rd Quartile	30th
4th Quartile	39th	4th Quartile	31st

In summary, the counties best equipped in terms of resources are those with a small length of PRoW and/or a relatively large population; and counties with small populations and substantial lengths of PROW are likely be seriously disadvantaged.

The deployment of resources may be affected by the level of available funding, and although there is a wide range of spending patterns within each set, the difference between 'rich' and 'poor' counties, (measured in terms of cash available per km of PRoW), seems to be an influential underlying factor (Table 6.2). In the country as a whole, Practical Work, (as distinct from Staff) accounts for 43% of all spending; but while the eleven richer counties spend equally on each, staff costs absorb 63% of the poorer counties' funds. Both 'rich' and 'poor' allocate half of their expenditure on Practical Work to 'routine maintenance' of paths, bridleways etc. However, this translates into an average of £30.12 per km by the rich counties and £6.26 by the 'poor' ones; and these differences are likely to be reflected in the quantity and quality of physical provision for countryside walking. There are, however, marked differences within each set of counties. For example, amongst the 'rich' counties, Nottinghamshire spent £63.67 per km on routine maintenance while Humberside spent £4.57; and amongst the 'poor' counties, Staffordshire spent £10.54 while Cambridgeshire spent only £2.66.

The development and promotion of paths generally receives the most parsimonious funding, comprising no more than 12% of all spending in the country as a whole. The 'poor' counties spent proportionally more (13%) than the rich ones (9%) but this translates into £4.3 and £11.3 per km respectively; and the difference shows in the product (Fig.6.5). With the exception of Lincolncolnshire (12%), all the poorer counties promoted less PRoW than the national average (12%). In contrast, while four of the richer counties performed below the national average, seven of them have distinguished achievements in this field:

County	All PRoW	Promoted PRoW in 1986/7	
		Length	*%*
Surrey	3279 km	1246 km	38
Devon	5000 km	1050 km	21
Cheshire	3327 km	965 km	29
Humberside	2082 km	958 km	46
Hertfordshire	2832 km	566 km	20
Nottinghamshire	2677 km	535 km	20
Cleveland	718 km	352 km	49

Five other counties promote 20% or more of their PRoW (Avon, 34%; North Yorks, 27%; Gloucs, 25%; I.o.W, 25%; and Oxford, 21%) while 11 promote less than 5%. The availability of adequate funding is an important factor; but determination to give priority to recreational use of PRoW is no less vital. For example, although Devon declared in 1987 that it did not expect to complete its definitive map until 2040, it had already positively promoted over 1000 km (21%) of its PRoW. Evidently concern for path-users figured more prominently in its priorities than PRoW maps. Lincolnshire, Cambridgeshire and Staffordshire also exhibit substantial concern for walkers through their significantly above-average allocation of funds (24%, 21% and 20%) to the promotion of routes. However, being 'poor' counties with extensive networks of paths, collectively they were able to promote no more than 7% of their 15,000 km of PRoW. The legacy of history no less than the paucity of funding denies evident expression of their ambition to serve path-users.

Imperfect though they may be, the main findings of all such recent enquiries into

	Total Spending £ per km	% of Total on Practical Work	% of Practical on Maintenance	% of Total on Promotion	% of PRoW Promoted
England	£69.9	43 %	51 %	14 %	12 %
& Wales	(£132.9)*	(43%)*	(56%)*	(15%)*	
All Counties	£63.9	43 %	48 %	12 %	12 %
'RICH' Counties	**£125.5**	**50 %**	**48 %**	**9 %**	**22 %**
1.Surrey	£176.8	39 %	69 %	7 %	38 %
2.Mid.Glam	£149.8	58 %	77 %	1 %	3 %
3.Sth.Glam	£149.7	48 %	31 %	9 %	3 %
4.Notts.	£140.0	71 %	61 %	19 %	20 %
5.Cleveland	£146.9	64 %	11 %	21 %	47 %
6.Devon	£103.9	47 %	50 %	11 %	21 %
7.Cheshire	£103.1	31%	68 %	6 %	29 %
8.Humberside	£99.4	46 %	10 %	16 %	46 %
9.Herts.	£98.9	43 %	48 %	2 %	20 %
10.Gwent	£98.2	72 %	29 %	4 %	6%
11.Berks.	£96.3	36 %	74 %	8 %	6 %
'POOR' Counties	**£33.2**	**37 %**	**51 %**	**13 %**	**5 %**
34.Lincs.	£45.5	46 %	48 %	24 %	12 %
35.Cambs.	£41.2	38 %	17 %	21 %	2 %
36.Clwyd	£41.1	14 %	75 %	11 %	3 %
37.N'thpton	£38.6	37 %	68%	12 %	6 %
38.Staffs.	£36.6	43 %	67 %	20 %	6 %
39.Wilts.	£33.3	22 %	53 %	9 %	2 %
40.Cumbria	£30.2	58 %	52 %	5 %	2 %
41.N'umberland	£29.5	39 %	33 %	5 %	6 %
42.Leics.	£26.4	18 %	91 %	4 %	4 %
43.Shropshire	£22.1	34 %	19 %	15 %	9 %
44.Powys	£20.5	60 %	39 %	15 %	9 %
11a Derbyshire*	£96.8	52 %	86 %	12 %	32 %

Table 6.2 Spending on PRoW by 'Rich' and 'Poor' Counties, 1987
*1991 data show Derbyshire as an additional 'rich county'.

the progress of rights-of-way work support the view that the Countryside Commission's aims and objectives in respect of the legal definition, condition and promotion of all PRoW and related paths were indeed 'unrealistic, unnecessary and unhelpful'. Secondly, they show that the dispersal of responsibility for interpretation, prioritisation and implementation of national policy amongst numerous local authorities with markedly different circumstances and capabilities has inevitably led to a wide variety of responses and conditions which, in turn, confounds the implementation of current policy. There is no 'logic' in the outcome. The development of fundamentally new approaches for the countryside as a whole and the nation are evidently overdue.

6. Which Way Forward ?
For the Countryside Commission there has been no turning back; and in 1987 it saw no need for new legislation nor any new approach to PRoW work:

> Problems surrounding the rights-of-way network are legion... Perhaps the greatest indictment is that much of the rights of way network is perceived as unavailable to those who wish to use it. People appear to be most worried about their rights in this area... The primary responsibility for both the rights of way network and for facilitating and managing wider access to open land rests with local authorities. It is right that this should remain so... *Further, we have concluded that there is no practical benefit in advocating major changes in legislation or to the extent of the rights of way network. This would divert attention from the real need which is to make the existing network fully available as a means for people to enjoy the wider countryside.* (CCP.225, 1987).

When it declared its policy that the entire rights of way network be legally defined, properly maintained, and well publicised by the end of the century, the Commission was not unaware of resource implications, but it understated needs to the point of trivialising them and made no attempt to systematically address the marked variety of conditions in different parts of the country:

> Of course this will cost money, but the sums involved are not large. A properly maintained rights of way network represents a good investment for the tourism and recreational benefits it can bring. Costs can be further reduced by involving Manpower Services Commission teams and volunteer groups. Farmers and landowners can also be used as local authority agents. The sharing of experience could be improved and more training courses set up for staff working in this field. (CCP.234, 1987).

However, determination to proceed was soon tinged with an increased element of realism if not doubt; but the dispersed locus of responsibility for progress was stressed:

> We shall continue to pursue the target of having all public footpaths and bridleways in good condition and usable by the year 2000. This target has been endorsed by the Government and main Opposition parties. We now look to all highway authorities to adopt the target in their own areas, with well thought-out programmes to attract Commission grants. (CCP.348, 1992).
> The target comprises a bold, ambitious challenge that has caught the imagination and received widespread support... The local authorities have, in the main, responded extremely well... and by 1991 annual expenditure on the network had risen from the 1987 figure of less than £14 million to £26.5 million... and the number of full-time equivalant staff working on rights of way has climbed from 581 in 1987 to more than a thousand.
> Nevertheless, the Commission felt that further assistance was needed to enable local authorities to see more clearly what they needed to do... The result was the

launch of *The Milestones* initiative in November 1993. Milestones encourage highway authorities to adopt a strategic approach to planning their work... and in the future grant aid will be linked to the production of a strategic planning document for rights of way work (Smith, 1994).

The Milestones Approach (CCP.435 & 436, 1993) calls for each highway authority to prepare a detailed year by year programme of costed work that will define, clearly and realistically, what remains to be done and will allow progress towards the national target to be monitored. At first sight, such 'marching orders' could hang millstones round their necks, especially during any period of declining resources; and could commit them to a long-distance challenge likely to exhaust the capability and commitment of many. On the other hand, if the Countryside Commission is able and willing to recognise harsh realities and admit a sufficient degree of flexibility, it could allow imaginative authorities to plot new directions (Kay, 1994).

The Approach re-presents the national target as 'three distinct components' rather than three successive phases; and this may allow steps towards achieving each of the objectives in three separate, parallel programmes, and progress to be plotted in each with reference to local priorities within the limits of available and anticipated resources rather than in relation to prescribed priorities and a single deadline. Such flexible approaches might emphasise PRoW as means to an end rather than an end in themselves; and admit schemes which give first priority to 'target three' which lies on the interface between 'people and place'. Purposeful selections of PRoW in relation to needs of identified sectors of the population could thus lead to the design, development and promotion of specific routes for countryside walking which, collectively, may serve the needs of the public as a whole. Granting priority to enjoyment of the countryside in this way could well exhaust available resources while embracing only a minority of PRoW; and this might extend the 'milestones' in respect of targets one and two into the distant future. While not surrendering any right of way, this might be read as subversion of the Countryside Commission's declared policy. On the other hand, it may be seen as an opportunity for the Commission to recognise and endorse the merits of approaches which it might not feel able to advocate openly.

Who will lead the way ? is an open question. In practice, several authorities and recreation officers have introduced people-oriented approaches and, to varying degrees, have set aside the Commission's target in order to serve people better. This, however, leads to piecemeal progress within the patchwork of local authority areas; and a comprehensive revision of national policy which identifies the real purposes of and priorities for PRoW is thus urgently needed. The Countryside Agency should address this need promptly rather than sustain flawed policies and approaches bequeathed by the Commission. The case for this will be explored further in the following chapters, first with reference to public paths before turning attention to routes and then to the promotion of walking as one of the principal means of enjoying the countryside.

Plate 6.4 Enjoying the countryside.
(Illustration from an Annual Report by Staffordshire's *Operation South Cannock*)

Attractive countryside is a pleasing product of man and nature; but a truly accessible countryside depends more specifically on quality provision and regular maintenance of at least basic facilities for walkers. Such provision requires substantial investment in terms of materials and, more particularly, managment and labour. These are essential for the creation and preservation of a marketable countryside which, in turn, is a prerequisite for the promotion of countryside walking to the nation as a whole.

7
PUBLIC FOOTPATHS - FIT FOR WHOM?

Only one respondent in ten rated the countryside as "good" for sign-posted walks and bridleways. (Ashcroft, 1996).

Over half of our public rights of way are unavailable to all but the most determined and agile person. (Blunden and Curry, 1989).

Far too many public footpaths have an atrocious surface - in critical places if not for extensive stretches and for lengthy periods if not continuously. They are waterlogged; ankle-deep in mud or worse; rutted; eroded down to rubble; overgrown with thistle and thorn. Many are beset with serious impediments to use, notably in the form of hindrances thrown up by nature run-wild and farmers intent on farming but also from obstacles provided in the guise of stiles, difficult flights of steps or stairs, plank-bridges and stepping-stones. While much of a route may be tolerable or even comfortable to most fit, able-bodied adults, the occurrence of half-a-dozen such 'black-spots' and barriers can ruin a short walk for many path users and deter thousands who understandably fear such conditions. (Kay & Moxham, 1996).

1. 'Natural' and 'Artificial' Paths

Footpaths should facilitate not detract from enjoyment of the countryside (Plates 1.1, 6.4 & 7.1). Such enjoyment depends substantially on interaction with the surrounding landscapes and one's companions; and any time necessarily spent negotiating obstacles or looking where to put one's feet must reduce the overall experience. The history of considered provision for recreational walkers (Ch.1.4) allows ready identification of the principal properties of an ideal path. The surface will be durable, smooth and even; firm but preferably yielding rather than hard; well drained and never water-logged. The path will be clearly visible; wide enough for at least two to walk side-by-side; and free from any physical obstruction or hindrance and extraneous impediment. Where necessary, it will be equipped with bridges, stepping-stones, gates, stiles, steps or stairways which are easily negotiable and have a carrying capacity consistent with above average traffic along the path. Integral aids for navigation along either prescribed or self-selected routes, such as sign-posts, way-marks, and basic information on relevant distances and the location of services and facilities, amenities and hazards, should all be clearly visible, readily intelligible and sufficiently frequent to reassure both novices and strangers to the area. Additional furniture and fittings such seats, information and interpretation boards, toposcopes and viewing platforms also contribute to walkers' enjoyment of the countryside.

Such ideal provision has substantial resource implications, but it should be the target on routes promoted for the public as a whole, including children, the aged, and the less able; and also in popular locations where intensive use justifies and requires quality provision to maximise enjoyment of both the landscape and one's companions. On the other hand, as noted above, experienced, determined and agile walkers, shod and equipped for all conditions that 'nature' may throw at them, do not need and probably do not wish for such comfort. They can cope with and even enjoy basic conditions. In short, investment in paths should relate to the market sector for which particular routes are intended and promoted; and this implies policies driven by people's needs rather than an historic pattern of PRoW.

Unfortunately, 'artificial paths' attract much unjustified criticism which reflects misplaced affection for 'natural paths', a concept that derives its legitimacy from the creation of footpaths by erosion comparable with that responsible for animal tracks (Plate 6.1). These time-honoured, no-cost products have considerable merit and an important role in much of the countryside. Many 'natural paths' of modest dimensions do blend with and contribute to the 'natural beauty' of their environs; and, though rarely ideal, many are satisfactory for well equipped, experienced walkers. However, in many cases they have become increasingly insufficient and inappropriate. Common deficiencies include a tendency to channel walkers into Indian-file, which is detrimental to social interaction; and if lightly used they are readily over-grown during the summer months. Also, where the surface soil and sub-strata cannot sustain heavy use, 'natural paths' are readily subject to excessive erosion which undermines their utility and inflicts damage on the ground.

Erosion is likely everywhere on steep slopes, no matter how short they are; and at all points, such as approaches to stiles and bridges, where there is a concentration of impact. In more fragile environments where the nature of the climate and weather, relief and geology, soils and vegetation, all conspire to admit powerful erosive forces, well worn paths are seriously vulnerable over extensive lengths. Formidable natural processes remove surface materials, excavate channels and expose uneven, often stony surfaces. Being uncomfortable if not unsafe, these are readily abandoned by walkers in favour of a nearby parallel line and a fresh surface which, temporarily, affords an easier passage. In the absence of managerial intervention and the provision of a stable path, walkers thus create yet another 'natural path'; and as successive paths become unacceptable, this process will be repeated while space is available (Plates 7.1, 7.5 & 7.6).

Such action may well involve trespass through departure from PRoW, but this is of little consequence to most walkers who simply seek to maximise their safety, comfort and enjoyment of the countryside. However, more extensive ecological damage and adverse visual effects also are inevitable, and will be extended as erosion widens the path or spreads to more supplementary paths. A delicate balance of processes has been disturbed without any precautionary or compensating provision of protective or remedial measures; but it is unreasonable that blame should be laid at the feet of walkers who were behaving rationally and reasonably in the given circumstances. Nevertheless, at least three sets of issues are evident: aesthetic, ecological and managerial; and farmers' may add a fourth concerning costs! The first two have readily acquired champions and excessive prominence which, in turn, have diverted attention and resources from the initial problem. The origins of this contentious amalgam lie in the history of inappropriate policies, under-funding and inadequate management of provision for countryside walking; and for too long this has left walkers heavily dependent on 'natural paths' of their own making and provided conditions which inhibit rather than promote enjoyment of the countryside.

Plate 7.1. Natural Paths... Overdue for Attention.

2. The Condition of Paths on PRoW in 1988 and 1994

Basic information is a vital aid to understanding, planning and management; and the Countryside Commission eventually organised surveys of paths on PRoW, though it has yet to survey the use of them. In 1988 all PRoW within 131 randomly selected 5x5 km grid squares in England and Wales were surveyed by 1200 volunteers; and in 1994 some 2000 volunteers surveyed 294 such areas selected to embrace each Highway Authority in England. The latter allowed a revised estimate of the length of PRoW in England which now comprises 169,000 km (105,000 miles) - some 10% less than the previous estimate but still 2.5 times as extensive as Britain's road network. These PRoW comprise 132,000 km of pedestrian rights (78%); 29,000 km of bridleways (17%); 5000 km of RUPPs and 3000 km of BOATS (5%).

Each survey required a significant element of judgement in classifying qualitative features, and consequently the perceptions of the surveyors are critical. Unfortunately, a random sample of the population could not be engaged; and dependence on volunteers meant that most were experienced path-users and 'many were members of the Ramblers' Association or other voluntary access groups' (CCP.504, 1996). Their views are likely to be markedly different, and generally more tolerant of discomfort, than those of occasional and novice walkers; and a broad-based behavioural approach to the assessment and interpretation of path conditions by the wider public is not yet available.

The surveys and their findings were structured to reflect a set of conditions walkers would encounter on each 'link' - or 'path' - on the PRoW maps, a link being a length of PRoW between successive junctions of any two 'highways'. They are mostly short and the average length of the 23,800 surveyed in 1994 was 397 metres (about a quarter of a mile). Finally, it is important to note that the 1994 survey covered significantly different proportions of types of farmed land. In 1988 arable and mixed farming (in which cropland has a substantial role) carried 37% of all surveyed PRoW and 54% of those on farmland. The comparable figures in 1994 were 24% and 42%; and these substantial reductions, by 24% and 22%, should be reflected in comparable reductions in path conditions associated with cultivated land.

The ease or difficulty of being able to follow a route is a matter of importance to walkers; and the surveyors, equipped with Path-finder (1:25,000) OS maps and the definitive PRoW maps, found that in 1988 and 1994, 82% and 89% of the links were accurately shown on the OS maps. The utility and limitations of such maps are thus confirmed and, valuable as they are, they can lead to difficulties in identifying and following PRoW. These will be compounded if paths are not clearly visible and if sign-posting and way-marking are deficient. In 1988 only 33% of PRoW leaving metalled roads had a signpost but 42% were so equipped in 1994. This still leaves the majority without signposts; and the observed rate of improvement will not complete the task until 2033. Way-marking at such junctions raised the proportion signed in one way or another to 45% in 1994; but 'vegetation obscuring signposts and damage to or removal of signs' reduced the proportion which were 'easy to find' to 41%. However, 27% of the junctions without any sign were easily found by the surveyors, bringing the total of visibly accessible roadside junctions to 68%.

While there is no legal requirement that the junction of two or more PRoW should be marked, it is important that they too should be clearly visible and each component of multiple junctions should be readily identifiable. These conditions are part of the official 'targets' for PRoW (CCP 436, 1993); but in 1994 only 22% of footpath junctions were equipped with signs, and only 50% were 'easy to find' by any means. This reflects a deterioration since 1988; and while it is easier to follow bridleways, byways and RUPPs because of their greater visual prescence, overall 'the data indicated a one-in-three chance of [experienced] users being unable to find the start of a link' (CCP. 504). However, generally, by 1994 ability to follow the paths had improved and 62%, rather than 51%, of all links were easy to follow.

Such data on route-finding is difficult to summarise in a meaningful fashion for the general public. On the other hand, it is all too simple to deduce, as the 1998 report did, that a random choice of a 2.5 mile walk would comprise, on average, ten 'links'; that only three of the nine junctions would be readily negotiated; two of the 'links' might be traced with the aid of a map, but one would be difficult or impossible to follow. Confident, experienced and well equipped walkers may readily tackle such a statistical probability; but most people will walk only where they believe the whole of their intended route will be evident without resort to any map, still less a compass. And if they did venture onto less certain ground and became 'lost', they probably would retreat in dismay and be more reticent in future. In short, prevailing conditions may be irksome to regular path-users but a positive deterrent to novices.

The physical condition of paths also is a matter of real importance to walkers. In 1994 73% of the footpath links were 'satisfactory', 15% were 'poor', 10% 'unusable' and 2% were not classified. However, the surveyors were not asked to record 'very good' or even 'good' conditions that might encourage inexperienced walkers to explore the countryside; and there is no explanation as to why such qualities were omitted. Consequently the bland conclusion that a large majority of the links were 'satisfactory' leaves no room for complacency; and provides no indication of the proportion of PRoW that might be attractive to the public as a whole.

> What is acceptable to hardened, hairy-legged and heavy-booted ramblers and athletic, lycra-clad challenge walkers in lightweight trailblazers should not be represented as being suitable for the public as a whole... (and)... it is unreasonable, even deceitful, to represent any Public Right of Way as a Public Footpath if it is not equipped with a path suitable for the public. (Kay and Moxham, 1996).

In fact, 25% of the paths were found to be 'poor' or 'unusable' by the surveyors because of (i) *unacceptable surface conditions* due to over-grown and over-hanging vegetation (7%); crops and cultivated ground (6%); muddy, boggy and flooded surfaces (3%); and rough surfaces (2%); and (ii) *barriers* - such as walls, fences and hedges - without satisfactory *'crossings'* over them (6%). Although 49% of all paths were entirely free of barriers, the walkers encountered 27,064 'crossings'. Stiles (12,162 - 45%) were the most numerous; and 10% of these were in need of attention and 2% were declared 'unusable'. Gates were the second most common (36%); and 11% were unsatisfactory and 5% unusable. Deficiencies in respect of bridges (11%) and flights of steps (5%) were less frequent; but other minor forms of crossings such as board-walks, stepping-stones, railings and culverts had above-average short-comings. Most barrier-crossings, whether in a good condition or otherwise, are often problematic to many people, notably the aged, very young persons, those whose standards of fitness and agility are below average, and the disabled. However, an assessment of the suitability of crossings with reference to their paticular needs will require further surveys.

Meanwhile, at face value the 1994 survey indicated a modest improvement since 1988 of 6% (from 67% to 73%) of paths which were satisfactory *at a basic level*, and, if there is no deterioration on the paths found to be satisfactory, this rate of change, if valid, would bring all paths on PRoW to a similar condition by 2020. However, the two surveys are not strictly comparable; and an apparently dramatic reduction in 'unusable' links due to 'crops, ploughed surfaces and impenetrable natural vegetation' must be partly due to the 25% reduction of arable and mixed agricultural lands in the 1994 survey. As the *Technical Report* put it, 'the *apparent* improvement may not necessarily reflect a real improvement on the ground' (CCP.504, 1996). Finally, neither survey was concerned with quality provision, which is so essential if countryside walking and enjoyment of the countryside are to be more accessible; and such ommissions, alongside that of the use of PRoW, bring into question the general purpose and design of the enquiries.

3. Survey Findings as Weapons and Tools

Information can be effective only insofar as it reaches and moves institutions and individuals with influence and power, authority and responsibilities in relevant fields; and any substantial body of new information should provide an opportunity for reflection and consideration of better means to serve fundamental purposes. However, each of the surveys was evidently intended to facilitate progress towards the declared aim that by the year 2000 all PRoW be equipped with paths that are *'satisfactory at a basic level'*. And if there was no initial hidden agenda in 1988, one soon emerged. It was to clarify and amend the distribution of power and duties between land-owners and farmers on the one hand and highway authorities and path-users on the other. This area of concern had been signalled in a report on *Ploughing Footpaths and Bridleways* (CCP.190, 1985) and in a code of practice in respect of *Ploughing and Rights of Way* (CCP.214, 1986) which achieved such a disappointing response that the Countryside Commission decided 'to look again at the whole issue of ploughing and cropping' after the winter of 1988/89 (Hickey, 1988; *Countryside 33*).

Even so, if read carefully with the interests of the wider public in mind, several of the summary conclusions from the 1988 survey could and should have informed a programme for widening access to more people, rather than making more paths more readily accessible to current users:

> More than one-half of all rights of way are effectively unavailable *to those without the skill to use a map and the confidence to assert their rights.*

> A major characteristic of the network is the unpredictability and uncertainty of what will be encountered. The condition of the network is *a strong deterrent to anyone using unfamiliar paths or exploring new areas.*

> The number of path links and length of rights of way that are unusable or usable only with great difficulty are a relatively small proportion of the total - *but these small sections spoil enjoyment of the whole network.* Re-establishing a right of passage over these unusable sections is not an unrealistic task and is achievable at a comparatively modest cost*. Dealing with these problems would have a dramatic effect, significantly increasing *the usability* [rather than *the use* GK] *of the entire network at a basic level.*

> The responsibility for carrying out the practical tasks that are needed rests, in broadly equal measures, *with highway authorities and the farming community.* (*Managing Rights of Way: An Agenda for Action*, CCP.273, 1989; italics by the author).

> * The 'modest cost' was estimated to be 'an extra £50,000 to £150,000 per year over the next ten years by each of the 103 highway authorities in England and Wales' (*Countryside 39*, 1989). At an average of £100,000 this would require an additional £10.3m p.a. whereas in 1986/87 total expenditure by all highway authorities on all PRoW work was £10.7m. (CCD.43, 1991).

It is self-evident that 'usability at a basic level' is adequate for regular and frequent walkers; and improving the worst paths provides more choice for the privileged few. More important questions concern what needs to be done to make carefully selected paths accessible for more people; but social equity was not on the agenda and the only path conditions fully explored in the body of the report are those produced by 'Ploughing and Cropping', which were evidently offensive to those who frequently encountered them.

> For **many people** the problems of rights of way that are ploughed and not adequately restored, or are affected by growing crops, are the single most important factor influencing their use, and enjoyment, of the network... Ploughing and cropping has a disproportionate and wholly unacceptable impact on **the public's** enjoyment of the rights of way network... Unless the problems of ploughing and cropping can be resolved, many of the resources invested elsewhere in the network will effectively have been wasted. The need is for immediate, coordinated action... the aim must be to ensure that every farmer is quickly made aware of the law and takes steps to comply with it as a matter of course. We do not see this as placing an unreasonably onerous burden on the farming community. (CCP.273, 1989).

Within the space of four lines, 'many people' was translated into 'the public'; and then *Countryside Commission News No.39* took up the cry and presented the problem in wholly unjustifiable behavioural terms, which could possibly apply to a walker dropped at random from a helicopter but not to a 'walk worked out at home from an OS map':

> Take a walk of two miles, *worked out at home from an Ordnance Survey map...* and you are very likely to run into at least one of a host of problems and difficulties that could spoil your enjoyment. *In fact, you stand a two in three chance of not being able to complete your walk at all...* Try a five-mile walk and the chances of getting through are less than 1 in 10. *How about a ten-mile walk?* Unless you already know the area like the back of your hand and are prepared to put up with a lot of bother, then *the advice has to be don't even try...*

> Top priority has to go to dealing with those problems that make paths unuseable... The job is not just one for highway authorities. Local communities and volunteers can play a part... But above all farmers must follow the 'Ploughing Code', quickly restoring ploughed paths and keeping them free of crops. If they do not, highway authorities will have no alternative but to enforce the law, a time-consuming, unpopular and expensive process.

The mass media heard the story and the press had a field day. A Private Member's Bill was at hand, won all-party support, and led to the *Rights of Way Act, 1990*, just in time to apply to the autumn ploughing of that year. The Ramblers' Association hailed this Act as the most significant piece of legislation on rights of way for many years (Hickey, *Countryside 46*, 1990); and the Countryside Commission's Chairman perceptively noted that 'people who *regularly walk in the countryside* should have fewer complaints'.

Although not blameless, the highway authorities were not subject to such pointed criticism as the farming community; and a growing awareness of the need for increased resources and of the complexity of superficially simple tasks may have contributed to the more measured approach to their responsibilities. Between 1987 and 1991 public expenditure on rights-of-way was increased by 90% and staff dedicated to such work, by

75%. Then *The Milestones Approach,* with its stick and carrot tactics, was introduced in 1993 'to help local authorities develop the full potential of the rights-of-way network'; and the second national survey of path conditions was directed at highway authorities rather than farmers (CCP.504, 1996). Its declared objectives were:

- to provide a statistically valid profile of the English rights-of-way network and to identify improvements on the ground since 1988;
- to provide information about the state of the network at the individual highway authority level; and
- to establish baseline information for local authorities to use for measuring their progress towards the National Target and for preparing their Milestones Statements.

Despite the substantial increases in resources and manpower, 'improvements on the ground since 1988' were modest if not minimal; but there was no protest or outcry. On the contrary, there was evident determination to disguise disappointment, to provide encouragement and, once again, to press onwards towards the National Target. This approach was neatly summarised in George Samuels' half-term report - *"Good progress being made but must continue to work hard"*. Some explanation and possibly a hint of apology also were offered:

> One thing seems to be certain... the scale of the task is far greater than that envisaged in 1987... (and) while many authorities are working systematically to open up paths and improve signing, others have been slowed down by protracted legal issues and negotiations... (Also) the considerable progress made by better-resourced highway authorities is obscured by the more limited achievements of poorly-resourced authorities. (*Countryside 74*, 1995).

The utilitarian rather than political use of the 1994 data is also evident in estimates of work required to achieve properly maintained paths on all PRoW. The basic 'shopping list' for England comprised the provision of an additional 184,000 signposts at path/road junctions; way-marking of at least 17,200 links which are 'difficult to follow'; the repair or re-building of 72,000 stiles, 30,000 gates and 6,000 bridges; and the removal of 30,000 other obstructions. Detailed lists were compiled for each county and metropolitan borough; and each was classified as 'average' or 'significantly better/worse than average' in respect of several parameters. A summary of conditions in counties with above and below average standings in respect of key criteria is offered in Table 7.1. Five of the seven metropolitan districts are high achievers but only nine counties win any significant accolade and only five of them score well in all areas. At the other end of the spectrum, six counties have uniformly poor conditions and five are significantly below average in one or two. Many factors must contribute to this diversity of conditions but the 'better-resourced' authorities are most likely to achieve the better results. Comparison of spending per km of PRoW in 1987 (Table 6.1) with path conditions in 1994 supports the key role of resource availability.

County or M.B.	Total Score	Signposts-Way-marks A	B	C	Easy to Follow	Easy to Use	Good Surface	£/km 1987
ABOVE AVERAGE								
Buckinghamshire	+39	+3	+3	+3	+10	+10	+10	£50.80
Berkshire	+36	+3	+3	a	+10	+10	+10	£96.30
Derbyshire	+36	a	+3	+3	+10	+10	+10	N.D.
Greater London	+33	p	+3	p	+10	+10	+10	£517.30
West Yorkshire	+33	p	+3	p	+10	+10	+10	£112.70
Surrey	+26	+3	+3	a	+10	+10	a	£176.80
West Midlands	+23	p	+3	p	+10	+10	a	£178.70
Greater Manchester	+20	p	a	p	a	+10	+10	£269.70
Hertfordshire	+19	+3	+3	+3	+10	a	a	£98.90
Oxfordshire	+19	+3	+3	+3	+10	a	a	£90.60
West Sussex	+16	+3	+3	p	+10	a	a	£81.90
Essex	+16	+3	+3	a	+10	a	a	£56.90
Hampshire	+16	+3	+3	a	+10	a	a	N.D.
Tyne and Wear	+13	a	+3	a	+10	a	a	£288.20
BELOW AVERAGE								
Northumberland	-36	-3	-3	a	-10	-10	-10	£29.50
Norfolk	-36	a	-3	-3	-10	-10	-10	£62.70
Shropshire	-36	-3	-3	a	-10	-10	-10	£22.10
Lincolnshire	-33	a	-3	g	-10	-10	-10	£45.50
North Yorkshire	-33	a	-3	a	-10	-10	-10	£55.00
Warwickshire	-33	-3	-3	g	-10	-10	-10	£90.80
Durham	-26	a	-3	-3	-10	-10	a	£51.40
Hereford & Worcester	-26	a	-3	-3	-10	-10	a	£59.90
Suffolk	-20	g	a	g	a	-10	-10	£58.10
Northamptonshire	-16	g	-3	-3	-10	a	a	£38.60
Gloucestershire	-13	a	-3	a	-10	a	a	£52.30

Table 7.1 Counties and M.B.s with Path Conditions Above and Below Average Standards in 1994

The scores reflect significant departures from average conditions in England in respect of the provision of signposts and/or way-marks at A - PRoW-Road junctions; B - PRoW-PRoW junctions, and C along PRoW links; and, more importantly, where general conditions provide paths which are Easy to Follow; Easy to Use; and have a Good Surface.

Each Authority achieving at least one score of +/- 10 is included. The occurrence of 'average' conditions is shown by 'a'; and where not indicated by the notional scores, above and below-average conditions are shown by 'g' (good) and 'p' (poor) ; but no adjustment has been made to the total scores. Sources: CCP.504, 1996 and, for expenditure/km of PRoW, CCD.43, 1991.

The spatial pattern of conditions is of some importance, and it will be of little comfort to the nation as a whole to learn that all but one of the nine counties with above average quality are in the South East; and, secondly, that none of the eleven with below average conditions is in that region, and only two are in the South-West. However, this apparently sharp North-South division should not distract attention from the more important message that there is no underlying spatial basis for progress in respect of path management; and, secondly, that there is an urgent need for policies which do relate to 'people *and* place' rather than to ancient rights, history and current spending power. Meanwhile, in contrast to the outrage generated by the 1988 survey of paths, the broadly similar findings of 1994 led to 'business as usual' in terms of 'a number of ways in which systems of managing the rights of way network could be improved, *to make better progress towards the National Target* and to ensure effective management beyond the year 2000' (CCP.506, 1996); and there is still no emphasis on quality provision in places best able to serve those who currently find enjoyment of the countryside largely inaccessible.

4. Responsibilities for Managing Paths on PRoW

History, geography and politics have created disparate sets of legal responsibilities and resource providers which confound path-management. The underlying problem is the need to obtain public sector provision of an unrestricted facility for diverse users on private property which has a variety of functions; and, secondly, a dearth of effective means to manage path-users. These problems distinguish PRoW to such an extent that they are perceived as being an independent category of highways rather than part of a national network; and most highway authorities have delegated their responsibilities for them to local government departments with interests in recreation. Nevertheless, highway authorities or their delegates are responsible for all legal processes necessary to create and maintain definitive maps of all PRoW. They also 'own' and should maintain the surface of all PRoW while the underlying ground remains the property of the land-owner; and they are responsible for the visible identification of PRoW, and this should be achieved whether or not PRoW are signalled by a path.

However, they are not responsible for traffic management over PRoW and users more or less manage themselves, relying heavily on visible paths which may or may not lie on PRoW. PRoW are fixed until altered by law but paths, and especially 'natural paths', are re-aligned and duplicated, mostly at very local levels, as users adjust their route in the light of prevailing conditions on the ground and their own immediate intentions. Also, unless in continuous and substantial use, paths are likely to disappear beneath crops or natural vegetation. Consequently, even when equipped with OS maps and compasses, most users are not usually aware of the precise line nor the prescribed width of the PRoW; and departures from them, and from paths which are in any way less attractive than adjacent ground, are commonplace. Walkers will cut corners, literally and metaphorically; and they will evade inconvenience and discomfort whenever possible. They are out to enjoy the countryside and the company of their fellows, not to observe niceties of the law. All such transgressions will have various effects on the ground, such as damage to crops, grazing and natural vegetation; and the widening and duplication of paths by erosion. Blame is often directed at path-users but the underlying causes often are ineffective marking of the PRoW, poor maintenance and clearing of surfaces, and the inadequate physical

Plate 7.2. Compliance with the Law can be Costly to Arable Farmers.

carrying capacity of the paths, particularly at crossings over barriers.

Responsibilities for keeping PRoW free from obstructions, hazards and hindrances and convenient for use, hopefully by the general public, are nicely shared between landowners and highway authorities or their agencies. In general terms, farmers are responsible for any inconvenience generated by their use of the land; and highway authorities are responsible for difficulties thrown up by 'nature'. Thus, within brief defined periods, farmers must make good the surface of any cross-field path damaged by ploughing or other disturbance; or blighted by any crop - other than grass which apparently is deemed to be innocent of any inconvenience despite the range of conditions it can provide. Unless otherwise stated in definitive documents, a cross-field PRoW designated as a footpath is granted a minimum width of one metre while a field-side or headland path, which must not be cultivated, has a minimum width of 1.5m. Bridleways have twice the width of footpaths. So, to provide for a 2.5 mile walk through cropland requires deliberate destruction by farmers of an acre of crops; and they are thus subject to a 'triple whammy' comprising the costs of ploughing and sowing, the costs of undoing the same, and the loss of income from space given over to walkers (Plate 7.2). The benefits to the public are in proportion to the use made of each path and while some may be heavily and frequently used, most are used lightly and infrequently. Implicit cost-benefit ratios are of some interest and practical concern to farmers - why should they sacrifice so much for so little ? - but they are of no consequence in law nor to path users.

Farmers must not plough or otherwise disturb or obstruct field-side PRoW; and they must keep them free from over-hanging obstructions by hedges and trees which they

Plate 7.3. An Obstacle in the Guise of a Stile !

own. Highway authorities are responsible for other conditions along these headland paths - and also on most other PRoW like those between two boundary hedges or walls. Given the paucity of public resources and the fact that headland paths are not readily accessible from public roads, many of them are seriously neglected; but their condition rarely generates a furore comparable to that directed at farmers who neglect cross-field paths. A walker's letter on *The Nightmare of Headland Paths* therefore is noteworthy.

> I have often found myself, by the end of summer, attempting to walk a headland path that is waist-high in docks and thistles. This jungle can hide brambles, discarded barbed-wire, large stones and clods of earth... It makes one's footwork a nightmare. Small wonder that I find ample evidence that fellow walkers have moved out from the field-edge and trampled the crop... Could the law not permit an occupier of land to plough or disturb the surface of the whole field, including any field-edge path, provided re-instatement is made in terms of the Rights of Way Act 1990 ? (Ron Fisher, Malvern, Worcs. *Countryside 78*, 1996).

In such circumstances, being too few to effectively combat rampant weeds and other wildlife, even hardened walkers naturally trespass and trample crops or grass to avoid the discomfort and difficulties of over-grown PRoW; and, in this case, at least one walker hopes that farmers might rectify the situation on behalf of local authorities. This is not fanciful thinking and, as an editorial footnote stated, 'several highway authorities were testing arrangements to pay farmers to maintain field-edge paths'.

This prospect is an extension of a 'radical new approach to maintaining and improving public rights of way by paying farmers to do work such as repairing stiles, clearing and resurfacing paths 'which was introduced on an experimental basis in 1987 following a pilot scheme in the North York Moors National Park (*Countryside 34*, 1988). Catriona Cook, 'a farmer and avid lover of the countryside' spelled out a logical conclusion of such developments and argued that 'If farmers were paid not only for the maintenance of rights of way but also for the existence of paths on their land... (they) would regard rights of way and the public as a business asset and would look after them'. (*Countryside 37*, 1989). This anticipated Pennington's wider argument that conservation and enjoyment of the countryside should be managed by market forces rather than quangos (Pennington, 1996); and changes in this direction may be viable *if applied selectively to paths where use justifies the expenditure*. However, such prioritisation would not only question the justice of requiring farmers to clear every cross-field path but also the merit of relentlessly pursuing the national target for all PRoW. It would, in fact, require a radical shift in policy and strategy to evaluate PRoW in terms of their utility for countryside walking, and selected routes would be more important than the alleged 'network' in its entirety.

Meanwhile progress has provided ample precedents for co-operation between local authorities and farmers, notably in respect of crossings over necessary barriers across PRoW. Land-owners or farmers are still responsible for the provision and maintenance of stiles, gates, etc on their property but they may now claim 25% or more of the cost from public funds. Some local authorities provide materials rather than payments and are thus able to influence the nature and quality of the crossing. Nevertheless, many stiles and gates comprise an obstacle rather than a facility (Plate 7.3); and when demand exceeds their carrying capacity, even those in good condition may impede walkers and generate queues. Frustrated individuals then take detours over 'alternative crossings' which may be dangerous to themselves and damaging to the property of others. Such action may be reprehensible and indefensible but it is understandable and reflects a need for ample quality provision; and this, in turn, raises questions concerning restrictions imposed or rather implied by the width of PRoW.

Crossings over 'natural barriers' such as rivers and streams, gullies, boggy and swampy ground generally fall on the highway authorities. In many cases, simple measures such as stepping stones, plank-bridges and board-walks may be adequate but substantial bridges and other structures often call for costly maintenance or re-building (Fig.7.4). Expenditure on such work can decimate annual budgets or lead to temporary closure of PRoW on grounds of safety; and, ultimately, to questions as to whether the route and its use, rather than the 'right' merit the necessary expenditure. Responsiblity for the onerous and expensive task of keeping the surface of all paths on PRoW in good repair raises similar questions, though in less dramatic fashion - except where water-logging is frequent (Plate 1.1) or erosion is rampant (Plate 7.5).

Plate 7.4. Woodside Bridge, Exmoor.

> Condemned after 40 years of service as unsafe, a replacement in 1994 cost only £8000, thanks to voluntary inputs by the Royal Engineers and National Park Staff. The full commercial cost of some £35,000 would embarrass most Highway Authorities.

Perhaps the most difficult duty for local authorities is enforcement of the law in respect of the condition and utility of paths on PRoW. This places them in an invidious position since they are a major partner in the provision and management of paths but often are unable to carry out their own duties to good effect. Nevertheless, they are required by law to assert and protect the public's rights to pass and re-pass along all public rights-of-way and to ensure that land-owners, farmers and other land users comply with the law in respect of PRoW. They not only have to be 'advisor and counsellor' to both parties but also to act as both 'police and prosecutor' in respect of any breach of the law which is drawn to their attention. And they have to accept assistance from victims of breaches of the law and from voluntary guardians of the law, who may be one and the same person and either a farmer or a rambler. This responsibility implies regular inspection of all PRoW - to identify any need for action in terms of maintenance by the authority itself or for persuasion and law enforcement in respect of offences by farmers and land-owners or path users and trespassers. Many highway authorities share this task of problem-spotting with parish councils, recognised local groups and self-appointed individuals; and the Countryside Commission's 'guide to rights and responsibilities in the countryside' positively encourages path-users to become involved:

> Report problems you find on rights of way to the highway authority... give them as much information as possible about exactly what was wrong, where and when. Give the exact location, including grid reference if you can, or mark

it on a map. A clear photograph of the problem, with the date and time it was taken written on the back can be useful, as can the names and addresses of any other witnesses... If you are unfortunate enough to have to complain about a number of problems, it is helpful to tell the authority any that you think need especially urgent action... The highway authority will normally investigate and respond to complaints as quickly as they can...(but)... If you feel the authority's officers are not responding as they should, then you may wish to raise the issue with one or more local councillors... or the chairman of the appropriate committee... Very exceptionally, it may be necessary to contemplate more extreme action... (CCP.186, 1990 & 1992).

This reads like an instruction manual for agents of a pressure group; and while it may well encourage and legitimise action by articulate protectors of peoples' rights, it is not likely to move the average path-user. The response therefore will be affected by the spatial activity and concerns of committed individuals; and this maverick element, in turn, affects the input of effort and resources by local authorities.

Any reported or observed breach by farmers of the 1990 Rights of Way Act can subject highway authorities to particularly onerous duties. Farmers have been advised that:

The Act removes the uncertainty that has existed about the authority's powers to take direct action to deal with a problem... The Act gives the authority power to enter onto your land, carry out any work it considers necessary, and to recover its costs. Such action may be taken whenever the authority believes an offence has been committed under the Act... The powers include a right to enter onto, and to cross with machinery or equipment any land you occupy... and providing the authority acts reasonably at all times, it will not be liable to you for any damage... Carrying out the work yourself, as and when it is required [by the Act] will almost invariably be cheaper and quicker than any default action by the authority. (CCP.299, 1990).

Given the practical difficulties local authorities encounter in carrying out their duties on headland paths, the bizarre prospect of them hiring neighbouring farmers to carry out 'default action' in respect of requirements of the 1990 Act on each others' land comes to mind as an option which might have some appeal to farmers. More intractable scenarios have generated litigation; and all such cases strengthen the argument that a radical review leading to more realistic strategies for the management of paths on PRoW selected with reference to their utility and use is long over due. As Harding might have said, 'Can it be that no-one knows what the 105,000 miles of English PRoW are really for ?'.

5. Manpower for Path Maintenance

Regular repair and maintenance is a key factor in determining the quality of paths and associated facilities and services - and in protecting the countryside from erosion; but there is no evident means to obtain and regulate the necessary inputs in relation to need. On the contrary, path maintenance presents an array of problems which make job-descriptions well nigh impossible and appointments very difficult. It is essentially lonely, low-

County	Manual Labour (person-years)	%	Acc.%	National Parks
Devon	13.8	8.6	8.6	Dartmoor
Gwynedd	12.4	7.7	16.3	Snowdonia
Derbyshire	12.0	7.5	23.8	Peak District
North Yorkshire	10.7	6.7	30.5	N.York Moors & Yorks.Dales
West Sussex	9.5	5.9	36.4	
Dyfed	8.9	5.6	42.0	Pembroke Coast
Cornwall	6.6	4.1	46.1	
Somerset	6.5	4.1	50.2	Exmoor
Hereford & Worcs	5.8	3.6	53.8	
Cheshire	5.0	3.1	56.9	
Cumbria	4.7	2.9	59.8	Lake District
Kent	4.6	2.9	62.7	
Clwyd	4.0	2.5	65.2	
Hertfordshire	3.4	2.1	67.3	
Northumberland	3.4	2.1	69.4	Northumberland

Table 7.2 Counties with Above Average Employment of Manual Labour for Path Maintenance on PRoW, 1987. (Source: CCD.43, 1991)

paid, unskilled manual work, exposed to all weathers and subject to seasonal rhythms. Also, unless done by volunteers for environmental well being, it carries little or no esteem; and unemployment may afford distinct advantages.

Furthermore, most of it is on inaccessible, narrow linear sites which defy all but the most portable power-driven tools; and in some celebrated cases vast quantities of materials have been flown in by helicopters. These characteristics are compounded by inadequate resource allocations which lead to 'make-do and mend' methods that grant the workers no sense of pride and give path-users little long-term satisfaction. They reflect the low priority given to resources for countryside walking and the current need to spread inputs thinly over all PRoW; and this generally deficient funding is compounded by the wide variations between local authorities in the availability and deployment of resources (Tables 6.1 & 6.2). These differences are accentuated by a piecemeal response to adventitious opportunities to supplement the work of paid employees, which in turn, accentuate spatial variations in achievements. Ironically, at the same time, some potential low-cost sources of labour are generally neglected, though their deployment also would probably provide an uneven pattern of inputs. In short, policy and provision for path maintenance on PRoW are in a parlous state and urgently require a comprehensive review.

During his endorsement of the National Target for PRoW in 1990, the Under Secretary of State for the Environment referred to the case for increased resources for PRoW - and suggested that the remedy lay in adjustment of local authority budgets.

The relatively small sum of £14 million a year spent by highway authorities on rights of way made a big return in providing recreational opportunity for millions... (but given that) the total leisure and recreation spending by local authorities is £1 billion a year, only a small reallocation of resources within authorities' budgets would allow significant benefits for informal recreation. (*Countryside 42*, 1990).

The piecemeal response was unlikely to be generous but it would probably increase the range of spending on path maintenance. At present PRoW work is dominated by professional, managerial and administrative staff who comprised 503 or 88% of all full-time employees in 1987. Labour drawn on an ad hoc basis from external sources doubled the input by manual workers to 215 person-years; but 25% of these were deployed in the wealthy Metropolitan Boroughs which had only 5% of the paths. The county councils, with 95% of all PRoW, generally were lightly staffed but expenditure on path maintenance extended from £63.67 per km in Nottinghamshire to £2.66 in Cambridgeshire. By 1991, increased funding and greater emphasis on practical work had effected some considerable change and manual inputs from all sources then comprised 1307 person-years; but, on average, this provided only one worker for every 365 km (228 miles) of PRoW.

1987 data allow some insight to the broad spatial pattern of inputs to path maintenance (Table 7.2). On average, each county employed only 3.4 person-years of labour but six, which embrace six National Parks, benefited from 42% of all inputs; and the 15 with 3.4 or more employed nearly 70% of all manual labour on PRoW. Thus 68% of the counties were served by only 30% of the manual employees; and at the lower end of the spectrum a dozen counties each employed less than one person-year. Was there really so little physical work to be done on paths in the greater part of the country; or was so much left undone?

The response to windfall opportunities offered by the Manpower Services Commission in the form of workers paid largely from central funds clearly shows there was - and is - ample work to be done but simply not enough employment opportunities nor cash to create them. In 1987 path maintenance benefited from 1670 person-years of MSC labour which added nearly eight workers for every one employed by the local authorities. However, the response was very uneven. 21 counties made negligible use of MSC labour; 5 ignored it; 8 took up no more than five person-years and a further 8, no more than ten (Table 6.1). Explanations for this neglect include 'trade union and political reasons'; administrative problems in terms of providing transport, tools, supervision etc; and a broader, perhaps not unreasonable view, that a marked temporary departure from normal inputs could be disruptive and, in the longer term, embarrassing if not detrimental. On the other hand, 12 counties siezed the day and each took on 50 or more person-years of MSC labour (Table 7.3). Collectively they employed 75% of all such workers deployed on PRoW work in 1987. In short, while these massive intakes of MSC labour highlight the need for manual inputs of this order, the variety of responses again reflect the diversity of approaches and circumstances in the several local authorities and the absence of an effective national policy in respect of PRoW. The public as a whole deserve better on a permanent basis.

The contribution of MSC labour was discontinued in 1989; but voluntary workers have continued to provide a supplementary source of labour, albeit on a very much smaller scale. They comprise a useful asset which deserves cultivation provided due recognition

County	Person-Years	%	Acc.%
Durham	200	14.0	14.0
Essex	132	9.2	23.2
Cheshire*	124	8.7	31.9
Lincolnshire	100	7.0	38.9
Devon*	90	6.3	45.2
Gwynedd*	85	6.0	51.2
Shropshire	70	4.9	56.1
North Yorkshire*	60	4.2	60.3
Dyfed*	58	4.1	64.4
Gloucestershire	58	4.1	68.2
Warwickshire	50	3.5	71.7
Hereford & Worcs*	50	3.5	75.2

* Significant regular employer of manual workers (Table 7.2).

Table 7.3 **Major Employers of MSC Manual Workers, 1987.**
(Source: CCD.43, 1991)

is given to its limitations and peculiarities. The report of the *Stockport Rights of Way Project 1989-92* identified volunteers as a source of cheap labour which, in addition to enthusiasm, brought familiarity with local paths, their history and problems; some knowledge of highway law; and ability to generate wider community involvement in path work. On the other hand, common disadvantages included inconsistency in reporting problems; willingness to work only when they wished and on their prefered tasks; limited skills and tools; no insurance; and a need for guidance and supervision. The British Trust for Conservation Volunteers was less encumbered with such disadvantages and offered more advantages - such as access to large pools of experienced volunteers with their own supervisors, transport and basic equipment. On the other hand, BTCV inputs had to be booked in advance, were available only for short, specified periods, and had to be paid for at prices above those for work done by farmers, though considerably less than those of local authoritiy Direct Services Organisations.

Inputs by volunteers have increased in recent years; in 1987 they provided 41 person-years or 16% of all manual workers and by 1991 they gave 109 person-years which comprised 19% of an enlarged labour force. However, the benefits of this adventitious resource also are very unevenly distributed. In the first place, some parts of the country generate more volunteers than others, and they are attracted to some places more than others. Secondly, their deployment is affected by the ability and commitment of local authorities to engage their services; and highly skewed patterns of participation are typical (Table 7.4). In 1987 14 counties engaged none and another 18 each used less than 1.0 person-year. In contrast, 15 counties benefited from 85% of the total input by volunteers; 5 of them received 54%. By 1991 substantial growth in the number of volunteers (from 41 to 109 person-years) and marked change in the leading users reflects the volatile nature of such inputs; but again 14 counties accounted for 71% of the total input (Table 7.4).

Devon is the most consistent major employer of manual workers and user of adventitious sources; and such evident concern for the condition of paths was matched by

(a) 1987	Person-years	%	(b) 1991	Person-years	%
Devon (x z)*	7.0	17.0	Gwent	25.0	23.0
Gloucestershire (z)	6.0	14.6	Essex (z)	16.8	15.4
North Yorkshire (x z)*	3.7	9.0	Devon (x z)*	10.2	9.4
Suffolk*	3.0	7.3	Shropshire (z)	4.0	3.7
Hereford&Worcs (x z)*	2.5	6.1	West Glamorgan*	3.0	2.8
West Glamorgan*	2.0	4.7	Clywd (x)	2.8	2.6
Surrey*	2.3	2.1	Surrey*	2.3	2.1
Berkshire	1.5	3.6	Lincolnshire (z)	2.2	2.0
lywd (x)	1.0	2.4	Suffolk*	2.1	1.9
Cumbria (x)	1.0	2.4	Hereford&Worcs(x z)*	2.0	1.8
East Sussex	1.0	2.4	Cambridgeshire	1.6	1.5
Gwynedd (x z)	1.0	2.4	Lancashire	1.6	1.5
Kent (x)	1.0	2.4	Leicestershire	1.5	1.4
Norfolk	1.0	2.4	North Yorkshire(x z)*	1.5	1.4
Powys	1.0	2.4			

Table 7.4 Leading Users of Volunteers on PRoW Work in (a) 1987 and (b)1991.
(x) - a major employer of manual workers; (z) - a major user of MSC labour.
* Major user of volunteers in 1987 and 1991

the promotion of more than 20% of all of its PRoW in 1987. This emphasis on serving people underlay its pioneering of a particular role for volunteers:

> In October 1986, Devon County Council decided to improve its extensive public rights of way network by developing a hitherto untapped resource - the enthusiasm, goodwill and interest in the countryside of the people of Devon. They were given the opportunity to become actively involved in the management of their paths through a scheme called *'Adopt-a-Path'*. This... encourages parish councils and volunteers to improve the path network by taking part in one or all of the following activities: (i) encouraging the proper use of paths; (ii) helping keep the paths clear and in good order; (iii) inspecting the paths three or more times a year; (iv) reporting on the condition of the paths; and (v) distributing and helping to produce leaflets about the paths. Volunteers come from all sections of the community... from nine-year old Brownies to octogenarians... from organised amenity groups such as the Ramblers' Association and the British Horse Society to an individual using his or her local public rights of way for recreation and exercise. There are also those interested in the service of the community - whether voluntary or otherwise - from Round Tables, Rotaract and Young Farmers' Clubs to the Probation Service for young offenders... Response to the scheme has been excellent. Over one-third of the parishes in Devon are involved. (Barnet, Slee and Townley, 1989).

Devon is a leading example but it was probably preceded in this particular initiative by South Yorkshire Metropolitan Council which had encouraged volunteers to 'adopt a path' for rather simpler reasons.

> *A problem arose from paths which were not being used regularly...* If we could encourage people to walk and ride these, our problems would lessen; and the mere fact that feet and hooves were going along them reduced our problems enormously. The fact that volunteers then reported problems was incidental to the original concept... and another unforeseen bonus was the number of manuscript maps of adopted walks which were then circulated by the council, and will be worked-up for publication as guides. (Gilmour, 1986).

There is a strange logic in this development - (to encourage people to walk unpopular routes) - and it would seem more rational to reverse the pattern and identify, develop and promote the most rewarding routes for the benefit of the public as a whole, while allowing unpopular PRoW to lie fallow. That, however, would challenge the national policy of equipping every PRoW with a path !

Building on such initiatives, in 1988 the Ramblers' Association published *Paths for People: A Guide to Public Paths for Members of Parish, Town and Community Councils*. This recommended that local councils:

> Form a Rights of Way Committee and coopt keen local path users to help carry out regular inspections of all rights of way in the parish; carry out basic maintenance work on behalf of the highway authority; try to resolve problems, such as ploughing and obstruction of paths, with the person responsible; and if this approach is not successful report the matter to the county council and see that the council takes action.

The Countryside Commission backed this initiative and introduced a 'low-cost grants scheme' to help voluntary groups undertake small projects costing upto £1500. This proved to be a testing-ground for the Commission's *Parish Paths Partnership* which links highway authorities, local councils and voluntary groups 'in schemes to keep rights of way open and in use'. Its key features are 'parish grants' paid by highway authorities for projects approved within a formal 'partnership agreement'; and an 'advisory service' via Parish Path Liason Officers who deliver advice, expertise and training at the local level and also administer the parish grant (CCP.370, 1992). The Scheme was launched in 1992 with £3,750,000 available for grants over the first three years. Bureaucracy had arrived; but upto 15 highway authorities were expected to win funding in the first year. 12 did so and a further 15 joined in the following year (Table 7.5).

The 10 English counties with substantial experience of MSC labour and 12 of the 18 with significant prior experience of employing volunteers were amongst the first 23 to join the Partnership scheme; and counties with one or both of these advantages comprise 15 of the 23 early starters. Perhaps it is inevitable that such prior experience should provide a springboard, but it is important to consider the underlying factors which generate such a concentration of initiative and its consequences for the distribution of benefits.

Started in 1992-93	Started in 1993-94
Buckinghamshire	Bedfordshire
Cambridgeshire (c)	Cheshire (a)
Devon (a b c)	Cornwall
Durham (a)	Cumbria (b)
Gloucestershire (a b)	Derbyshire
Hereford & Worcester (a b c)	*Essex (a c)*
Hertfordshire	Hampshire
Kent (b)	Humberside
Leicestershire (c)	*Lincolnshire (a c)*
Suffolk (b c)	*North Yorkshire (a b c)*
Barnsley	*Shropshire (a c)*
Leeds	Somerset (South)
	Warwickshire (a)
(a) *Major MSC employer, 1987.*	Knowsley
(b) *Major employer of volunteers, 1987.*	Wirral
(c) *Major employer of volunteers, 1991.*	

Table 7.5 Counties and MBs in the Parish Paths Partnership Scheme by 1994.

The early success of the scheme confirmed the Commission's original belief that the Parish Paths Partnership has an important role to play in achieving the year 2000 target... Despite cutbacks in other areas, the Commission is maintaining the Partnership as a priority over the next four years... with around £750,000 for every year until 1997/98; *this will enable a quarter of the 8,000 parish councils in England to join the scheme.* While this will allow new highway authorities to join, *the Commission's main priority during this time will be to support the expansion of existing schemes.* (CCP.380, 1994).

The Commission's determination to give priority to existing schemes and the consequent exclusion of 75% of all English parishes must give grounds for concern regarding the factors affecting the spatial occurrence of investment by volunteers in the maintenance and management of paths and, indeed, in all kinds in PRoW work. Which parishes are most and least likely to throw up the requisite cohort of volunteers ? Which sections of the population will benefit from the improvements ?

Such questions are not intended to be critical of practical inputs by volunteers or voluntary organisations *per se*. These generally are commendable and valuable. They not only provide a public service in an under-funded field but benefit the participants too. This is true even, and perhaps especially, in the case of unlikely sources of volunteers. For example, since 1986 teams of mentally handicapped persons have been involved in Surrey; and in 1989/90 they provided 74% of the 3728 'volunteer days' spent on PRoW work in that county. "Their work has given a big boost to the county council... It has also been of great benefit to the team members, many of whom have shown marked improvement in their physical fitness, mental health, communication skills and self-esteem". (Sperrin, 1990). The deployment of young persons on probation on PRoW work in Devon had similar mutual benefits; and the Itchen Hamble Countryside Project also gained from and gave benefits to low security prisoners from a training annex at Winchester Prison (Watson, 1991). Evidently a wider search for 'volunteers' or even for 'pressed men/women' could effect more widespread benefits; and those required to give 'community service' might simultaneously pay their dues and benefit themselves in a variety of ways if they were deployed on PRoW work.

However, it would be a contradiction of terms if genuine volunteers gained neither job-satisfaction nor ancillary benefits; and currently most voluntary workers have their own agenda for participation which, almost inevitably, includes specific rather than general interests in access to the countryside. Therein lies a need for caution and reflection. A preponderance of committed regular path-users and other persons with essentially local interests will affect both the spatial distribution and nature of the benefits for 'the public'. Similarily, schemes devised wholly or in part by them and calculated to appeal to sponsors, including county councils and the Countryside Commission, are likely to favour their own preferences within current policies and targets. In short, voluntary groups are unlikely to be impartial or give priority to the needs of the large majority who are currently disadvantaged in terms of access to the countryside. In summary, the increased and diverse inputs by the voluntary sector undoubtedly go some little way to reducing resource deficiencies; and they add another dimension to enjoyment of the countryside. However, the efforts of volunteers generally support and reinforce existing policies and, secondly, intensify rather than reduce spatial differences in the overall deployment of resources for path maintenance and improvement.

6. 'Natural Paths' and 'Managerial Disasters'

It is odd to the point of being paradoxical that path surfaces should receive so little attention in the surveys of 1988 and 1994. It was noted that 'the surface condition of a path is critical to its enjoyment... and conditions may vary with the seasons... Links deep in mud in winter may turn into dusty hard-caked ruts in the summer'. (CCP.504, 1996); but surface conditions were merged with obstruction of the surface, and the reasons for 22% of all links having a poor or impassable surface in 1994 were as follows:

Condition	% of all links	% of poor or impassable links
Crops/cultivated surface	7 %	32.7 %
Overgrown natural vegetation	6 %	28.0 %
Muddy/boggy/flooded	5 %	23.4 %
Rough surface	<2 %	8.4 %
Erosion of surface	<2 %	7.5 %

The need to make path surfaces accessible by clearance of crops and vegetation and to improve drainage were thus highlighted; but the very real, highly emotive and much publicised problem of eroded paths was reduced to apparently miniscule dimensions. It merits more attention than it received.

The essential context has been outlined above (Ch.7.1); and the critical issue is when and how Man should intervene to prevent Nature siezing the opportunity of bare 'natural paths' to unleash eternal erosive processes whereby 'every valley shall be exalted and every mountain and hill made low'. Typically, the process begins slowly and is most

Plate 7.5. A Natural Path and a Managerial Disaster !

easily arrested by decisive action in its early stages. However, in locations prone to erosion, once top-soils are breached it gathers independent momentum and accelerates until underlying bed-rock presents more stubborn resistance and a durable, though often intolerable, surface (Plate 7.5). Meanwhile, walkers will have side-stepped onto more even ground to develop alternative 'natural paths', which are often braided to circumnavigate particular obstacles. Scarification of wider swathes is thus initiated and erosion will continue on both new and abandoned paths since the latter rarely have the means to heal themselves. Damage is particularly severe where heavy precipitation conspires with long, steep slopes and also in fragile environments such as peaty moorlands where the surface material, though often deep, has no inherent stability beneath its vegetative cover.

There is nothing new in this scenario, and British highway history shows both the need for and benefits of the construction of durable, well drained surfaces which are suitable for the expected traffic (Plates 6.2 & 6.3). Constructed paths afford a simple though not necessarily cheap means of serving public needs and simultaneously preventing 'natural disasters'. Delay is expensive since remedial measures are more costly, more difficult, more extensive, and have a greater environmental impact. The key is good management, early action and adequate funding; but for many years the provision of constructed paths has been overlooked, too readily questioned and too often compromised. This begs questions as to the proper locus of responsibility for the physical condition of PRoW paths. By law this lies with Highway Authorities per se but the delegation of PRoW work has generally relocated it where there is responsibility for a range of countryside matters, including its conservation, but little or no expertise or interest in civil engineering. Consequently 'natural paths' have been widely prefered to 'artificial products'; and during a review of *The Coasts of North-West England,* a provider of effective paths for people felt obliged to adopt a defensive tone: "Blackpool has been criticised for the apparent harshness of its use of concrete, but how else could one preserve an area, particularly the cliff paths, which so many people wish to use ?" (Rodgers, 1973). There should be no need for any apology for sound management; and more pertinent questions relate to the general failure during the following decades to apply comparable measures more widely in the service of the public and protection of the countryside.

Unfortunately, since 1949 both policy and resource allocations for countryside walking seem to depend heavily on the assumption that 'natural paths' are self-sustaining, even though the National Parks and many National Trails were located in evidently vulnerable environments. As use of paths increased, environmental scientists invoked the concept of an 'ecological carrying capacity' as a measure of wear and tear on the land. Conservation and aesthetic issues were thus quickly perceived; but no lesson was learned from Blackpool. Knowledge of an 'ecological carrying capacity' is of no practical use in the absence of effective measures to ensure use of the path is consistently below the critical limits. As the Romans and the cliff manager at Blackpool knew, a surface commensurate with the burden placed on the path should be provided; but generally neither the will nor the resources were available to equip PRoW with durable surfaces. Consequently, 'make do and mend' strategies have prevailed; and although rough, uneven surfaces are a deterrent to casual users, the outcome has generally been accepted by regular, seasoned walkers. This partial success and apparent ability to cope on minimal resources may have undermined the case for a more radical approach. The implicit insult and injury to many walkers and the deterrent to potential walkers were readily ignored; but when management crises emerged, mythical hordes were made scapegoats for 'environmental damage', adding another theme to the multi-part chorus raised in protection of the countryside and of vested interests therein (Plate 4.2).

By the early 1970s serious and difficult problems had emerged in predictable locations, and conditions on significant stretches of the Pennine Way and the Lyke Wake Walk, both essentially moorland routes 'over the tops' of extensive uplands and hills, were destined to become notorious. Delay in addressing evident needs promoted accelerating deterioration; and some 10-15 years later many disasters reached headline proportions. National Parks and National Trails were the principal focus of attention, reflecting their vulnerability and neglect no less than their status and esteem; and eventually *Paths as Wide as Roads* were publicised:

> In 1985 (when) surveys confirmed the worst fears, alarm bells were sounded over the deteriorating conditions of footpaths on 'The Three Peaks' - Ingleborough, Penyghent and Whernside. Of the 63 kms of footpaths that gave access to the peaks, 24 km were in a severely damaged state and a further 30 km required immediate remedial work if progressive erosion on a similar scale was to be avoided... It is particularly distressing that 50 % of the area traversed by the eroded paths is a Site of Special Scientific Interest, renowned for its botanical and geomorphological interest... The National Park Committee decided that the erosion problem was so serious that it shoud be tackled "urgently and comprehensively" in a special project costing £600,000 [revised to £800,000 in 1990]. (Wood, 1986).

It now appeared that 'this green and pleasant land (was) being increasingly trampled underfoot by hordes of well-meaning but heavy-booted pilgrims'; and 'the national parks were in danger of being loved to death by the millions of people who visit them each year' (Tim Jones, *The Times*, 8.6.82). To reduce both problems, 'Britain's most popular Parks were to go under wraps' (Plate 4.2).

> Footpath erosion and traffic congestion are common to all Parks... (and) the head of the Countryside Commission's national parks unit said *"We are in danger of destroying the very fabric of what makes our national parks important. The tourist industry is consuming the countryside and contributing virtually nothing"*. In the Peak Park the start of the Pennine Way is now an eight-lane highway known to the park rangers as the Pennine Motorway... The car-park at Dovedale has been halved to reduce visitor numbers... Five paths up Snowdon are crumbling away under 500,000 visitors a year [estimated cost of repairs - £1.5m]... So beauty spots are being deliberately omitted from future tourist promotions in an effort to prevent them being destroyed by sheer weight of numbers. Several of the Lake District's most popular attractions have already vanished from promotions by the Cumbria tourist board... In Devon, the West Country tourist board marketing manager said *"We won't mention Widecombe... and there are some other fragile areas which are absolutely taboo"*. However, national parks officers face a serious dilemma. They want to alleviate 'honeypot areas' and spread tourism to lesser-known regions but are frightened of opening the way to further devastation by visiting hordes. As a result, some parks are keeping quiet not only about the busiest beauty spots but also about most unspoilt, wild country. (Richard Caseby, *The Sunday Times*, 4.6.89).

Such retreat from responsibilities is regrettable and blaming innocent parties for problems due to inappropriate policies, under-funding and poor management is deplorable. It evidently did nothing to promote wider enjoyment of the Parks and questioned John Dower's belief that 'there can be few national purposes which, *at so modest a cost,* offer so large a prospect of health-giving happiness for the people'.

Eventually, the diverse problems of Parks 'crowded to crisis point' were investigated by the National Parks Review Panel; and its less emotive Report was 'broadly welcomed by a whole range of pressure groups who see it as a viable blueprint for the next century' (Colthurst, 1991). Typically, the Panel's views on footpath erosion give support to a range of viewpoints, but at last some commitment to positive path management does emerge:

> We recognise the serious problem of erosion on some routes, even if these eroded sections represent only a small fraction of the total path length. Erosion must be tackled, and the resource implications will be considerable... In some cases, access will need to be discouraged to facilitate recovery, and in others, provision of alternative routes will need to be made so as to limit use to a level that is sustainable without recurrent damage.
> *Recommendations*: 5.3.4 Where it is a problem, or emerging as one, path ero-

sion must be tackled sensitively and in sympathy with the local environment...
5.3.7. Government should provide additional resources to national park authorities... to tackle the problems of footpath erosion. (Edwards, 1991).

However, the basic dilemma and difficulties were compounded rather than resolved; no new direction is discernible, there is no overt reference to path construction; and additional resources were, as ever, dependent on government priorities. The Report did emphasis that work on PRoW in the Parks was a matter of the highest priority and recommended an increase in excess of 50% over current expenditure (£2,132,000 in 1990-91). This may have been a key factor in facilitating a belated appreciation of the merits of 'artificial' paths.

For example, a National Trust team copied the construction of an ancient packhorse route in a £50,000 footpath restoration scheme at the head of Borrowdale in the Lake District (*National Parks Today 27*, 1990). 600 tonnes of Lancashire mill flagstones were air-lifted in 1992 to four problem sites on the Pennine Way where some 3 km of path were being restored at a cost of about £30 per metre - £48,400 per mile (*Countryside 79*, 1992). By 1994 2350 tonnes had been dropped by helicopters as part of a £3m project to resurface some 10% of the Pennine Way. And at last the worth of constructed paths was acknowledged:

> Flag-paths, using flat stone slabs that integrate well with the landscape, provide walkers with a hard, durable surface in areas of severe footpath erosion. About 23 km of path were laid between 1989 and 1994 and nearly 5000 tonnes of stone had to be airlifted in for the job. The operation has played a major role in the success of the Pennine Way Project... By 1994, where new paths had been built, the trampled zone had, in some places, been narrowed from over 11 to 1.6 metres... The restoration programme is two years ahead of schedule and - (due to new and more cost-effective techniques developed along the way) - 40% below the cost estimated in 1989. (*Countryside*, No.79 1996).

Also in 1996 Ronald Faux reported 'on how artificial paths can save the Lake District':

> Peter Davies, the area manager of the Lake District National Park, says the solution to erosion of footpaths in the upland areas is not to stop people enjoying the hills but to find ways of minimising the damage from walkers' boots and protecting the landscape. He talks about creating "sensitive paths" which can carry the number of people using the hills... Sir Chris Bonnington, the president of the Council of National Parks and a resident in the Lake District, insists that reducing the numbers of people going into the hills, apart from being difficult to achieve, must never be seen as a solution... 'Building upland footpaths in a sensitive way actually enables an ever-increasing number of people to enjoy our British hills without doing them severe damage'. (*The Times*, 16.11.96).

Inevitably, such a shift of emphasis in favour of 'artificial paths' to make amends for preventable disasters has not been universally welcomed; and antipathy to man-made paths

Plate 7.6. Aesthetic Concerns Misdirect Path Management.

> An eroded path was rebuilt to be aesthetically pleasing; but it does not please most walkers. They prefer to use a more even, softer surface and thus create a new 'natural path', which will be used until exposed bed-rock persuades the walkers to step aside again ... Unless effective management intervenes to provided the best available option and include measures to persuade walkers to adhere to it.

in the countryside is probably undiminished in particular quarters. This must not deter wider adoption of rational policies and effective management of footpaths in the best interests of the public and the countryside, for these are not incompatible if precedence is given to an overview of both rather than to special interests of numerous minorities and to ill-founded opinion.

It would be a mistake to conclude this section leaving the impression that only upland areas and eroded paths are in need of careful and often expensive management; and perhaps brief reference to one exceptional case of water-logging may be sufficient to make amends.

> Waterwynch Lane, on the Pembrokeshire Coast Path, used to live up to its name, becoming a quagmire for nearly a mile after heavy rain. The National Park

Authority has drained and resurfaced it. The Footpaths Officer said 'This was a major piece of engineering work but we took great care to preserve the distinctive character of this age-old lane'... At £48,000 per mile this must be a serious contender for the title of Britain's most expensive path. The cost of the work was grant-aided by the Countryside Council for Wales. (*National Parks Today* 34, 1992).

Finally, the apparent need to concentrate on 'management disasters' in National Parks also must be qualified. Collectively the relatively anonymous but widespread occurrence of local and often limited stretches of severely damaged path surfaces has more adverse effects on current and potential walkers than the celebrated cases in well known places. Typically, the latter have received publicity, generous funding and remedial attention, while numerous, equally or more important needs in mundane places continue to be largely overlooked and neglected.

7. Paths for the Public ?

Having for long purposefully connived with claims that the countryside is threatened by hordes of visitors, the Countryside Commission found itself in a delicate position in 1995 when required to address the House of Commons Environment Committee on *The Environmental Impact of Leisure Activities on the English Countryside*, but its evidence is generally frank and fair:

> The Countryside Commission would like the Committee to set the incidence of problems in its proper perspective against the normal situation of recreation taking place with no cause for concern... For the vast majority of England, recreation forms a natural and harmonious component of the legitimate activity of the countryside. It delivers considerable economic benefits, which are increasing. It is easy but misleading to use evidence from a comparatively small number of celebrated and often quoted localities or areas to draw false conclusions that overstate problems associated with recreational use of the countryside... *Problems, so far as they exist, can usually be resolved by straightforward local management and planning solutions. It is possible to accommodate and even increase the quantity of recreation activity without detriment to environmental quality by deploying relevant expertise and management measures.*
>
> Adequate resources are, however, necessary if leisure in the countryside is to be adequately provided for and managed. In many cases lack of resources is restricting the ability of local managers to act. The costs of managing the countryside to accommodate recreational use are good value. The Committee is asked to endorse the Year 2000 Target to ensure the public rights of way network is legally defined, properly maintained and well publicised. *To ensure that this major asset continues to be well managed and maintained to a high standard, the Committee is asked to recommend that adequate resources be devoted to it by Government and the Highway Authorities.* (Countryside Commission, April 1995; italics by GK).

The infamous pseudo-case for restricting participation in countryside recreation is set aside; and the critical need for 'adequate resources' is stressed, with special reference being given to the needs of PRoW work. On the other hand, the weaknesses and failings of policies and management in respect of provision for countryside walking are white-washed; and the implication that paths on PRoW currently are 'well managed and maintained to a high standard' is untenable. New approaches, new policies and new priorities no less than additional resources are urgently needed; but the subsequent *Agenda for Action* focused on 'the action and investment necessary to ensure that *the whole path network is available at the most basic, minimum level*" (CCP.273, 1989).

Will this 'minimum level' meet the needs of the people as a whole ? Wilkinson *et al* (1985) stress that 'to attract new recruits, it is vital to design attractive walks suited to their needs, expectations and limitations'; while Kay (1989) argues that 'occasional walkers and would-be walkers prefer to be cosseted, and catering for their needs does not come cheaply'. Quality provision is not only a key factor in the promotion of countryside walking as a means of widening participation but also as a major factor in the enjoyment of most path users. On the other hand, it is evident from their behaviour that regular and frequent hikers and long-distance walkers generally do accept current conditions with all their limitations and difficulties; and some may wish for nothing better. Therefore if all paths on PRoW can eventually be maintained at a basic level, they will all meet the needs of this minority, if not satisfy their hopes; but they will not attract novices, social walkers nor families with young children. The 'Milestones Approach' (CCP.435 and 436) requires that the 'surface of every PRoW is *in proper repair, reasonably safe and suitable for the expected use*'. This implies some positive understanding of and relationship with current and anticipated usage; but while current use is accepted as an indicator of 'expected use' the present exclusion of the disadvantaged majority will persist (Ch.4.4-5); and the labelling of PRoW as Public Footpaths will continue to be inappropriate if not, in many cases, libellous. The management of each PRoW should be determined with reference to its utility and purpose within a scheme that gives full and fair consideration to the population as a whole; and the promotion of access to the countryside calls for policies related primarily to the people rather than to PRoW.

Plate 8.1 Long Distance Walkers on the Anglezarke Amble in Winter (Photo by R. Coleman)

8
NATIONAL TRAILS, REGIONAL ROUTES AND LONG DISTANCE WALKERS

The concept of long distance routes (LDFPs) is somewhat confused and perhaps dated. Their use is much more varied than their name suggests, and their appeal is wider too, yet not recognised in their planning, management and promotion. (CCP.253, 1988).

National Trails... are set apart by their national quality... and by virtue of their character and quality (they) reflect the grandest, wildest and most beautiful landscapes the nation has to offer... The Commission intends that the routeing, maintenance and promotion of National Trails should reflect the highest standards... (And) will continue to take the lead in exploring the feasibility, planning and development of National Trails, and in securing their funding. (CCP.266, 1990)

1. National Trails and Regional Routes

The creation of any route has a purpose related to an identified or anticipated market which may be an individual, a special interest group or a substantial section of the public. Public sector provision should serve the public, identifying and responding to needs in order of priority. However, provision for countryside walking has been led by particular demands of effective advocates pursuing their own vision and interests. Thus the National Trails can be traced to the late-19th-century quest for fitness and adventure and the topicality of 'moorland tramping' in the 1930's (Ch.1.8). Aficionados, then and now, created their own long distance routes and there was no need for massive intervention by the government. However, pressure groups siezed the opportunity to bundle proposals for Long Distance Footpaths into the National Parks and Access to the Countryside Act of 1949 (Ch.4.3); and since then public sector provision for countryside walking has been seriously distorted.

Much credit or blame for the National Trails may be attributed to Tom Stephenson; and, perhaps, beyond him to the heritage of John Muir, wilderness sage of the USA. Muir had inspired others to 'think big' in terms of provision for outdoor recreation.

> James Taylor founded the *Green Mountain Club* in 1910 with the objective of cutting The Long Trail through virgin forest to create a 265 mile high-level route from Massachusetts to the Canadian border... The Appalachian Trail also was the result of one man's vision: Benton MacKaye's proposal for a 2100 mile route was published in 1921, and was completed in 1937... the challenge of its existence proved irresistable and soon each year about 100 hikers walked from end-to-end; and it was first 'thru-walked' in 1948....

In 1935 two young women, having walked part of the Appalachian Trail, wrote to Tom Stephenson, a journalist on the Daily Herald, asking if there was an equivalent in the UK. Tom's response was to write an article in June 1935 - 'Wanted: A Long Green Trail' - suggesting a similar trail along the crest of the Pennines. This led to the formation of *The Pennine Way Association* at Hope in Derbyshire in 1938 where it was recorded that: *The wide, health-giving moorlands and high places of solitude, the features of natural beauty and the places of historical interest along the Pennine Way give this route a special character and attractiveness which should be available at all time as a natural heritage of the youth of the country and of all who feel the call of the hills and the lonely places.* Voluntary organisations prepared a survey of the route which indicated that some 70 miles of new footpath were required to turn Tom Stephenson's vision of a 250 mile trail from the Peak District to the Cheviots into reality. (CCP.253, 1988).

American experience showed that long distance routes serve only the ambition of their creators and small numbers of exceptional walkers (Plate 8.1); and the Pennine Way project should have been left with its authors. However, the post-war campaign for access to the countryside provided the opportunity to transfer the task to the public sector; and, as secretary of the Ramblers' Association, Tom Stephenson was well placed to press the case for the Pennine Way and other LDFPs. Proposals for National Parks and long-distance paths were partly fused, and the Hobhouse Committee of 1947 recommended that there be continuous footpaths along the coasts of the national parks and that six other specified routes be developed (Ch.4.3 & Fig.8.1).

'Tom Stephenson's Pennine Way' was granted priority. It was approved in 1951 and opened in 1965, four years before the Cleveland Way but ten years after the Lyke Wake Walk. Ten more LDFPs followed in the '70s; then output slowed with only two additions in the '80s and, after a ten-year break, the Thames Path in 1996 (Table 8.1). Outstanding commitments comprise Hadrian's Wall Walk, the 340-mile Pennine Bridleway, the Cotswold Way and Glyndwr's Way. This tapering of the programme disappointed the Ramblers' Association which, in 1985, 'stressed the need to provide more... and nominated seven new paths for development before the end of the century' (Sports Council, 1986). But for some time there had been a growing recognition that National Trails were an expensive investment; and that the voluntary sector is capable of adequate if not excessive provision of long routes.

The Commission met the cost of establishing each Trail and 95% of all maintenance costs, tapered to 75% in the late '80s. Greatly increased repair bills were incurred as the more vulnerable Trails, notably the Pennine Way and the Cleveland Way, deteriorated rapidly; and expenditure on the Trails increased from an average of £653,000 p.a. in 1986-89 to £1.47m in 1993-94. At that time all grants related to provision for walking comprised £4.06m and the distribution of this sum places spending on the Trails in perspective.

PRoW and Permissive Routes	£1,540,000	37.9 %
National Trails	*£1,469,000*	*36.2 %*
PRoW Staff and Definitive Map Work	£651,000	16.0 %
Parish Paths Partnerships	£382,000	9.4 %
Access Agreements	£19,000	0.5 %

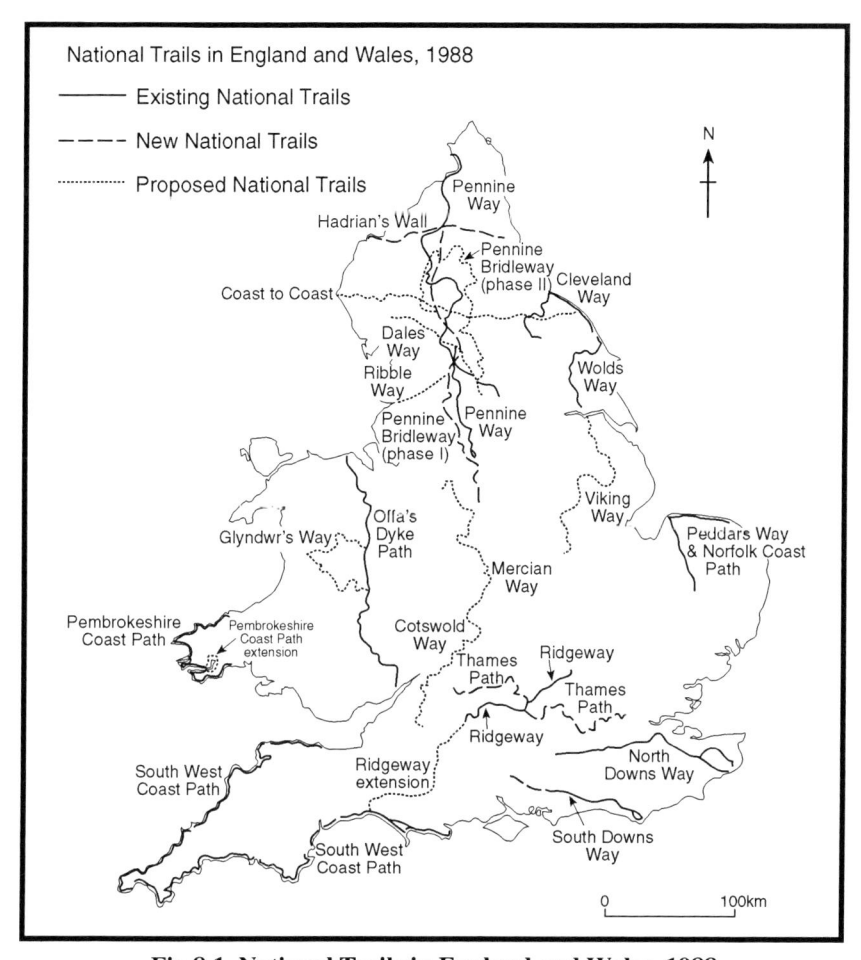

Fig.8.1. National Trails in England and Wales, 1988.
The locations and concentrations of these routes show a close correlation with John Dower's proposals for National Parks and other valued places and, in broader terms, with Cyril Fox's 'Highland Britain' (Fig.4.2).

The Trails embrace only 2% of all PRoW but they received 36% of all relevant central funds. More recently, £750,000 has been dedicated to upgrading the Cotswold Way (*Countryside, 86,* 1998); and the Lottery Sports Fund has contributed £1.84m towards the £3.84m required for the southern section of the Pennine Bridleway (*Countryside 89,* 1998) and £1.62m towards the £4.5m for Hadrian's Wall Walk (*Countryside Focus,* 1999). These massive investments extend a long history of generous allocations to National Trails; and neither the injustice nor the spatial occurrence of such largesse passed entirely unnoticed.

Many local authorities were thus inspired to equip their own territory with 'unofficial' Long Distance Footpaths, believing that such projects would bring their own reward and hoping that they might also benefit from national recognition and funding. For example, in 1971 Staffordshire County Council expressed the view that:

Route	Length (miles)	Approved	Opened
1 Pennine Way**	250	1951	1965
2 Cleveland Way*	109	1965	1969
3 Pembrokeshire Coast Path*	186	1953	1970
4 Offa's Dyke Path**	176	1955	1971
5 South Downs Way** (+ extension)	106	1963	1972
6 Ridgeway**	85	1972	1973
7 (a) North Cornwall Coast Path	135	1952	1973
8 (b) South Cornwall Coast Path	133	1954	1973
9 (c) South Devon Coast Path	93	1959	1974
10 (d) Dorset Coast Path	72	1963	1974
11 (e) Somerset & N. Devon Coast Path*	82	1961	1978
7-11 South West Coast Path	515		
12 North Downs Way**	153	1969	1978
13 Wolds Way	81	1977	1982
14 Peddars Way & Norfolk Coast Path	93	1982	1986
15 Thames Path**	214		1996

+ Hadrian's Wall Path; Pennine Bridleway; Cotswold Way; Glyndwr's Way.

Table 8.1. The National Trails, 1999
** Trails individually recommended by the Hobhouse Committee.
* Those similarly recommended as coastal routes within National Parks.
+ Trails approved and being developed.
   In 1986 the Coast to Coast Walk, the Cotswold Way, the Dales Way, Glyndwr's Way, the Mercian Way, the Ribble Way, and the Viking Way were nominated for elevation to national status and this has been granted to two of them.

A system of recreational paths is needed offering a range from long distance routes to medium and short distance circular routes... The Staffordshire Way was immediately adopted since it was felt that such a path would have considerable educational value in introducing young people to some of the best scenery in Staffordshire and that it would be well used if effectively publicised.

Work on this 93-mile route began in 1971; a feasibility study was completed by 1973; and a Footpaths Officer was appointed to the project in 1974. The northern section was opened in 1979, the middle section in 1981 and the southern section in 1983. Guide books were published for each stage and then replaced in 1992 with a comprehensive volume sponsored by the Countryside Commission. Progress was constantly hampered by inadequate funding, even though the project was given pride of place and absorbed the greater part of available resources for more than a decade (Moxham, N. 1993 and 1997). In 1987 Staffordshire promoted 6.1% of its rights-of-way (CCD.43, 1991); and the Staffordshire Way accounted for 60% of these favoured parts. More recently, some priority has been given to linking the Staffordshire Way with the Worcestershire Way and the Heart of England Way in the south and with Cheshire's Gritstone Trail and the South Cheshire Trail to the north. This investment will contribute to a growing network of long-distance routes developed by local authorities, for Staffordshire was by no means alone in emulating national policy and envying the funding of National Trails.

However, growing concern that the status of 'official LDFPs' was being undermined by 'unofficial long-distance walks' was addressed in 1976 within a rare but commendable appeal for a review of general principles and priorities for the use of PRoW. The Countryside Commission asked local authorities:

Route	Miles	Route	Miles
01 Angles Way (Norfolk)	78	24 Oxfordshire Way	65
02 Calderdale Way	50	25 Ribble Way	72
03 Cambrian Way	274	26 Robin Hood Way	105
04 Centenary Way (York-Filey)	83	27 Saints Way	37
05 Cheshire Ring Canal Walk	97	28 Saxon Shore Way	135
06 Coast to Coast Walk	190	29 Shropshire Way	125
07 Cotswold Way **	103	30 Solent Way	60
08 Cumbrian Way	70	31 Staffordshire Way	93
09 Dales Way	81	32 Taff Trail	55
10 Dyfi Valley Way	108	33 Tarka Trail	180
11 Essex Way	81	34 Three Castles Path	60
12 Glyndwr's Way **	128	35 Two Moors Way	103
13 Greensand Way	106	36 Vanguard Way	63
14 Heart of England Way	100	37 Viking Way	140
15 Hereward Way	103	38 Wayfarers Walk	56
16 Ickneild Way	105	39 Weald Way	80
17 Isle of Man Coastal Path	75	40 Weavers Way	56
18 Isle of Wight Coastal Path	65	41 Wessex Ridgeway	136
19 Landsker Borderlands Trail	60	42 West Mendip Way	30
20 London Countryway	205	43 Wye Valley Walk	107
21 Mercian Way	125		
22 Nidderdale Way	53	** *selected to be a National Trail.*	
23 North Bucks Way	39		

Table 8.2 Regional Routes, 1999

Wainwright's famous 190-mile Coast-to-Coast Walk traverses three National Parks and spans the breadth of the land; and without his initiative there would be no National Trail or Regional Route in the Lake District. The defence of that District has been resolute. However, Howard Beck (1998) has also addressed this situation with his *William Wordsworth Way*, a 180-mile walk in the Lake District visiting more than 80 places associated with the poet. This might occupy an active tourist for 7, 10 or 14 days; and if it should become as popular as Wainwright's walk, will Wordsworth and the Friends of the Lake District be well pleased by the enjoyment it provides?

- to give greater priority to the planning and management of footpaths as part of a total recreation strategy;
- to identify and improve footpath routes suitable for 'intensive use' (major recreation paths); and
- to identify and improve footpath networks suitable for 'extensive use'.

(CCP.99, 1976).

This attempt to address the purpose and optimal use of PRoW was virtually ignored; and a decade later the Commission returned to the need for some rational policy and priorities but, at a time when some 300 long distance paths were being promoted, it was faced with a demand that more routes be recognised as National Trails:

> Many candidates were put forward for National Trail status... The distinction between 'unofficial' long distance routes and the Commission's national trails was seen by some as artificial... (but) it was generally recognised that the Commission could not fund all desirable routes. Nevertheless there was a desire for 'recognition' to be given to all high-quality routes in their marketing and promotion. (Report on 'The Consultations' in response to CCP.253, 1988).

Recognition as a *Regional Route* was subsequently granted to selected candidates, including the Staffordshire Way; and more than 40 long distance walks are now distinguished as such and receive some support from central funds for their promotion (Table 8.2).

The 6175 miles of National Trails and Regional Routes embrace only 5.5% of all PRoW but they comprised 41% of PRoW promoted by local authorities in 1988 (CCD.43, 1991). Regional Routes now provide 67% of the designated long distance paths and, given their wider geographical distribution, they have greater potential to serve the nation as a whole. Also, on average, they are considerably shorter (96 miles) than the Trails (186 miles) and this too may improve their utility, especially since some of the shorter routes are within a day's walking by hardened aficionados. The case for differentiating one from the other therefore may be seen to lie in accidents of history, associated policies and resource allocations; and to what extent these Trails and Routes do serve the needs of long distance walkers and the public at large may be assessed by locating them in the wider context of all long distance walks.

2. Long Distance Walkers and Long Distance Walks.

The 19th-century quest for fitness and adventure led many individuals and organisations to devise long-distance routes for regular exercise or occasional use; and guide books, such as those by William Crossing and Alfred Brown, no doubt inspired many others to participate in long-distance walking (Ch.1.7). Walkers and writers of today have extended the proliferation of 'unofficial' long distance routes, and while any selection is invidious, some case material may be useful.

John Merrill is one of the world's greatest exponents of long distance walking, and his achievements were not dependent on public provision of quality footpaths.

> Over 15 years he walked more than 100,000 miles... In 1978 he became the first person to walk the entire coastline of Britain - 6824 miles in ten months... In

1982 he walked across Europe - 2806 miles in 107 days - crossing seven countries, the Swiss and French Alps and the Pyrennean Chain... In America, he used the Appalachian Trail as a training walk; and during the summer of 1984, he set off from Virginia Beach on the Atlantic Coast and walked 4226 miles without a rest-day to Santa Cruz and San Francisco on the Pacific Ocean. (Merrill, 1988).

At home in the Peak District John Merrill walks and writes; and sales of his 90 publications on walking exceed two million. He designs and promotes both short circular walks and challenge walks, typically the 25-mile *White Peak Challenge* (Merrill, 1988). He understands the needs of the market no less than his own achievements; and he does not press the latter as a model for the public.

In contrast, many others have campaigned for their particular vision to be imprinted on the ground; and the most famous National Trail is faithful to Tom Stephenson's concept of a crest-line walk along 'the back-bone of England'. However, the *Alternative Pennine Way* (APW) may offer a better option. It does not keep to 'the tops' and thus embraces less bleak moorland but entails more climbing; it is 17 miles longer; and it might well afford the greater challenge. But its authors recommend it on quite different grounds. It is a product of practical experience rather than dreams; and it is more varied in terms of landscapes and place-related experiences.

> The APW does not always seek the high hills... and is not frightened of the odd mile on minor roads. It seeks out places of interest where a day could be spent on local exploration instead of forging ahead; and it passes through man-made as well as natural environments... The route is arranged in 20 stages so that each is a good day's walk finishing at a place where accommodation is possible... We are modest gourmets... and we like to think that your days on the APW will be like our ideal: a breakfast to suit your preference; the day's walk 'cracked' by midday, when a light lunch can be taken; an afternoon's 'stroll' to complete the walk in time to find accommodation; a hot bath... a preprandial drink... an excellent dinner... We are not masochists or backpackers; nor do we subscribe to the proposition that to be a 'proper walker' you have to be covered in mud as well as being a purist. We walk to enjoy the whole journey and ourselves; and we do not set out to prove anything... We want you to enjoy your walking and to do it your way. Backpack if you will... or gourmet like us... Above all, enjoy yourselves. (Brook and Hinchliffe, 1992).

The APW has much to offer as a challenge and a tourist attraction, and at least one experienced walker agrees. For Ben Evens (1996), APW stands for 'Absolutely Perfect Walking' and he recommends it to 'those who want to savour rather than conquer the Pennines'. But during his walk Evens met no other 'APW walker'. Popularity depends heavily on image and publicity, and the APW is unlikely to rival the National Trail; but this will hide rather than deny its qualities.

The importance of image and promotion is well illustrated in the story of Bill Cowley's *Lyke Wake Walk*, 'the first and foremost challenge walk in the country' (Wimbush,

1981). Born in 1955 of romance and adventure laced with northern humour, it comprises a 42-mile crossing of the North York Moors along the watershed from Osmotherley to Ravenscar. It thus has much in common with the Pennine Way but, being negotiable within a day, it is more marketable; and in 1965, when the National Trail was opened, there were 2813 recorded crossings. Ten years later the Lyke Wake Walk was the most popular and most infamous long-distance route in England; and its problems should have sent early warnings to managers of the Pennine Way.

Bill Cowley, a north Yorkshire farmer and scholar of the local region, was digging peat high on Glaisdale Moor when his thoughts turned to the 20 miles of virtually trackless heather-clad moor between him and his farm and another 20 beyond him leading to the coast. Walking would be better than digging; and the notion of trail-blazing 'over the tops' within 24 hours was planted in the pages of *The Dalesman* of August 1955. The challenge was irresistable and on 1st October Bill Cowley was joined by a dozen enthusiasts. A noon start granted a night on the moors and in the small hours one member encouraged his fellows with a medieval chant, mentioned by John Aubrey in 1686 as being favoured at funerals by vulgar people in Yorkshire. This 'Lyke Wake' dirge thus lent its name and a wealth of imagery, much being fantastic rather than factual, to enrich the Walk and related experiences; and the Lyke Wake Club was established to celebrate its resurrection and enjoy its future.

> The Club confines its activities to collecting information about the Walk... furthering the interests of those who do the Walk... and encouraging members to learn all they can about the moors, their history and folk-lore, and assist in safeguarding them... The Club gradually built up, with more humour than seriousness, its own rather macabre traditions... Its crest is a silver coffin and three silver tumuli on a black shield. The cloth badge is a silver candle and two tumuli on a black coffin. The tie is black, with silver coffins, candles and tumuli.... From the early days a few enthusiasts used to gather for a post-mortem on the year's efforts. This became the Candlemas Wake... and the first Midsummer Wake was held on 24th June 1961... and the 21st Anniversary Wake was appropriately held in the Haunted Castle, Kirby Misperton on 2nd October 1976. (Cowley, 1983).

There is an evident emphasis on fun; and amongst other strange things, the Lyke Wake Walk 'seemed to inspire everyone who does it to a peak of literary achievement'.

A verse by the Chief Dirger, who died in 1994, aged 79.
Storm Longing
Come, friends o' my heart, to the hills we'll fly,
Where the high winds never rest,
But storm and cry on the Riggs that lie
To the eastward crest on crest;
Where rain and sleet in tempest beat
Round many an ancient Cross,
From Crookstaff Hill to Wheeldale Gill,

> From Bloworth to Yarsley Moss.
> When the sea-roke spread on Botton Head
> Rolls down to the dale beneath,
> And our way we thread with careful tread
> Through the gloom of the trackless heath;
> When the sea-wind snarls from Stony Marls
> And the sky's a leaden cloud
> That hides the brow of Shunner Howe
> Like a Norseman's funeral shroud.
> But what reck we of roke or storm
> Or the furies overhead ?
> A song we'll sing as on we swing
> With sure and steady tread.
> Though boggets growl and ratchets howl
> As we tramp on side by side,
> Through the night that's black with storm and wrack
> Our steps the gods shall guide.

Beneath this camaraderie lay a commitment to the concept of the walk as an adventure (Ch.1.7); and it probably was the first of the now numerous 'Anytime Challenge Walks' which set basic rules and a testing route for walkers to pursue at their leisure. It is designed to test physical and mental strength, endurance, navigational skills, and that less definable quality comprising 'hill-craft' or 'the art of moorland walking'. The time-limit provides guidance in terms of logistics and a minimum standard of fitness; and opens the door to comparisons and competition which add another element of interest, while special achievements create wonders and attract attention.

The Lyke Wake Club thus became a pioneer of the now popular 'Challenge Events', organised on a specified date for registered, fee-paying walkers and runners. Nor is the link with fund-raising without significance, for the age of 'Charity Walks' was at hand; and the Lyke Wake Walk became a target of numerous large groups walking for a memorable experience which would also tug at both heart and purse strings. Popularity is a product of sound marketing and effective promotion; and personal experience of both place and event can affect this relationship. Special occasions, action and achievements, memorabilia and memories, all generate stories and reports which repeatedly circulate into wider spheres. Personal accounts can be the life-blood of promotion; and they underpin the fame of the Lyke Wake Walk, which spread slowly for a while and then gathered momentum.

Initially, the Walk's clientele was drawn from the local region; it was small, grew slowly and 25% of the walks were 'repeat crossings' by devotees (Table 8.3). In the late '60s it snowballed and the 16,322 recorded in 1967-69 exceeded all walks in the preceding 12 years. In the '70s, repeat crossings fell markedly but the number of recorded walks grew relentlessly as the 'Lyke Wake' became a major attraction for charity walks. Furthermore, as time progressed more walkers were content with the field experience and did not report to the Club; but independent surveys indicate that by the late '70s there were some 16-20,000 walks a year on the more popular sections of the route. In the absence of any effective path management, such ample enjoyment inevitably led to a physical disaster;

	First Crossings	Repeat Crossings	Total Crossings	Mean Annual Crossings
1955-59	265	38	303	61
1960-64	4,439	1,451	5,890	1,178
1965-69	17,321	5,074	22,395	4,479
1970-74	27,122	3,531	30,653	6,131
1975-79 *	39,791 *	2,487*	42,278*	8,456*
(1975-79)*	(42,870)*	(2,506)*	(45,376)*	(9,057)*
1980	8,109	637	8,764	8,764
1981	7,513	459	7,972	7,972
1982	5,217	328	5,545	5,545

Table 8.3. Lyke Wake Walks reported to the Lyke Wake Club
1955-79 and 1980-82
* The figures in brackets are a product of 'smoothing' to eliminate the effects of the serious fires of 1976.

> In 1957 Arthur Puckrin did a crossing in 10hr.10min. and the double in 23.19. In 1961 Eric Derwin did 8.38 but Arthur replied with 6.40... and the following year lowered this to 6.19 and 16.17 for the double. Later he managed 6.13 and did a triple in 32.15... In 1970 M.Turner and C.Garforth, international athletes of Cambridge University, reduced it to 4.58.07... Only in 1979 did the great fell runner Josh Naylor get the record down to 4.53... then Mick Garratt of Guisborough lowered it in 1981 to 4.51.. [Meanwhile] in 1964 the Osmotherley Summer Games Committee had asked the Club to organise a Lyke Wake Race from east to west to end at the village cross, and for any profits to go to a fund for the new village hall... (Cowley, 1983).

and the progression from virtually track-less moors to braided 'natural paths' and then to serious environmental damage and associated dangers to walkers was particularly rapid.

Although the Countryside Commission was simultaneously engineering a comparable disaster on the Pennine Way, blame was laid at the feet of the walkers. No-one was more distressed at this outcome of the Walk's popularity than Bill Cowley, but his reasonable intention and remarkable achievement in promoting enjoyment of the countryside was bedevilled by vacuous policies for and non-existent management of provision for walkers (Ch.6 & 7). Where the 'natural paths' created on the crest of the Moors lie on PRoW, their surfaces were and are the responsibility of the appropriate highway authorities, who had done nothing to reinforce them. However, where the route presumed 'a right to roam' or departed from PRoW and trespassed over private property, no public body is directly responsible for making good any damage; nor is any landowner. It is fortuitous but fortunate that the Walk lies within a National Park; and in the mid-70s, a 'Lyke Wake Walk Working Group' was formed to consider management of the route as part of the North York Moors National Park Plan. Various measures were adopted, including steps to greatly reduce use of the Walk; and much has been achieved to improve what continues to be a problematic - and instructive - situation.

The Lyke Wake Walk is exceptional for many reasons but the underlying issues and problems, in varying degrees, are commonplace. It illustrates the power of effective marketing and promotion; and it highlights the need for a regulatory role and wider managerial responsibilities by both central and local authorities. It would have been more appropriate for the Countryside Commission to develop and administer these than to participate directly in the provision of walks over much longer distances. In broader terms, it also illustrates the very real difficulties of managing or even supervising people in pursuit of countryside recreation, whether through promoting routes or walking them; and this too should have been an early and central concern of the Commission.

3. The LDWA and its Directory of Long Distance Walks

The network of long distance walks was destined to grow like Topsy - rapidly in all directions and beyond comprehension; but the small market for this product remained an enigma. The number, nature and behaviour of long distance walkers are not well known; and precise definitions of long distance walks were slow to emerge. Even the constitution of the Long Distance Walkers' Association (LDWA) retains some flexibility on these points:

> The Association's interests shall lie mainly in extended walks in rural areas and especially those walks that exceed 20 miles. Whilst such walks may be competitive in the sense of a challenge, no emphasis shall be placed on any form of racing or road walking.

This suggests that *completion within a day of a recreational walk of 20 miles or more* might identify both long distance walkers and long distance walks. These criteria suggest that 15% of the Ramblers are long distance walkers (Fig.5.1), and most members of the LDWA also qualify; but general surveys show that distances in excess of 10 miles attract a very small proportion of all walkers and a tiny fraction of the public (Fig.5.1). Nevertheless, Chris Steer circulated the first 'LDWA Newsletter' in 1972; 200 walkers responded; the LDWA was born; and data from its journal, *Strider*, informs this study.

For 15 years about 600 joined the LDWA each year but 270 resigned, leaving some 5000 members in 1987 (Table 8.4). By then, steady growth and stability had won the Association recognition as 'the governing body in the UK' for long distance walking (Sports Council, 1986). During the 1990s recruitment averaged 978 pa but a fall-out of 791 left an annual growth of only 187; and while 20,000 walkers have joined the LDWA, only recently has its current membership approached 7000. Evidently committed long distance walkers are a very small group; and the substantial turn-over suggests that particular activities of the LDWA exert a strong but short-lived attraction for perhaps half of all those who join, while they are perpetually magnetic for the hard core of some 5000 long-standing members. It is, however, abundantly evident that long distance walkers per se have never been able to justify the preoccupation with and investment in National Trails and Regional Routes.

In any case, long distance walkers have always been able to provide for their own needs (Ch.1.7); and in 1980 two founder members of the LDWA, Alan and Barbara

Date	Current Members	Change No.	%	Last No. Issued*	(a) Enrolment & (b) Fall-out (a)	(b)	Fall-out as % of Enrolment
Nov.87	'5000'	—	—	9,582	482	482	100 %
Nov.88	'5000'	—	—	10,311	729	729	100 %
Nov.89	5048	48	1.0	11,250	939	891	95 %
Nov.90	5397	349	6.9	12,210	960	611	64 %
Nov.91	5585	188	3.5	13,080	870	682	78 %
Nov.92	5864	79	6.9	14,125	1045	966	92 %
Nov.93	6213	349	5.6	15,123	998	649	65 %
Nov.94	6385	172	2.8	16,156	1033	861	83 %
Nov.95	6779	394	6.2	17,254	1098	704	64 %
Nov.96	6884	105	1.5	18,249	995	890	89 %
Nov.97	6984	100	1.5	19,162	913	813	89 %
Nov.98	6929	-55	-0.8	20,051	889	944	106 %
Nov.99	6743	-183	-2.6	20,728	677	860	127 %

Table 8.4. Trends in the LDWA Membership, 1987 to 1998.
* Each member has a unique serial number; this is the key to the above analysis.

Blatchford published the first national directory of promoted walks of 20 miles or more in the UK. It comprised 130 walks while the 2nd edition of 1982 identified 150. Then, with Countryside Commission support, the LDWA set up and publicised the *National Register of Long Distance Paths;* and 240 routes and 40 'anytime challenge walks' were recorded by 1986. Thereafter additions probably record current growth rather than pre-existing products. The 4th edition of 1990 contains 350 routes; that of 1994 describes nearly 500; and another hundred were added in the next four years (LDWA, 1998). These figures suggest that during the 1990s about 25 new long distance walks have been created and publicised each year. These are predominantly products of the voluntary sector whose output clearly indicates that public sector provision in this field was never necessary and has never suppressed the appetite of individuals to provide for themselves and their peers

Individual authors express their particular interests but their collective output may provide an overview of practising walkers' preferences; and all current provision may be evaluated in the context of market needs (Table 8.5). The aggregate length of the 402 routes, including unidentified multiple use of paths, is 24,392 miles; and the 55 National Trails and Regional Routes (with an average of 186 and 96 miles respectively) account for 6488 miles or 27% of the total. The other 347 walks, which include 42 of more than 100 miles, have an average length of 52 miles.

The length and difficulty of a route are major determinants of its utility and use; and most long distance walkers regularly undertake walks of up to 30 miles which are capable of providing both a challenge and a full day's enjoyment of the countryside. Many authors recognise this and 34% of the 402 routes are of 20-29 miles. However, particularly fit, experienced walkers are able to cover greater distances in a day and 50 miles or even 100 km is within the compass of the more energetic. This too is well recognised, and

Length	All L-D Paths*			Regional Routes			National Trails		
Miles	No.	% of paths	% of miles	No.	% of paths	% of miles	No.	% of paths	% of miles
020-029	138	34.3	13.7	-	-	-	-	-	-
030-039	64	15.9	8.8	3	7.0	2.4	-	-	-
040-049	37	9.2	6.5	-	-	-	-	-	-
050-059	26	6.5	5.5	5	11.6	6.5	-	-	-
060-079	37	9.2	10.4	10	23.3	16.2	-	-	-
080-099	30	7.5	10.9	6	13.9	12.5	3	25.0	12.7
100-129	33	8.2	14.9	12	27.9	31.9	3	25.0	10.5
130-159	17	4.4	10.0	3	7.0	10.0	1	8.3	7.5
160-199	6	1.5	4.4	2	4.6	9.0	2	16.7	17.7
200+	14	3.5	15.1	2	4.6	11.6	3	25.0	51.5
Totals	402	100.0	100.2	43	99.9	100.1	12	100.0	99.9

Table 8.5 All Long Distance Walks, Regional Routes and National Trails in England and Wales by Length of Walk, 1994
* The National Trails and Regional Routes are included in the data for all Walks. The Pennine Bridleway is included with the National Trails. (Source: LDWA, 1994)

32% of the routes are between 30 and 60 miles. Longer walks of 60-100 miles (17%) are for exceptional people on a day's outing; and for others, only on special occasions such as walking holidays which extend over several days, perhaps in successive years. The annual LDWA 100-mile challenge walk is a special occasion . It comprises a specified route, usually circular and over varied, often difficult terrain but with the advantage of staffed service points at well spaced intervals. Each year a handful of 'runners' complete the walk in less than 24 hours; but it is intended for upto 500 walkers who are able and willing to cover at least 50 miles a day, more or less continuously, on two consecutive days. It is rarely over-subscribed (Table 8.7).

Against this analysis, it is difficult to justify in practical terms the 70 routes of more than 100 miles which comprise only 18% of the options but cover 44% of the paths occupied by long distance walks (Table 8.5). These are the stuff that dreams are made of; and the voluntary sector has duly acknowledged romantic notions and the lure of heroic feats by producing 42 routes in excess of 100 miles, including 9 of more than 200. These cost the public purse little or nothing that would not otherwise be spent on PRoW; but the 55 National Trails and Regional Routes dominate public expenditure on direct provision for countryside walking. The profile of Trails is particularly incongruous; all but three are in excess of 100 miles and three have a combined length 1062 miles, which exceeds that of the other nine. The Regional Routes are somewhat less extraordinary, but the seven (16%) which are in excess of 130 miles account for 36% of the paths committed to this category of walks (Table 8.5).

It may well be that the incredible commitment to excessively long Trails, which was triggered by American tourists and pressed upon the government in 1949, has allowed no easy opportunity for withdrawal. Consequently, even now support is being given to projects that will enmesh Britain within European Trails of proportions that bear comparison with the longest in the USA; and this may encourage further emulation of American ideas, such as Long Distance Hikers Association. This is for those who are interested in walking long trails, particularly the 2600 mile Pacific Crest Trail, the 3000 mile Continental Divide Trail, and the 2150 mile Appalachian Trail. For those who have walked all three, [and at 21 miles per day this would require just one year of continuous walking], there is a 'Triple Crown Award' (Townsend, 1995). Surely such peripheral interests are the province of fringe groups rather than national governments.

The Long Distance Walkers Association is a very effective 'fringe group' that serves its clientele in a rational and effective manner. Its 1994 *Directory of Long Distance Paths* describes 402 walks, and their spatial occurrence on the OS Landranger maps is recorded in 1080 citations. This data allows an overview of the spatial distribution of all LDWs in England and Wales (Fig.8.2). The mean density is 8.8 per map but the range is from several which offer contact with only one walk, to one where 42 LDWs may be encountered. This is *Sheet 109 Manchester* which embraces parts of a major urbanised area with a long history of upland walking and parts of the West Pennine Moors and the Peak District which afford excellent walking country. This conjunction of tradition, people and place with an extraordinary concentration of walks is not without interest; but the national picture affords more useful information.

	Walks per Map	*% of Maps*	*% of LDWs*
(1)	1 to 3	19.5 %	5.0 %
(2)	4 to 5	22.8 %	11.6 %
(3)	6 to 8	20.3 %	15.7 %
(1-3)	*1 to 8*	*62.6 %*	*32.3 %*
(4)	9 to 11	16.3%	18.7 %
(5)	12 to 17	12.2 %	20.4 %
(6)	19 to 42	8.9 %	28.6 %
(4-6)	*9 to 42*	*37.4 %*	*67.7 %*

The Spatial Pattern of 402 Long Distance Walks, 1994.

37% of the country with above average access to LDWs offers contact with 68% of the walks, while 63% with less than average access nevertheless has contact with 32% of them; and nowadays no place is far removed from at least one LDW. The relatively sparse distribution of National Trails and Regional Routes and its correlation with Dower's valued landscapes (Figs.4.2 & 8.1) have been overwhelmed by the massive voluntary sector provision; and the more populous regions now have the greater densities of walks. Thus the apparent focus of attention on the uplands of northern England (other than Northumberland and Cumbria) is equally coincident with closely settled regions of the 'industrial north'; and the secondary areas of above average provision occur along the London to Birmingham axis. Proximity to people is important and has been recognised; and most of those who enjoy a long walk may do so relatively close to their home - or elsewhere as they wish.

The occurrence of lighter densities of LDWs in the more distant rural regions complements this message. The well farmed lowland counties of eastern England may

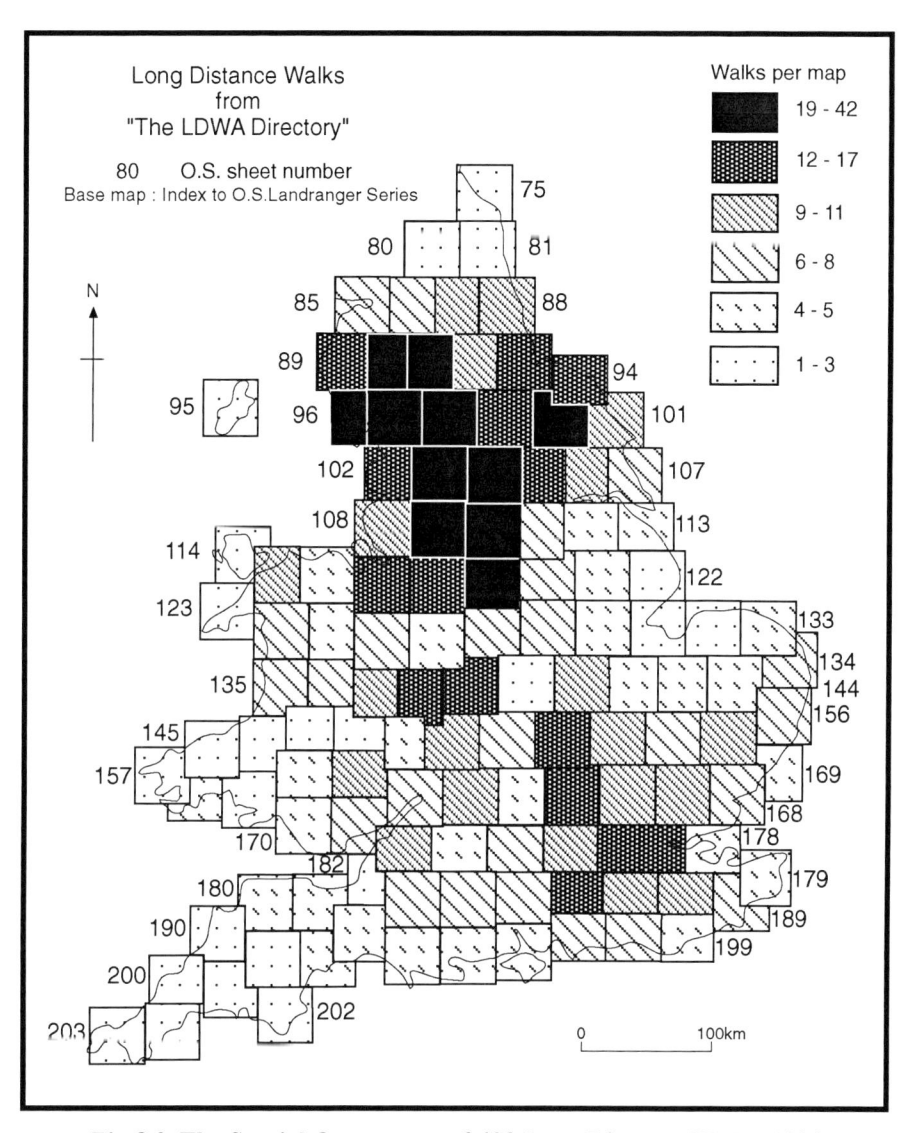

Fig.8.2 The Spatial Occurrence of 402 Long Distance Walks, 1994.

lack valued landscapes, but they are also sparsely populated and relatively remote. The latter factors probably are also responsible for the relative dearth of LDWs in Wales, the South-West peninsular and 'Wessex', Northumberland and Cumbria - notwithstanding the reputation of these parts of the country for their landscapes, moorlands and mountains, and their National Parks (Fig.4.2). In summary, the voluntary sector has responded much better than the public sector to people's needs in terms of proximity, as well as the length of walks.

183

County/MB	A .% of LDWA	B .% of Pop'l	A/B x100	LDWA Groups	Group Walks	National Events
1. North Yorkshire	5.7	1.5	380	3	66	34
2. West Yorkshire	9.1	4.3	212	2	26	12
3. E.Yorks/Humberside	3.5	1.8	194	1	30	4
4. Devon	3.5	2.1	167	0.5	11 *	3
5. Surrey	3.3	2.0	165	1	26	8
6. Shropshire	1.3	0.8	160	1	19	4
7. Cleveland	1.9	1.2	158	1	13	0
8. Cumbria	1.5	1.0	150	2	18	8
1-8	**29.8**	**14.7**	**200**	**30%**	**27%**	**37%**
9. Sussex	4.2	3.0	140	1	24	5
10. Hertfordshire	2.7	2.0	135	0.5	10 *	4
11. South Yorkshire	3.6	2.7	133	1	12	6
12. Cornwall	1.3	1.0	130	0.5	11 *	1
13. Greater Manchester	5.1	4.0	128	2	29	0
14. Lancashire	3.4	2.9	117	4	105	22
15. Berkshire	1.7	1.6	103	1	25	1
16. Hampshire	3.3	3.2	103	1	26	1
17. Greater London	9.4	9.3	101	1	42	1
9-17	**34.7**	**29.7**	**117**	**32%**	**37%**	**21%**
18. Suffolk	1.3	1.3	100	0.5	18 *	2
19. Cheshire	1.9	2.0	95	0	0	0
20. Isle of Wight	0.3-	0.3+	93	0	0	1
21. Kent	2.9	3.2	91	1	18	4
22. Cambridgeshire	1.2	1.4	86	0	0	1
23. Buckinghamshire	1.1	1.3	85	0.3	6 *	3
24. Tyne and Wear MB	2.0	2.4	83	0	0	—
25. Bedfordshire	0.9	1.1	82	0.3	6 *	1
26. Nottinghamshire	1.7	2.1	81	1	15	2
27. Staffordshire	1.7	2.1	81	1	25	2
28. Somerset	0.8	1.0	80	0	0	1
29. Avon	1.5	2.0	75	1	19	—
30. Essex	2.4	3.2	75	0.5	10 *	4
31. Gloucestershire	0.8	1.1	73	0	0	2
32. Dorset	0.1	1.4	71	1	12	5
33. Warwickshire	0.7	1.0	70	0	0	0
18-32	**20.2**	**23.7**	**87**	**18%**	**17%**	**14%**
34. West Midlands MB	3.8	5.6	68	0	0	0
35. Durham	0.8	1.2	68	0.5	12 *	2
36. Oxfordshire	0.8	1.2	67	0	0	2
37. Derbyshire	1.2	1.9	63	1	13	8
38. Lincolnshire	0.7	1.2	58	1	30	2
39. Wiltshire	0.6	1.2	50	1	14	4
40. Leicestershire	0.8	1.8	44	0	0	3
41. Wales	2.3	5.9	39	1	13	22
42. Northamptonshire	0.4	1.2	33	0.3	6 *	5
43. Merseyside MB	0.9	3.1	29	1	18	0
44. Hereford & Worcs.	0.4	1.4	28	1	14	4
45. Norfolk	0.3	1.6	19	0.5	18 *	3
46. Northumberland	0.1	0.6	17	0.5	12 *	3
34-46	**13.1**	**27.9**	**47**	**21%**	**20%**	**29%**

Table 8.6. LDWA Members, Groups, Local Outings and National Events by Counties and Metropolitan Boroughs, 1998

A sample of 1072 members' addresses shows that 1.8% lived in Scotland; and the distribution of the 1053 resident in England and Wales is summarised in Column 1 and compared with the distribution of the population as a whole in Columns 2 and 3 and Fig.8.3.
*Where a single Group serves two or more counties, the Walks it organised are divided between them.

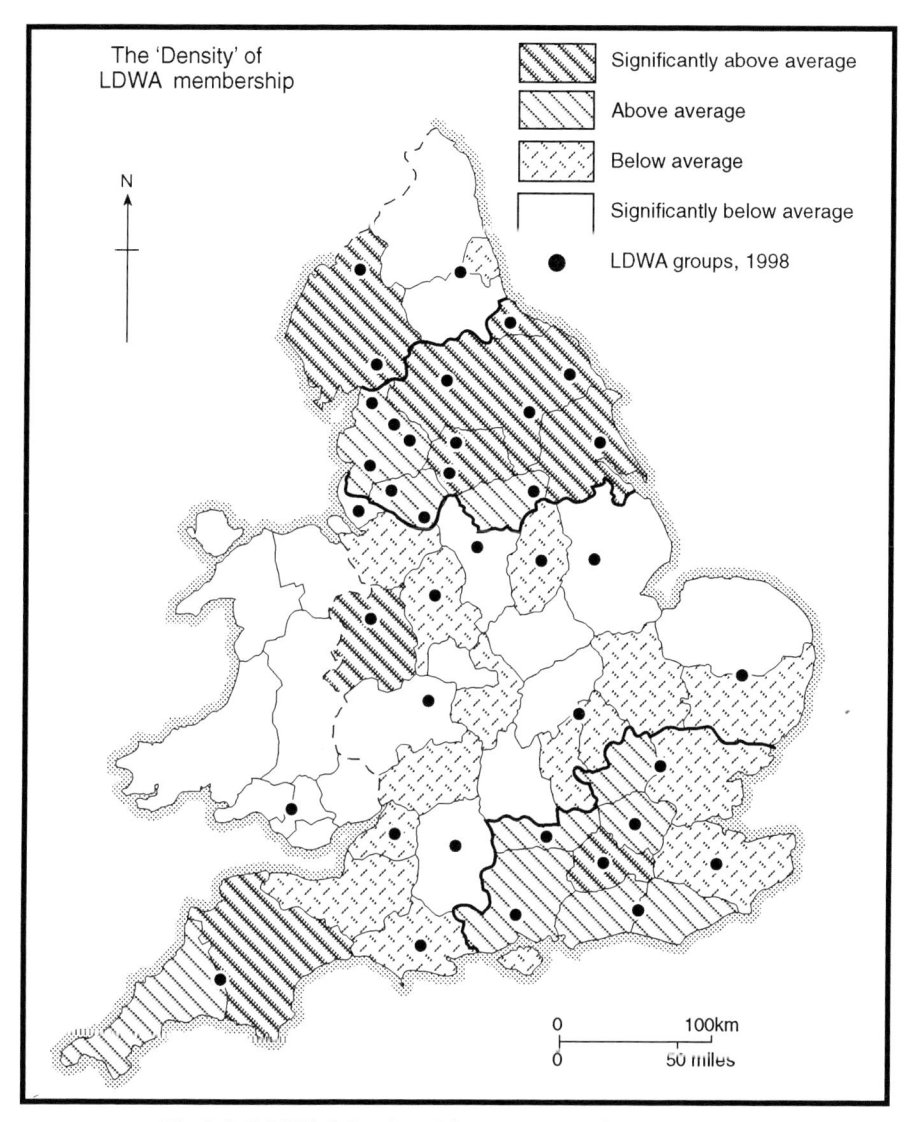

Fig.8.3 LDWA Membership and Local Groups, 1998.

4. The LDWA and the Promotion of Walking

The promotion of routes, often referred to as 'walks' 'ways' and even 'paths', is not synonymous with the promotion of walking; and many may scarcely ever be walked. However, the LDWA exercises a positive outreach to serve the wider community of long distance walkers; and this may be illustrated by spatial analysis of its membership, its organisational structure, and its programmes of local and national events (Table 8.6)

The spatial pattern of LDWA members reflects the strength of interest in long distance walking; and the Association's Local Groups, comprising capable and committed individuals, similarly reflect the strength of the organisation (Fig.8.3). Each Group de-

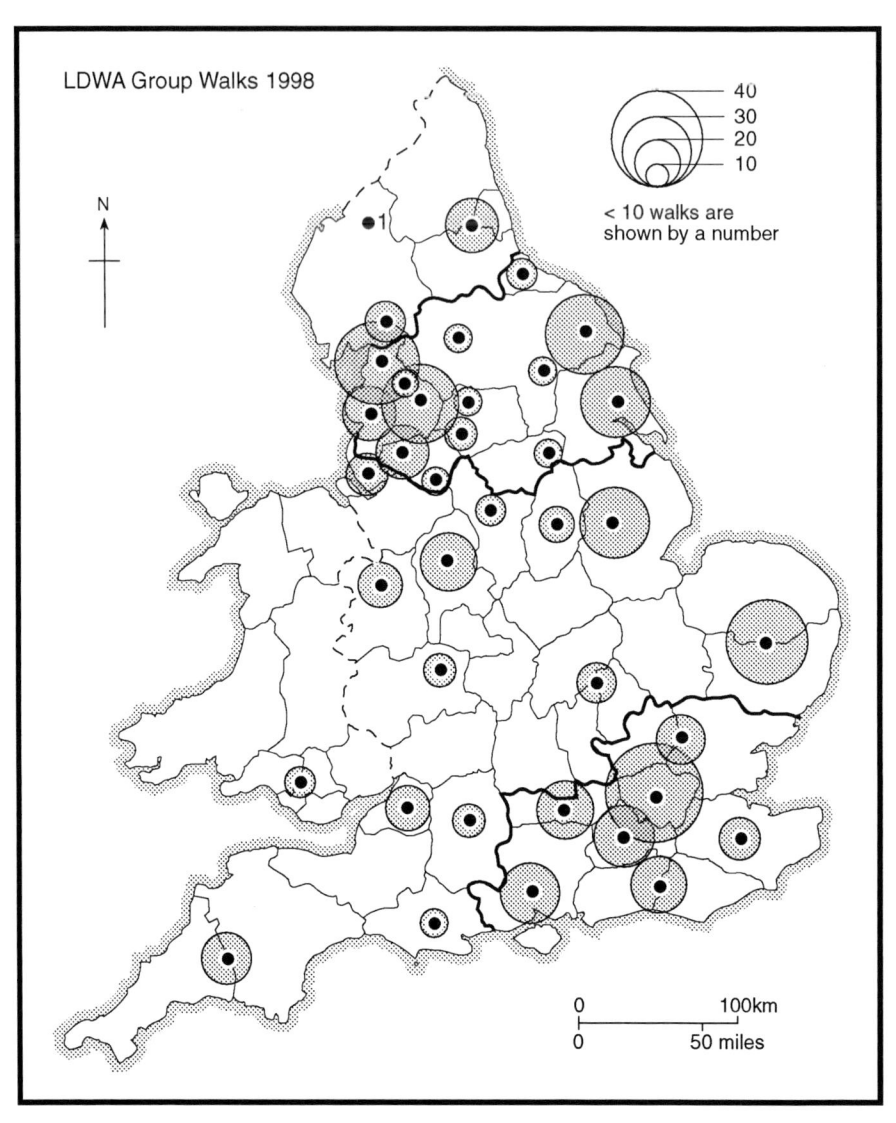

Fig.8.4 Local Walks Organised by LDWA Groups, 1998.

signs its own programme of local walks to serve the everyday interests of long distance walkers, and generally they are sociable occasions rather than competitive events. In 1998 the 38 Groups provided 771 walks; and the output ranged from that of the Cumbria Group, which was able to organise only one walk as a prelude to its AGM, to the London Group's regular weekend and mid-week walks comprising 42 events. Between these extremes, 21 Groups provided 11-20 walks; 11 provided 21-30; and 4 provided 31-36. In all cases there is a seasonal rythm; and the long leisure time-slots of summer weekends are the most popular, though 11 Groups also provided mid-week evening walks in summer.

While some Groups organise visits to distant places, most walks are within their own region and local needs are well served by the LDWA (Fig.8.4). Lancashire with Manchester has the most active membership. Only 8.5% of the LDWA live there but they provide 16% of the Groups and 134 or 17% of the Group Walks. Yorkshire, with Humberside and Cleveland, has a larger population and more LDWA members (23.8% in 8 Groups) and achieves similar performances in terms walks (147 or 19%), though these are spread over a much wider area. In summary, this 'northern bloc', already indentified by its density of long-distance routes (Fig.8.2), has only 18% of the population but accounts for 32% of the LDWA, 37% of the LDWA Groups and 36% of all Group Walks. Long-distance walking is also popular in the South-East where 28% of the population produce 30% of the Association's members, and seven Groups (18%) provided 181 (23%) of the 1998 walks. Members in Greater London (9.4%) just outnumber those in West Yorkshire (9.1%); but in proportion to its population, Surrey is the most active county in the South East and its 3.3% of the membership organised 26 walks (Table 8.6).

These concentrations of members and activities in the North and the South-East leave the greater part of the country (78%) and more than half of the population (53%) with only 38% of the long-distance walkers; and the latter are not evenly distributed. There are significant concentrations in Devon and Cornwall, Shropshire and Cumbria - all charismatic counties of 'Highland Britain' (Fig.4.2); which leaves the greater part of rural England and all of Wales with very few members (Fig.8.3 and Table 8.6). Even so, there are active Groups in some rural counties; and the Norfolk & Suffolk, the Lincolnshire and the Staffordshire groups provided 36, 30 and 25 walks respectively. But the corollary of such local concentrations is less elsewhere; and much of England and all of Wales appear to suffer from their 'rurality'. However, it is also clear that the Tyne & Wear, West Midlands, Merseyside and South Wales conurbations have not produced such a positive response to long-distance walking as that evident in urban regions of Lancashire, Yorkshire and the South-East. In short, the origins of these spatial patterns reflect a variety of factors - historical and geographical (Ch.1.8); but more to the point, they summarise current market demand and the voluntary sector's response in terms of carefully targeted provision.

The LDWA also promotes 'national events which are not restricted to its members but serve the needs and aspirations of all long distance walkers who relish a challenge at any time of the year. However, there is a seasonal rythym and a clear response to temporal factors affecting demand (Fig.8.5). May and September, on either flank of the holiday season and with generally favourable weather and long hours of daylight, are the most popular months; and May, with the benefit of two bank-holiday weekends, is particularly favoured. There is a lull in August at the heart of the holiday season; and a comparable fall in the lower level of winter activity occurs in December (Fig.8.5).

The programme of national events also is sensitive to preferences in terms of the length of walks; and this sensitivity extends to special recognition of charismatic distances such as 25 miles and the 26 mile 'marathon'. Beyond 30 miles, demand decreases and the task of organising walks increases, exponentially in each case. Consequently there were only a handful of walks in each class above 40 miles; and none above 70, save two special events at 100 miles - another 'magic' distance. Walks of 40 miles or more serve a small countrywide clientele and forge a camaraderie between regular participants which is consolidated by repeated meetings at annual 100-mile events. The LDWA recognises the need to succour and sustain these enthusiasts; but it dedicates the greater part of its

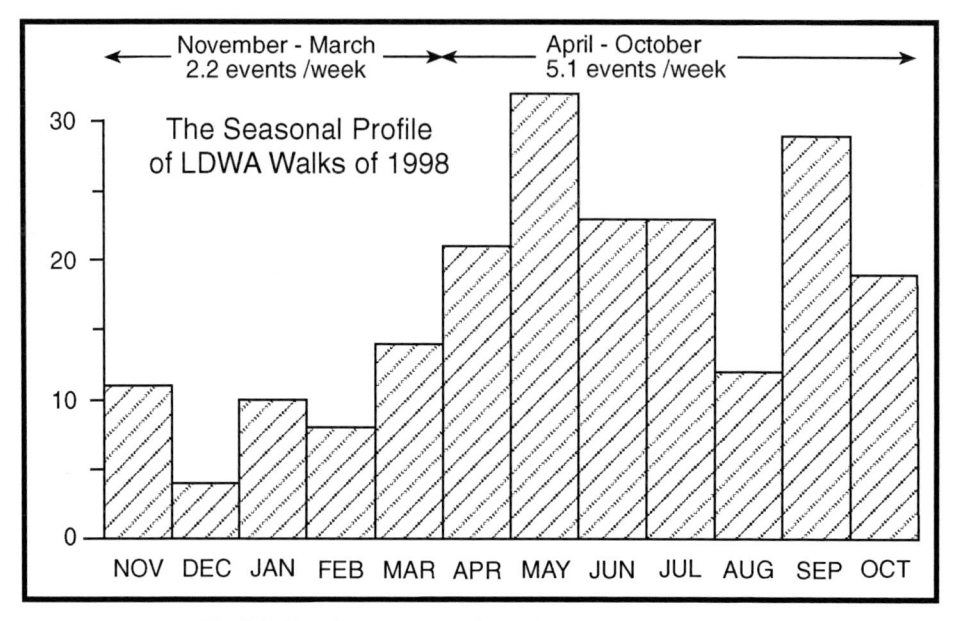

Fig.8.5 The Seasonal Profile of LDWA Walks, 1998.

Length	No.	%	Length	No.	%
20-24 miles	36	17.5%	30-39 miles	28	13.6 %
25 miles	53	25.7%	40-49 miles	8	3.9 %
26 miles	47	22.8%	50-59 miles	8	3.9 %
27-29 miles	19	9.2%	60-69 miles	7	3.4 %
20-29 miles	155	75.2%	*30+ miles*	*51*	*24.8 %*

The Length of the 206 LDWA National Challenge Walks of 1998.

programmes to the greater number of long-distance walkers. Furthermore, it recognises that every long distance walk is to some extent a special event, and many organisers simultaneously provide walks of more manageable dimensions. Thus the 1998 calendar included 139 supplementary options. 39 of these were of no more than 10 miles; and 79 were between 10 and 20 miles. Paradoxically, 21 or 15% were long distance walks in their own right, being in excess of 20 miles, but they offered options substantially shorter than the main walk.

    The spatial distribution of the LDWA's national challenge walks (Fig.8.6) differs significantly from the collective pattern of Group walks (Fig.8.4); and this reflects a range of factors. First, each walk must be within the province of a competent cadre, able and willing to manage and promote the event. Secondly, the venue must be accessible and attractive to sufficient walkers to make the event viable. Thirdly, the lie of the land and nature of the terrain, not just the distance, should contribute to the challenge and enjoyment of the walk; and in a similar vein, the pathways and environment should be sufficiently robust to support the event. Finally, since most long distance walkers are neither purists nor masochists but sensitive, sociable individuals with a strong appreciation of the

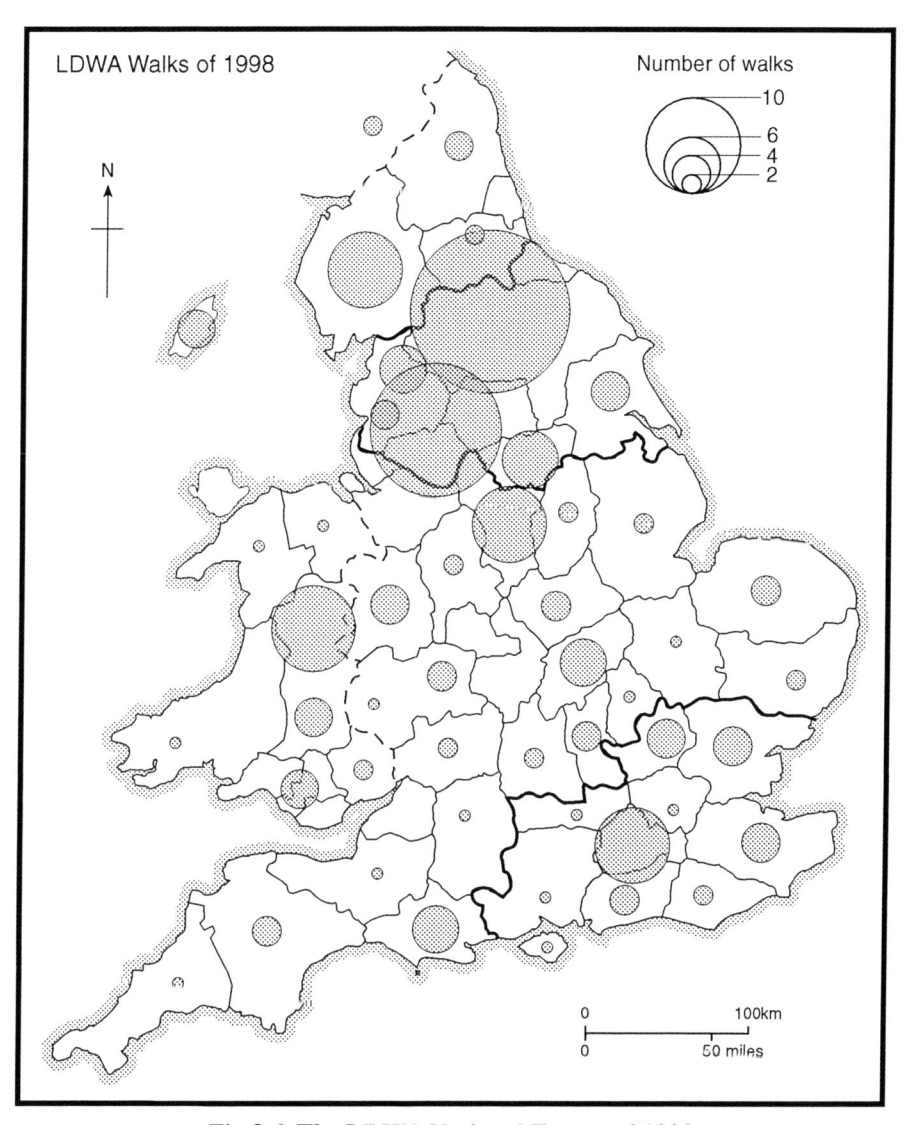

Fig.8.6. The LDWA National Events of 1998.

countryside, the character and quality of the landscape should significantly enhance the overall experience of the participants. The pattern of the 1998 programme of 206 events illustrates the net effect of these factors (Fig.8.6).

The national events are more widespread than the Group walks, and no part of the country is without reasonable access to at least one LDWA walk. However, they are particularly numerous in the northern block of long-distance walking country; and where 32% of all members, 37% of the Groups and 36% of the Group walks are to be found, it is not surprising that there should also be 38% of the LDWA's national events - even though this region accommodates only 18% of the national population. Furthermore, Cumbria with only 1.0% of the population, and 1.5% of the LDWA, figures prominently with 3.9% of the national events; and Derbyshire is similarly well used. Again, history and geography are important, and this varied territory lies astride the Pennines, includes four National Parks, the Yorkshire Wolds and a magnificent heritage coast; and it has become a mecca for long-distance walkers. In contrast, the South East, which is comparable in many relevant respects (28% of the population, 30% of the LDWA and 23% of the Group walks), was host to only 14% of the national programme of 1998; and perhaps it is too far south for northern walkers ! Nevertheless, it offers sufficient to establish it as a major contributor and venue, reflecting qualities of both its LDWA Groups and the land. These two regions, comprising little more than one-fifth of the country but accommodating 63% of the LDWA, accounted for more than half of the LDWA walks.

Elsewhere, despite the paucity of members and Group activity (Figs.8.3 & 8.4), the whole of rural England - from East Anglia, across the Midlands and down into the South-West peninsular - is equipped with 37% of the national events. These are spread widely but each is located carefully with reference to qualities of the land and landscape; and the Association responds to the best prospects in each county to make optimal provision for a national rather than a local clientele. Wales may present the best example of this balance of forces. It has few members and its only Group provided less than 2% of the 1998 local walks; but it was host to 22 (11%) of the national events, mostly in mid-Wales - reflecting the quality and accessibility of this highly varied, upland region.

Given that the Association's national events generally show a strong correlation with exceptional landforms and landscapes, a greater concentration in the National Parks might be expected. The cost and difficulty of access to some of the Parks may be a deterrent; but the greater part of the explanation may lie with a self-denial order that the LDWA will not promote events in areas known to be fragile or perceived to be under excessive pressure without explicit approval of the relevant land-managing authorities. This may be laudable, but it would be unfortunate if it excluded major events from highly valued locations. Fortunately, the prestigious LDWA 100-mile events are limited to 500 walkers and each follows a unique route designed for the event. Therefore, they can be planned in consultation with land-managing authorities and many have been granted access to National Parks over agreed routes. Such charismatic landscapes add significantly to these occasions, and the list of events reads like a catalogue of valued places (Table 8.7). However, such locations do not guarantee comfortable paths; on the contrary, path conditions in many parts of the National Parks and elsewhere in areas of exceptional quality often present a challenge to any walker - and, perhaps, a deterrent to any but a challenge walker.

The promotion of walking by the LDWA illustrates the ability of a well organised minority group to provide not only for its own members but also to generate interest and participation in its particular field bys others. This is undoubtedly true of many other capable organisations, such as the Ramblers' Association at national and local levels, and the Surrey Walking Club at a local level. Such committed, capable organisations and individuals are dedicated to their particular interests, and understandably so. However, ostensibly neutral governments and their agencies, with national responsibilities, should respond not primarily to the needs of such minorities but at least equally to the less able who stand in greater need of positive outreach if they are to enjoy access to countryside walking in any of its diverse forms. And this begs questions concerning the priority given to

Year	Event	Walkers	Completions	Best time
1973	Downsman	123	53 %	22.20
1974	Peakland	074	45 %	19.30
1975	Downsman	200	62 %	18.58
1976	Cleveland	200	41 %	24.10
1977	Downsman	215	66 %	18.31
1978	Cleveland	187	40 %	21.16
1979	Dartmoor	228	46 %	25.37
1980	Downsman	275	67 %	16.13
1981	Cumbrian	288	54 %	20.25
1982	Pilgrims Way	355	61 %	22.05
1983	Snowdonia	278	64 %	22.58
1984	Dartmoor	310	66 %	20.23
1985	Yorkshire Dales	461	51 %	21.45
1986	Downsman	434	86 %	16.32
1987	Snowdonia	423	69 %	21.00
1988	White Peak*	472	76 %	17.59
1989	Brecon Beacons*	417	72 %	21.42
1990a	Chilterns*	341	76 %	22.37
1990b	Shrops.Marches*	155	59 %	23.40
1991	Lancastrian*	460	85 %	18.48
1992	Invicta (Kent)*	447	75 %	22.01
1993	Cleveland*	499	66 %	22.50
1994	Dartmoor*	469	84 %	21.35
1995	Shropshire*	484	79 %	22.40
1996	Yorkshire Dales*	484	76 %	20.35
1997	Downsman*	475	85 %	20.17
1998	White Peak	494	71 %	21.50
1999	Durham Dales	474	77 %	22.40
2000	Canterbury	449	65 %	22.15

Table 8.7 The LDWA '100-mile Challenge Walks', 1973-2000.

This list provides a window onto the development of the LDWA and of long distance walking in recent years. (* completed by the author).

National Trails and Regional Routes, for which there has always been very limited demand.

5. The Utility and Use of Long Distance Routes

The utility of the National Trails, Regional Routes and other excessively long routes has been questioned on grounds of their length and, in many cases, their peripheral locations. Long linear walks also present logistical difficulties and, ideally, the walkers should be self-contained, which implies back-packing. This fits the concept of adventure walking that underpins their origin; but nowadays it is more common for walkers to deploy a support team or a shuttle service by members of their party at the beginning and end of each day's walk, when access to accommodation is often required. The walk is thus further embedded in an expedition; and all this may add to the adventure for the minority of walkers attracted by a challenge. However, the merit of the investment in any such route is best tested in terms of the enjoyment it provides; and the worth of a long distance walk may be measured by its use.

There is no evidence of any market research prior to the repeated commitment of substantial resources to National Trails and Regional Routes; and in 1988 a letter in *Strider* raised the vital question *"Are long distance paths used ?"*.

> Each May since 1976 I have walked a long distance path with a friend... There has been much enjoyment and variety in the walks. However, I have been surprised at how few other walkers we have met except on the Pennine Way and Coast to Coast Path. For example, on the South West Coast path from Minehead to Land's End in two one-week walks, we met less than ten people. On the Viking Way, Hereward Way and Somerset Way, we met no other walker. Have other readers any comments ? (D.S. of Bristol, Strider No.51, August 1988).

Visual impressions can be misleading; 2000 walkers in well spaced groups travelling in the same direction at the same pace would see no other walker, but 1000 travelling in each direction may give the impression of a busy path. The 'orientation' of maps and guides has created a strong bias as to where linear routes 'begin' and 'end', so most walkers do tend to follow each other. Also, those taking a stroll at a popular location on the route of a long distance walk might be persuaded that the whole route was well used. In short, walkers' impressions are unlikely to address the important underlying question; and therefore the present author put the question in a more structured form to the membership of the LDWA.

Each member was invited to report on a few contextual matters and their use and appreciation of 24 long distance paths, including all the National Trails. 953 (c.20%) replied; and it must be recognised that they are a committed cohort of long distance walkers with substantial experience of long routes. Men (87%) comprised a large majority; and while those over 60 were relatively few (5.8%) most respondents (67.7%) were of mature years (40-59) and only 9.9 % were under 30. Their post-codes broadly confirm the spatial prominence and paucity of long-distance walkers noted above (Fig.8.3); and this, in turn, may affect the spatial pattern of their activity.

The 24 routes comprise the 17 National Trails of the day, 6 Regional Routes and the Lyke Wake Walk (Table 8.8). Although each had completed at least one walk of 50+ miles, 137 (14%) of the respondents had walked none of the specified routes. This immediately affords support for DS's doubts as to the use and utility of National Trails and other LDFPs. The other 816 had completed 4616 walks on the 24 named routes, an average of 192 walks on each. But this represents an average of only 5.66 walks per person throughout their 'life-history' as a long-distance walker. Given their age and status as committed walkers, an average 'life-time' of 10 years may well be an under-estimate, but it would indicate 566 completions a year by 1000 such walkers. *If* there were or are 10,000 such

Yorkshire and Humberside	23.7 %
The North West	11.0 %
The North	8.9 %
The 'Northern Block'	*43.6 %*
London and the South East	*29.0 %*
East Midlands	7.5 %
West Midlands	7.0 %
East Anglia	2.3 %
The South West	7.8 %
The rest of England	*24.6 %*
Scotland, Wales and N.Ireland	2.8 %

The Residential Location of Respondants by Standard Regions

walkers, there would be 5660 walks to distribute over the 24 routes - an annual average of 236 on each, which hardly seems sufficient to justify any of them.

While such averages must carry weight, the actual distribution of use between routes is of greater interest; and as DS implied, this is very uneven (Table 8.8). Bill Cowley's 42-mile Lyke Wake Walk was the most popular and it sustained or suffered 25% of all walks on these 24 paths. 50% of the respondents had walked it at least once, and returnees accounted for 65% of the 1171 crossings of the North York Moors on this route. The Pennine Way was a close second in terms of customers (44%) but it attracted few returnees and carried only 10% of the walks. Wainwright's Coast to Coast Walk held third place with 33% of the walkers but, like the Pennine Way, few of its customers had returned and it provided only 6% of the walks. It is therefore arguable that the shorter South Downs Way, which served 32% of the walkers but supplied 12% of the walks is a stronger contender for 'third place' overall. The Cleveland Way, which carried as many walks as the Coast to Coast Walk and served nearly 30% of the walkers, completes the five routes which might lay some claim to popularity with experienced long distance walkers.

Offa's Dyke Path, the Ridgeway, the Cotswold Way, the Pembrokeshire Coast Path, the North Downs Way and the Dorset Coast Path follow in order of usage, but it would require a very sympathetic approach to describe any of them as 'popular'. The other 13 (54%) account for only 17% of the walks; and only the Wolds Way and the North Cornwall Coast Path attracted 10% of the walkers. However, the image of five coastal Trails has now been improved by cosmetics; and the merger of these would allow the 600-mile South West Coast Path to claim to 11.6% of the declared walks - though few would have been through-walks over the new Path. On the other hand, honest arithmetic will show that the path along the northern edge of the North York Moors which is simultaneously host to Cowley's Lyke Wake Walk, Wainwright's Coast to Coast Walk and the Cleveland Way did indeed carry 37.8% of all reported walks. The effects on the 'natural path' were noticeable; and, of course, more walkers noticed each other and, unlike DS, they might have taken away an impression that National Trails are busy places.

Route, Length and Status	Walkers			Frequency of Walks*						All Walks		
	No.	%	Rank	1	2	3	4	5	6	No.	%	Rank
Lyke Wake Walk 42 —	404	49.5	1	207	65	42	22	14	54	1171	25.2	1
Pennine Way 250 NT	357	43.8	2	294	41	12	4	4	2	468	10.1	3
Coast to Coast 190 RR	270	33.1	3	253	15	1	0	1	0	291	6.3	5
South Downs Way 106 NT	260	31.9	4	157	51	15	12	9	15	547	11.8	2
Cleveland Way 109 NT	240	29.4	5	203	30	4	1	1	1	294	6.3	4
Offa's Dyke Path 176 NT	209	25.6	6	190	13	2	1	0	3	256	5.5	6
The Ridgeway 85 NT	163	20.0	7	126	19	9	2	3	4	254	5.5	7
Cotswold Way 103 RR-NT	133	16.3	8	124	6	1	2	0	0	147	3.2	8
Pembrokeshire Coast 186 NT	105	12.9	9	97	6	1	1	0	0	116	2.5	12
North Downs Way 153 NT	98	12.0	10	85	6	3	0	1	3	141	3.0	10
Dorset Coast Path 72 NT	88	10.8	11	68	10	4	3	0	3	142	3.1	9
Wolds Way 81 NT	82	10.0	12	78	2	1	1	0	0	89	1.9	15
North Cornwall Coast 135 NT	80	9.8	13	65	8	1	2	1	3	127	2.7	11
Somerset/N.Devon Coast 82 NT	67	8.2	14	57	6	1	1	1	1	91	2.0	14
South Cornwall Coast 133 NT	65	8.0	15	52	7	1	3	0	2	101	2.2	13
The Two Moors Way 103 RR	64	7.8	16	58	2	2	1	0	1	82	1.8	16
South Devon Coast 93 NT	51	6.3	17	42	4	2	1	1	1	75	1.6	17
Cambrian Way 274 RR	43	5.3	18	42	1	0	0	0	0	44	0.9	19
Peddars Way & Norfolk Coast 93 NT	39	4.8	19	33	5	1	0	0	0	46	1.0	18
Hadrian's Wall Walk 75 RR-NT	35	4.3	20	34	1	0	0	0	0	36	0.8	20
Staffordshire Way 93 NT	27	3.3	21	25	1	1	0	0	0	30	0.6	21
Viking Way 140 RR	24	2.9	22	23	1	0	0	0	0	25	0.5	23
Thames Way 180 'NT'	22	2.7	23	17	4	1	0	0	0	28	0.6	22
Heart of England Way 100 RR	15	1.8	24	15	0	0	0	0	0	15	0.3	24

Table 8.8. The Popularity and Use of 24 Long Distance Walks by 816 Experienced Members of the LDWA.

> *Technical Note: The frequency of walks over the entire route is a key dimension, reflecting the popularity of a particular route and the experience it granted. The inquiry had not anticipated numerous completions and invited respondents to state the actual number if more than 5 had been made. The 92 responses were varied and included descriptive phrases such as 'several times'; evidently rounded figures such as 10/10+, 20, 25 and 40 which occur too frequently to be accepted at face value; and a range of specific, hopefully truthful numbers such as 8, 9, 12, 17 - and one of 118 by a Lyke Wake Walk addict. Excluding this one and taking all other numerical statements at the lowest option, the entries for the Lyke Wake Walk average 16 and that for the other eleven routes affected routes is 12. For the sake of simplicity, and to avoid over-stating the merit of repeat walks on selected routes, a somewhat arbitrary value of '10' has been allocated to all occurrences of 'more than 5' The Lyke Wake Walk is thus credited with 540 repeat walks (rather than the 864 which may have been done). The South Downs Way also is a 'loser' while the other 11 with few repeat walkers have generally benefitted.

The duration of walks and the size of groups provide additional perspectives on the use of the several routes (Tables 8.9 & 8.10). Respondents reported on their last complete walk over each route and collectively 2173 walks provided 17,122 days of enjoyment; and the data-set deserves close attention with reference to the diverse experiences sought by the walkers on different routes. These range from short, sharp challenges which test stamina and speed and involve some degree of navigational skill, through to expeditions or holidays which call for organisational skills, endurance and the commitment of numerous days, often spread over a series of visits. In each case, there is room for solitary endeavour, and singletons comprised 30% of the parties and 7% of the walkers; or, at the other extreme, for gregarious groups of 10 or more which accounted for only 11% of the parties

Route and Length	Walks	Duration of walks in days									Total days	Mean days
		1	2	3	4	5	6	7	10 *	17 * 24 *		
Lyke Wake Walk - 42	356	343	9	3	0	0	1	0	0	0 0	376	1.1
Pennine Way - 250	338	0	2	2	2	1	3	9	148	166 5	4526	13.4
Coast to Coast - 190	249	0	1	1	3	1	12	9	209	12 1	2475	9.9
South Downs Way - 106	210	53	44	25	26	22	19	12	9	0 0	718	3.4
Cleveland Way - 109	210	1	5	7	26	54	39	36	42	0 0	1312	6.2
Offa's Dyke Path - 176	193	0	3	1	2	6	1	17	150	8 ?	1874	9.7
The Ridgeway - 85	132	22	16	12	31	21	14	8	8	0 0	539	4.1
Cotswold Way - 103	110	1	1	2	14	27	23	33	9	0 0	659	6.0
Pembroke Coast - 186	91	2	1	1	3	5	6	9	57	6 1	839	9.2
North Downs Way - 153	72	8	11	5	5	5	8	6	23	1 0	427	5.9
Dorset Coast Path - 72	67	4	9	6	13	12	8	7	8	0 1	329	4.9
Wolds Way - 81	63	7	5	11	21	9	5	4	1	0 0	247	3.9
N.Cornwall Coast - 135	62	3	3	7	2	13	4	10	19	1 0	404	6.5
Somerset & N.Devon - 93	55	2	4	2	4	13	8	8	14	0 0	341	6.2
S.Cornwall Coast - 133	52	2	3	2	3	13	4	8	17	0 0	341	6.6
Two Moors Way - 103	58	1	2	3	4	14	17	10	6	1 0	349	6.1
S.Devon Coast - 93	38	1	1	4	4	5	7	7	8	1 0	244	6.4
Cambrian Way - 274	39	0	0	0	4	5	3	3	8	13 3	453	11.6
Peddars & Norfolk - 93	33	3	6	2	4	7	5	6	0	0 0	144	4.4
Hadrian's Wall - 75	29	4	2	5	3	5	4	4	2	0 0	132	4.6
Staffordshire Way - 93	24	0	4	6	2	6	1	2	3	0 0	114	4.8
Viking Way - 140	16	1	1	0	1	3	4	2	4	0 0	100	6.3
Thames Way - 286	16	0	2	2	2	0	0	2	7	1 0	119	7.4
Heart of England - 100	14	0	0	4	4	3	2	1	0	0 0	62	4.4

Table 8.9 LDWA Walkers on Long Distance Paths : The Duration of Walks
(* Rounded numbers)

but 46% of the walkers. However, long-distance walks do not exclude a preference for sociable companionship, and 33% of the parties and 15% of the walkers were couples, while groups of 3-9 persons comprised 26 % of the parties and 32% the walkers.

Most routes serve a range of purposes, but some have a special role and reputation, and the current data set embraces a variety of situations. Cowley's vision evidently matched a substantial need and the utility and popularity of the 42-mile Lyke Wake Walk is beyond question. It is essentially a 'challenge walk' and 96% of the walkers made their crossings within Cowley's limit of 24 hours. It generates short visits rather than expeditions, and only one walker spent more than a weekend on it. Also, more than any other route, it served large groups and organised outings. Groups of 11 or more comprised 34% of all parties and accounted for 68% of the crossings. Singletons comprised less than 10% and made less than 1% of the crossings. The South Downs Way also attracts challenge walkers and organised events. 19% of its groups comprised more than 10 persons and accounted for 71% of all users; and the *'South Downs 80'*, a well established trail race, may explain many of the completions achieved within 24 hours. The Ridgeway has some claim to a similar role, and 22 (17%) of its users covered its 85 miles within a single day.

Since 1973 the annual 'LDWA 100' has provided a popular annual challenge walk and, together with other LDWA events, this may have deprived or relieved National Trails and other routes of some, perhaps many,competitive customers, thus reducing their use and utility. Nevertheless, the Pennine Way is seen to be *the place* to prove one's worth;

Route	1	2	'4'	'8'	'15'	'25'	Walkers	Groups	Mean
Lyke Wake Walk	36	62	72	80	67	53	3418	370	9.2
Pennine Way	99	128	82	10	24	1	1148	344	3.3
Coast to Coast Walk	67	106	65	15	10	-	809	263	3.1
South Downs Way	73	58	25	7	10	28	1195	201	6.0
Cleveland Way	71	78	43	15	10	5	794	222	3.6
Offa's Dyke Path	62	75	47	7	9	-	544	200	2.7
The Ridgeway	52	50	23	7	9	-	435	141	3.1
Cotswold Way	42	42	22	4	5	-	321	115	2.8
Pembrokeshire Coast	30	32	20	8	4	2	348	96	3.6
North Downs Way	36	13	13	3	3	8	383	76	5.0
Dorset Coast Path	29	33	6	2	1	-	175	72	2.4
Wolds Way	18	20	12	5	10	3	371	68	5.4
North Cornwall Coast	30	29	7	2	2	-	162	70	2.3
Somerset & N.Devon	23	22	13	-	1	1	159	59	2.7
South Cornwall Coast	25	25	5	1	1	-	118	57	2.1
Two Moors Way	18	16	15	8	2	-	204	59	3.5
South Devon Coast	21	13	2	4	2	-	117	42	2.8
Cambrian Way	10	13	11	3	2	-	134	39	3.4
Peddars & Norfolk Coast	16	11	8	1	1	-	93	37	2.5
Hadrian's Wall Walk	9	10	8	3	1	-	100	31	3.2
Staffordshire Way	8	11	1	2	-	2	75	24	3.1
Viking Way	7	5	1	3	1	-	60	17	3.5
Thames Path	8	8	2	-	-	-	32	18	2.0
Heart of England Way	8	3	3	-	-	-	26	14	1.9

Table 8.10 LDWA Walkers on Long Distance Paths : The Size of Groups
Groups of 3-5 are given a value of '4'; those of 6-10, '8'; those of 11-20, 15; and those of 21 or more - '25'.

and those who have done it twice, once in each direction, stand tall, even amongst Lyke Wake Walk addicts. The survey embraced a few superb athletes who covered the 250 miles in less than 5 days, but for most the Pennine Way is a test of endurance, durability and organisational ability. 44% of the walks took 7 to 13 days, 51% occupied more than a fortnight and five continued into a fourth week. Together, they provided 338 walkers with some 4500 days of walking - 35% more than the combined contribution of the 14 less popular walks (Tables 8.9-8.10).

However, this forbidding provider of ascetic adventure is a source of much disappointment to many, and *The Pennine Way Management Project* reported that:

> Some 5000 walkers head north from Edale each year... and there is a drop-out rate of 70% around Standedge and Mankinholes, this massive defeat being the result of exertions on the first two days... Few experienced walkers have not been confused and exhausted at some time in their lives by the mires and maze of goughs on Kinder, Bleaklow and Black Hill. (CCP.297, 1991).

Such dismal news indicates that the attraction of the concept inflicts massive pressure on the southern, highly vulnerable stages of the Way and that the reality of the truncated experience disappoints the majority of its users - and is not reported in the survey of LDWA walkers. Paradoxically, the failure rate may enhance its reputation as the premier challenge walk. As A.J. Brown indicated in 1938, it is the 'sustained lyric thrill', if not the horror of moorland tramping, that lends such uplands their peculiar attraction (Ch.1.8). In which case the Countryside Commission's expensive intention that maintenance of the Trail should reflect the highest standards could be misplaced but for the prior need to limit environmental damage, which in turn begs the question as to why this 250-mile route was given the highest priority in the first place.

The 190-mile Coast to Coast Walk is less demanding, embraces a greater variety of landscapes and is more appealing to countryside walkers. Nevertheless, it too calls for commitment over lengthy periods and, on average, it entertained its 249 walkers for ten days and provided 2475 days of enjoyment. The 176-mile Offa's Dyke Path was similarly used for 1874 days by 193 walkers; but all of the other very long routes - Pembrokeshire Coast Walk, the Cambrian Way and the undeveloped Thames Path - attracted very few (Table 8.9).

The shorter Trails show a similar range of popularity. The attraction of the dual-purpose 106-mile South Downs Way and the 85-mile Ridgeway has been noted above; and both the 109-mile Cleveland Way, where 210 walkers enjoyed 1312 days and the 103-mile Cotswold Way, where 110 walks occupied 659 days, may be recognised as popular walks. The best of the rest are the North Downs Way, where 72 walkers spent 427 days, the Dorset Coast Path and the Wolds Way, which entertained 67 and 63 users for 329 and 247 days. None of these can be described as popular options with the LDWA walkers, but they are within the upper half of the list (Table 8.9). Hadrian's Wall Walk, the Staffordshire Way, the Viking Way, and the Heart of England Way each attracted less than 30 walkers and, collectively, they provided only 527 days of enjoyment during the combined life-time experience of 953 members of the LDWA.

Such limited use may defy rather than deny their utility, but these walks were evidently surplus to current requirements of long distance walkers and they point to over-provision and a dearth of market-research if nothing else. Furthermore, no matter how good or poor they maybe, their inherent properties have been experienced by so few that they cannot be promoted, or criticised, by any substantial body of users. Success breeds success; and minimal use too readily implies limited utility, whereas it might comprise criticism of suppliers who have glutted the market with routes which may never attract sufficient custom to evaluate their worth or justify their existence. This situation calls for a regulatory role by a central authority; and whereas the current *LDWA Directory of Long Distance Walks* is deliberately descriptive, its utility may be improved if some systematic judgement on quality could be introduced. This, however, is a task which should not be left to the voluntary sector.

In addition to the actual use of the 24 routes, the survey explored some contextual factors, notably their location in relation to the source of walkers; and, secondly, the path users' evaluation of their walks, which may affect their role as advocates of particular routes. The northern four of the five most popular walks benefit from proximity to the greatest concentration of walkers . The Lyke Wake Walk derived 38% of its users from

Yorkshire and Humberside; and the three northern regions together provided 59%. Even so, it served the national market, and the southern counties supplied 22% of its users. The Cleveland Way drew 58% of its walkers from the North and 26% from the South, reflecting a substantial dependence on its home region while serving the country as a whole. The Coast to Coast Walk and Pennine Way are less dependent on their local region and drew 29% and 31% of their users from the South, thus establishing a stronger claim to 'national' status.

The popular southern routes similarly depend heavily upon their regional market while also attracting users from further afield. The South West Coast paths derived 63% of their walkers from the South-East and the South-West, and another 11% from the Midlands. The comparable figures for the South Downs Way are 63% and 12%; for the Ridgeway, 62% and 12%; and the Cotswold Way, 43% and 22%. The two walks in Wales, on the Pembrokeshire Coast and Offa's Dyke, have no sizeable local support and consequently may have the greater claims to national stature; they each drew 43% of their walkers from the South, 15% and 16% from the Midlands, and 36% and 34% from the North. In summary, while proximity to a major source of walkers inevitably provides a regional bias, each of the few popular walks draws clients from all parts of the country; and their reputations must be widespread

In contrast, walkers on the least used routes are mostly drawn from limited areas and, being few in number, their voice will have limited impact even in their own locality. For example, 69% of the 110 who had walked the North Downs and/or the Thames Path were from the South; 61% of the 39 with experience of the Peddar's Way and Norfolk Coast Path came from East Anglia or the South; 58% of the Viking Way's walkers were from the East Midlands or Yorkshire & Humberside; 54% of walkers on the Wolds Way were from Yorkshire and Humberside; 53% of the Two Moors' walkers were from the South; and 48% of the handful who had walked the Staffordshire Way or Heart of England Way were from the Midlands. Clearly, a problem of the less popular walks is the paucity of their users.

The reputation of a route also may be affected by the opinion of its users no less than the weight of their voices; and the survey asked respondents to summarise their views on a five point scale from 'very poor' to 'excellent' in respect of their last walk on each route in terms of three parameters:

- *(a) **The Recreational Experience*** (scenic quality, enjoyment,sense of satisfaction and achievement, etc).
- *(b) **The Quality of the 'Way'*** (condition of the path,signposting, facilities, etc);
- *(c) **The Weather*** during the walk.

Many walks had been made some considerable time earlier, and this apparently simple task was not seen to be easy, partly because many respondents felt constrained to recall the evidence rather than report their memories which, in fact, are the continuing part of their experience and an effective determinant of their current impression of the event (Fig.1.3). Nevertheless, most undertook it and the data merits attention (Table 8.11).

The walkers were highly appreciative of the general outcome, and nine of the 24 routes provided excellent experiences. The best of these were obtained on very long,

Route	Exp.	Path.	Wthr.	All 3	Rank	Rpt.Users
Dorset Coast	5.1	4.6	4.3	14.0	1	23 %
Pembrokeshire Coast	5.1	4.6	4.3	14.0	2	8 %
N. Cornwall Coast	5.2	4.5	4.2	13.9	3	19 %
S. Cornwall Coast	5.1	4.4	4.4	13.9	4	20 %
S. Devon Coast	5.1	4.6	4.1	13.8	5	18 %
Somerset & N.Devon Coast	5.1	4.6	4.1	13.8	6	15 %
Coast to Coast	5.3	4.2	3.9	13.4	7	6 %
Cambrian Way	5.3	4.4	3.7	13.4	8	5 %
South Downs Way	4.6	4.4	4.4	13.4	9	40 %
Offa's Dyke Path	4.9	4.4	4.0	13.3	10	9 %
Pennine Way	5.6	3.8	3.6	13.0	11	18 %
Cleveland Way	4.8	4.1	3.8	12.7	12	15 %
Cotswold Way	4.4	4.2	3.8	12.4	13	7 %
Peddars Way & Norfolk Coast	4.2	4.1	4.1	12.4	14	15 %
Two Moors Way	4.6	3.7	3.8	12.1	15	9 %
North Downs Way	4.1	4.0	4.0	12.1	16	13 %
The Ridgeway	4.3	3.9	3.7	11.9	17	23 %
Hadrian's Wall Walk	4.3	3.6	4.0	11.9	18	3 %
Wolds Way	4.1	3.9	3.8	11.8	19	5 %
Thames Way	4.3	3.7	3.7	11.7	20	23 %
Staffordshire Way	4.4	3.6	3.4	11.4	21	7 %
Lyke Wake Walk	4.3	3.1	3.7	11.1	22	47 %
Heart of England Way	3.7	3.3	3.9	10.9	23	0 %
Viking Way	4.0	3.3	3.4	10.7	24	4 %

Table 8.11 LDWA Walkers' Evaluation of (1) the Experience, (2) the Path and (3) the Weather provided by 24 Long Distance Routes.

7185 items of information have been reduced to 72, three for each route. Descriptive labels have been reduced to give categories:

Score	Label	Occurrences
5.0 - 5.4	Excellent	9
4.5 - 4.9	Very Good	17
4.0 - 4.4	Good	22
3.5 - 3.9	Poor	19
3.0 - 3.4	Very Poor	5

The routes are ranked on their combined score for the three parameters; if this is equal, the best score for the experience is taken into account and then the percentage of repeat walkers, which is taken as an indicator of 'satisfaction'.

upland walks: the Pennine Way, the Coast to Coast Walk and, despite the fact that it attracted only 43 walkers, the Cambrian Way. Evidently the challenge these afford is rewarding to those who succeed. The other six were all coastal paths, and their clients clearly endorse John Dower's selection of picturesque coasts. At the other end of the scale, only the Heart of England Way was seen to be 'poor' and, perhaps coincidentally, this was the least popular walk. The Viking Way, the Wolds Way, the North Downs Way with the Peddars Way & North Norfolk Path complete the lowest quartile; and it will be noted that three of the five are National Trails.

The quality of the path is an important variable in its own right but it also has a significant effect on the overall experience. Even hardened long distance walkers are sensitive to conditions underfoot, and the paths on 10 routes were found to be poor or very poor. None was excellent but 9 were good, and 5 were very good. These particularly favourable conditions all occurred on the coastal paths of the South West and South Wales; and they fortify or underpin the quality experiences enjoyed there. Poor paths were more widespread; the Lyke Wake Walk had the worst but those on the Viking Way and the Heart of England Way also were very poor. These three are at the bottom of the table, and nine of the paths in the lower half had unsatisfactory paths while the Pennine Way was the only route in the upper half to suffer such conditions. With this notable exception, there is a strong suggestion that the overall experience and path conditions are related; and the latter is capable of being managed to improve the former.

Weather conditions are an independent variable and given the duration of outings on long distance walks, choosing fine days is not always an option. Even summer weather is variable and the walks are split evenly between 'good' and 'poor' conditions except for two, the Viking Way and the Staffordshire Way, where very poor weather prevailed. There is, however, a clear 'North-South' divide, which may be reinforced by an upland-lowland dichotomy. All the southern coastal walks, with good paths, enjoyed good weather; and these must be favourite places for holiday-makers. And all of the northern walks are associated with poor weather, except the Viking Way and the Staffordshire Way where very poor weather prevailed and, paradoxically, the most northerly upland walk by Hadrian's Wall where 75 walkers generally enjoyed good weather.

This final part of the survey offers useful messages though, by their very nature, they are higly qualitative; and some appear to be in conflict with the popularity ratings based on usage. Thus the two most popular walks, the Lyke Wake Walk and the Pennine Way, are ranked 22nd and 11th respectively, but each is a special case. Both essentially present a challenge for those in search of ascetic adventure; and although afflicted by poor paths and poor weather, the Pennine Way was the most highly rated of the 24 routes in terms of overall experience. It is glorious in its awfulness, and the enormity of the challenge and the achievement underpin its image and popularity. This also applies to the Lyke Wake Walk, which has the worst paths and poor weather, but is the most frequently used and has the highest rate of repeat users. Its length (40 miles) is a key factor and 96% of its users complete the walk within 24 hours; they do not have to endure successive days in high, wild places; but a day's experience provides highly valued recollections

The key to its popularity therefore may be its length, and a brief note on another well known, short route may support this important indicator as to why the very long walks are relatively unused. The 24-mile *Three Peaks Walk*, embracing Pen-y-ghent (2278 feet), Whernside (2416 feet) and Ingleborough (2376 feet) is very popular with a wide range of users, including many who enjoy a short, sharp challenge (Fig.8.7). Heavy use caused excessive wear to 'natural paths' and, being in the Yorkshire Dales National Park, its condition caused considerable distress, publicity, investigation and expenditure (Ch.7.6). Consequently it was subject to close attention (Fig 8.7).

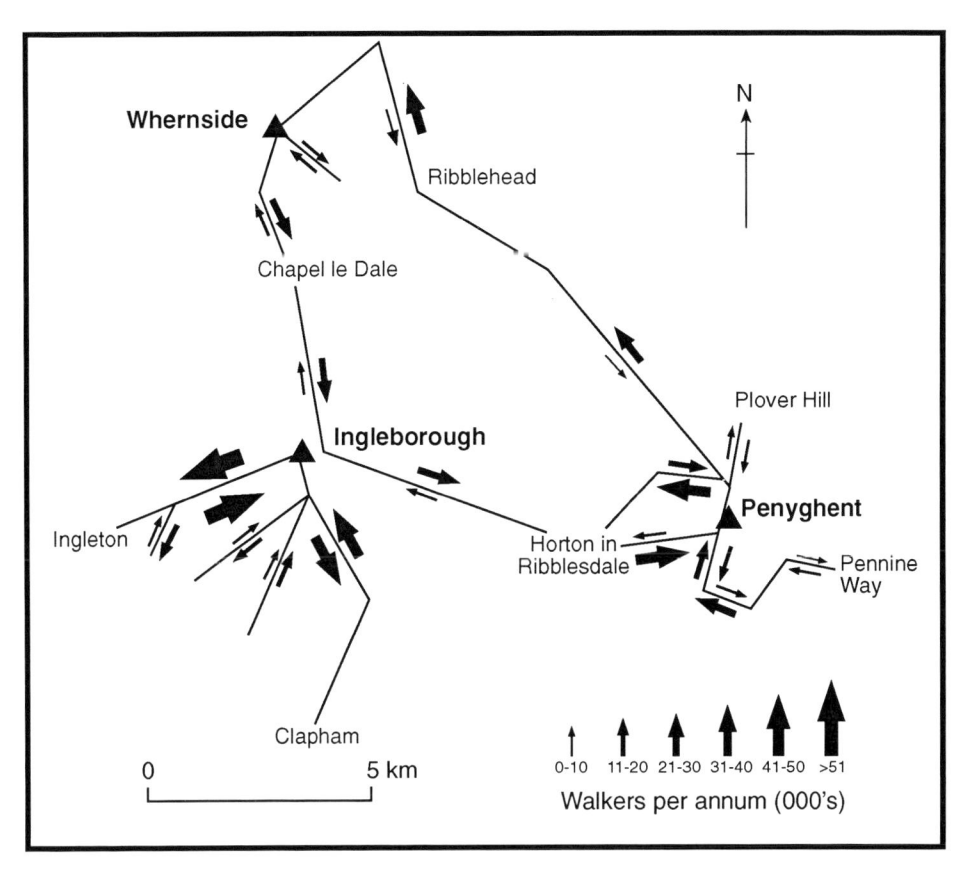

Fig.8.7 Path Usage on the Three Peaks Walk and adjacent paths, 1985.

A survey in 1985 indicated that 250,000 people per annum were using the major paths in the Three Peaks areas comprising:

Fell Runners	1.8 %
Pennine Way Walkers	5.1 %
Challenge Walkers	26.1 %
All long-distance walkers	*33.0 %*
Day Walkers	57.0 %
Educational Visits	3.5 %
Other visitors	6.5 %.

Ingleborough was the most popular peak (150,000 visitors), followed by Peny-ghent (60,000) and Whernside (40,000)... The levels of path-use also varied widely... and some paths are more popular for one direction of travel than the other. (Yorkshire Dales National Park, 1993).

28% of the users, some 83,000, are properly identified as long distance walkers since they are enjoying the full 24 miles of the Three Peaks; and they are six times more numerous the Pennine Way walkers, who pass over part of the circular walk. So the case material provided by the *Lyke Wake Walk* and the *Three Peaks Walk* allows a dual response to DS's question which refers to the use of very long distance routes. All the evidence supports his doubts and fears; and, with three or four possible exceptions, the National Trails and Regional Routes are used only by a handful of long distance walkers, including those who distribute their walk over several visits. Supply of such long routes greatly exceeds demand, and even the relatively popular routes are very lightly used - although contrary, impressions have been given much publicity when and where the low carrying capacity of some 'natural paths' generated environmental concerns. On the other hand, there is clear evidence, if only from two data sets, that long distance walks of 20 to 30 miles and possibly upto 40 miles are substantially more popular. They provide a better service for walkers and a better return on investment; and they comprise the greater part (89%) of the provision by the LDWA for long distance walkers.

6. Site Surveys and 'SDUs' on National Trails

However, the long-overdue need to face the naked truth that 'the concept of long distance routes is confused and dated' has yet to be properly addressed; and in 1988 the official LDFPs were translated into National Trails, Regional Routes were created, and the image of each was enhanced. There is now no room for a U-turn, but a commitment to retrieve the situation and a strategy for doing so is urgently required. Site surveys on particular routes provide complementary data to that set out above and, together, they indicate a basis for a new approach to the National Trails and Regional Routes.

It is ironic that the use and utility of long distance footpaths were not investigated until wear and tear on 'natural paths' raised environmental issues and management crises (Ch.7.6). A spate of surveys ensued; and a collation of data from surveys carried out between 1990 and 1996 on six National Trails - the Pennine Way, the Cleveland Way, Offa's Dyke Path, the North Downs Way, the Thames Path and the South West Coast Path - provides key material and usefully differentiates 'SDUs' from 'LDUs':

> Around three million visits are made each year to the six Trails surveyed. 39,000 of them are by 'long distance users' (LDUs), spending several days or weeks walking all or part of the trail. The remainder are by 'short distance users' (SDUs), out for just a day's walk or less. (CCP.524, 1997).

Spread over the 1570 miles of these six Trails, the 39,000 LDUs provide a density of 25 walkers per mile per annum, which confirms the very light use of them for their original and present ostensible purposes. On the other hand, the SDUs are lightly dismissed as 'the remainder' because they are just out for a short walk; but they generate 98.7% of the visits and 2,960,000 short walks, with a mean density of 1885 per mile. In practice their walks are concentrated on selected short sections of the Trails in particularly accessible locations, often adjacent to resorts or other settlements and at places noted for their scenic qualities. For example, just south-east of Whitby, the Cleveland Way carried 112,000 walkers in the five summer months of 1989 (Keirle, 1990). In short, the SDUs are adventitious users; and the existence of the Trail is likely to be coincidental rather than central to their visit; but their use of the Trails is central to any justification of the massive investment in them.

The SDUs, in fact, are the principal customers of the National Trails, and it would be appropriate if their particular needs were directly addressed and given priority in planning for the use of the Trails and in their promotion. 'A quarter of the SDUs on the South West Coast Path were using the Trail as part of a circular walk'; and the obvious compromise is the provision of short circular walks coincident in part with the sections of the Trails which are already popular with the SDUs. These short walks should be equipped throughout with quality paths, furniture and fittings; but the longer, intervening stretches of the Trails need be no more than adequate for their expected use by a small number of LDUs comprising experienced, hardy walkers. Promotional materials would need to be amended to reflect the dual purpose of the Trails; and part of the solution is to publicise a series of individual brochures and/or a volume of 'Short Walks on the....Way'. Staffordshire Ramblers have provided a pointer in this direction with their volume of 16 circular walks on *The Best of the Staffordshire Way;* and if only in this context, the merit of restoring the 600-mile South-West Coast Path to its original component parts deserves careful consideration (Table 8.1).

None of this calls for originality, merely for the commonsense and courage first, to recognise the National Trails and Regional Routes as the white elephants they have always been and which irrefutable data now show them to be; and, secondly to devise a new strategy which will recognise and promote their individual utility and use, for not all of them will attract holiday-makers and thousands of SDUs. A report on users of the South West Coast Path (1994) seems to be on the brink of such an approach:

> Some of the results do no more than quantify what was already known... For example, most people could have told us that a majority of users in the summer are holiday-makers... We now know that 687,000 people (64% of all users) are in this category... (and this) will be put to good use, informing local authorities and the tourism industry, to make them more aware of the importance of this 'green tourism resource'; and it will help the Countryside Commission to attract additional funding... and to market the Trail more effectively and sensitively.

'National Trail users on holiday tend to spend longer away from home than the average holiday maker' and 'nearly two-thirds (of them) come from socio-economic Groups A or B who bring significant economic benefits to the rural communities through which they pass'. Alas, many SDUs are day visitors and, like LDUs who are 'camping rough or staying with friends and relatives... they spend nothing at all on accommodation'; and they also spend 'considerably less during the daytime' (CCP.524, 1997). Individually, each SDU may give less support to the local economy, but collectively nearly three million SDUs must have an economic impact in excess of that of 39,000 LDUs. The future of most if not all National Trails lies very largely with short distance walkers, whether holiday-makers or day visitors; and they make the greater contribution to the new image and role of some Trails as 'green' tourist attractions. However, there should be no new fetish and, useful though they are, it would be unfortunate if the use of the National Trails is perceived in terms of LDUs and SDUs. Provision for walking should serve the needs of all types of walkers (Fig.1.2) in proprotion to their numbers and needs; and the promotion of walking should serve the nation as a whole. Hitherto the investment in National Trails and Regional Routes has conspicuously failed to achieve these objectives and steps to redress this situation are long overdue.

Plate 8.2 Strollers or Hikers ? LDUs or SDUs ?

Countryside tourism and leisure activities are making an important contribution to the rural economy...In 1998 £11.5 billion was spent...by day visitors from home (77%), UK tourists (17%) and overseas visitors (6%)... on eating and drinking (46%), travel (20%), attractions and entertainments (15%), shopping (11%) and accommodation (8%). (*Countryside Focus 7*, May 2000). This evidence, and the survey of National Trail Users (CCP.524, 1997) highlight the key role of day visitors (SDUs). Yet the media all too often give prominence to the image of expert, long-distance walkers (LDUs). The truth deserves more respect.

Plate 9.1 Making Countryside Visitors Welcome ?
All too often, the promotion of walks and walking inhibits rather than
facilitates participation by inexperienced visitors.

9
PUTTING PEOPLE FIRST?
'RECREATION 2000' AND CIRCULAR WALKS

The Countryside Commission's task is to make an attractive countryside truly accessible and its benefits available to the whole public.. Opportunities to enjoy the countryside are of no use unless people are aware of them.. Alongside awareness there needs to be a confidence and ability to enjoy the countryside.. Traditional ways of involving people through activities such as guided walks and natural history clubs cater for a small, interested section of the population.. The most important target should be the 50% of the population who make few trips to the countryside.. We therefore propose.. to improve and extend opportunities for the public to enjoy the countryside. (CCP. 225, 1987).

1. 'Recreation 2000' - Putting People First ?

These worthy sentiments and intentions were aired in the final consultation paper on policies for *Recreation 2000: Enjoying the Countryside**; and, given a prior statement that 'Public enjoyment of the countryside should rank in importance as a land use with food and timber production.' (CCP.224, 1987), some real hope for people-oriented policies must have been kindled. The Commission had the advantage of its joint study with the Sports Council into *Access to the Countryside for Recreation and Sport* (CCP.216, 1986) and of a conference report on *New Approaches to Access in the Countryside* (CRRAG, 1986). And it was evidently aware of key messages from its own surveys concerning the division of countryside visitors into the 'privileged few' and the 'disadvantaged majority' (Ch.4.5).

Each of these sources highlighted the complexity and dynamic diversity of countryside affairs and the related range of vested interests and underlying differences in beliefs and values (Ch.2-4). Only the disadvantaged majority had no direct voice, but the question of social equity was aired. Sidaway (1986) specifically asked 'Is it right that more resources should be given to those groups who are already well provided for and are the main beneficiaries of existing policy ?.. This is an important issue to be debated in the context of the Commission's *Recreation 2000* initiative'. The case for a major shift in policy and practice was clear, and the intention to pursue it was evident in draft policies for *'Recreation 2000'*.

---

* The concept of *Recreation 2000* may owe something to Peter Melchett, a Norfolk farmer and member of several conservation and amenity organisations. In 1984, at a time of great confusion about the future of the countryside, he convened *The 1999 Committee*. This informal group, embracing a range of interests, compiled 'a coherent set of policies' entitled *The Countryside We Want : A Manifesto for the Year 2000*. This was edited by Charlie Pye-Smith, an environmentalist, and Chris Hall, chairman of the Ramblers' Association; and was published by Green Books in 1987.

Draft policies were expressed in terms of *Objectives* and priorities were set out as *Targets*. 'People' were the subject of a single objective and three complex targets.

OBJECTIVE: *To ensure that the general public is more aware of the opportunities for recreation in the countryside and has the confidence, ability and understanding to enjoy it in a considerate way.*

TARGET 1 · Improving Awareness: By the year 2000 we expect to see:
- countryside information services in the major cities;
- countryside media correspondents working with local radio stations;
- the creation of local countryside information packs for the areas of highest visitor demand;
- effective use of local information networks to convey countryside information.

SUCCESS *will be measured by better awareness by the occasional visitor of the opportunities for enjoying the countryside.*

TARGET 2 : Creating Confidence and Ability. By the year 2000 we aim to see established:
- programmes and events of broad appeal located within easy reach of towns to introduce people to the countryside;
- public transport systems which provide effective access to countryside recreation opportunities for people living in urban areas;
- camping and bunk-house barns in remote yet attractive parts of upland England and Wales.

SUCCESS *will be measured in the use of these new services and the extent to which they reach those now poorly served in terms of access to the countryside.*

TARGET 3 : Promoting Understanding. Our aims are that:
- by 1990 local authorities and other public bodies working in this field are fully conscious of their powers and duties;
- by 1992 farmers and landowners are familiar with their responsibilities and rights in relation to public access to the countryside;
- by the year 2000 people wishing to explore the countryside are aware of their basic rights and responsibilities.

This is one of our key target areas.

Target 3 is an unfortunate but key appendage which provided the means to undermine the other two. Local authorities would be required to give priority to the 'powers and duties' pressed upon them by the 1949 Act and supplementary legislation (Ch.6). Farmers and landowners were singled out for their responsibilities in relation to paths on PRoW (Ch.7.3). And people wishing to explore the countryside would retain their priority over those who need positive assistance to gain access to and enjoyment of it. 'Improving awareness' and 'creating confidence and ability' amongst the disadvantaged were sacrificed; and, except for the provision of bunk-house barns for hardy countryside visitors, Targets 1 and 2 were set aside.

Furthermore, the nascent concern for *People* was over-shadowed by a more substantial discussion of *Place;* and attention was focused on three particular aspects of access which all refer back to and beyond the Act of 1949. First, 'the national system' of 120,000 miles of rights-of-way was identified as 'the most important single means by which the public can enjoy the countryside'; and the Commission was persuaded to give pride of place to its uniform, tripartite policy 'that the entire rights of way network should be legally defined, properly maintained and well publicised by the end of the century (CCP.234, 1987). This sustained the interests of experienced walkers and those 'wishing to explore the countryside', but it did nothing for the disadvantaged (Ch.6).

The second relic of 1949 to be addressed was the future of the LDFPs; and a commitment to rationalise and extend the current situation was confirmed as a high priority (Ch.8.1). The inconsistency of giving priority to National Trails and Regional Routes with the intention to serve 'the general public' was brushed aside on grounds that 'under the 1949 Act the Commission has a specific duty to identify and propose for approval long distance routes'. Blind allegiance to bad law prevailed; and the fact that a minority interest had triumphed in 1949 apparently granted it preferential treatment in perpetuity.

Fortunately, the third item of unfinished business from 1949 was received with greater scepticism, and the proposal 'to secure [open] access to wider areas of countryside for quiet enjoyment' was not pursued vigorously. Agreements negotiated since 1949 had proved to be expensive; and it was noted that 'much existing access is informal and unregulated, being on a de *facto* basis'; in other words, trespass by small numbers was being tolerated. Nevertheless, since pressure groups rarely surrender, the 'right to roam' has been resurrected yet again and will now misdirect policy and priorities for countryside walking well into the 21st century (Kay, 1998).

Beyond these three contentious 'access issues', *Recreation 2000* also addressed the future of some particular places which are relevant to opportunities for countryside walking. It observed that Country Parks were 'expensive to provide and maintain and took less than 10% of all countryside visits'; so the modest objective would be 'to fill gaps in provision that can attract intensive use for a range of activities and provide a gateway for access to the wider countryside'. Given that the original concept may have been to contain people within the Parks, their ability to absorb upto 10% of all countryside visits identifies them as an effective filter; and the proposed shift to a gateway function was overdue but welcome. However, to be effective any such initiative must incorporate positive measures to create confidence and ability amongst occasional and infrequent visitors; and similar initiatives should have been built into proposals and plans for the creation 'of new, multi-purpose recreational forests'.

Finally, the 'urban fringe' was cited alongside National Parks, Heritage Coasts and Areas of Outstanding Natural Beauty as a place deserving special attention. The latter were required to 'contribute to countryside recreation in ways that sustain and enhance their particular character'; and this may imply protecting them from most people (Plate 4.2). On the other hand, the urban fringe was seen to be 'particularly important for countryside recreation because it is heavily used'. Indeed, in terms of serving people the urban fringe may well be deserving of higher priority and greater resource inputs than the National Parks; but this was not noted. And, in summary, *Recreation 2000* continued to give priority to particular components of the countryside and the interests of minority groups rather than develop a nascent concern for the people as a whole and for their capacity to enjoy an accessible countryside. A promise faded; an opportunity was lost; and a new initiative is still awaited.

2.Parish Paths and Local Walks: Policies and Priorities

In 1976 the Countryside Commission had invited local authorities 'to give greater priority to the planning and management of footpaths as part of a total recreation strategy' (CCP.99); and in 1988 its consultation paper on *Paths, Routes and Trails* (CCP.253) repeated this suggestion by noting that 'it is time to go back to first principles and to examine the whole rights of way network and the purposes it serves'. This was sound advice; but key minority groups did not want radical change, and being burdened with a history of inappropriate provision and its new tripartite policy for all PRoW, there was little room for a fresh start.

Consequently, the consultation paper, which is beggared by vague concepts and confusing labels, first reviewed the historic and apparently inescapable commitment to LDFPs; and then proposed that *the entire PRoW network* be distributed between National Trails, Regional Routes, and Local Paths - subdivided into Parish Paths (which were not to be promoted) and Local Networks, or Walks, which were to be promoted. Since the force of history, the strident voice of minority interests, and pressures from local authorities for recognition of their long-distance routes could not be denied, the outcome was largely predetermined. The 'official' LDFPs were destined to become National Trails and other selected long-distance paths would be elevated to Regional Routes (Ch.8).

The dedication of all other PRoW to 'Parish Paths' or 'Local Walks' was more debatable, but established path users and local authorities dominated the consultation process.

> There was a strong consensus that the priority for action should be directed at the parish path... A number of respondents made the point that this would give enthusiastic individuals almost unlimited freedom to devise and follow their own routes. Others drew attention to the financial implications of looking after the whole network properly. To meet even basic standards involves high initial expenditure... and there is also an ongoing maintenance cost... [Also] local walks could help to meet what many see as the overwhelming need for a choice of short, well presented circular walks. (From*The Report on the Consultations,* June 1989).

Conflicting interests and concerns are evident, and in pursuing those of 'enthusiastic individuals' the more deserving needs of the silent majority were largely overlooked. Commitment to the tripartite policy for all PRoW (Ch.6) effectively supported the 'strong consensus' in favour of the ubiquitous but enigmatic 'Parish Paths', which embrace all PRoW not committed to the well defined National Trails and Regional Routes or the ill-defined Local Walks. These universal 'parish paths' are to be 'legally protected, kept open, marked on Ordnance Survey maps, and signposted where they leave the road *but not otherwise promoted*'; and work to these ends has dominated the deployment of resources in most if not all local authorities (Ch.6). Their title might imply provision for the people of each parish, who probably do make highly selective use of them; but, in fact, Parish Paths as an entity are for the small minority of enthusiastic individuals 'who wish to devise and follow their own routes... and find their own way through the countryside'.

> The use [of Parish Paths] will often be light, but this is not to imply that they are of little value. Indeed, for those who look for the quiet beauty of the countryside, wish to explore it for themselves and respect its life and work, such paths will be prized above all others... They also constitute a reservoir on which to draw for future development and promotion of walking. (CCP.266, 1990).

'Parish Paths' thus ensure that the greater part of all PRoW and most of the countryside are accessible to the small map-reading communities of highly active, experienced walkers; but they are unlikely to be suitable for the people as a whole and, for the sake of clarity if not honesty, perhaps they should be re-styled as Ramblers or Explorers Paths.

The 'Local Walks' are scarcely less enigmatic but potentially much more useful. They comprise 'paths [or PRoW] capable of attracting use by all sections of the general public for a day out in the countryside - whether from home or a holiday base' that *have been selected by local authorities for promotion.* It was properly suggested in the consultation paper that such routes have the potential to serve 'the overwhelming public need for a choice of short, well presented circular walks'. Their merit had been demonstrated in a report compiled for the Countryside Commission and Sports Council on *The Marketing of Circular Walks* (Wilkinson et al, CCP.195, 1985); and there is a clear case for such 'Recreational Walks', whether promoted by local authorities or other agencies, to be granted precedence over all others (Fig.5.1). Their relegation to the lowest priority is explicable only in terms of history, the dominance of minority interests, and preoccupation with PRoW as an entity; but it is inexcusable in terms of its disregard for the needs of most people.

3.The Marketing and Promotion of Short Circular Walks

> Marketing is the process of matching the product or service to the consumers needs... And, above all a walk must be *attractive*... this does not mean that it has to be pretty... but it must attract people to it and it must attract people to continue along it; and at the end it must confer a feeling of pleasure and satisfaction which will attract them to repeat the experience, either here or on another route (Wilkinson, Atkins and Brewer, 1985).

A recent survey of Public Attitudes suggests that 'the countryside is not providing the quality and range of facilities which people expect' (Ashcroft, 1996). This is particularly so in respect of provision for walking; and perhaps PRoW should be signposted as such, since a right-of-way carries no promise of a path fit for the public. 'Public Footpath' signs should then be deployed for paths suitable for the general public, that is for able-bodied persons of all ages, including those with less than average fitness and little or no experience of countryside walking, but excluding those with special needs for whom special provision is necessary. In particular, short circular walks intended for the public as a whole do require marketable paths which afford quality provision in every respect (Plate 6.4); and these walks, rather than the National Trails, should reflect the highest standards if Britain is to provide an accessible countryside that is attractive to all.

To serve the public well, the location and the site must be right. The principal entry point(s) must be physically accessible to all, suitably equipped with car-parks and, if possible, with public transport from local centres of population. They require basic ancillary services such fixed information points, seating, picnic tables and, perhaps, toilets and litter disposal facilities. The route should traverse landscapes which are attractive if not charismatic; and varied, especially at the local level where the detail of their constituent parts should complement a range of wider views and prospects that should be readily visible. At strategic points, sites with pleasing views and interesting surroundings should be equipped with seating and, perhaps, with some play-space and natural or constructed shelter from sunshine and showers - all to encourage walkers to stop and stare or to rest awhile and chat. And, like the entry-points, such locations evidently require more space than that offered by PRoW. The terrain also should be varied but without any unavoidable section that is likely to place excessive demands on those with less than average fitness.

The paths should be user-friendly all-year-round and in all but the most exceptional weather conditions; and wide enough to allow sociable interaction within small groups and a free flow of walkers in each direction. All crossings of obstacles, whether by gates, stiles, steps or bridges, must be easily negotiable and seen to be safe by all users. They should have a physical carrying capacity to cope with above-average levels of use, and queueing should rarely be necessary. Lanes and rural roads should be used, not only where necessary but wherever they enhance the overall experience of the walk; and appropriate measures should be taken to remind motorised users that pedestrians have the right of a safe passage along all of the Queen's highways. For example, the 'line' of a promoted walk could be marked on the road surface; and all 'No Footway' signs should be replaced with 'Walkers Ahead'.

To serve a range of needs and to optimise use of the chosen location, the walk should comprise not only the obvious self-determined short, 'out and back' options along parts of the main circuit, but also several designed subsidiary routes of different lengths and, perhaps, difficulty. The main route might usefully cover some 5-7 miles but there should be a choice of shorter, partially over-lapping but separately identifed 'circles', including a couple of no more than two miles. Each option should be positively identified or named - (avoiding pejorative terms such as 'cop-out' or 'short-cut') - and individually signposted or waymarked throughout its length, preferably so that it may be walked in either direction. Other services and facilities may be desirable and may be provided if regular demand justifies them; but scarce resources should not be lavished on extravagant features. As Jack Wilkinson and his colleagues put it in 1985:

> Let's face it, refreshments are a basic requirement during or after a walk of several hours, and the perfect walk will have somewhere to eat and drink en route or at least at the end... but perfect walks cannot be provided everywhere. In many cases the nearest refreshments will be off the route... but they should be referred to in whatever guide or information is provided.

In short, creating a marketable product calls for careful consideration not only of customers' and potential users' needs but also of their reasonable wishes too; but it responds by giving priority to quality in key areas and does not sacrifice standards by over-extending provision. Quality provision is expensive; and the 1985 costs of creating and maintaining the *Ditchling Walk(s)* over 8.63 miles of paths illustrate this point (Wilkinson, 1985):

(1)	All 'establishment' costs - from survey to opening:		£1547 per mile.
(2a)	Maintenance costs @ £500 p.a.		£58 per mile.
(2b)	Replacement costs - based on an average life of 15 years for all furniture and fittings - @ £290 p.a.		£34 per mile.
(2a/b)	*Annual maintenance/replacement costs:*		*£92 per mile.*

Translated into 1999 prices these indicate establishment and recurrent costs per mile of £2772 and £330 respectively; but these may be put into some context by the recent estimate of £7353 per mile to upgrade the 103-mile Cotswold Way from a Regional Route to a National Trail (Countryside 86, 1998).

The Ditchling Walk (Fig.9.1) was designed for a wide range of users who may well enjoy both the quality provision and the pleasing countryside to which it gives access; but it stops short of inviting those who have not yet ventured into the wider countryside to do so. They may well require an approach that is more directly related to their circumstances, including specific assurance that at least some of the routes are within their competence and some explicit advice on how to prepare for and conduct themselves on such a walk. The product is evidently marketable; but the promotion of walks is not the same as the promotion of walking, and both the experience and how to win access to it have to be positively publicised amongst the disadvantaged, inexperienced public. It is also important to note that not all short circular walks should endeavour to accommodate all sectors of the highly varied public. On the contrary, the full range of capabilities and interests of all walkers and potential walkers, including those with special needs, deserve attention *in proportion to their numbers* and in locations that facilitate their enjoyment of the countryside.

> Thus, while accepting that a Circular Walk is not intended as the ultimate test of endurance, there is scope to make some of them more difficult than others... The knee-bending, leg-stretching, heart-pounding-climbs and the sock-sodden, foot-sliding, boot-sucking damp patches are within the rules - so long as your customers are warned in advance... and it is possible to vary the degree of difficulty within a single network by, for example, including a choice of easy and more difficult paths - which may also serve as alternatives for wet and dry weather. (Wilkinson, 1985).

Evidently, both marketing and promotion relate to the interface between people and product, and this raises the need for a simple but standard system of classifying promoted walks into broad categories according to their nature and difficulty no less than their length, and for the provision of appropriate signals on site as well as in all supporting documentation. The inappropriate universal deployment of 'Public Footpath' signs has been noted; and careful consideration of a more refined and systematic approach to the

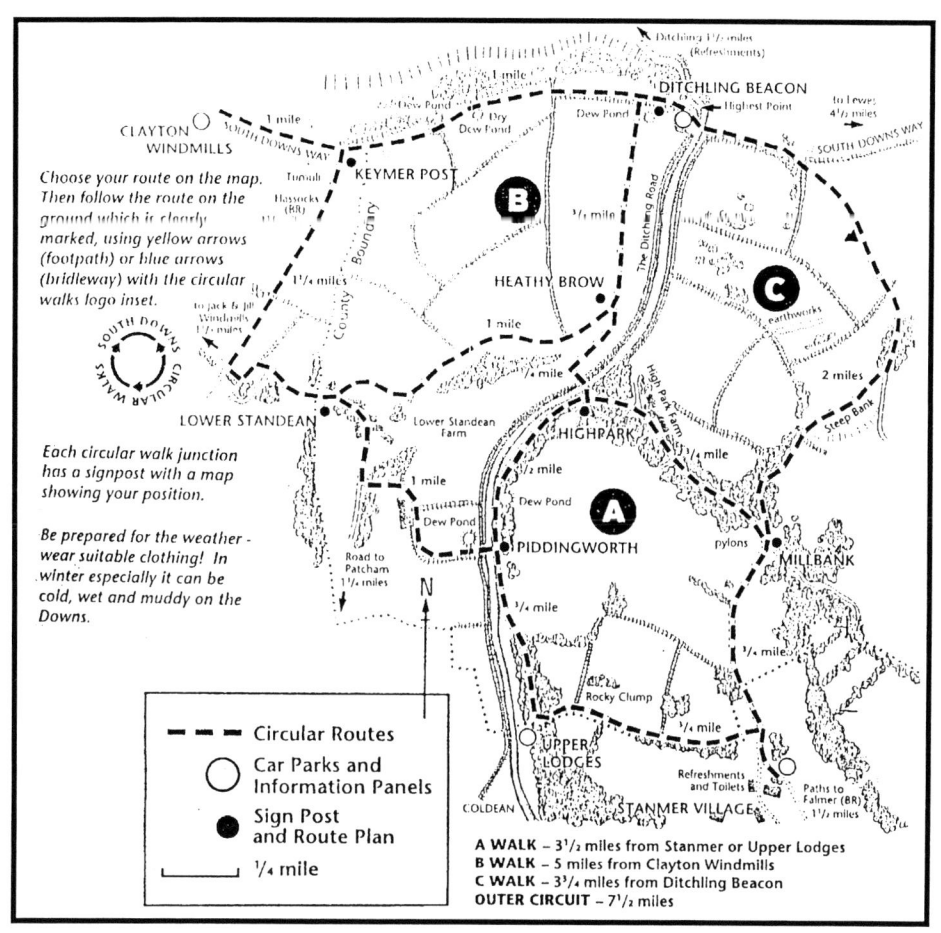

Fig.9.1 The Ditchling Beacon Walk, 1999.

> The original scheme (by Wilkinson et al, 1985) has been extended by development of the path between Piddingworth and Millbank; this economically increases the options at a site which has proved to be popular.
> "The routes offer a variety of walks suitable for everyone - from the experienced rambler to the Sunday stroller. All the paths are clearly marked and connect together so that you can choose a route and a distance to suit you and your companions. The paths will take you right to the top of the South Downs and down into the bottom of tranquil valleys... through mature woods, beautiful parkland and past historic sites and landmarks. It is all on the edge of Brighton, yet it is like another world, a much quieter, slower place - like stepping back in time". (Wilkinson, 1985)

promotion of walks is long overdue. This is a neglected responsibility which calls for intervention by an authoritative national body, such as the Countryside Agency.

Unfortunately, preoccupation with the comprehensive tripartite target for all rights of way effectively precluded any such new initiative; and the 'Milestones Approach' was introduced in an attempt to expedite progress during the closing years of the 20th century (CCP.435 & 436, 1993). This Approach admitted some flexibility insofar as the three targets - to have all PRoW legally defined, properly maintained and well publicised - were redefined as distinct components rather than successive phases (Kay, 1994); but central funding remained dependent upon an acceptable, comprehensive plan or 'Milestones Statement' by each local authority. The terms of reference for these effected a direct link with *Recreation 2000* by asking for 'a programme to develop and promote a range of routes meeting the criteria set out in *Paths, Routes and Trails*' - which gives Parish Paths priority over Local Walks and thus emphasises the aim of developing all PRoW at a very basic level.

Local authorities may try to do this; but while they may have a duty to publicise PRoW, they have no duty nor an exclusive right to promote 'walks'. Indeed, as noted in

---

THE
FAIR BRITAIN SERIES

A delightful Series of books illustrated with beautiful photographs and with interesting descriptive commentaries

Bound in stout boards, $11\frac{1}{2}'' \times 9\frac{1}{2}''$. With attractive pictorial Jackets in Photogravure.

Each 6/- net.

UNSPOILED DORSET
Foreword by Horace Annesley Vachell

THE ISLE OF WIGHT
Foreword by Lord Mottistone

THE CHARM OF THE ENGLISH LAKES
Foreword by Sir Hugh Walpole

THE SPELL OF OXFORD
Foreword by Sir A. T. Quiller-Couch

COTSWOLD COUNTRY
Foreword by Horace Annesley Vachell

EDINBURGH
Foreword by Sir J. I. Falconer

SHAKESPEARE'S COUNTRY
Foreword by Lord Willoughby de Broke

LORNA DOONE COUNTRY
Foreword by Lord Gorell

THE GLORY OF NORTH WALES
Foreword by Lord Harlech

WARD, LOCK & CO., LIMITED, LONDON, W.C.2

Plate 9.2 The FAIR BRITAIN SERIES of Guides
Such Guides shaped both social and spatial patterns of post-war rural tourism.

the case of long-distance walks, routes promoted by the public sector are exceeded by more practicable contributions from voluntary organisations and commercial concerns (Ch.8). However, these bodies have no responsibility for PRoW and they cannot directly affect path conditions on their routes. In short, they may select and publicise routes but they cannot effect development along them, unless they own the relevant land. Managing the overlap and inter-face between the complex voluntary and private sectors and the local authorities is thus a matter of some importance, and some appreciation of the current position in respect of promoted walks may inform priorities for future responsibilities.

4. The Countrywide Pattern of Promoted Walks

Countryside guides have a long history but the promotion of specific routes for countryside walking is essentially a 20th-century phenomena. It has its roots in the voluntary sector, supported and then followed by commercial enterprises. The Holiday Fellowship (founded in 1913), the YHA, the YMCA and various rambling or walking clubs were early leaders, each providing for its own clientele. They worked alongside enthusiastic and highly literate individuals; and William Crossing's 1909 *Guide to Dartmoor* is a classic amongst books written primarily for walkers and students of the countryside. Dartmoor is divided into 12 'districts'; within these, 46 'excursions' and 121 'shorter excursions' are described in detail; so too are 66 'routes' connecting 'centres' in the several districts - giving a total of 233 walks in this upland region. Similar guides followed, including A.J.Brown's influential *Moorland Tramping* (1931) and *Tramping in Yorkshire* (1932); and the Forestry Commission Guide to the *Argyll Forest Park*, where coloured discs were used to identify several routes (Edlin, 1939).

In the post-war period, as motorists increased and walking became more popular, guides to serve both became more numerous. Again, these were to inform no less than direct a highly literate clientele. Thus, for example, Odham's *Historic Britain* was intended:

> To show how the wayfarer in Britain's varied countryside can piece together the things he sees on his journeys and reconstruct the story of Britain's historic past, the changing pattern of social life through the ages and the character of the peoples who have made Britain what it is today. (Fisher, c.1948).

The companion volume on *The Countryside and How to Enjoy It* has been examined in some detail (Ch.1.6); and many others, including the popular *Shell Country Book* (Grigson, 1962), exercised a comparable educational role directed at the middle classes. Increasingly, more guides targeted particular parts of the countryside (Plate 9.2). The Batsford-Methuen series of *Little Guides* to selected counties began in 1900; and revised editions for Devonshire, Dorset, Gloucestershire, Hampshire, Norfolk, Somerset, Sussex and Wiltshire were still available in 1949, though by then the Ward Lock [Red] Guides were rapidly becoming more popular. By following demand and directing customers, all such books did much to inform attitudes towards the countryside and shape both the social and spatial patterns of post-war rural tourism.

By the 1970s guides to specific walks were more common but they too reinforced usage of the more popular parts of the countryside. The 1979 list of Warne Gerrard Guides illustrates the point. It comprised 25 volumes of *Walks for Motorists*; each providing descriptions and sketch maps of 30 short circular walks, typically covering 3-10 miles. This awareness of established walker's habits no less than the spatial distribution of the 750 walks served the needs of the privileged, regular users of valued places.

The 1979 Warne Gerrard "Walks for Motorists"

Lake District Walks (3 vols - 90 walks)
Pendleside and Bronte Country Walks (1 vol - 30 walks)
Yorkshire Dales Walks (3 vols - 90 walks)
North York Moors Walks (2 vols - 60 walks)
Peak District Walks (1 vol - 30 walks)

Snowdonia Walks (1 vol - 30 walks)
Cheshire Walks (1 vol - 30 walks)
Midland Walks (1 vol - 30 walks)
Wye Valley Walks (1 vol - 30 walks)

Cotswolds Walks (2 vols - 60 walks)
Chilterns Walks (2 vols - 60 walks)
London Countryside Walks (4 vols - 120 walks)
Exmoor Walks (1 vol - 30 walks)
South Downs Walks (1 vol - 30 walks)
Jersey Walks (1 vol - 30 walks)

A more recent (1991) product of the Ordnance Survey and Automobile Association promotes 149 *Village Walks* and it has a similar but more pronounced spatial imprint

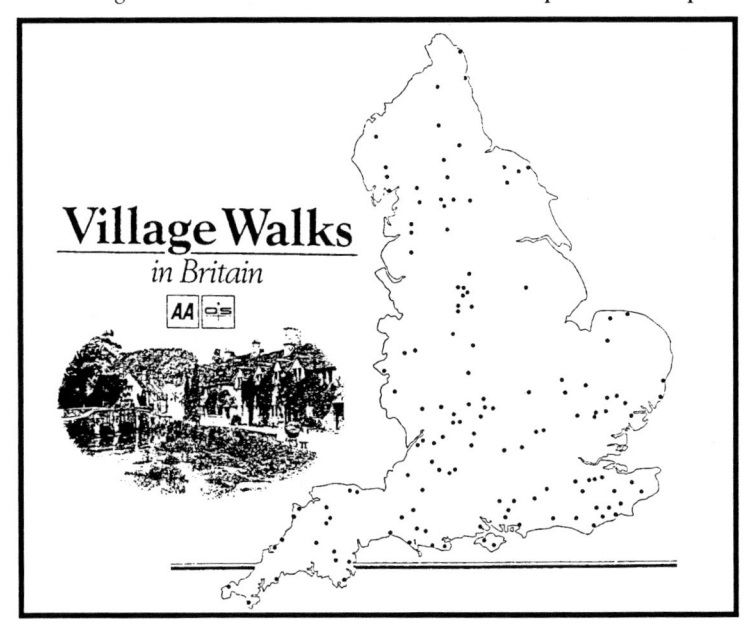

Fig.9.2 Village Walks pinpoint 149 Prized Places in England.

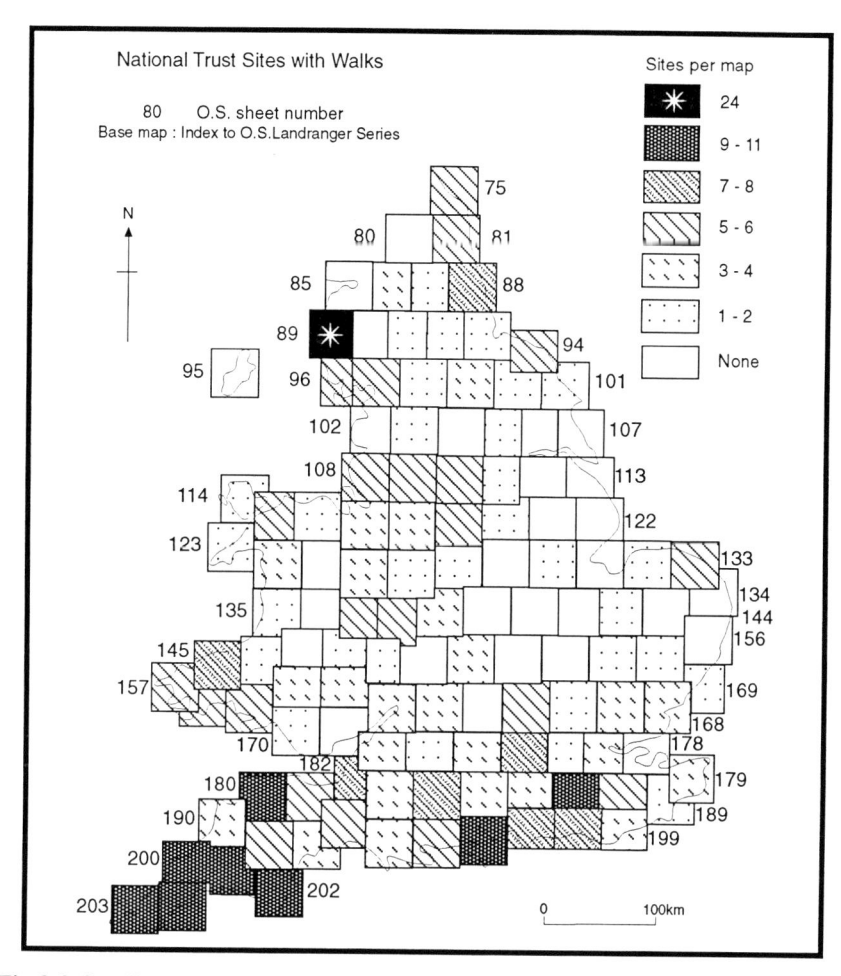

Fig.9.3 Quality provision by the National Trust serves walkers well in parts of 'Beautiful Britain'.

(Fig.9.2). There is an emphasis on historic and cultural heritage, and the list of locations evokes a romantic approach to the countryside. The walks are designed for family groups of strollers; and users are advised which routes are not suitable for prams and push-chairs. The average length is 1.8 miles and only 33 (22%) exceed two. A longer option is available at 29 locations but only 11 of these exceed 3 miles and the longest is five. The routes are mostly on roads and lanes; and they afford more opportunities to support local economies than practise any navigational skill. They would not meet with Mike Harding's approval nor that of the typical Rambler (Ch.1.2); but such products do serve a sizable segment of regular countryside visitors, who may have benefited further if introductory walks into the wider countryside had been grafted on to the village walks - provided, of course, that quality paths suitable for family groups were available along these extensions.

The National Trust provides a third and evidently a special case study. The Trust has a reputation for rewarding sites and quality provision; and, given its origins and purposes, the spatial imprint of its 'sites with walks' inevitably reflects the occurrence of favoured and favourite places (Fig.9.3). It too thus promotes a fine selection of parts of 'beautiful Britain' rather than the countryside as a whole; and, given its substantial and largely middle-class membership, it fortifies current patterns in respect of the promotion and the usage of the countryside.

While any such qualitative review of promotional materials may be persuasive, systematic analyses might afford more convincing statements on the spatial pattern and

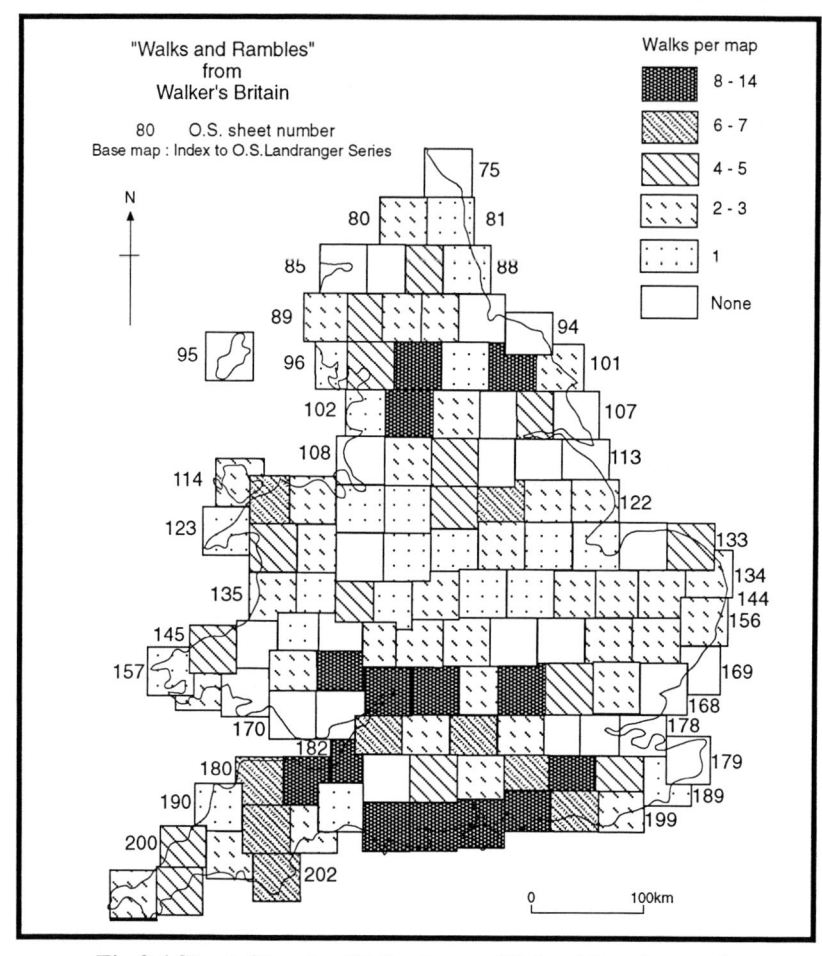

Fig.9.4 Short Circular Walks favour 'Valued Landscapes' in England and Wales.

role of promoted routes. Unfortunately, there is no national register of promoted 'short walks', and any arbitrary selection from an unknown quantity cannot be truly representative of the whole. However, the two volumes of *Walkers' Britain* produced by the Ordnance Survey and Pan Books in 1982 and 1986 permit a spatial analysis of 357 walks within the framework of the 123 OS maps covering England and Wales (Fig.9.4). These walks have an aggregate length of 2198 miles and an average of 6.2 miles each. They are thus directed at walkers rather than the more numerous strollers (Fig.5.1); but while all of them are mostly on paths, inevitably very few are entirely off-road. An even distribution of these walks would provide 2.9 on each map; but the actual distribution is very uneven:

The Spatial Imprint of 357 Short Circular Walks

28 maps (23 %) with 000 walks have 00 or 00 % of all walks.
21 maps (17 %) with 001 walks have 21 or 06 % of all walks.

36 maps (29 %) with 2-3 walks have 88 or 25 % of all walks.
15 maps (12 %) with 4-5 walks have 66 or 18 % of all walks.

09 maps (07 %) with 6-7 walks have 56 or 16 % of all walks.
14 maps (11 %) with 8-14 walks have 126 or 35 % of all walks.

In contrast to the spread of long distance walks, there is no ready access to any of these short walks in a quarter of the country; and 40% has only 6%. At the other extreme, 35% occur within 11% of the country; and 51% are to be found in 18%. In broad geographical terms, southern England is highly favoured; but a more discerning view may recognise a relationship throughout the country with 'valued landscapes' such as those identified by John Dower (Fig.4.2). Picturesque and grand places with an established reputation are heavily targeted; and commercial concerns evidently serve regular countryside visitors and encourage the use of popular places. In contrast, areas close to urban populations needing encouragement to walk in the countryside evidently are not a priority.

5. Promoted Walks in Staffordshire

The countrywide case material highlights the input by commercial concerns which focus on the preferred places of regular and frequent walkers; and it may be complemented and qualified by a more comprehensive analysis of promoted walks in Staffordshire, which draws heavily on work by Moxham (1997). This is a large county with a population in excess of one million and a variety of distinctive landscapes ranging from part of the Peak District National Park and the Cannock Chase AONB through designated areas of 'great landscape quality' to other notable places, namely the Staffordshire Moorlands and the Churnet Valley in the north, the Hanchurch Hills and Downs Banks between Stoke and Stone, and Kinver Edge in the extreme south (Fig.9.5).

Staffordshire's farmlands fall into three broad categories comprising upland dairying and stock-farming on the more broken land of the north, through mixed livestock and arable farming in the central areas to good quality arable land in the south. This sequence is matched, from north to south, with a decrease in visually attractive features and an increase in difficulties for walkers. Within this varied expanse of countryside there is the urban sprawl of the Potteries and Newcastle-under-Lyme with a population of 330,000; five substantial urban areas - Stafford (56,000), Cannock (66,000), Lichfield (32,000), Burton-on-Trent (48,000) and Tamworth (72,000); and several smaller country towns. In summary, Staffordshire provides a good context for a study of walking and walks (Fig.9.5).

In 1988 the County Council prepared a preliminary overview of *Staffordshire Country Walks* which embraced 115 promoted routes, including the 93-mile Staffordshire Way. The county and its constituent local authorities, independently or with voluntary organisations, promoted 75 (66%) of the walks; Kinver Civic Society provided 9 (8%); and the remainder - 30 or 26% - comprised a book on *Staffordshire Walks - Simply Superb* (Lumsden, 1988). Rapid growth and change lay ahead and in 1996 the County's revised and more comprehensive list identified 66 sources and 504 walks. Ten items by commercial publishers embraced 291 (58%) of the routes; and although the public sector provided 76% of the publications, these contained only 31% of the walks. Five contributions by the voluntary sector provided 42 (8%) of the walks; and a joint enterprise by volunteers and Stafford's Tourism Bureau accounted for 14 (3%).

Sources	Public Sector	Voluntary Sector	Commercial Sector	All
All Publications	74 (63%)	17 (14%)	27 (23%)	118
(a) Pamphlets	64	12	—	76
(b) Magazines	—	—	10	10
(c) Books/Booklets	10	5	17	32
No. of Walks	164 (29%)	73 (13%)	327 (58%)	564
Publications				
Pre-1990	18 (55%)	2 (14%)	4 (20%)	24 (36%)
1990-95	15 (45%)	12 (86%)	16 (80%)	43 (64%)
Price				
Free	67%	None	None	—
Upto £1.00	27%	86%	4%	—
£1.00 - £3.00	6%	14%	45%	—
Over £3.00	——	——	51%	—

Table 9.1. Moxham's 1995 Catalogue of Promoted Walks in Staffordshire.

Meanwhile, an exhaustive search by Moxham, concluded early in 1995, identified 118 current and discontinued publications, ranging from ephemeral pamphlets to substantial books, which collectively refer to 564 walks. (Moxham, 1997 and 1998). This data set illuminates the dynamic situation noted above and highlights differences between the several providers (Table 9.1). Until recently, the public sector was the senior partner in promoting walks and more than half of its publications appeared before 1990. Since then its annual output has increased but has been outstripped by the voluntary sector and, more particularly, by commercial enterprises which were responsible for 58% of the 564 walks.

The public and voluntary sectors' publications are mostly pamphlets; they are mostly free or sold at very modest prices; and the principal outlets for them are tourist information centres, libraries and council offices. In contrast, the commercial sector sells books and magazines, mostly at affordable prices, by mail order and through shops. The format affects the contents and use. On average, each public and voluntary sector publication presents two and four walks respectively while the more durable, commercial publications have an average of 12; and most books promote, and often illustrate, large numbers of routes. Pamphlets are easy to use in the field but are not durable. Substantial publications offer a wider choice, are capable of selective photo-copying for field-use and are more likely to be retained.

The underlying grounds for and effects of the rapid and probably continuing increase in the promotion of walks have not been researched. Within the public and voluntary sectors growth may be attributed in part to *Recreation 2000*. In the wider world, new technologies in and approaches to publishing allow a viable response to small markets; and the recent growth of interest in rural and 'green' tourism and increased awareness of walking as a major recreational activity of the middle classes may underlie the greater participation by commercial concerns. The availability of many highly literate walkers as a ready source of authors may also be a factor, and one which, in turn, may affect the contents and presentation of the material. Whatever the balance of causes, one evident effect is that market-led initiatives will not sit comfortably with any scheme for the promotion of all PRoW; nor are they likely to address the needs of 'the 50% of the population who make few trips to the countryside and should be the most important target' of promotional efforts (CCP.225, 1987).

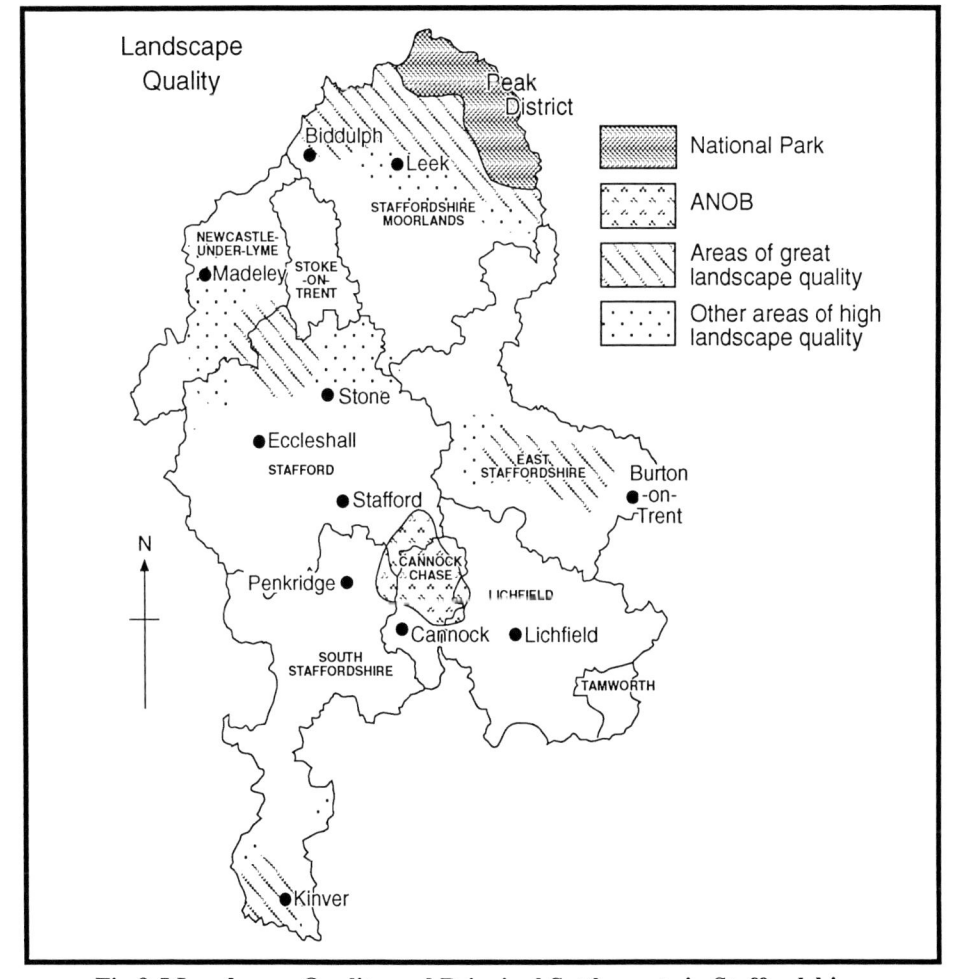

Fig.9.5 Landscape Quality and Principal Settlements in Staffordshire.

Staffordshire has been particularly affected by *Sigma Leisure* books from Sigma Press in Wilmslow, Cheshire, which may be representative or even a leader of the new publishers. Its website and Spring Catalogue of 1999 offer 154 books on walking, most of them published in the last five years. And while the location of the press is clearly a factor, the regional distribution of these illustrates a focus on regions and places already popular with the intended market:

North-West England	- 44 books (11 on the Peak District)
Midlands & Heart of England	- 34 books
The Lake District	- 19 books
Yorkshire	- 16 books (8 on 'the Dales')
South-East England	- 13 books
South-West England	- 12 books
Wales and the Welsh Borders	- 11 books
North-East England	- 5 books.

The Press favours a series of 'themed walks' which serve key market segments; and this point is illustrated in the list of books on Staffordshire:

Pub Walks in Staffordshire (1993)
Best Staffordshire Walks (1996)
Town and Village Discovery Walks in Staffordshire (1996)
Best Pub Walks in South Staffordshire and the Vale of Trent (1997)
Walking On and Around the Staffordshire Way (1997)
Tea Shop Walks in Staffordshire (1998).

Tea Shop Walks offers 'a wide selection of routes between 3 and 10 miles exploiting Staffordshire's scenery from the Peak District to Kinver Edge'; and the 16 circular walks of 4 to 12 miles on the Staffordshire Way, contributed by local Ramblers, are similarly aimed at established walkers. However, the *Town and Village Discovery Trails* are 'for walkers with shoes, not boots'; and although *Walks for Children* is ostensibly 'aimed at young walkers, with plenty of questions and answers about what to look for in the countryside and simple maps - so that the grown-ups don't get lost!', it will appeal to parents who already know the benefits of walking. Most recently *Sigma* has sought 'to cater for those who prefer a whistle-stop tour of 17 or 18 points of interest and natural beauty with a minimum of walking through a fabulous new series of Tape-Drive guided tours, currently available for Exmoor, The Lake District and The Peak District'. Sigma Press evidently responds to and supports prevailing spatial and social patterns of participation in countryside walking, but it does little to extend enjoyment of the countryside to the uninitiated.

The full effects of the explosion of publicity must await further research; but meanwhile Moxham's work allows analysis of spatial patterns of promoted walks in Staffordshire. The location of 314 walks were plotted within a grid of 80 x 3.5 mile squares and mapped according to their source within the voluntary, commercial and public sectors and all three combined (Figs.9.6-9). None of the sectors nor the combined provision afford an even distribution of walks across the county. The voluntary sector leaves nearly 80% of Staffordshire without any walk; and both the commercial and public sectors neglect 60% of the county, though the combined provision equips 61% of the units with at least one walk. The most striking features are highly localised concentrations. The voluntary and commercial sectors each locate 55% of their walks in just two grid squares; public sector walks are more widespread, but 77% of the 314 walks occur in just 22% of the county and 61% are within 12% of it.

Walks per Unit	Voluntary Sector (40)		Commercial Sector (101)		Public Sector (173)		All 314 Walks	
	Units	Walks	Units	Walks	Units	Walks	Units	Walks
Zero	78%	None	59%	None	59%	None	39%	None
1 - 4	20%	45%	38%	45%	25%	28%	39%	23%
5 - 9	1%	17%	None	None	11%	36%	10%	16%
10 +	1%	38%	3%	55%	5%	36%	12%	61%

These favoured locations probably relate to particular characteristics of the countryside, and they have been analysed with reference to landscape quality, land-use regions, and proximity to concentrations of population (Fig.9.5 & Table 9.2). The landscapes are ranked in terms of their quality and attraction, which is explicit in their labelling. The marked effect of landscape is immediately evident and it is the most important determinant of the distribution of promoted walks. The National Park and AONB have three-and-

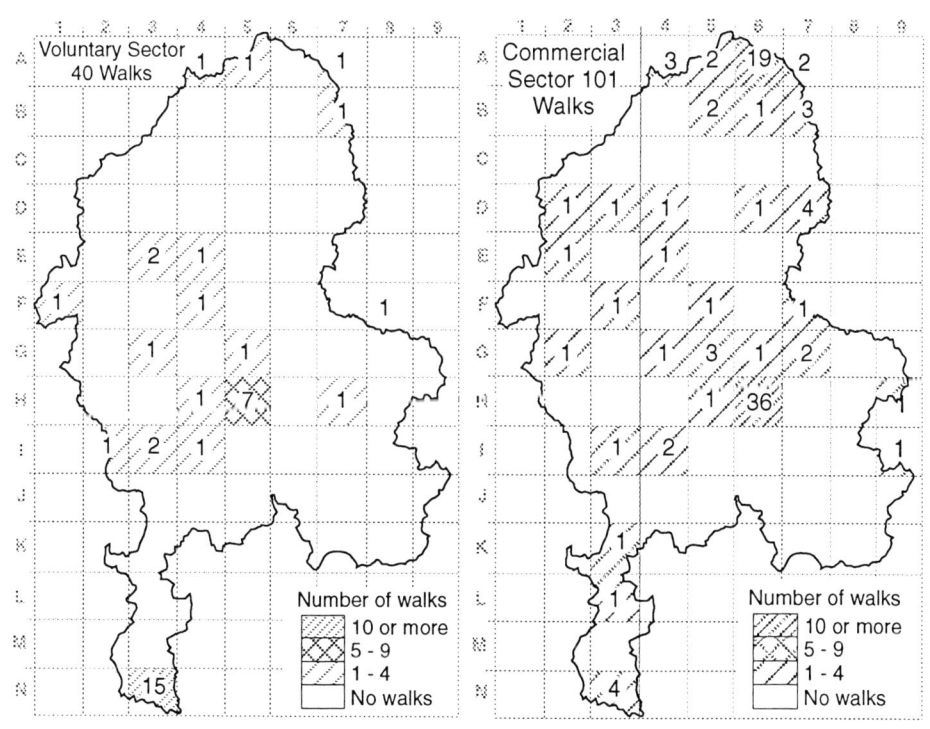

Fig.9.6 Walks in Staffordshire, 1995 Promoted by the Voluntary Sector.

Fig.9.7 Walks in Staffordshire, 1995 Promoted by the Commercial Sector.

223

a-half times as many walks as an even distribution or 'fair share' would grant them. The voluntary and public sectors favoured them with 25% and 21% of their walks but they were particularly targeted by the commercial sector which located 67% of its walks in this 10% of the county.

Areas of 'Great' and 'High' landscape quality embrace 34% of the county and have 50% of the walks. Here the public sector is the main provider with 113 or 73% of the walks; and by locating 65% of its walks in these categories it complements the emphases of the other sectors which placed only 42 walks in these attractive areas. Furthermore, 15 of these (comprising 38% of the voluntary sector's walks) occur in one unit embracing Kinver Edge. This reflects the maverick element associated with such provision. Enthusiastic, energetic and capable people, acting on their own initiative or, as in this case, within a voluntary organisation can equip a locality of their choice with an ample if not superfluous supply of walks. Similar effects have now occurred at Biddulph, Eccleshall and Stone; and the 'canal town' has also been equipped with a suite of 'health walks'. Such contributions may be admirable but they are not unproblematic. They may not fit comfortably within any rational plan for the county; and if they command a prior allocation of resources for path maintenance, they may adversely affect the quality of provision elsewhere. On the other hand, in the absence of any strategic plan for the county, it is difficult to guide and unreasonable to deny any such enterprise by voluntary organisations.

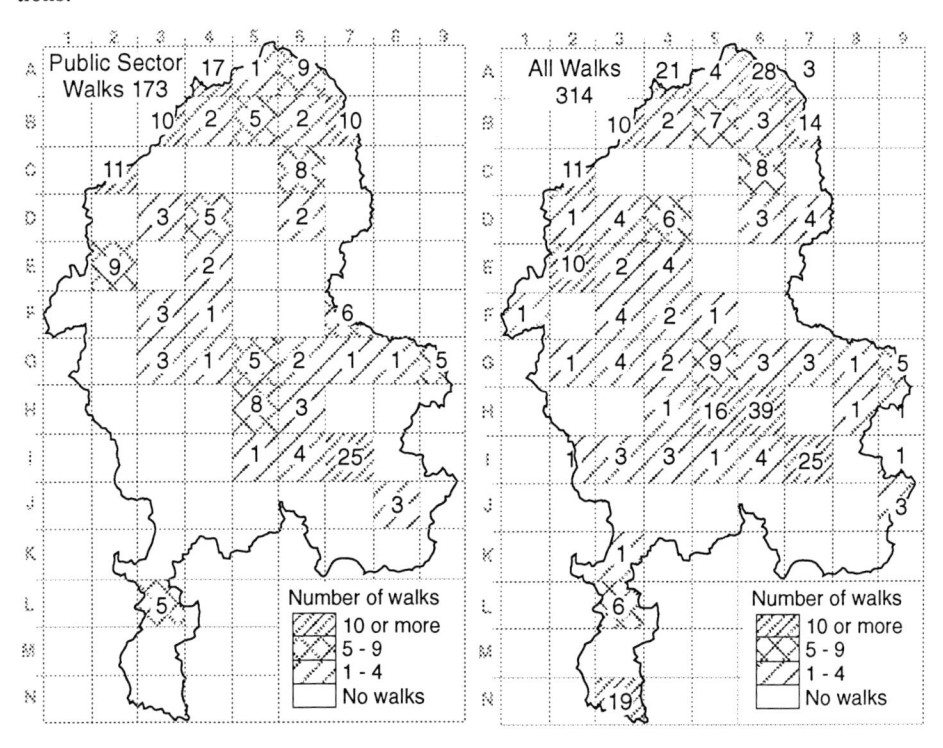

Fig.9.8 Walks in Staffordshire, 1995 Promoted by the Public Sector.

Fig.9.9 All Walks Promoted in Staffordshire, 1995.

	(a) Share of the County	(b) Share of the Walks	(b) / (a) x 100
(A) Landscape Regions			
(1) Peak District National Park	5 %	16 %	320
(2) Cannock Chase AONB	5 %	19 %	380
(3) Areas of Great Landscape Quality	15 %	23 %	153
(4) Areas of High Landscape Quality	19 %	27 %	142
(5) Other Countryside	56 %	15 %	27
(B) Land-use Regions			
(1.a) Upland Livestock Farming	20 %	34 %	170
(1.b) 1.a *outside* the National Park	15 %	18 %	120
(2) Mixed Stock and Arable Farming	26 %	21 %	81
(3) Arable Farming	34 %	21 %	62
(C) Distance from an Urban Centre			
(1) Within 2.5 miles	6 %	5 %	83
(2) 2.5 - 5.0 miles	19 %	17 %	89
(3) 5.0 - 7.5 mile	29 %	20 %	69
(4) 7.5 - 10.0 miles	27 %	31 %	115
(5) More than 10 miles	19 %	27 %	142
(6.a) The Urban Fringe	20 %	24 %	120
(6.b) The Urban Fringe *less* the AONB	15 %	5 %	33

Table 9.2 Promoted Walks and (A) Landscape Regions, (B) Land-use Regions and (C) Proximity to People in Staffordshire, 1995.

In contrast, the greater part of Staffordshire (56%) is undistinguished countryside though not, for the most part, unattractive; but the combined contribution of all three sectors grants it only 15% of the promoted walks, just 27% of its 'fair share'. This may or may not be sufficient for the people's needs, but the apparent neglect of more than half of the county raises questions concerning the perceived utility of its rights-of-way. On the other hand, the concentration of walks in the National Park and AONB is so pronounced that their effects need to be separated in any review of the provision of promoted walks within the several categories of land-use regions and the urban fringe. The relationship with the agricultural regions emerges as anticipated but the differentials are much less pronounced than those generated by landscape quality, a point which is emphasised by removing the effect of the National Park from the upland farming region. Similarly, the exclusion of Cannock Chase from the urban fringe reveals the generally sparse provision of promoted walks in this region, which has just one-third of its proportional entitlement. This begs the question as to how the pattern of provision relates to the distribution of the population.

'Proximity to people' is explored by assuming that the rural population is uniformly distributed and classifying each grid square according to its distance from the nearest of the six major urban centres (Fig.9.5). There is a relatively narrow range of densities of promoted walks in the five zones but the peri-urban areas are less well served than more distant ones. Furthermore, there is no evident initiative to systematically provide walks close to the major concentrations of people. Taken as a whole, territory within 2.5 miles of an urban region does have 83 % of its 'fair share' of walks but the significant contribution of Cannock Chase has been noted, and other clusters of walks close to urban areas now invite comment. The promotion and funding of Country Parks has been influential; and in Staffordshire these, and associated walks, are located either in areas of high scenic quality or, paradoxically, on selected sites in the urban fringe. Additionally, the national drive to reclaim derelict industrial land has provided significant support for the Newcastle and the South Cannock Countryside Projects, which have effected major improvements in peri-urban provision for recreation. Such special initiatives have provided some parts of the urban fringe with above average densities of walks. This, however, is not an effective substitute for a policy decision to give a high priority to ample provision of well promoted walks on quality paths in close proximity to where most people live.

6. The Utility and Use of Promoted Walks

These several patterns raise as many questions as they answer concerning the underlying reasons for the location of promoted walks, their utility and use, and their effect on participation in countryside walking; and only systematic data collection can provide definitive answers. Each set of providers has its own mix of motives; and the voluntary sector's satisfactions may lie largely in the production of artefacts reflecting personal preferences for favourite places. Some such products may serve people similar to their creators; and others may relate to charismatic special needs, as has been the case recently in providing 'health walks' and walks for disabled persons.

Commercial publishers have an evident interest in sales and profits. They respond to the current market; and there are some clear efforts, including the production of magazines, to reach subsets of regular walkers. On the other hand, many may relate to a wider market for attractive documentation, such as expensive coffee-table guides and countryside calendars backed with maps. These exploit and reinforce middle-class aesthetic, romantic and even intellectual interests in the countryside but they may do little in practical terms for any but arm-chair walkers.

In contrast, although too readily led by national policies and priorities and limited by available resources, the public sector may be the best servant of the public; but its efficacy in serving even regular countryside visitor is not proven. Indeed, in all three cases, printing and distributing promotional materials will be of limited value if they do not reach and motivate their intended customers.

The sources of information used by countryside visitors in selecting their destination and activities have been recorded in many surveys; and the response is often partly a product of the method of enquiry (Kay, 1996). Nevertheless, a review of three sets of findings may be useful. The National [Household] Survey of Countryside Recreation of 1990 found that only 3% of the visitors' destinations had been identified by documentary sources (Walker, 1994). Prior knowledge was the principal determinant; and the report noted that 'countryside visitors are very much creatures of habit and little influenced by marketing or publicity'. This finding is an indictment of the process of promotion, but it is consistent with the fact that most walkers are frequent and regular users of their favourite places.

(1) National Household Survey of Countryside Recreation, 1990

Previous visit	40 %
Always known the place	19 %
Went with family	8 %
Recommended	7 %
Organised trip	6 %
Found by chance on journey	3 %
Guide books	1 %
Tourist Information Centre	1 %
Newspapers	1 %
Others	14 %
ALL	100 %

(2) North York Moors National Park Visitors Survey, 1991

	Home-based Visitors		Holiday-based Visitors	
	All	1st-time	All	1st-time
Prior knowledge	78 %	23 %	44 %	5 %
Friends/relations	6 %	27 %	12 %	11 %
Maps	23 %	19 %	43 %	31 %
Brochures/guides	4 %	6 %	31 %	31 %
Visitors Newspaper	1 %	2 %	6 %	4 %
Press/TV/Radio	1 %	4 %	1 %	1 %
Information Centre	5 %	4 %	13 %	11 %
Advertising	2 %	8 %	8 %	4 %
All *	120 %	93 %	158 %	98 %

* Categories are not mutually exclusive; totals less than 100 indicate that an unknown number of respondents cited no source.

(3) Moxham's Survey of 208 Staffordshire Walkers, 1995

	Citations	Walkers
OS maps	100	48 %
Leaflets	79	38 %
Walking book	71	34 %
Word of mouth	56	27 %
Walk map	37	18 %
Magazine	29	13 %
Other (personal) sources*	29	13 %
Signposts	21	10 %
Radio/TV	13	6 %

* Respondents were given a fixed menu of eight items and an option to state other sources. On average, the 208 walkers named 2.1 sources, a total of 435 citations.

Table 9.3 Three Surveys of Sources of Information
Used in Planning Countryside Visits/Walks

On-site surveys, the use of a check list and segmentation of the respondents may capture more detailed data sets; but each will relate to a particular time and place (Table 9.3). A 1991 survey of home and holiday based visitors to the North York Moors, with first-time visitors separately identified in each case, is revealing. Prior knowledge was the most important determinant for experienced, home-based visitors but first-time local visitors also depended heavily on friends and relations. In contrast, only 5% of first-time holiday-makers used prior knowledge and less than half of the returning tourists did so. Indeed, all holiday visitors were quite heavily dependent upon maps and other documentary sources; and many home-based visitors also made substantial use of OS maps, probably because 40% of them went for a long walk and needed a map for navigation (Kay, 1996).

Moxham's (1997) Staffordshire research requires a cautionary note since 'prior knowledge' was not included in the proffered options and it was focused on active walkers. 136 were interviewed while walking in popular places - Dovedale (30%), Cannock Chase (20%), at Tittesworth Reservoir (11%) and in the Churnet Valley (4%); and the other 72 (35%) were active members of walking clubs in South Staffordshire. Nearly half of the respondents used OS maps; and, on average, they each cited the use of 1.5 documentary sources. Promotional materials evidently are appreciated; and use of published works is matched by awareness of where to find information on walks - 63% cited Tourist Information Offices while bookshops (11%) libraries (9%) and civic offices (9%) also were recognised as suppliers.

The weight of the evidence reviewed above suggests that while many regular visitors and walkers enjoy reading about the countryside and countryside walking, most do not depend heavily on documentation to locate their visit except when on holiday or in relatively unknown territory. On the other hand, most regular countryside walkers are acutely aware of the value of maps, especially OS maps, and to a lesser extent of practical guides of all kinds. Finally, first-time home-based visitors are greatly influenced by friends and relations and by prior knowledge, no matter how limited and limiting this may be. This suggests that relevant publications are not reaching them or are unintelligible to them.

Furthermore, the efficacy of each and every promotional effort is not known; and it is reasonable to ask *'Are promoted paths used ?'*. There is no analysis of the use of short walks comparable with those of long distance routes (Ch.8.5-6); and it is disappointing that the 1988 and 1994 surveys of paths on PRoW included no systematic measure of their use. Such information is vital for a valid assessment of the utility of PRoW (and other highways) for countryside walking; but it may well be that in some quarters there is a vested interest in its non-availability. However, in the absence of evidence to the contrary, it is safe to deduce from spatial patterns of visitor use that some few are heavily used, others are lightly used, and most are rarely or never used (Ch.5.2). And, secondly, that if the promotion of short walks proliferates on lines identified for long distance walks (Ch.8.3), it is likely that the differential will widen, because personal testimonials are likely to be more effective than documentary materials. More importantly, neither is likely to affect the disadvantaged majority who 'do not know what the countryside is for'; and it is important to repeat that promoting 'walks' is no substitute for promoting walking as a means to enjoy the countryside. The initial promise in *Recreation 2000* to 'put people first' has yet to be addressed.

10
Promoting Enjoyment in a Countryside for All

Access and exclusion are complementary concepts which inform this study as a whole; and although diverse forms of countryside walking developed within the upper and middle classes of the 17th-19th centuries (Ch.1.4-7) their dissemination has been slow, partial and deliberately hindered. Resistance grew as participation increased; and exclusion, on various grounds, became a common cause of diverse parties which otherwise were often antipathetic. A range of key issues of continuing importance emerged; and they are summarised as a prelude to an appraisal of the National Parks and Access to the Countryside Act (Ch.4.2-3). Parts of this Act and related legislation were generated by particular groups of walkers concerned with ancient rights which could be deployed to their advantage. These privileged minorities have benefitted substantially; but the needs of the disadvantaged majority who enjoy little or no access to the countryside continue to be denied and neglected (Ch.4.4-5).

The motives and arguments which underlie the reluctance to actively promote enjoyment of the countryside are varied, but self-interest and 'conservation' are particularly prominent. On the other hand, the mechanisms whereby exclusion has been sustained are more obscure. First, there is a widespread pretence or assumption that 'access' is readily available and that non-participation therefore reflects a considered choice. In fact, neither countryside walking nor access is a simple matter (Ch.1.2-3); and it follows that positive promotion of each is an onerous duty which has been unduly neglected. Secondly, a major strategy for 150 years or more has been to deploy scare stories concerning an alleged threat to the well being of the countryside which increased numbers of visitors would engender. These superficially plausible arguments have proved sufficient to justify doing little or nothing to promote participation. However, more specific measures arise from the persistent domination and manipulation of relevant legislation, policies and priorities by minorities with powerful pressure groups and lobbies. And without some significant change in relevant decision-making processes, there can be little confidence that people's needs will be put first in the foreseeable future.

1. Ancient Rights versus Current Needs in the 21st Century

Legislation and policies in respect of physical access to the countryside are sharply focused on rights from bygone days with little or no reference to their utility in respect of current recreational needs of the public and their impact on other uses of the countryside. This narrow orientation was conceived 200 years ago in a climate of conflict generated by agricultural improvement, enclosures and 'stopt paths' (Ch.2.2 & Plate 0.1). Subsequent campaigns for 'the preservation of ancient public footways' and similar rights continue today with little or no regard for social equity. An obsession with history and self-interest are the driving force of dominant minorities; and it is a measure of the power of modern pressure groups that a Labour Government, apparently committed 'to break down the barriers that deny opportunity and hold people back', should replicate events of 1949 and present parliament with a *Countryside and Rights of Way Bill* designed, in part, 'to give greater freedom for [some few] people to explore open countryside' on grounds of an alleged ancient 'right to roam' (Ch.4.1).

While English Nature expressed 'a need for caution', the Countryside Agency greeted this distraction from more deserving matters with some misplaced enthusiasm:

> From our perspective, the Bill's single most important element is the new access to open countryside. This fulfils the Government's manifesto commitment and tackles unfinished business from the landmark 1949 Act... Millions of people will benefit from new legislation that will open up access to large areas of countryside... (Countryside Focus: Special Issue, March 2000).

The Bill may bring 200-years of war to an end by throwing open some 4 million acres of mountain, moor, heath, down, and common land to those few confident walkers and ramblers able and anxious to exercise such liberties. This may threaten vulnerable terrain; it will certainly divert scarce resources from more deserving needs; and it will do nothing for the disadvantaged millions who currently have little or no access to the countryside as a whole. There are many more important countryside issues; but this minority interest was pressed into the Labour Party's election manifesto, and apparently no such promise can be treated lightly. Political expediency ousts commonsense.

The same Bill includes further fine tuning of rights-of-way legislation. The tripartite policy for all PRoW could not be achieved by the target date; but the production of peculiar, patchwork patterns across the country will continue (Ch.6), with the marginal advantage of 'ways in which systems for managing the rights of way network [will] be improved, both to make better progress towards the target, and to ensure effective management beyond the year 2000'. The case for this unfinished business was set out in *Rights of Way in the 21st Century* (CCP.543, 1998) and in the Countryside Commission's related recommendations to the Government in March 1999.

The latter comprise three purposes and ten objectives which summarise symptoms and intended relief but, with one exception, do not address the fundamental issue concerning the merits of the policy. The purposes are:

> 1. To make it easier to achieve a more extensive and more useful network for all users, by creating a framework for the resolution of differences over rights of way as amicably and efficiently as possible;
> 2. To make the job of highway authorities achievable, at a realistic level of resources, by reducing the cost and complexity of rights of way management; and
> 3. To make the record of the existence and status of rights of way more universally accurate and readily available at reasonable cost.

The ten objectives and action needed to achieve them illustrate the cost and the complexity of pursuing the tripartite target:
- 1. *Meeting and subsequently sustaining the National Target throughout England.* This will need new money... (£150m over five years)... All highway authorities need to adopt a rigorous planning approach, ie *Milestones* or an equivalent scheme...

- The Commission should establish a practical definition of 'meeting the Target' and... once achieved, the authorities need to draw up costed strategies for maintaining it.
- 2. *Providing a more extensive network, particularly for riding and cycling.*
Highway authorities should identify proposals for a better network of bridleways and cycle tracks where there is demonstrable need... and implement them by 2005... (And) make the 'hidden network' of some 10,000-15,000 km of unclassified carriageways fully available for public use.
- 3. *Making the legal processes for recording and changing rights of way quicker, cheaper, less bureaucratic and less adversarial.*
This is a particularly difficult area...but the time is right now to make progress by means of a negotiated package of changes to rights of way legislation... and the Government should work towards 'closing' definitive maps to further amendments based on historical evidence.
- 4. *Improving the mapping of rights of way, the quality of the legal record, and the availability of information to the public.*
- 5. *Dealing with the current mis-match between rights of way duties of highway authorities and the resources allocated for rights of way management.*
We need... to streamline highway authorities' duties and to ensure that those duties are accurately costed and adequately resourced. Highway authorities... should maximise efficiency and value for money by working through parish groups and local groups... and by using local farmers as contractors.
- 6. *Concerning the need for more effective sanctions to encourage underperforming highway authorities to carry out their statutory duties.*
- 7. *Establishing rights of way as part of a sustainable transport network and integrating their management with that of minor roads to the benefit of all users.*
- 8. *Promoting a more effective approach to managing vehicular use of rights of way.*
BOATs, some RUPPs and unclassified roads carrying vehicular rights..but their recreational use should focus on walkers, riders and cyclists; low-key motorised recreational use should be accommodated as long as it is compatible with other recreational uses and is sustainable in terms of route management.
- **9. *Understanding the demand for and use of rights of way.***
The cost and feasibility of monitoring the usage of the rights of way network should be explored.
- 10. *Making rights-of-way management more self-sufficient and increasing its cost-effectiveness.*
It is not the Commission's job to subsidise highway authorities' statutory duties... In the short term... the Commission should continue to support the development and implementation of Milestones Strategies... but in the longer term the Commission's grant programme will be used mainly to support non-statutory work.

This last testament largely reiterates established dogma but it also confesses some sins of ommission and commission. Thus, for example, the Commission recommends the closing of PRoW maps to amendments on historical evidence (Objective 3). There should be no more looking back for ancient rights; and this may be as contentious as the intended 'right to roam', with ramblers opposing the former while pressing for the latter. Objectives 1, 5 and 10 now acknowledge that the tripartite policy was always 'unrealistic in the absence of any reliable estimate of the costs involved and of ways and means of funding this operation' (Kay, 1989); but the Government's cautious response will effect little real improvement. DETR has commissioned its own appraisal of the merits of any special 'one-off' allocation of funds and it is also careful to report that:

> 'under the Revenue Support Grant system it is for individual local authorities to decide how much they will spend on services, including rights of way, although they clearly have to do so within the framework of their statutory obligations. The Government has no power to require local authorities to increase - or decrease - expenditure on particular items'.

Parliament thus lays down the law but responsibility for its implementation is located with individual authorities. Their diverse capabilities and priorities generates a multifarious patchwork pattern of provision with scant regard for the nation's needs (Ch.6.5). Also, given stringent resource limitations, the idea of 'providing a more extensive network' for walkers and other path users (Objectives 2, 7 & 8) may have little appeal - unless selective use of the hidden network of 'green lanes', of minor roads and, indeed, all appropriate highways provides better value than the least useful PRoW. This may well be the case (Ch.6.2); and an assessment of the merit of each and every section of all 'highways' (including PRoW) would raise constructive questions as to which are the least and most useful parts, and what should be done with each of them. The comprehensive tripartite policy for PRoW denies any such selective approach; but path-users' preferences for parts of the total network ridicule this policy (Ch.5.2: Figs.5.2-3).

In this context the 9th objective is the most revealing. It hesitantly suggests that it may be useful to understand the *'demand for and use of rights of way'*. This simple proposition should not require consideration by parliament; but the persistent failure to address the need for such basic information may well justify a public inquiry. The utility and use of PRoW should have been explored in some depth before 'preoccupation with the total network distracted attention and resources from a more useful plan for walking... and aligned the Commission with the interests of a small number of crusaders for the total recovery of every yard of the rights of way' (Kay, 1989). The use of PRoW could and should have been addressed within the 1988 and 1994 surveys of the condition of paths on PRoW (Ch.7.2-3); and in the comparable survey of 2000. When available, data on path usage will certainly challenge the relevance of current policies for PRoW, just as survey data on the use and utility of long-distance walks question the priority granted to National Trails (Ch.8.5-6). In summary, attention continues to be focused on ancient rights and minority interests rather than on people and their current needs.

2. Pseudo-Democracy Distorts Policy and Planning

The persistent failure to relate policy, priorities and provision for walking to needs of the people as a whole is central to the purpose of this study; and the recurrent correlation between national policy and interests of influential minorities is evidently a key factor. The precise nature of this relationship is a field for further research; but the influence granted to particular groups by consultation processes deployed by the Commission and by DETR merits attention now.

The Commission's discussion paper on *Managing Rights of Way* (CCP.506, 1996), which led to its 'position statement' on *'Rights of Way Beyond 2000'*, attracted 133 responses. 64 or 48% were from 'users associations'; 32 from local authorities; 19 from individuals; 5 from landowners and farmers organisations; 4 from conservation organisations; and 9 from other bodies. Proposals concerning definitive maps of rights-of-way generated most interest; and 'two ideas attracted almost universal criticism; that there should be a cut-off date for the submission of new claims to amend the map or, alternatively, that a highway authority could apply for a Ministerial directive that the definitive map was up-to-date and that no more claims could be submitted'. In contrast, only 30% of the respondents chose to comment on 'what needs to be done to publicise opportunities offered by the rights-of-way network'; and their response was generally negative:

> Publicising the network ...must not take precedence over opening all rights of way at a basic level... it must not result in the network becoming over-publicised... nor lead to path erosion... or a loss of solitude or sense of discovery.

The net outcome in the light of the consultations comprises the three purposes and ten objectives set out above; and while the 'particularly difficult area of closing PRoW maps' is addressed (Objective 3), there is no reference to publicising opportunities offered by PRoW. Evidently reducing pressure on resources by partial closure of PRoW maps warrants disagreement with current path-users; but their concerns over 'publicising the network' evidently eliminated the proposed outreach to the public.

DETR's consultations on *Access to the Open Countryside* [ie the Right to Roam] generated a more substantial response. 2132 submissions were received; 65% were from 'recreational users' and 6% from 'recreational user organisations'; 13% were by local authorities and local authority organisations; and 8% by land owners and managers.

> On the question of whether voluntary arrangements could deliver sufficient access, 80% of respondents commented, of whom 11% supported a voluntary approach, 84% opposed it, and 5% stated no preference. Almost 90% of those opposing voluntary arrangements were recreational users... Nearly 80% of those who commented agreed that walkers should not have to pay for the right to roam'... Some 54% (recreational users, National Park Authorities and others) agreed that there should not be general compensation for access; but landowners and others supported the case for compensation, for example, for reduction of land value, increased management costs and increased insurance costs.

All such consultation processes evidently empower interested minorities that can raise large numbers of signatories; but the general public has no voice and the silent majority are readily over-looked. Democracy would be better served by a 'jury system', whereby a random selection of (N x 12) households from each county and municipal borough were systematically interviewed by professional surveyors. Such data collections would probably reveal just how small the parties with vested interests really are; but they may be usefully supplemented by a single submission from each major organisation with a particular, acknowledged interest in the specific issue.

Meanwhile, the power of diverse pressure groups and lobbyists in pursuit of their own interests remains a major determinant of policies, priorities and patterns of provision; and the constant failure to positively promote walking and achieve a greater measure of social equity in enjoyment of the countryside is an indictment of the whole process. The demolition of the best intentions to put people first in the Commission's initial proposals for *Recreation 2000* supports this dismal conclusion (Ch.9.1-2). Furthermore, *The Countryside and Rights of Way Bill (2000)* is evidently a product of self-centred minorities; and the consultation process inspires no confidence that constructive proposals for the best provision for countryside walking and for the benefit of the public as a whole will be adopted. Until the preoccupation with ancient rights is dismissed and the prevailing hegemony and mythology are broken, commonsense will not prevail and democracy will continue to be dispossessed (Plate 0.1)

Consequently no effective strategy for access to the countryside for recreational walking has been achieved by the Countryside Commission. On the one hand, it has favoured 'visions' which convey a broad philosophy and afford a sensible basis for a comprehensive approach to policy and provision. Thus, in the 1990s it sought:

> A thriving, environmentally healthy, beautiful, diverse and accessible countryside, which should be seen as a whole ...where... an integrated strategy would take into account farming, forestry, rural development, tourism and leisure provision, and how these interests would relate to one another in harmony with the natural environment ... and would help us all to pursue our objectives with greater confidence. (CCP.336 & 351, 1991).

On the other hand, its specific quest for 'an accessible countryside for all to enjoy' has remained focused on the myopic perception that 'the rights of way system is the best way of providing for informal recreation... and our principal priority (is) the national target for the network as a whole'. This is seriously at odds with its recognition of 'a diverse countryside' since the 'national target' takes nothing into account except the location, rather than the utility, of ancient rights and the demands of particular pressure groups (CCP.435. 1993).

The surrender of its role as 'the national leader in encouraging people's access to and enjoyment of the countryside' to the new-born Countryside Agency provided the Commission with a final opportunity for a *Policy Statement on Countryside Recreation* (CCP.544, 1999). This legacy is summarised in half-a-dozen key statements:

> *To achieve sustainable countryside recreation there needs to be:*
> - (a) increased opportunity for people to enjoy the countryside, especially near to where they live and spend most of their 'free time';
> - (b) fewer barriers to people wishing to enjoy the countryside, whether these are physical barriers, insufficient information, or lack of personal confidence;
> - *(c) attractive alternatives to the car for travelling to and within the coun-*

tryside;
- *(d) high quality recreation opportunities, which match the full range of people's expectations;*
- *(e) measures to help services and enterprises to protect the basic countryside resource;*
- *(f) leadership from local authorities who should prepare strategies for informal recreation, analysing existing provision and demands, and showing how sustainable countryside recreation can be delivered.*

Four of these (a, b, d & f) are particularly important in respect of provision for and promotion of enjoyment of the countryside; but this apparent intention for a new approach to informal recreation is promptly set aside as the legacy of ancient rights is again singled out for special attention.

> The Commission is anxious to see completion of the national target for the rights of way network... and that the long term future of the network, (comprising nearly 170,000 km [105,600 miles] of footpaths, bridleways and byways in England), be secured by ensuring that efficient, effective and adequately resourced management systems are in place. (CCP.544, 1999).

Established but ill-founded priorities are thus recommended for the 21st century and the more important need for a rational, holistic approach to access and provision for countryside walking, focused on the people's needs and optimal means to serve them, continues to be neglected. Furthermore, while current decision-making and consultation processes persists, there can be no confidence that the Countryside Agency will be able to proceed where its predecessor has failed to tread. In this context, the Commission's last wish that local authorities might provide the leadership to produce 'strategies for informal recreation' may be an acknowledgement of its own failure to do so. However, while local involvement will be always be necessary, a countrywide approach is a prerequisite for any policy 'to help everyone, wherever they live, to enjoy the countryside without damaging its future'; and two key areas will now be explored. The first comprises a tentative spatial strategy for provision for walkers; and the second considers the need for outreach to the population as a whole.

3. Towards a National Strategy for Countryside Walking

Countryside walking, in all its forms, is a means to enjoy diverse experiences (Ch.1); and prime determinants of walkers' outings include both physical and visual contact with the broad expanse and intimate detail of their selected locations. Planning for countryside walking therefore should be guided by key factors underlying the spatial patterns of current participation (Ch.5), while also bearing in mind the potential demand of the disadvantaged majority (Ch.4). The intrinsic qualities of valued countryside or landscapes are evidently a major attraction but, in practice, proximity to home and major holiday resorts is a stronger determinant of the location of walks, though local outings are generally shorter than those to more distant places (Tables 5.2-3). In each and every case, off-road countryside walking shares space with other uses of rural land, notably farming and forestry.

(A) Proximity to People	Priority Points
(1) The urban fringe, within 3 miles of all cities, towns and major resorts.	+9-10
(2) The wider peri-urban zone, 3-6 miles from a major a centre or resort.	+7-8
(3) Accessible countryside, within an hours drive (25 mls) of a major centre or resort.	+5-6
(4) Distant regions, requiring 1-2 hours driving (25-65 mls) of a major centre or resort.	+3-4
(5) Remote countryside, the remainder.	+1-2

(B) Landscape Character and Quality	Priority Points
(1) Exceptional 'beauty spots'- eg: the 'highlights' of National Parks and AONBs.	+9-10
(2) Charismatic and distinctive - eg: highly varied landscapes with considerable relief; cliff coasts; and significant waterside locations.	+7-8
(3) Pleasant, undulating terrain that is varied at macro, meso and micro levels.	+5-6
(4) Ordinary - with its own intrinsic interest but limited relief and variety.	+3-4
(5) Poor - featureless, flat, monotonous; including upland moors.	+1-2

(Zero and negative values may deserve consideration for ugly, obnoxious and dangerous areas).

(C) Commercial Land Use : Quality and Productivity	Protective Points
(1) Very Good - eg: intensive, predominantly arable farming and horticulture.	- 5
(2) Good - eg: largely arable but with some dairy and intensive stock farming.	- 4
(3) Average - eg: mixed faming with much ley grassland and livestock.	- 3
(4) Low - eg: mainly grassland and stock farming.	- 2
(5) Marginal - eg: predominantly permanent grassland and rough grazing for stock rearing.	- 1
(6) Hardy permanent 'vegetation' - eg: rough grazing, moorlands and forests.	Zero

(a) The value of agricultural land may be a surrogate for land-use or an additional dimension.

(b) Temporal variations in access may be deployed in respect of particular conditions; for example, where ley grass alternates with crops; when fire-risk is high; and when special activities, such as lambing and shooting, justify limited access or temporary exclusion. Areas susceptible to such periodic or occasional occurrences should be permanently labelled as such and equipped with specific exclusion notices as and when appropriate.

Table 10.1 Rating the Countryside for Recreational Walking.

Most of these functions have prior rights, often derived from ownership of the land; and insofar as the intrusion of walkers is detrimental to the property and rights of others, provision for recreational walking should be sensitive to all other forms of land-use.

These three key aspects of the diverse countryside as a venue for recreational walking may be summarised as follows:
- **(A)** *Proximity to people* - whether at home or in holiday resorts;
- **(B)** *Landscape character and quality* - best available options within leisure time-slots;
- **(C)** *Commercial land-use* - its nature and productivity. (Table 10.1)

All three properties occur in every part and parcel of the countryside. Therefore identifiable spatial units derived from the OS national grid may be graded within a quasi-quantitative tri-partite scheme that allocates positive *priority points* (from 1 to 10) in respect of a range of conditions with reference to proximity to people and, similarly, to landscape quality; and with negative, *protective points* (-5 to 0) to reflect limitations on provision for access that should be granted in respect of the prevailing use and associated value of the land (Table 10.1). The maximum and minimum combined scores are 20 and -3, indicating that the most suitable areas merit the capacity for at least twenty times more walking than is justifiable in other, remote places which are unattractive and/or where the land-use merits protection. For example, parts of the Peak District National Park and Cannock Chase AONB may achieve the maximum score, and thus justify a close network of clearly identified high quality paths. On the other hand, parts of East Anglia might achieve a negative score and qualify for protection from all but a few natural paths.

Pending detailed research, the three criteria may be plotted for identifiable spatial units derived from Ordnance Survey maps; and 3kmx3km squares, embracing 3.5 square miles, may provide an appropriate preliminary framework. The three individual scores A, B and C and the total score (A + B - C) should be recorded for each unit; and units may be variously aggregated to provide summary data for larger functional or administrative areas. Each parameter is independent and has its own merits, but the combination of all three indicates the overall priority of a place in respect of provision for walkers. Contrasting areas may achieve the same aggregate points score, which implies comparable provision for walkers:

	A	B	C	A + B - C
Case 1	*Proximity* +10	*Landscape* +4	*Productivity* -3	*Priority Points* 11.
Case 2	*Proximity* +2	*Landscape* +10	*Productivity* -1	*Priority Points* 11.

An urban fringe location (Case 1) may have very ordinary landscapes and support much horticulture and intensive farming, while an exceptionally beautiful area (Case 2) supporting only marginal hill-farming may be so remote that it serves only small numbers of summer holiday-makers. Each scores 11 points; and this indicates grounds for somewhat above average provision, which should be strategically located to achieve optimal enjoyment by walkers in each area.

The scheme is essentially simple and capable of immediate adoption and application in principle anywhere by anyone; and although a wide range of interpretations would probably emerge, any such piecemeal rating of parts of the countryside in respect of provision for walking would institute a comprehensive reform of current policy. On the other hand, a national map of *Priorities for the Provision of Paths for Pedestrians* could underpin systematic adoption of this approach and a new countrywide policy. Its preparation would require some substantial research, including refinement of the methodology; and its implementation would require some considerable time and money. Furthermore, it could delay dissemination and adoption of the underlying policy precepts; and at this point in time, some preliminary discussion of ways and means to implement them is all that need be offered.

The rating is necessarily in comparative terms (Table 10.1), and the translation of the aggregate scores of 'priority' and 'protection' points for each part of the countryside into actual densities and specific patterns of real paths is no easy matter. Basic data relevant to these problems, notably on path usage, is scarce and is not readily transferable beyond its specific context. For example, in the vicinity of North Yorkshire's *Three Peaks* (Fig.8.7), survey data show that some paths carry at least 50 times more walkers than others; some carry in excess of 50,000 in a year; and at some points peak use has required the provision of multiple stiles. This information indicates that demand probably exceeds the current capacity of some paths, if only periodically at critical locations; but while some paths are often crowded, others within the same locality may be so lightly used at all times as to be redundant. Such survey findings can inform a strategy for provision in the area to which they refer; but they contribute little to any national scheme; and the persistent failure to systematically survey the use of paths on PRoW - and country lanes - leaves a serious gap in the basic information relating to the need for provision in contrasting locations.

The continuing national policy for the provision of paths evades all such issues, particularly by giving priority to National Trails and Regional Routes (Ch.8) but more generally by virtually ignoring all highways other than PRoW while insisting that there is a path on every PRoW and that each is 'in proper repair, reasonably safe to use and suitable for the expected use' (CCP.435, 1993). The spatial pattern of provision for countryside walking in the 21st century is thus being largely determined by the location of ancient rights of way; and whether this comprises over or under provision in parts or all of the countryside is not seen to be an issue. The variable spatial outcome is evident in Fig.6.2 and may be illustrated further by a simple mathematical model (Fig.10.1). The mean density of PRoW in England and Wales is about 1.3 km per ha or 2.7 miles per square mile (Table 6.1). If all PRoW were arranged in straight, parallel lines no part of the countryside would be more than 385 metres (420 yards) from a path, while a more useful rectilinear network would move the most distant point to 543 metres (594 yards). However, ancient rights have no sense of spatial equity or social justice. Thus, for example, in North Yorkshire and Devon, Humberside and Norfolk PRoW densities are relatively low and more than half of their countryside lies between 500 and 1000m from a path. Yet none of them has a reputation for insufficient pathways and at least two of them are highly regarded by walkers. At the other extreme, Bedfordshire is blessed or burdened with enough PRoW to bring every point within 160m of its path users. Any such analysis of PRoW challenges the comprehensive adoption of all PRoW as the basis of provision for the needs of today and tomorrow; and a systematic approach to rating the countryside for recreational walk-

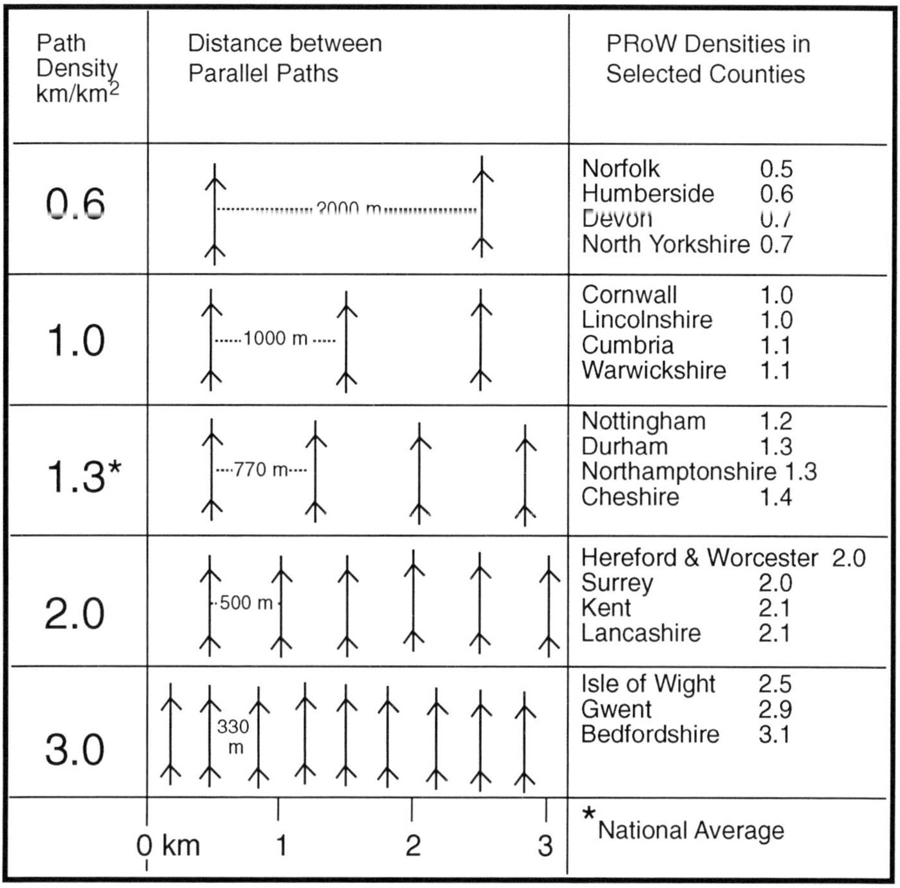

Path Density km/km²	Distance between Parallel Paths	PRoW Densities in Selected Counties
0.6	2000 m	Norfolk 0.5 Humberside 0.6 Devon 0.7 North Yorkshire 0.7
1.0	1000 m	Cornwall 1.0 Lincolnshire 1.0 Cumbria 1.1 Warwickshire 1.1
1.3*	770 m	Nottingham 1.2 Durham 1.3 Northamptonshire 1.3 Cheshire 1.4
2.0	500 m	Hereford & Worcester 2.0 Surrey 2.0 Kent 2.1 Lancashire 2.1
3.0	330 m	Isle of Wight 2.5 Gwent 2.9 Bedfordshire 3.1

*National Average

Fig.10.1 Densities of PRoW in Selected Counties of England and Wales.

> 37 of the 47 counties have densities above the national average. This is due to particularly low densities in most of the more extensive counties. The full data set is available in Table 6.1 which is derived from CCD.43 (1991) and CCP.393 (1993).

ing must afford a more rational foundation for spatial planning.

The scheme outlined above (Table 10.1) indicates the relative need for paths in different places; and the next step is to identify the optimal, affordable selection of pathways to serve current and potential walkers of all kinds in relation to their numbers and needs (Fig.1.2). The choice lies within the total network of *all highways* other than those forbidden to pedestrians by law (Ch.6.1-2); and while PRoW, with RUPPS and BOATS, comprise the greater part (c.125,000 and 6-9000 miles in England and Wales) their utility must be considered alongside that of lanes and roads (32,000 miles) and that of canal towpaths, reclaimed railway lines and private roads to which public access is granted. No legal option should be ignored; and given the fact that many country lanes and roads are heavily used by walkers and provide additional, highly valued perspectives on the countryside, there should be positive protection rather than implicit surrender of pedestrian rights on highways carrying vehicular traffic.

National planning must relate to the role of highway authorities or county councils and municipal boroughs which interpret and implement policy, provide the management of footpaths and 'decide how much they will spend on [such] services'. However, any national scheme must incorporate priorities; set over-riding guidelines; facilitate co-ordination between adjacent authorities; and distribute any central financial support to the best advantage of the nation. Primary questions therefore relate to the proportion of highways to be selected for development to different levels; for their distribution between the several highway authorities; and, finally, their location within each county or MB. All walkers probably appreciate high quality provision, but many are not dependent upon it; and some prefer 'natural paths'. Therefore, *positive provision for countryside walking* might embrace upto 60% of all PRoW and 30% of the metalled roads, to be variously deployed in the provision of graded pedestrian pathways, classified as A, B or C, and universally signposted and way-marked as such, and separately identified on PRoW and OS Maps (Table

Category of Path.	*Characteristics*	Share of (a) PRoW, BOATS and RUPPS and (b) Roads and Lanes.
Class A	Excellent in all respects throughout the year and wide enough for free movement by groups of walkers. Comfortable for all able-bodied persons, including young children and the elderly; and negotiable without special footwear or maps.	(a) 20% c.26,800 miles (b) 10% c.3,200 miles (a+b) c.30,000 miles
Class B	Good quality paths at least 1 metre wide, suitable in all respects for fit, able-bodied persons. Durable footwear and maps may be advisable but these paths should be negotiable without them.	(a) 20% c.26,800 miles (b) 10% c.3,200 miles (a+b) c.30,000 miles
Class C	Basic provision, as outlined in the 'Milestones' Approach', suitable for the expected use by fit, experienced, map-reading walkers.	(a) 20% c.26,800 miles (b) 10% c.3,200 miles (a+b) c.30,000 miles
Class N	All PRoW excluded from A-C. Undeveloped except for basic crossings where necessary. 'Natural paths' may be created by experienced walkers and adventurers, intent on exploring such undeveloped countryside.	(a) 40% c.53,600 mls*. (b) 70% As necessary. * Some may be subject to approved extended, re current or occasional closures.

Table 10.2 Paths for Countryside Walkers.
Graded Categories and their Deployment on Highways.

10.2 and Fig.10.2).

The 80,400 miles of PRoW and 9,600 miles of roads and lanes to be purposefully developed as Class A, B or C 'recreational paths' should be distributed *between* the several highway authorities in proportion to their share of the national total of *priority points,* which reflect the case for paths in terms of proximity to people and preferred landscapes (Table 10.1). It would be prudent to hold 20% in reserve until each authority responded with provisional plans for the deployment of its apparent entitlement and in case the formula should leave any authority with an unacceptably low allocation. *Within* each County or Municipal Borough the location of its share of the Class A, B and C paths should reflect the net score of *priority and protection points* in each unit of 3.5 square miles or, in more

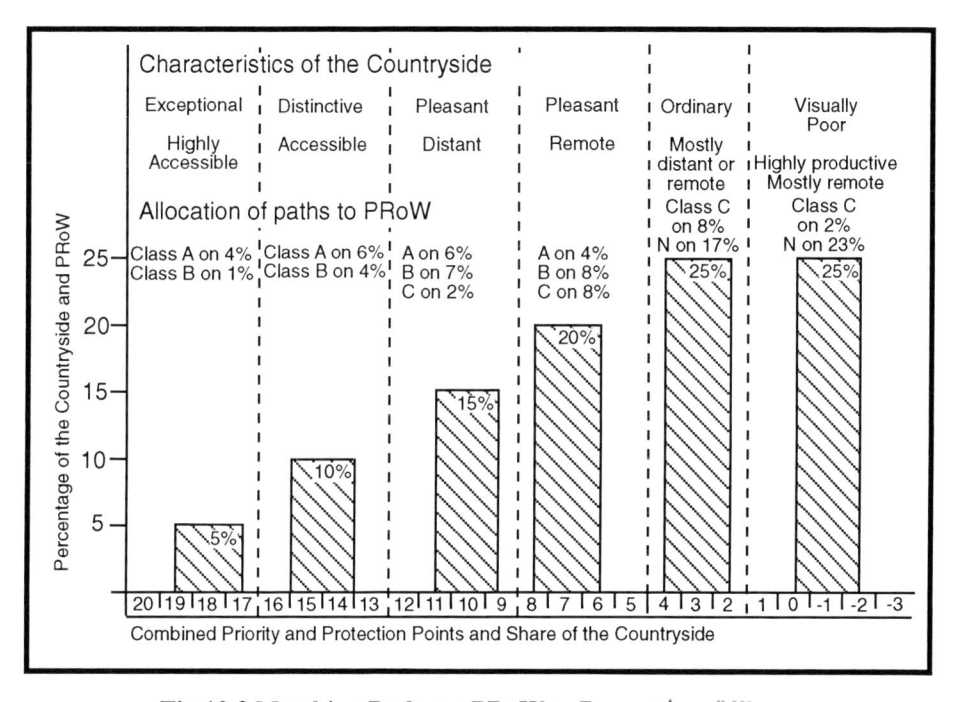

Fig.10.2 Matching Paths on PRoW to Properties of Place.

Key features of the national scheme for the provision of paths for countryside walking are summarised. The spatial extent of the six categories of place and the assumed uniform density of PRoW are largely hypothetical; but the allocation of A, B and C paths to 60% or some 80,400 miles of PRoW illustrates a principal feature of the strategy. Subject to resource availability, all PRoW in the more highly valued parts of the countryside would be equipped with these variously developed paths; but in the 'other half' only a carefully selected 10% of PRoW would have a basic, *Milestones* path; 40% might carry 'natural paths' created by use; and 50% might be mapped but closed and held as a 'reservoir' for future development when sound evidence of need was available togther with resources for the appropriate development.

practical terms, within appropriate 'patches' of units with similar scores (Fig.10.2).

The 40% of all PRoW and 70% of all roads and lanes excluded from the status of Grade A, B or C 'walkways' are thus set aside for the minimal provision, notably crossings over physical obstacles, necessary to allow the emergence of 'natural paths' in the wake of walkers intent on exploring them. Furthermore, where use is evidently negligible land owners or users and highway authorities should be granted the right to apply to a local adjudicating panel for temporary seasonal or all-year closures for periods of upto 5 years. These should be indicated by appropriate, effective signage for the duration of the closure at the applicant's expense. This could allow cultivation over the PRoW and suspend the risk of damage to crops, livestock and property by any walker other than a wilful trespasser; and if fees were levied for this privilege, they should be dedicated to the maintenance of heavily used paths in adjacent areas.

If any such scheme is adopted for practical rather than educational purposes it would require refinement as information emerges during the collection and mapping of basic data, analysing the outcome, and running pilot 'paper' and perhaps 'field' exercises. The immediate objective is to demonstrate that, as exhibited in some few parts of the countryside, there is a much better basis for policy, priorities and practice in respect of provision for walking than those generally deployed at present. This suggestion will be rejected out of hand in some influential quarters on grounds that ancient rights and current law relating to them are sacrosanct; and, secondly, that any such new start will be too difficult, too expensive and, above all, too embarassing. Such opinions may perpetuate simplistic approaches based on out-dated rights; and until wiser counsel prevails no such model based on people's needs and preferences is likely to win favour with policy makers.

On the other hand, it is important to stress that quality provision (Plate 6.4) is not only preferred by most walkers of today but is also essential if participation is to be fostered amongst those who currently have little or no access to the countryside (Ch.4.4). Recent data show that they still comprise more than half of the nation (CRN 19, 2000) and the potential for extending the diverse benefits of walking for the well being of individuals and society as a whole thus continues as a major challenge to those responsible for facilitating enjoyment of the countryside. Effective promotion and out-reach also are long over-due.

4. Promoting Access for Countryside Walking : A Neglected Need

In 1949 The Times reported that parliamentary action would 'provide urban populations fuller access to and enjoyment of the countryside'; but no positive step was taken then, nor later, to initiate such progress. Access for 'untutored townsmen' was not promoted on grounds that common folk cannot benefit from the finer experiences offered by natural beauty, heritage and wildlife; and that their presence in numbers would destroy the countryside and the enjoyment of sophisticated users (Ch.2.5 & Ch.4.4-5). In a democratic society this is untenable; and good management should not only protect the countryside but also create quality provision and promote access for all. The latter have yet to be achieved; and the increased promotion of walks has done little or nothing to increase participation in countryside walking.

On the contrary, even short walks are generally publicised as a service for established walkers (Ch.9.6); and they largely fail to connect with the needs and aspirations of

Plate 10.1 Images of the Countryside for 'Discerning Minds'.
(from Walker's Britain, 1982).

the majority whose capabilities, confidence and interests are significantly different. Typically, promoted walks relate to 'discerning minds' and present an highly selective, intellectual approach to the countryside, focused on 'natural beauty', 'wildlife' and 'cultural heritage' (Plate 10.1). 'Untutored minds' - and most young people - prefer less cerebral, more sociable, fun-filled and even boisterous outings. All too often these legitimate needs have not only been neglected but also rejected in favour of quiet, and preferably contemplative enjoyment of the countryside; and the existence of 'two nations' in terms of access to and acceptance within the countryside has been fortified rather than eliminated.

This bias has a long history. It shaped the early development of countryside walking; it was firmly established and popularised during the Victorian era; and it has been widely propagated during the latter part of 20th-century (Ch.1 & Ch.2). Thus, for example, even introductory educational products have reflected the prevailing doctrine; and when C Mill's (1977) 'Henry the Hedgehog Discovers the Countryside' he meets many different animals, birds and insects but encounters no livestock. *Gale's Book of Countryside Projects* (Colman's Foods, 1975) provided a broader but similar agenda for older children; and in 1976 Robertson's much-loved golliwog introduced a quartet of 'guides' that embraced *British Butterflies, Wild Flowers of the Hedgerows, Birds of the Woodlands, and Seashore Life on Sandy Beaches;* but the countryside as an entity and farmland in particular were ignored. More mature minds were similarily misdirected by Warne's

243

extensive series of *Observer's Books**, which did embrace *Horses and Ponies* but overlooked all the diverse breeds of cattle and sheep, pigs and poultry and other farm animals, and all the varied crops, grassy swards and pastures which clothe much of the British countryside. In short, the countryside as it really is, with its potential wealth of interest for children no less than adults, has been neglected in most if not all promotional materials.

This highly selective, quasi-erudite approach was reflected in an ambitious attempt, sponsored by the Countryside Commission, to enhance enjoyment of the countryside within and around the West Midlands conurbation.

> This was to be achieved during 1978 and 1979 through an experimental programme of 1000 walks each summer, in which a guide conducts a party around an area of natural or historical interest at 14 popular destinations. Off-site publicity comprising press releases, radio interviews, posters and leaflets could have reached 4.6 million people, while on-site notice-boards at 27 starting points may have been seen by 250,000. The latter invited visitors to "Explore Your Countryside...*to discover the history and wildlife of the area with the help of a local guide... Its an ideal activity for the whole family and costs only 30p for adults with accompanied children free".*
>
> Initially, walks were offered on Saturday afternoons and Sunday mornings and afternoons... but morale fell sharply as returns came in for the first weekend: 47 walks had attracted 82 people (22 of them children) with 28 walks totally unattended. The following weeks were a little better... the programme was modified and events reduced to Sunday afternoons. Some participants began 'doing the rounds'; word-of-mouth publicity gradually had some effect; and £1,200 were invested in newspaper advertising. The response was sufficient to re-kindle hope; and in 1979 a curtailed programme was more successful ... but over the two seasons 3,500 participants provided an overall average of only 5.1 per walk.
>
> With few exceptions the walks... generated a predominantly middle-class following from amongst those with a natural inquisitiveness about their environment. Certain guides commented on the predominance of middle-aged and elderly customers... and in most cases the age and socio-economic profile of participants seemed to bear little relationship to that of the site users as a whole... It was clear at many sites that few of the users were in fact potential customers. (CCP.135, 1980).

This extravagant experiment was ill-conceived and evidently designed for a very small number of middle-class walkers with discerning minds who were willing to surrender their freedom for the benefit of tuition. The derogatory conclusion that few of the visitors were 'potential customers' also is an indictment of the scheme, which clearly failed to connect with the 'general countryside goer'; and any similar approach within the conurba-

---

**Footnote: The Observer's Books* embraced the following subjects: Birds; Wild Flowers; Butterflies; Trees and Shrubs; Wild Animals; Freshwater Fishes; Grasses, Sedges and Rushes; Dogs; Horses and Ponies; Geology; Ferns; Architecture; The Larger Moths; Common Insects and Spiders; Birds' Eggs; Common Fungi; Mosses and Liverworts; and Weather.

tion to those who rarely if ever visit the countryside would surely be doomed to failure.

However, careful diagnosis of the format and the outcome could have provided salutory lessons; and eventually, in 1987, the Countryside Commission did acknowledge that its prime task should be 'to make an attractive countryside truly accessible and its benefits awailable to the whole public... [and that] the most important target should be the 50% of the population who make few trips to the countryside'. Its proposals for *Recreation 2000* therefore included a range of measures for 'improving awareness, creating confidence and ability, and promoting understanding' (CCP.225, 1987); but these were systematically undermined during the consultation process; and thus 'a promise faded; an opportunity was lost; and a new initiative is still awaited' (Ch.9.1). Meanwhile, the *Countryside Code* and the Commission's documentation of people's rights and responsibilities in the countryside (CCP.186, 1990) are likely to deter participation amongst those who were regarded as 'unsuitable customers' in 1980 but who were rightly identified in 1987 as 'the most important target' (Plate 10.2); and there is still no positive approach to promotion amongst them.

Furthermore, a more subtle argument has now been propagated to undermine the case for positive promotion of wider enjoyment of the countryside. It comprises an unjustified and unproven claim that non-participants abstain by choice, and that this reflects a cultural trait which should be respected. This may be valid in the case of some small immigrant communities but it cannot be sustained in respect of 50% or more of the population; and much evidence denies this argument any general validity. Indeed, it is self-evident that both culture and behaviour are amenable to change; and given that the purpose of 'promotion' is to effect change, failure to do so comprises dereliction of duty by the Countryside Commission/Agency.

An excuse for doing nothing has been found in the widespread superficial affection for the countryside. This may be traced to commercial exploitation of Victorian romanticism (Ch.2.3); and it is now argued that 'for hundreds of years, our English countryside has given us such ideas as we have of what paradise might be like.' (Shoard, 1980). Consequently, the countryside is widely seen as 'a British equivalent to the American *Motherhood and Apple Pie* - something that everyone unthinkingly supports.' (Evans in Pennington, 1996). However, such sentiments provide no foundation for participation in countryside recreation, nor any reason for not promoting enjoyment of the countryside. Indeed, the real case for action lies with the contradiction between prevailing attitudes towards the countryside and the widespread failure to gain access to and interaction with it (Ch.1.3 and Fig.10.3).

This contradiction is not only self-evident but it is also well supported by survey data. In 1977 'only 17% of the NSCR respondents said that they preferred to spend leisure time in town rather than the countryside' and 89% denied that 'being in the countryside soon gets boring'; furthermore, *75% of those who had not visited the countryside expressed these views* (Duffield and Walker, CCP.127, 1979). More recently, the 'people's love affair with the countryside' was similarly documented, and '93% of the population [stated that they] personally value the countryside, *regardless of whether they visit or not*'; and 85% declared that 'the countryside is an important part of my life'. (Ashcroft, 1996 & CCP.481, 1997). Such findings are often a product of the diet of 'questions' offered to respondents but they also reflect an almost universal readiness to echo respectable con-

Plate 10.2 The Countryside Code and Conventions for Walkers Conspire to Inhibit the Promotion of Walking.

> A friendly 'welcome' is essential because visitors [especially newcomers] want to feel that they are wanted; and a succession of *No Parking, No Dogs, No Entry, No Children, No Staying after 6 pm, No Nonsense* notices means one thing to most visitors - *No Good Times Here !* (Lawson, *Countryside*, 58, 1992).

ventional views.

However, they provide no evidence that failure to participate in countryside recreation is a product of a considered decision not to do so; and when solicited opinions are inconsistent with behaviour, the latter is the better guide for policy. Indeed, the case for a major commitment to promoting access to the countryside for recreational walking and thus to enjoyment of the countryside is self-evident and long over-due. The decision-making process in the adoption or rejection of a novel option is not a simple matter (Fig.10.3); and a thorough understanding of its complexity will facilitate appreciation of

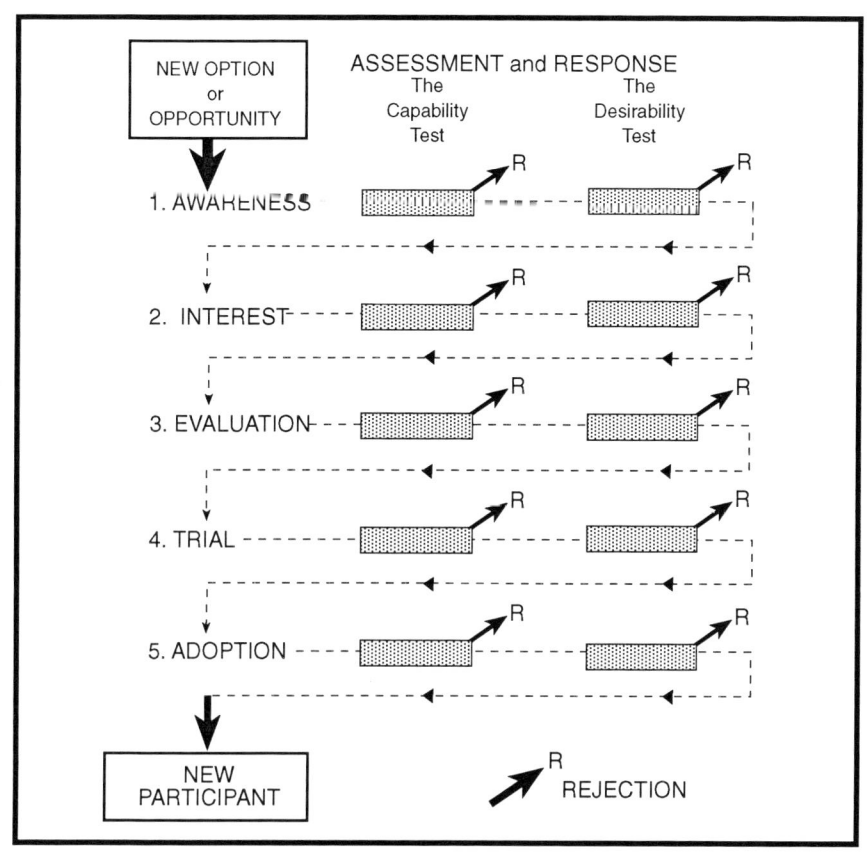

**Fig.10.3. The Gateway to Participation:
A Decision-making Process in the Adoption or Rejection of a Recreational Activity.**

This model is under-pinned by Roger's (1962) ideas on the diffusion of innovations. It highlights the key role of intelligible information; education and promotion; and the outcome of early experiences. The first three stages are dependent upon information and persuasive argument. *Awareness is a prerequisite for* assessment of whether or not the activity lies within one's ability and means to participate and to what extent it may satisfy a perceived need or desire. Awareness may arouse *interest* and this may lead to an informed *evaluation*. Each stage may well require more information and persuasion to develop a deeper understanding of both the requirements for and the benefits of participation.

At each stage, progression will depend on the client being persuaded that he/she is capable of participation and that the overall experience will be rewarding. However, the critical fourth stage requires a commitment of time and, perhaps, a small investment in clothing and equipment for some *exploratory participation* in the activity, preferably in the company of supportive companions and an experienced leader. The on-going evaluation will now depend more on the overall experience rather than information (Fig.1.3); but continued exploratory involvement may lead to *adoption* of the activity by a potentially regular participant and devotee - or to the retirement of a disappointed apprentice.

the task of promoting any recreation. It is not a matter to be undertaken lightly; and carefully prepared information appropriate for and readily intelligible to each target audience is of vital importance, but the sympathetic delivery of such information, together with guidance, encouragement and direct assistance also have a key role (Fig.10.3).

In 1987 the Countryside Commission was close to recognising the need for outreach to the general public:

> Survey data show that only 26% of the people felt they knew even their local countryside well... In the past our main approach has been to concentrate on providing 'on-site' information and interpretation. Less effort and resources have been put into *delivering information to the general public*... Much is available on maps, but only 15% are able to read and habitually use them... There are clear information gaps... and we shall encourage more 'consumer research' and imaginative methods which deliver relevant and useful information to people... (CCP. 225, 1987).

Consequently, although the *Recreation 2000* proposals 'to extend opportunities for the public to enjoy the countryside' were seriously undermined (Ch.9.1), the Commission continued to explore the delivery of 'countryside information'. Its relevant consultation paper was focused on *Visitors to the Countryside* rather than on those who rarely if ever participate in such recreation; and it embraced four initiatives: to stimulate care of and caring for the countryside; to deepen understanding of the places visited; to provide information on recreation opportunities; and to foster confidence (CCP.341, 1991). The first two reflect the ongoing importance attached to conservation and the intellectual approach to appreciation of the countryside. Nevertheless, the subsequent advisory booklet on *Delivering Countryside Information* (CCP.447, 1994) does provide a useful general 'guide for promoting enjoyment'; and it outlines the importance of 'understanding the customers'; of 'knowing who wants what'; and of 'tailoring the approach to market needs'.

However, it draws particular attention to minority groups, notably ethnic communities and people with disabilities; and politically correct responses have led to some particular initiatives in respect of these, Indeed, these minorities continue to attract special attention, and recently the director of the Black Environment Network has argued that 'more should be done to encourage ethnic groups to use the countryside'.

> Unless attitudes change significantly at senior level, most disadvantaged British ethnic persons will not be able to claim the right to enjoyment and use of the countryside for years to come... We need commitment and leadership at senior levels to bring about policies which ensure ethnic involvement... Organisations whose remit says they are for everyone need to take a pro-active stance... They need to work at projecting a philosophy of inclusion... They should encourage and support their personnel in generating targeted projects with properly resourced programmes of outreach by trained staff... Access to the countryside will make an enormous difference to our quality of life. (Judy Ling Wong, *Countryside 88*, 1998).

Furthermore, while a concern to deploy countryside walking as a health measure has a significantly longer history (Ch.3.3), it has recently enjoyed a revival and focussed attention on another minority group. This may have begun in 1992 when 'an exercise in holistic health promotion' was organised by North Derbyshire Health and the Peak District National Park Rangers.

> The aim of the Peak Park Leisure Walks is to promote health and increase access to the countryside by encouraging disadvantaged groups living in the Peak District to take advantage of their local environment through a programme of supported walks. In short, *by removing barriers*, a whole new recreational experience and improved physical and mental well-being could be gained by people who would benefit most. A 1998 evaluation of the Walks showed that social rewards - 'companionship', 'meeting nice people', 'making new friends' - were valued most highly; and the second most popular factor was 'the countryside' and 'scenery', which indicates that simply being out in pleasant, open green space is health promoting. These rewards are more immediate and more memorable than the physical rewards. (Hirst and Prendergast, *Countryside Recreation News*, 1999).

A more widespread provision of graded *Health Walks* has emerged in response Dr William Bird's more recent initiative at Sonning Common Health Centre. He hopes to foster a national scheme comprising some 200-300 'partnerships between local health centres, district councils, local businesses, ramblers and historians' that will identify, publicise and support 5-10 graded 'health walks' in their area. His project emphasises the physiological benefits of walking, which are particularly pertinent to victims or potential victims of stroke, coronary heart disease, osteoporosis or blood pressure; and his promotions provide quantitative indices whereby dynamic physiological conditions may be monitored. Nevertheless, he is sensitive to the benefits of visual inputs by pleasant scenery; and is keen to develop interests in natural and local history to help people to focus outside themselves, to relax, and to develop a sense of belonging to their community. Such elements create a more holistic approach to health; and presumably Dr Bird takes for granted the highly valued social benefits of walking with companions.

Dr Bird's *Healthy Walking* initiative has now won support from the Countryside Agency and the British Heart Foundation and funding from the New Opportunities Fund and Kia Cars for an effort 'to get more than a million people walking for the good of their health... using attractive places in town and country because that provides the essential motivating factor of enjoyment'. £12,000,000 is available for the five-year plan to achieve this objective; and dedicated staff in the Countryside Agency's regional offices will offer advice and help to get local schemes up and running. (Countryside Focus 10, 2000).

Such careful attention to two minority groups is admirable. However, charismatic cases and special responses should not divert attention nor resources from the more fundamental need to promote enjoyment of the countryside for the benefit of the nation as a whole, and in particular for everyone who currently lacks effective access. Democracy calls for attention to the needs of all; and hitherto the less obvious needs of the far more numerous but less distinguished people who rarely or never achieve the benefits of a countryside walk have won very little attention.

For this highly varied but very large proportion of the population, motivation is probably more critical than information, and 'alongside awareness there needs to be a confidence and ability to enjoy the countryside' (CCP.225, 1987). Developing these latter qualities is a diffcult and demanding task; and reticent people require face-to-face encouragement, persuasion and assistance from agents who understand their particular constraints and fears. The key to success therefore is sustained out-reach by institutions and individuals who believe in their mission, have a thorough understanding of the extended process of promotion, and can achieve empathy with each of their various target audiences, since the disadvantaged comprise a wide diversity of people. This was recognised in the 'Access Study' of 1986:

> Hitherto, countryside recreation policy has been concerned more with resource management issues than social policy issues... (and) the analysis of accessibility raises the question as to whether an indiscriminate 'access for all' policy provides a credible or realisable goal ... The issue is as much about deprivation as about low and infrequent participation... and there is a need for a selective approach aimed at specific target groups. (CCP.216, 1986).

Relevant lessons may be derived from the campaigns to promote *Sport for All*. For example, the diversity of the non-participating population should be recognised in a way comparable to that whereby the Sports Council identified over-lapping 'target groups', including school-leavers, young people, the unemployed, women, the over-'fifties, and ethnic minorities. Secondly, within each group and across the several groups account must be taken of a range of key personal properties, such as levels of fitness, literacy and skills; household and peer group relationships; current recreational and cultural characteristics; and, perhaps, levels of disposable income and access to a car. It follows that no single campaign will be effective, and the particular nature of the promotion and of the personnel delivering it must be in sympathy with the characteristics and capabilities of their particular client group. Indeed, the first step for any promoter or motivator should be to identify the characteristics, capabilities and relevant experience (if any) of his/her clients; and there should be no prior assumption in respect of apparently basic knowledge and simple skills. Furthermore, promoters will probably be most effective, not on people's doorsteps, but when they are face-to-face with indiviudals within a wide diversity of existing institutions, organisations and groups which, collectively, afford contact across the full spectrum of the target population.

Carefully prepared information, ideas and inspiration are important aids for the conversion of each target group; but only experience will test commitment (Fig.10.3). Therefore organising and leading walks for groups of novices with a common background and, perhaps, a nodding acquaintance with each other is a key element in promoting countryside walking. The route must be chosen with close reference to the capabilities of the participants; and careful consideration must be given to the demands of distances and gradients, the quality of the footpaths, and the nature of the landscapes to which they give access. However, the capacity to enjoy the countryside depends primarily on the walkers' current abilities to interact with each other and to respond to that which they encounter;

and their initial response to the countryside is likely to be sensual rather than intellectual, adjectival rather than factual (Ch.1.3). Positive experiences, including the sociable company of one's peers, comprise the essence of enjoyment; and although such fundamental appreciation of a countryside walk may be enhanced by knowledge and understanding of that which is seen, any intellectual element comprises an optional extra and should be supplied in relation to the customer's appetite.

Indeed, any erudite approach to promoting enjoyment of the countryside is likely to have limited appeal amongst those with 'untutored minds' and little or no experience of rural life and scenes. Thus, the choice of 'history and wildlife' as the theme for the widely publicised programme of guided walks in the West Midlands during 1978-79 was an abject failure. Numerous such walks are still readily available, particularly in the National Parks but also in many other parts of the country; but most of them still attract very small numbers, mostly from amongst people with a prior interest in and knowledge of the specified field. They serve tiny minorities and do little or nothing to extend participation in countryside walking. Furthermore, by placing an emphasis on selected elements of the natural world or historic heritage, such intellectual interpretations generally neglect the greater part of the visible landscapes. Warne's *Observer Books* thus served aficionados with interests in selected minutiae; and while pupils of *Henry the Hedgehog* may well be able to recognise a red squirrel, stoat and fallow deer (p.243), their chances of seeing them during a countryside walk are rather limited.

If enjoyment of the countryside as an entity is to be made accessible to all, a less esoteric and a more fun-filled approach to recreational walking is necessary. For example, optional extras may add a valuable dimension provided they are carefully planned with reference to the characteristics of the participants and the venue. Mixed groups of children and adults may benefit from 'games', such as *I Spy... in the Countryside,* played with reference to clearly visible items such as types and breeds of livestock; types of crops - and their use; types of farm machinery and buildings - and their use (NFU, 1989). Indeed, children may be allowed, even encouraged, to breach the convention of 'taking nothing from the countryside and leaving nothing but footprints' in order to collect a specimen of each wild flower they encounter or one leaf from each type of tree and bush. Such direct experiences provided a great deal of enjoyment in the latter part of the 19th-century (Ch.3.4-5); and they could well serve a useful role in promoting access to and enjoyment of the countryside today.

Even such a tentative discussion of positive means to promote countryside walking is probably premature prior to a national commitment to 'put people first'. The Countryside Agency is taking steps in that direction in respect of residents in rural areas and other special groups (CA.41, 2001), but it will require a sea-change in policy, strategy and practice to give priority to the promotion of access to and enjoyment of the countryside by the people as a whole. This is long over-due and deserves at least parity with conservation and with appropriate physical provision for access. The latter is of paramount importance since quality pathways are not only desirable for the benefit of current walkers but also a prerequisite for effective promotion of countryside walking amongst the majority of the population. A critical appraisal of history, policy and practice in respect of physical access therefore comprises the principal subject matter of this text; and it is evident that significant changes in policy and practice in this field are necessary to obtain and maintain a high quality and cost-effective product that will properly support and foster countryside walking. However, the more important underlying questions relate to the purpose, utility and use of physical provision for countryside walking and to the current inequitable achievement of access. The politics of promotion therefore deserve no less attention than the politics of provision.

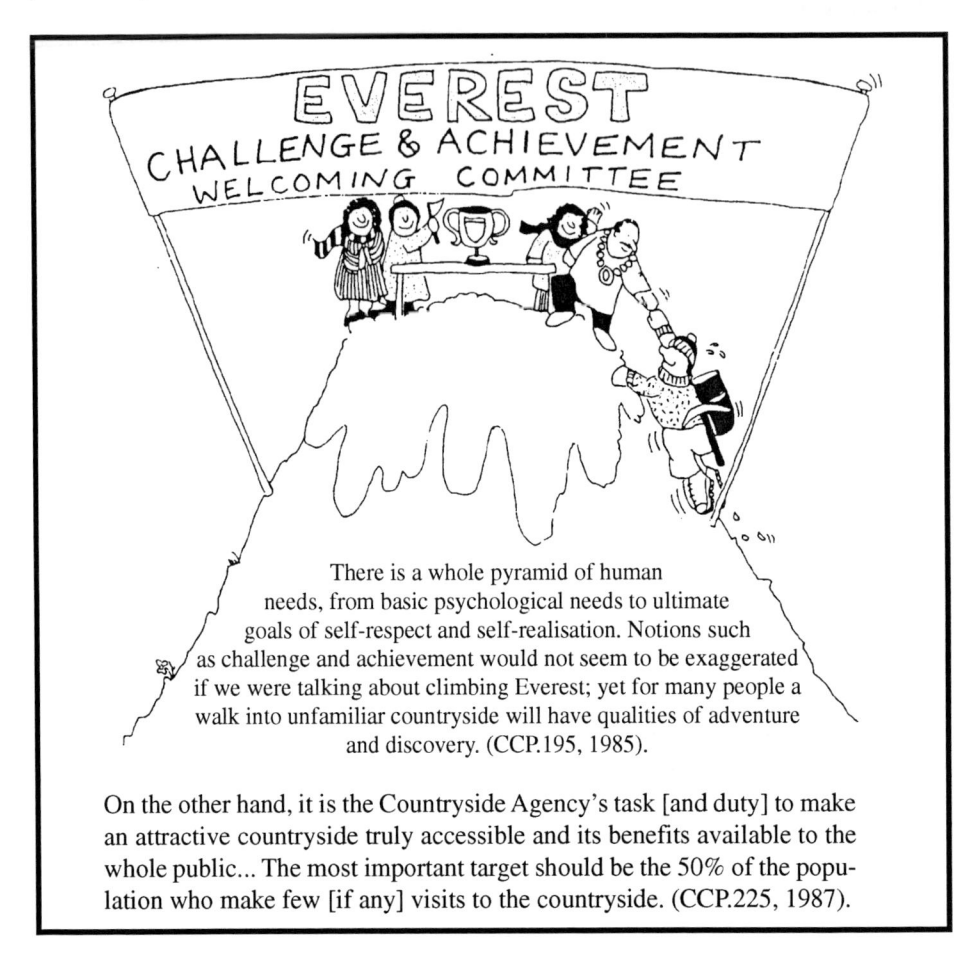

> **EVEREST CHALLENGE & ACHIEVEMENT WELCOMING COMMITTEE**
>
> There is a whole pyramid of human needs, from basic psychological needs to ultimate goals of self-respect and self-realisation. Notions such as challenge and achievement would not seem to be exaggerated if we were talking about climbing Everest; yet for many people a walk into unfamiliar countryside will have qualities of adventure and discovery. (CCP.195, 1985).
>
> On the other hand, it is the Countryside Agency's task [and duty] to make an attractive countryside truly accessible and its benefits available to the whole public... The most important target should be the 50% of the population who make few [if any] visits to the countryside. (CCP.225, 1987).

Bibliography of References and Sources

Arvill, R. 1967 *Man and Environment : Crisis and the Strategy of Choice,* Penguin Books.
Ashcroft, P. 1996 'Love Affair with the Countryside', *Countryside 77.*
Balogh, T. 1969 'Foreward' to Dumont, R. & Rosier, B. *The Hungry Future, M*ethuen, London.
Bayfield N.G. & McGowan G.M. 1986 *Three Peaks Project Footpath Survey, 1986*, Yorkshire Dales National Park, Grassington.
Barber, D, 1990 'The Future Countryside: Visions for the South', *Royal Society of Arts Journal,* Sept.1990.
Beckett, J. 1990 *The Book of Nottingham*, Barracuda Books, Buckingham.
Bicknell, P. 1984 (1992) *The Illustrated 'Wordsworth's Guide to the Lakes',* Webb and Bower, Selecta Book, Devizes.
Blackie, J.A. et al. 1979 *The Leisure Planning Process*, Sports Council and SSRC, London.
Blatchford, A, & B. & the LDWA 1980-1998 *The Long Distance Walker's Handbook & LDWA Directory of Long Distance Paths,* A & C Black, London.
Blunden, J. & Curry, N. 1988 *A Future for Our Countryside*, Basil Blackwell, Oxford.
Blunden, J. & Curry, N. 1990 *A People's Charter ? Forty Years of the National Parks and Access to the Countryside Act, 1949,* H.M.S.O.
Brandon, P.F. 1979 'The diffusion of designed landscapes in South-east England' in Fox, H.S.A.& Butlin R.A. *Change in the Countryside*, Institute of British Geographers, London.
Breakell, W. 1987 *Old Pannier Tracks*, North York Moors N.P. Authority, Helmsley.
Briggs, A. 1959 *The Age of Improvement,* Longman, London.
Briggs, A. 1963 *Victorian Cities,* Penguin Books, Harmondsworth.
Briggs, A. 1983 *A Social History of England,* Weidenfeld & Nicholson, London.
Brook, D. & Hinchcliffe, P, 1991 *The Alternative Pennine Way*, Cicerone Press, Milnthorpe.
Brown, A.J. 1938 (Revised 1949) *Striding Through Yorkshire*, Country Life, London.
Brown, S. 1999 *Unbroken Contact : One Hundred Years of Walking with Surrery Walking Club, 1899-1999*, Surrey Walking Club.
Butler, S. 1986 *A Gentleman's Walking Tour of Dartmoor, 1864*, Devon Books, Exeter.
Chamberlain, R. 1983 *Great English Houses*, Weidenfeld & Nicolson, London.
Channon, H. 1975 *A Pride of Parks,* Recreation and Open Spaces Dept. City of Liverpool.
Cherry, G.E. 1972 *Urban Change and Planning - A History of Urban Development in Britain Since 1750*, G.T.Foulis, Henley-on-Thames.
Cherry, G.E 1975 *National Parks and Recreation in the Countryside; Environmental Planning Vol II* HMSO.
Colthurst, R. 1991 'The Failure of Success', *Geographical Magazine, (June).*
Cook, C. 1989 'The Access Business', *Countryside, 37.*
Country Landowners Association, 1991, *Recreation and Access in the Countryside: A Better Way Forward*, CLA, London.
CRRAG, 1986 *New Approaches to Access in the Countryside*, Proceedings of the CRRAG Conference, School for Advanced Urban Studies, Bristol.
Crane, N. 1989 *Nick Crane's Action Sports,* Oxford Illustrated Press.
Crossing, W. 1912 *Guide to Dartmoor : A Topographical Description of the Forest and Commons*, 2nd Edition, David & Charles, Newton Abbot.
Conduit, B. & Brooks, J. 1989 *Dartmoor Walks*, Ordnance Survey, Southampton.
Coppock, T. 1973 Contribution to the Discussions in Rodgers, H.B. et al. *op cit*
Cowley, B. 1983 *The Lyke Wake Walk*, Dalesman Books, Clapham
Crofts, B. 1990 At *Satan's Throne : The Story of Methodism in Bath*, White Tree Books, Bristol.
Csikszentmihalyi, M. 1975 *Beyond Boredom and Anxiety*, Jossey-Bass, San Fancisco.
Csikszentmihalyi, M. & J.S. 1988 *Optimal Experience*, Cambridge University Press.

Cunningham, F.F. 1979 'James D. Forbes' Alpine Tour of 1832' *Scottish Geographical Magazine, 95(3)*.
Curry, N. 1991 *Countryside Recreation, Access and Land Use*, E. & F.N. Spon, London.
Curry, N. 1996 *Review of Local Authorities' Charging for Public Path Orders*, Rural Research Monographs No.2, Cheltenham & Gloucester CHE.
Daniels, S. & Seymour, S. 1990 'Landscape Design and the Idea of Improvement 1730-1900' in **Dodgshon, R.A. & Butlin, R.A.** An Historical Geography of England and Wales, Academic Press, London.
Denbigh, K. 1981 *A Hundred British Spas: A Pictorial History,* Spa Publications, London.
Denman, J & Clarkson, S, 1992 *Rights of Way : An Action Guide*, CCP.375.
Dept of Transport, 1983 *National Travel Survey: 1978-9 ,* HMSO.
Dept. of Transport, 1996 *Developing a Strategy for Walking*, HMSO.
Dower, J. 1945 *National Parks in England and Wales*, HMSO
Dower, M. 1965 *The Fourth Wave : The Challenge of Leisure*, Civic Trust, London.
Dower, M. 1970 'Leisure - Its Impact on Man and the Land', *Geography 55(3)*.
Dower, M. 1993 'A Gift for the Future', Co*untryside, 64*.
Duncan/Peterson Associates. 1982 & 1986 *Walker's Britain* and *Walker's Britain 2*, Pan Books & the Ordnance Survey.
East, W.G. 1951 'England in the Eighteenth Century' in **Darby, H.C**. *An Historical Geography of England before A.D.1800,* Cambridge University Press.
Edwards, K.C. 1962 *The Peak District*, Collins, London.
Edwards, R. 1991 *Fit for the Future: Report of the National Parks Review Panel*, CCP.334.
Edlin, H.L. 1939 *Forestry Commission Guide to the Argyll Forest Park*, HMSO.
Elson, M.J. 1974 'Some Factors Affecting the Incidence and Distribution of Weekend Recreation Motoring Trips', *Oxford Agrarian Studies, 11*.
Elson, M.J. 1978 *Countryside Trip-Making*, Sports Council & SSRC, London.
Evans, A.W. 1996 *Foreword* to Pennington, M. 1996, *op cit.*
Evens, B. 1996 'The Alternative Pennine Way', *Strider 76.*
Fairbanks, R. 1997 'Health Walks', Co*untryside Recreation Network News, 5(2).*
Fearon, M. 1990 *Filey : From Fishing Village to Edwardian Resort,* Hutton Press, Beverley.
Fisher, G. 1948 *Historic Britain : Britain's Heritage of Famous Places and People Through the Ages*, Odhams, London.
Fisher, R. 1996 'The Nightmare of Headland Paths', *Countryside 78.*
Fox, C. 1932 (1952) *The Personality of Britain*, National Museum of Wales, Cardiff.
Garner, J.F. & Jones, B.L. 1991 *Countryside Law*, Shaw & Sons, London.
Gittins, J.W. 1973 'Recreation and Resources : Conservation and Capacity : The Snowdonia National Park', G*eographical Journal, 139 (3).*
Glyptis, S. 1991 *Countryside Recreation*, Longman, London.
Goldsmith, F.B. & Warren, A. *Conservation in Progress*, John Wiley & Sons, Chichester.
Gratton, C & Taylor, P. 1987 *Leisure in Britain*, Leisure Publications, Hitchin (Herts).
Gratton, C & Tice, A. 1994 'Trends in Sports Participation in Britain, 1977-87', *Leisure Studies 13.*
Graham, H. 1986 *When Grandmama Fell Off the Boat: The Best of Harry Graham*, Methuen, London.
Gruen V. 1964 *The Heart of Our Cities - The Urban Crisis: Diagnosis and Cure,* Simon and Schuster, New York.
Glyptis, S. 1991 *Countryside Recreation*, Longman, Harlow.
Gutkind, E.A. 1971 *Urban Development in Western Europe: Vol VI The Netherlands and Great Britain,* Collier-Macmillan, London.
Harding, M. 1986 *Rambling On,* Robson Books, London.
Harrison, C. 1991 *Countryside Recreation in a Changing Society*, TMS Partnership, London.

Hawkins, 1987 'From Awareness to Participation : New Directions in the Outdoor Experience', *Geography, 72(2).*
Heathcote-Amory, D. 'Government Backs Rights of Way Target', *Countryside, 42.*
Hickey, R. 1988 'Furrowed Brows', *Countryside 33.*
Hickey, R. 1990 'Vision of a New Way', *Countryside 46.*
Holden, E.B 1906 (1977) *The Country Diary of an Edwardian Lady*, Michael Joseph/Webb and Bower, London/Exeter.
Hoskins, W.G. 1951 *Chilterns to Black Country : About Britain No.5*, Collins, London.
Hoskins, W.G. 1955 *The Making of the English Landscape*, Hodder and Stoughton, London.
Hunt, J. c1990 *In Search of Adventure : A Study of Opportunities for Adventure and Challenge for Young People*, Talbot Adair Press.
Jarvis, P.J. 1979 'Plant introductions to England and their role in horticultural and sylvicultural innovation, 1500-1900' in Fox, H.S.A. & Butlin R.A. *Change in the Countryside*, Special Publication No.10, Institute of British Geographers.
Joad, C.E.M. 1946 *The Untutored Townsman's Invasion of the Countryside*, Faber & Faber, London.
Kay, G. 1962 'The Landscape of Improvement: A Case Study of Agricultural Change in North East Scotland', *Scottish Geographical Magazine, 78(2).*
Kay, G. 1989 'Routes for Recreational Walking' *Town & Country Planning, 58(3).*
Kay, G. 1990 *Recreational Behaviour and Perceptions of Visitors to Smaller Resorts of North East Yorkshire, 1989*, Report for the *Cleveland Way Project,* Dept of Geography & Recreation Studies, North Staffordshire Polytechnic.
Kay, G. 1994 'The Milestones Approach to Public Rights of Way - Marching Orders or New Directions ?' *Town & Country Planning, 63(4)*
Kay, G. & Moxham, N. 1996 'Paths for Whom ? Countryside Access for Recreational Walking', *Leisure Studies, 15.*
Kay, G. 1996 *Detecting Patterns of Countryside Recreation*, Occasional Papers in Geography: New Series A, No.8, Staffordshire University.
Kay, G. 1998 'The Right to Roam - A Restless Ghost', *Town & Country Planning, 67(7/8).*
Kay, G. 2000 'On Wordsworth, the Lake District, Protection and Exclusion', *Area, 32(3).*
Keirle, I.1990 *Cleveland Way Management Strategy*, North York Moors National Park Authority, Helmsley.
Lata, K, N.D. *I Spy... In the Countryside*, NFU, London.
Lockhart, R.H.B. 1937 *My Scottish Youth*, Putnam, London.
Lowenthal, D. & Prince, H.C. 1964 'The English Landscape', *Geographical Review, 54(3).*
Lowenthal, D. & Prince, H.C. 1965 'English Landscape Tastes', *Geog.Review, 55(2).*
Lumsden, L. 1988 *Staffordshire Walks - Simply Superb*, Sigma Leisure, Wilmslow.
McEwen, A & M, 1987 *Greenprints for the Countryside ? The Story of Britain's National Parks*, Allen & Unwin, London.
Mais, S.P.B. et al 1948 *The Countryside and How to Enjoy It*, Odhams, London.
Mais, S.P.B. & Stephenson, T. c.1935 *Lovely Britain*, Odhams, London.
Martin, B & Mason, S. 1993 'Current Trends in UK Leisure: New Views of Countryside Recreation', *Leisure Studies 12.*
Maslow, A.H. 1943 'A Theory of Human Motivation', *Psychological Review 50.*
Maslow, A.H. 1970 *Motivation and Personality,* Harper and Row, New York.
Mathieson, J. 1991 *Participation in Sport,* GHS Series No.17 (B), Social Survey Division of OPCS, HMSO.
Mercer, D. & Puttnam, D. 1988 *Rural England : Our Countryside at the Crossroads*, CPRE, MacDonald & Co, London.
Merrill, J.N. 1988 *The White Peak Challenge Walk,* John Merrill Publications.

Millward, R. 1955 *Lancashire : An Illustrated Essay on the History of the Landscape,* Hodder and Stoughton, London.
Mortlock, C. 1973 (1978) *Adventure Education,* Private Publication.
Mortlock, C. 1984 *The Adventure Alternative*, Cicerone Press.
Moxham, N. 1993 *The Status and Value of the Staffordshire Way*, BA Dissertation, Staffordshire University.
Moxham, N. 1997 *The Provision and Promotion of Countryside Walks with Special Reference to Staffordshire*, M.Phil thesis, Staffordshire University.
Moxham, N & Kay, G. 1998 'The Efficacy of the Promotion of Countryside Walks : A Case Study in Staffordshire', *The Journal of Regional and Local Studies, 18 (2)*.
Muir, J. 1992 *John Muir's Eight Wilderness-Discovery Books (1913-1918),* Diadem Books, London.
National Trust, 1985 & 1996 *Properties of the National Trust* and *The National Trust Handbook,* The National Trust, London.
Nicholls, P. 1998 'The National Trust: A Spatial Audit of Conservation Progress', *Geography, 83(4)*.
North York Moors N.P., 1981 *Patterns of Informal Recreation in the North York Moors National Park.*
North York Moors N.P., 1993 *North York Moors Visitor Survey 1991.*
OPCS, *General Household Surveys of 1965, 1973, 1977, 1987 &1990,* HMSO.
Pacione, M. 1984 *Rural Geography, Harper and* Row, London.
Patmore, J.A. 1970 *Land and Leisure in England and Wales,* David Charles, Newton Abbot.
Patmore, J.A. 1983 *Recreation and Resources: Leisure Patterns and Leisure Places,* Basil Blackwell, Oxford
Peak District N.P. 1975 *The Way Ahead.*
Peak Park Joint Planning Board, 1988a *Peak National Park Visitor Survey 1986/87 &* 1988b *Peak National Park Plan: First Review.*
Pearce, D. 1987 *Tourism Today : A Geographical Analysis*, Longman, Harlow.
Pearsall, W.H. 1950 *Mountains and Moorlands*, Collins, London.
Pennington, M. 1996 *Conservation and the Countryside ; By Quango or Market ?* Studies on the Environment No.6, Institute of Economic Affairs, London.
Pimlott, J.A.R. 1947 *The Englishman's Holiday,* Faber and Faber, London.
Plog, S.C. 1973 'Why Destination Areas Rise and Fall in Popularity', *Cornell H.R.A. Quarterly (4)*.
Puttnam, D. in **Mercer, D**. 1988 *Rural England : Our Countryside at the Crossroads*, CPRE and Queen Anne Press, London.
Pye-Smith C. & Hall, C. 1987 *The Countryside We Want; A Manifesto for the Year 2000*, Green Books, Bideford, Devon.
Raistrick, A. 1967 *Old Yorkshire Dales*, Pan Books, London.
Ramblers' Association, 1984 *KEEP OUT ! The Struggle for Public Access to the Hills and Mountains, 1884-1984*, R.A. London.
Ramblers' Association, 1994 *A Survey of the Membership of the Association*, RA. London.
Ramblers' Association (Staffs.Branch), 1997 *Walking On and Around the Staffordshire Way,* Sigma Leisure, Wilmslow.
Redfield, R. 1953 Th*e Primitive World and its Transformations*, Cornell University Press.
Riddall, J. and Trevelyan, J. 1992 *Rights of Way : A Guide to Law and Practice*, The Open Spaces Society, Henley-on-Thames & The Ramblers' Association, London.
Roberts, K. 1978 *Contemporary Society and the Growth of Leisure*, Longman, London.
Rodgers, H.B, Patmore, J.A, Gittins, J.W, & Tanner, M.F. 1973 'Recreation and Resources', *Geographical Journal, 139 (3)*.
Rodgers, H.B. 1973 'The Demand for Recreation', in Rodgers et al, 1973.
Rogers E.M. 1962 *The Diffusion of Innovations, MacMillan, New York.*

Rose, C. 1993 'Achieving Change' in Goldsmith, F.B. & Warren, A. *Conservation in Progress*, John Wiley & Sons, Chichester.
Ryder, J. & Silver, H. 1970 *Modern English Society : History and Structure 1850-1970*, Methuen, London.
Samuels, G. 1995 'Rights-of-Way Survey', *Countryside, 74.*
Schama, S. 1995 *Landscape and Memory*, Harper & Collins.
Sheail, J. 1975 'The concept of National Parks in Great Britain 1900-1950', *Transactions & Papers of the Institute of British Geographers, 66.*
Sheail, J. 1981 *Rural Conservation in Inter-war Britain*, Clarendon Press, Oxford.
Shercliff, W.H. 1987 *Nature's Joys Are Free For All : A History of Countryside Recreation in North East Cheshire*, W.H. Shercliff, Stockport.
Shivers, J.S. 1981 *Leisure and Recreation Concepts : A Critical Analysis*, Allyn & Bacon.
Shoard, M. 1980 *The Theft of the Countryside*, Temple Smith, London.
Shoard, M. 1987 *This Land is Our Land*, Paladin.
Sidaway, R.M. et al, 1986 *Access to the Countryside for Recreation and Sport*, Countryside Commission, Cheltenham & Sports Council, London.
Smith, D.H. & Theberge, N. 1987 *Why People Recreate: An Overview of Research*, Life Enhancement Publications, Champaign, Illinois.
Smith, P.R. 1987 'Outdoor Education and its Educational Objectives', *Geography*, 72(2).
Smith, R. 1994 'Milestones Measure Progress: Making Tracks', *Countryside, 68.*
Smout, T.C. 1969 *A History of the Scottish People, 1560-1830*, Collins, London.
Sperrin, G. 'Pioneering Teams Lead the Way', *Countryside 43.*
Sports Council, 1986 *A Digest of Sports Statistics for the UK*, Information Series No.7.
Spratt, D.A. and Harrison, B.J.D. 1989 T*he North York Moors: Landscape Heritage*, David & Charles, Newton Abbot.
Stamp, L.D. 1946 *Britain's Structure and Scenery*, Collins' New Naturalist Series, London.
Stamp, L.D. 1955 *Man and the Land*, Collins' New Naturalist Series, London.
Taylor, E.G.R. 1951 'Leyland's England' & 'Camden's England' in Darby, H.C. *An Historical Geography of England before A.D. 1800*, Cambridge University Press.
Thompson, E.P. 1963 *The Making of the English Working Class*, Penguin Books, Harmondsworth.
Tranter, R.B. 1994 'Valueing Woodland Walks', *Countryside Recreation Network News 2 (2).*
Travis, A.S. 1979 *The State and Leisure Provision*, Sports Council & SSRC, London.
Wallace, A.D. 1993 *Walking, Literature and English Culture.*
Walker, S. 1993 'The 1992 UK Day Visits Survey', *Countryside Recreation News 2(1)*, Cardiff.
Walker, S. 1994 'The 1993 UK Day Visits Survey', *Countryside Recreation News 2(2)*, Cardiff.
Walker, S. 1995 *National Survey of Countryside Recreation : 1990*, Countryside Commission.
Walker, S. 1996 *The UK Day Visits Survey 1993*, Countryside Recreation Network, Cardiff.
Walton, J.K. 1983 'Municipal Government and the Holiday Industry in Blackpool, 1876-1914' in
Walton, J.K. & Walvin J. *Leisure in Britain, 1780-1939*, Manchester University Press.
Walvin, J. 1978a *Beside the Seaside : A Social History of the Popular Seaside Holiday*, Allen Lane, London.
Walvin, J. 1978b *Leisure and Society, 1830-1950*, Longman, London.
Walvin, J. 1983 'Children's Pleasures' in Walton, J.K. & Walvin, J. *Leisure in Britain, 1780-1939*, Manchester University Press.
Waterhouse, K. 1994 *City Lights : A Street Life*, Hodder and Stoughton, London.
Watson, J. 1991 'Inside Out at Winchester', *Urban Wildlife News 8(2).*
Whitby, H.C. et al 1974 *Rural Resource Development*, Methuen, London.
White, W. 1851 *A History, Gazetteer and Directory of Staffordshire*, W.M. White, Sheffield.
Wilkinson, J. Atkins, B & Brewer, E. 1985 *A Step in the Right Direction : The Marketing of Circular Walks*, Sports Council & Countryside Commission (CP.195).

Williams, C.H. 1991 'Language Planning and Social Change: Ecological Speculations' in Marshall, D.F. *Language Planning Vol III*, John Benjamins, Amsterdam/Philadelpia.
Williams, R. 1973 *The Country and the City,* Chatto & Windus, London.
Wimbush, T. 1981 *Long Distance Walks : The North York Moors and Wolds*, Dalesman Books.
Wimbush, T. 1987 *Moorland Challenge*, The Earnest Press, North Yorkshire.
Wood, C. 1988 *Paintings of English Country Life and Landscape 1850-1914*, Barrie & Jenkins, London.
Worth, J. 1988 'Test Role for Farmers Clearing the Way', *Countryside 34.*
Wright, G.N. 1985 *Roads and Trackways of the Yorkshire Dales*, Moorland Publishing Co., Ashbourne, Derbyshire.
Yorkshire Dales National Park 1993 *The Three Peaks Project, 1986-92,* YDNP, Grassington.

Countryside Commission/Agency Publications

CCP.99, 1976 *Footpaths for Recreation : A Policy Statement.*
CCP.117, 1978 *Countryside for All : CRRAG Conference Report.*
CCP.127, 1979 *CRRAG Conference Report.*
CCP.135, 1981 *Explore Your Local Countryside.*
CCP.151, 1982 Countryside Issues and Action: Prospectus of the Countryside Commission.
CCP.152, 1982 *Participation in Informal Countryside Recreation, 1977 and 1980.*
CCP.166, 1984 *Access Study : Issues for Consultation.*
CCP.186, 1985/1990 *Out in the Country.*
CCP.190, 1985 *Ploughing Footpaths and Bridleways.*
CCP.195, 1985 *A Step in the Right Direction : The Marketing of Circular Walks..*
CCP.201, 1985 *National Countryside Recreation Survey : 1984.*
CCP.202, 1986 *Rights of Way Legislation: First Monitoring Report.*
CCP.214, 1986 *Ploughing and Rights of Way.*
CCP.216, 1985 *Access Study : Summary Report..*
CCP.224, 1987 *New Opportunities for the Countryside.*
CCP.225, 1987 *Recreation 2000: Enjoying the Countryside: A Consultation Paper on Future Policies.*
CCP.234, 1987(1989) *Recreation 2000: Policies for Enjoying the Countryside.*
CCP.235, 1987(1989) *Recreation 2000: Enjoying the Countryside*; *Priorites for Action.*
CCP.237, 1987 *National Parks: Our Manifesto for the Next Five Years.*
CCP.253, 1988 *Paths, Routes and Trails : A Consultation Paper.*
CCP.254, 1988 *Changing the Rights of Way Network.*
CCD.43, 1991 *Local Authorities' involvement with Rights of Way in England and Wales*, (Peter Scott Planning Services).
CCP.265, 1989 *A Countryside for Everyone.*
CCP.266, 1989 *Paths, Routes and Trails : Policies and Priorities.*
CCP.273, 1989 *Managing Rights of Way : An Agenda for Action.*
CCP.297, 1991 *The Pennine Way Management Project.*
CCP.299, 1990 *Rights of Way Act 1990 : Guidance Notes for Farmers.*
CCP.301, 1990 *Rights of Way Act 1990 : Guidance Notes for Highway Authorities.*
CCP.334, 1991 *Fit for the Future : Report of the National Parks Review Panel.*
CCP.335, 1991 *Fit for the Future : Executive Summary.*
CCP.336, 1991 *An Agenda for the Countryside.*
CCP.341, 1991 *Visitors to the Countryside.*
CCP.348, 1992 *At Work in the Countryside.*
CCP.351, 1991 *Caring for the Countryside: A Policy Agenda For England in the Nineties.*
CCP.361, 1992 *Pennine Way Survey 1990 : Use and Economic Impact.*

CCP.370, 1992 *Parish Paths Partnership.*
CCP.375, 1992 *Rights of Way : An Action Guide* (by Denman, J. & Clarkson, S.).
CCP.380, 1994 *Parish Paths : An Outline.*
CCP.395, 1990 *Local Authorities Expenditure on Rights of Way.*
CCP.426, 1993 *Rights of Way Condition Survey : A Practical Guide.*
CCP.435, 1993 *National Target for Rights of Way. A Guide to the Milestones Approach.*
CCP.436, 1993 *National Target for Rights of Way: The Milestones Approach.*
CCP.447, 1994 *Delivering Countryside Information : A Good Practice Guide for Promotion of the Countryside.*
CCP.449, 1994 *A Guide to Procedures for Public Path Orders.*
CCP.450, 1994 *Managing Public Access : A guide for Farmers and Landowners.*
CCP.459, 1995 *Roads in the Countryside.*
--- —,   1995 National Su*rvey of Countryside Recreation, 1990: Summary of Results.* [No Code]
CCP.470 1995 *Quality of Countryside : Quality of Life.*
CCP.481, 1996 *Public Attitudes to the Countryside.*
CCP.503, 1996 *Visitors to National Parks: Summary of the 1994 Survey Findings.*
CCP.504, 1996 *Second National Rights-of-Way Condition Survey : 1993-94.*
CCP.505, 1996 *The Condition of England's Rights of Way : A Summary of the 1994 Survey.*
CCP.506, 1996 *Managing Rights of Way : A Discussion Paper.*
CCP.513, 1997 *The Cotswold Way.*
CCP.524, 1997 *The National Trails User Survey : A Summary.*
CCP.543, 1998 *Rights of Way in the 21st Century.*
CCP.544, 1999 *Countryside Recreation : Enjoying the Living Countryside.*

CA.03, 1999 *The State of the Countryside, 1999.*
CA.22, 1999 *Tomorrow's Countryside - 2020 Vision.*
CA.41, 2001 *Towards Tomorrow's Countryside.*